EARLY FOCUS

EARLY FOCUS

**Working with
Young Children
Who Are Blind or
Visually Impaired
and Their Families**

SECOND EDITION

RONA L. POGRUND and
DIANE L. FAZZI, Editors

PRESS
NEW YORK

Printed in the United States of America

Library of Congress Cataloging-in-Publication Data

Early focus : working with young children who are blind or visually impaired and their families / Rona L. Pogrund and Diane L. Fazzi, editors.—2nd ed.
    p. cm.
Includes bibliographical references.
ISBN 0-89128-856-2
    1. Children, Blind—Rehabilitation.   2. Children with visual disabilities—Rehabilitation.   3. Children, Blind—Services for—United States.   4. Children with visual disabilities—Services for—United States.   I. Pogrund, Rona L.   II. Fazzi, Diane L.   III. American Foundation for the Blind.
HV1596.5 .E27 2002
362.4'1'083—dc21

                                                     2002025593

Photo credits: Blind Childrens Center, pp. 213, 230. All others, Vincent G. Fazzi.

The American Foundation for the Blind—the organization to which Helen Keller devoted more than 40 years of her life—is a national nonprofit whose mission is to eliminate the inequities faced by the ten million Americans who are blind or visually impaired.

It is the policy of the American Foundation for the Blind to use in the first printing of its books acid-free paper that meets the ANSI Z39.48 Standard. The infinity symbol that appears above indicates that the paper in this printing meets that standard.

Dedicated with loving memory to

Rona's father,

WALTER LAZARUS

and

Diane's mother,

CHARLOTTE ANNE PHIPPS

CONTENTS

FOREWORD

The profound impact of blindness or severe visual impairment on early growth and development is understood and acknowledged by most professionals today. Yet it was not too many years ago that we were telling parents of infants and preschool children with visual impairments to treat them as though they were not disabled, and everything would be all right. This advice was given by the innocently ignorant—those of us who were so focused on school-age children that we had given little thought to the needs of children birth to 5 years of age. Nor had we thought much about the needs of their parents.

Fortunately, a number of leaders in this area emerged over time, and by the 1970s, we knew that if we didn't provide guidance to parents and loving intervention to babies and preschool children, we would see these children entering our school programs at great risk for developmental delay. The young child who has not had a wealth of experiential learning by age 6 may have serious difficulties in school.

Many exciting programs began, both home-based and center-based. However, the leaders and teachers of these early programs developed curricula and learning experiences through trial and error. For a number of years after recognizing the vital importance of early intervention for babies and preschoolers who are blind or visually impaired, we had no written curriculum, no research data, no definitive guidance on what we should be teaching. We were in the era of "folk art." Teaching techniques and suggestions were passed on from one generation of teachers to another, almost always verbally or by example.

Then we began to see a gradual increase in research and writing about the education of visually impaired children. Even after the education of school-age children moved from "folk art" to profession, services to infant and preschool children who are blind were struggling to develop a professional foundation. Recently, a steady stream of publications has moved early intervention to the status of "profession." The first edition of *Early Focus* was a major contribution to this movement.

Now the editors and authors have provided us with an entirely new, greatly expanded second edition of *Early Focus*. This new book is a major contribution to our profession. There is material in this book that many of us have thought about for a long time and may have even attempted to put into writing. But Rona Pogrund and Diane Fazzi have completed a remarkable job of bringing together, in one publication, a variety of concepts, facts, thoughts, and techniques that will enrich the knowledge of any professional or family member. Here are a few examples:

- The impact of parents' emotional reactions to the birth of a baby who is visually impaired—or to the diagnosis of a visual impairment soon after birth—is presented in a sensitive, compelling manner.

- References to cultural differences and how they affect parental nurturing of a visually impaired baby are vital information for anyone serving as an early intervention specialist. The authors also deal with issues of racism.

- There is in this book a very clear description of the difference between a clinical vision examination and a functional low vision assessment. Invaluable samples are provided.

- The contributors and editors never forget that the majority of children who are blind or visually impaired today have multiple disabilities, and they draw on their extensive knowledge and experience to make certain that this publication addresses the entire population of blind and visually impaired children.

- There is appropriate emphasis on what we have learned about early childhood development from Piaget in this book.

- There is a very important reference in the social focus chapter to the issues of circadian rhythms and sleep patterns of children who are blind. Some may think that this is minor, but the fact that it is dealt with at all is a pleasant surprise.

The chapters in this book are outstanding contributions to the knowledge base in early intervention. For instance:

- A chapter devoted to literacy is a unique contribution to a book on early intervention. This chapter is full of ideas for teachers and family members as they work together to provide a rich environment for the development of early skills for reading and writing.

- The chapter on social skills emphasizes manners, a sometimes forgotten but vital part of social interaction.

- The chapter on motor skills is outstanding. Readers will be pleased with the detailed information presented on motor development in children with visual impairments and strategies for intervention.

- The mobility chapter represents one of the most extensive compilations of strategies for developing early O&M skills for infants, toddlers, and preschool-age children available anywhere.

- The overview of service delivery systems and models pulls together in a very effective manner most of the information and concepts about this topic.

Indeed, it is a temptation to tell the reader a bit about each chapter, but that would be a long and unnecessary process. Suffice it to say that each chapter is rich in research, background information, and excellent suggestions and tips. Indeed, the format of this book, with its "focus points" and "focus on effectiveness" boxes, and other highlighted information will bring the reader back again and again for practical information on teaching techniques.

There are books that contain a wealth of information, theory, and research about a topic, and often these publications serve as excellent college and university textbooks. There are others that serve as curriculum guides—helping the parent or the teacher with practical suggestions and guidelines. This book does both. It is a "must-read" for future teachers and other professionals, as well as individuals already serving families and children with visual impairments. And, if you own this book, you will find yourself referring back to it countless times as you encounter teaching situations where you could use some sound, creative ideas and suggestions.

I believe that this book will become a classic in our profession.

Phil Hatlen
Superintendent
Texas School for the Blind and Visually Impaired
Austin, Texas

PREFACE TO THE SECOND EDITION

The second edition of *Early Focus: Working With Young Children Who Are Blind or Visually Impaired and Their Families* is a comprehensive resource on early childhood visual impairment. It addresses the needs of children who are blind or visually impaired from the age of birth to 5. These young children are in need of early intervention and early education services and are on the caseloads of educational vision specialists more frequently than ever before. Their numbers are increasing, and they are being identified at an earlier age. Other specialists are being asked to serve these young children with visual impairments more often as well. The amount of information on this young population of children has increased over the past 10 years, but this edition of *Early Focus* provides an in-depth yet synthesized presentation of the most relevant and practical information available in an easy-to-read, organized manner. In an age of information overload, it is often helpful to have one primary resource to turn to for knowledge and answers. *Early Focus* has this purpose as its goal.

It is our hope that this second edition of *Early Focus* serves as a valuable resource to the many different professionals who work with young children who are blind or visually impaired, as well as the families of these children. The target audiences for this book are teachers of students who are visually impaired, orientation and mobility specialists, early childhood interventionists, and other specialized professionals who work with children with visual impairments such as occupational therapists, physical therapists, speech and language therapists, behavior specialists, psychologists, and social workers. The information is designed to be useful for both preservice and in-service personnel. In addition, administrators of programs serving these young children and classroom teachers, day-care center workers, and instructional assistants who may have a child who is visually impaired in their program will also find beneficial information in this book. It can also serve as a significant resource for medical personnel such as ophthalmologists, optometrists, pediatricians, nurses, and health-care aides who may be seeing a particular child who is visually impaired, and who would like to have a broader understanding of the impact of vision loss on development and learning. All of these team members are important to the growth and development of the child, and the more each of them understands about early childhood and visual impairment, the more they can each contribute to the team. Families, being the most significant members of any educational team, will also find a wealth of information in this book to help them better understand their child's visual impairment and ways to work more effectively with the professionals who serve their child.

The first edition of *Early Focus* was a compilation of information shared by professionals from various disciplines and parents and represented a new resource to the field. As our field has grown in its capacity to provide appropriate services to young children who are blind or visually impaired and their families, the need for greater depth, currency, and a stronger focus on strategies in the book became apparent. These needs served as the impetus to rewrite and update *Early Focus.* Four new chapters were added in areas we felt had not been thoroughly addressed in the first edition: "Refocus," "Literacy Focus," "Independence Focus," and "Motor Focus." In addition, the majority of the chapters have been either totally rewritten to reflect current best practice or significantly updated and revised. The reader will find a wealth of new information in this edition.

The second edition of *Early Focus* is a comprehensive overview of all of the developmental areas that may be affected by vision loss. *Early Focus* provides the theory and knowledge base for sound educational practices, accompanied by specific examples and suggestions for implementation of concepts. It is not intended to be a curriculum or a "cookbook," as the editors feel strongly that it is most important for teachers or other specialists to apply a theoretical basis in developing best intervention practices on an individual basis for young children and their families. *Early Focus* can serve as a springboard for the creativity that is the art of teaching. The book is full of strategies that can be used as guidelines for high-quality intervention and has many examples throughout which serve as models for interventionists to use along with their own creativity in serving individual children. Some of these suggestions and strategies are highlighted in boxes entitled "Focus on Effectiveness" in each chapter. Others are highlighted within the text. A wide range of additional resources is offered at the end of the book for further study and ideas.

As with any collaborative project, the end product is much richer than it ever could have been without the many contributions from the various writers. Multiple perspectives brought fresh ideas and added important dimensions to the book. The variety of voices gathered in writing this second edition also helped to create an interesting array of terminology. Readers may notice a variety of terms used to describe similar concepts or populations (such as "children who are blind or visually impaired," "children with visual impairments," and "children who are visually impaired"; or "infants, toddlers, and preschoolers" and "young children"). Similarly, there are some regional, professional, and personal differences in how various professionals are addressed (such as "education vision specialists" versus "teachers of students who are visually impaired" and "orientation and mobility specialists" or "early interventionists," "preschool teachers," and the like). Families, parents, caregivers, and siblings are all terms used throughout the book to describe those people who love, nurture, and care for young children. Even the services provided by professionals are referred to both as early intervention and early education somewhat interchangeably. Most of the terms used in this book reflect terms that are commonly used in the field, and it is our hope that readers will accept the variety of ways in which terms have been used. Perhaps this approach will help to promote a degree of flexibility that will assist families and professionals in communicating and working together more effectively.

Many people have contributed to the completion of this edition, either directly or indirectly. Appreciation goes first to our husbands, Rich Pogrund and Vince Fazzi, for their support and patience during the many hours we have spent on this book. It equally goes to our children, Ben and Amy Pogrund and Kathryn Fazzi, who have sacrificed time and attention from their moms throughout this project. We sincerely thank our families for their understanding. Additional gratitude goes to Vince Fazzi, the Azusa Unified School District, the Blind Childrens Center, and families and children for their assistance in taking and providing photographs for the book. Thanks also go to Linda Donovan for her many hours of deciphering illegible handwriting, arrows, and scribbles and for her superb word processing skills. We would like to acknowledge Natalie Hilzen, Director and Editor in Chief at AFB Press for all her wisdom, guidance, and patience, along with all the other staff members at AFB Press who assisted us in the publication process.

In addition to wanting to revise and update the first *Early Focus* for the field of visual impairment, part of the original motivation to rewrite the book was so that we could once again work together as colleagues and friends on a joint project. We are happy to say that after long weekly phone calls and daily e-mails, we are still the best of friends. We have had a great excuse to stay connected on a regular basis over the past years even though we are more than 1,000 miles apart—and for that we are thankful!

A final note of thanks goes to all of the contributors to the book, without whom this book would not have been possible, who each spent a great deal of time writing, editing, and revising their sections to make the second edition of *Early Focus* a significant contribution to our professional literature. We hope it fulfills the needs in the field by serving as a rich and vital resource on early childhood visual impairment. Of course, our greatest hope is that it helps in meeting the needs of the young children who are blind or visually impaired who depend on us as families and professionals to know how to help them be all that they can be.

Rona L. Pogrund
Diane L. Fazzi

ABOUT THE EDITORS

Rona L. Pogrund, Ph.D., COMS, is a private consultant in visual impairment in Austin, Texas. She was previously Associate Professor in the Division of Special Education and Director of the Orientation & Mobility Specialist Training Program at California State University, Los Angeles. Dr. Pogrund is the co-editor of the first edition of *Early Focus: Working with Young Blind and Visually Impaired Children and Their Families* and the co-author of *TAPS: Teaching Age-Appropriate Purposeful Skills: An Orientation and Mobility Curriculum for Students with Visual Impairments.* In addition, she has co-authored book chapters and articles and made numerous presentations on preschool orientation and mobility, advocacy issues, and students with multiple disabilities. She has worked as an orientation and mobility specialist, a teacher of students who are visually impaired, and a special education administrator.

Diane L. Fazzi, Ph.D., COMS, is Professor in the Division of Special Education, Charter College of Education and coordinator of the Orientation & Mobility Specialist Training Program at California State University, Los Angeles. Prior to joining the faculty of California State, she was an orientation and mobility specialist and teacher of students who are visually impaired in public school districts in Southern California, as well as at the Burwood School for the Blind in Melbourne, Australia. Dr. Fazzi is a peer reviewer for the *Journal of Visual Impairment & Blindness,* a member of the Research Committee of the Blind Childrens Center in Los Angeles, and is active in both state and national professional organizations. She is the co-editor of the first edition of *Early Focus: Working with Young Blind and Visually Impaired Children and Their Families* and co-author of *Imagining the Possibilities: Creative Approaches to Orientation and Mobility Instruction for Persons Who Are Visually Impaired,* as well as the author of numerous book chapters, journal articles, and conference presentations on working with young children who are visually impaired.

ABOUT THE CONTRIBUTORS

Tanni L. Anthony, Ed.S., COMS, is State Consultant on Visual Impairment and Project Director of the Colorado Services to Children with Deafblindness of the Colorado Department of Education in Denver. She has written articles, taught courses, and presented papers on working with infants and young children who are visually impaired and multiply disabled. She is currently a doctoral candidate at the University of Denver.

Hannah Bleier, COMS, M.A., is an orientation and mobility specialist and a teacher of students who are visually impaired in California. She has presented at both state and national conferences on the topic of teaching echolocation to young children who are blind.

Vivian I. Correa, Ph.D., is Professor in the Department of Special Education, College of Education, University of Florida at Gainesville, and held the 2000–2001 Matthew J. Guglielmo Endowed Chair in Mental Retardation at California State University, Los Angeles. Dr. Correa is the coauthor of *Interactive Teaming: Enhancing Programs for Students with Special Needs,* has published numerous book chapters and articles, and was co-editor of *Teacher Education and Special Education.* She has been involved in many research projects in the areas of early childhood and special education.

Jane N. Erin, Ph.D., is Professor in the Department of Special Education, Rehabilitation, and School Psychology at the University of Arizona, Tucson. She is co-editor of *Diversity and Visual Impairment,* co-author of *Visual Handicaps and Learning,* and past editor-in-chief of the *Journal of Visual Impairment & Blindness.*

Robert L. Gordon, O.D., F.A.A.O., is Associate Professor at the Southern California College of Optometry in Fullerton and on the medical staff of Cedars-Sinai Medical Center in Los Angeles. He has authored papers on low vision, vision testing for infants, and developments in ophthalmic technology.

M. Cay Holbrook, Ph.D., is Associate Professor in the Faculty of Education at the University of British Columbia in Vancouver, BC,

Canada. She has prepared teachers of students with visual impairments at Johns Hopkins University and the University of Arkansas at Little Rock and has taught children with visual impairments in public school programs. Dr. Holbrook is co-editor of *Foundations of Education* and editor of *Children with Visual Impairments: A Parent's Guide*.

Sherwin J. Isenberg, M.D., is Lantz Professor and Vice-Chairman of the Department of Ophthalmology at the Jules Stein Eye Institute and Professor of Pediatrics at the University of California, Los Angeles, School of Medicine. He is editor-in-chief of the *Journal of the American Association for Pediatric Ophthalmology and Strabismus* and has written numerous books, book chapters, and research papers.

Daniel Kish, M.A., COMS, is Executive Director and Senior Instructor at World Access for the Blind in Long Beach, California. He has given numerous presentations and workshops in professional and public forums.

M. Diane Klein, Ph.D., is Professor and Coordinator of the Early Childhood Special Education Program at California State University, Los Angeles. She is the co-author of *Working with Young Children from Culturally Diverse Backgrounds* and *Strategies for Including Children with Special Needs in Early Childhood Settings*.

Alan J. Koenig, Ed.D., is Professor of Special Education at Texas Tech University in Lubbock, where he coordinates the teacher preparation program in visual impairment. A leading researcher on the selection of appropriate literacy media for students with visual impairments, he is co-author of *Foundations of Braille Literacy, Learning Media Assessment of Students with Visual Impairments: A Resource Guide for Teachers,* and *New Programmed Instruction in Braille,* and co-editor of *Foundations of Low Vision* and *Foundations of Education*. Dr. Koenig is also editor-in-chief of the *Journal of Visual Impairment & Blindnesss*.

Evelyn A. Paysse, M.D., is Assistant Professor of Ophthalmology at Texas Children's Hospital and Assistant Professor in the Department of Pediatrics at Baylor College of Medicine in Houston, Texas. She is the author of numerous articles on vision loss and strabismus.

Kay M. Pruett, Ph.D., COMS, is Special Programs Teacher at the Texas School for the Blind and Visually Impaired. Dr. Pruett was adjunct faculty member at San Francisco State University's Department of Special Education and has also worked as a private consultant in blindness. She has co-authored articles and made presentations on the topics of developing communication skills and spatial skills for children with multiple disabilities.

Patricia Sacks Salcedo, M.A., is a Program Specialist in the SEEDS Project, Sacramento County Office of Education and has also worked as a teacher of students who are visually impaired. She is a contributor to *First Look: Vision Evaluation and Assessment for Infants, Toddlers, and Preschoolers, Birth Through Five Years of Age* and has made professional presentations on topics that include early literacy, family assessment, and transdisciplinary teamwork.

Chris A. Strickling, M.A., OTR, is an occupational therapist and doctoral candidate at the University of Texas, Arlington. She is the author of *Impact of Vision Loss on Motor Development: Information for Occupational and Physical Therapists Working with Students with Visual Impairments*. In addition, she has participated in performance programs with a disability focus and has participated in conference sessions on disability and identity.

REFOCUS

Setting the Stage for Working with Young Children Who Are Blind or Visually Impaired

CONTRIBUTOR

Rona L. Pogrund

It has been 10 years since the first edition of *Early Focus: Working with Young Blind and Visually Impaired Children and Their Families* was published in 1992. The field of visual impairment and blindness has entered a new century, and the need for appropriate services from qualified professionals who know how to meet the unique needs of children who are visually impaired is greater than ever. Some things have changed, and some have not. There has been a contined increase in the number of children who need to be served, a continued shortage of professionals qualified in both visual impairment and early childhood education, an improvement in laws and policies supporting services to young children with visual impairments, and an overall increase in knowledge of best practices in early intervention for children with disabilities.

The current status of early intervention will be reviewed in this chapter, along with the basic principles of early intervention with young children who are visually impaired. An overview of the laws and regulations affecting the service delivery to this population of young children will also be covered. A description of the children and families being served will be included. There will also be a summary of some of the key issues professionals and families face as they try to meet the needs of these children who are visually impaired.

CURRENT STATUS OF EARLY INTERVENTION

The term *early intervention* is commonly used to describe services provided to children with disabilities from birth to 3, as well as their families, to enhance their early development. However, the term has

FOCUS POINTS ON EARLY INTERVENTION IN THE FIELD OF VISUAL IMPAIRMENT

The following key ideas are addressed in this chapter.

➜ The value of early intervention services to all young children with disabilities and to society in general has been increasingly established, as the federal legislation supporting early intervention services to children from birth to age 5 has steadily improved over the past 25 years.

➜ Understanding the unique ways that vision loss affects development and learning is critical when providing early intervention services to young children who are visually impaired.

➜ The numbers of young children who are visually impaired and their families that are being served are increasing, with over half of these children having additional disabilities.

➜ The increase in the numbers of various ethnic groups, teen births, and premature births are factors that affect the demographics of the children and families served.

➜ The increasing population and changing demographics of young children with visual impairments and their families make it essential for professionals in the field to stay current with best practices in early intervention.

➜ Key issues facing families and professionals in the field of visual impairment include specialized versus generalized services, personnel shortages, cross-cultural competence, provision of services in natural environments, caseload size, direct service versus a consultation model, and the needs of children with multiple disabilities.

been used more globally in this book because many of the strategies described may be appropriate for children birth to 5. The reader will also find the terms early education and preschool services used when referring to children ages 3 to 5. Ideally, these services follow a prescribed sequence, which is outlined in "The Process of Early Intervention and Early Educational Services" in this chapter.

The significance of early intervention in the lives of young children with disabilities has been established over the past decade (Hanson & Lynch, 1995; Rosetti, 2001). The fields of developmental psychology and early childhood education, as well as recent brain research studies, all support the importance of early intervention in the first years of a child's life to maximize cognitive, motor, and social development. Observable changes in a child's behavior and de-

THE PROCESS OF EARLY INTERVENTION AND EARLY EDUCATIONAL SERVICES

The basic process of both early intervention and early education for children who are visually impaired ideally includes the following components:

1. Identification and referral of the child in need of early intervention or early education.

2. Screening and assessment of the child's visual impairment to determine his or her visual functioning and eligibility for services.

3. Assessment of the child's needs in all developmental areas and the family's needs for support.

4. Planning of an intervention program to meet the identified needs and to promote the child's development and the family's well-being.

5. Identification of and referral to all appropriate specialists who can assist in meeting the needs of the child and family.

6. Implementation of a program in the appropriate setting for a particular child and family.

7. Ongoing evaluation of the appropriateness of the services provided in meeting the needs of the child and family.

Rona L. Pogrund

velopment are not always a good measure in determining whether early intervention services are effective, because it is difficult to tell what changes were due to the intervention and what were due to maturity and natural development in the individual child. A key finding in the literature is that caregiver involvement is the most significant factor in early intervention efficacy (Carnegie Corporation, 1994; Mahoney, Boyce, Ferrell, Spiker, & Wheeden, 1994). The other crucial factor that contributes to the efficacy of early intervention is the age of identification of a disability. The children who are identified early and receive appropriate services do better than those who are found later or receive services at a later age. The earlier the intervention, the better for the child. Successful early intervention programs are also found to be more highly structured than less successful ones, regardless of the curriculum model being used (Shonkoff & Hauser-Cram, 1987; Hauser-Cram & Krauss, 1991). A greater intensity of services also appears to more positively affect outcomes as well as individualizing instruction for each child. Other measures that can be used in evaluating the effectiveness of an early intervention program include attainment of individual child goals, outcomes of family variables, and environmental aspects such as staff training and retention.

There has also been increasing support for the contention that the dollars put into early intervention for children with disabilities and those at risk for developmental delay are a wise investment that ultimately saves society money in later years as these children enter adolescence and adulthood. It has been shown that for every dollar a school district spends on a child with a disability or an at-risk child under 3, $6.00 are saved by that district later (Rosetti, 2001). The

FOCUS ON EFFECTIVENESS

BEST PRACTICES IN EARLY INTERVENTION

Some of the best practices and priorities that are seen in early intervention programs for children with disabilities include the following:

➜ A family-centered approach: When an early intervention program is planned and implemented, it reflects the particular family's values, concerns, priorities, and cultural background.

➜ Collaboration with families and other professionals: Everyone involved with the child is working together in meeting the child's individual needs.

➜ A team approach in assessments and program implementation: Working as a team promotes a more cohesive program and less fragmentation.

➜ Written Individualized Family Service Plans (IFSPs) to identify family and professional priorities (mandated by federal law P.L. 99–457): IFSPs serve as written guidelines to the goals, objectives, and specific services to be provided for each child.

➜ Provision of services in natural environments to the maximum extent appropriate: Natural environments are defined as environments in which children would naturally be if they did not have disabilities.

➜ Coordination of services by a lead agency in each state: A designated entity in each state oversees all funds authorized for early intervention and all services provided to these young children with disabilities.

➜ Provision of a comprehensive child-find system to increase early identification of children with disabilities and those at risk for developmental delay: A specified plan is put in place to provide information in the community (for example, at medical facilities) to help identify and locate children with special needs so they can be referred for appropriate services.

Rona L. Pogrund

long-term costs in terms of welfare, unemployment, and adult rehabilitation are indeterminable.

Early intervention services are more universally accepted today as a primary contributor to optimal development for children with disabilities and their families. Many of the concepts identified in earlier legislation have become common practice in most places. Some of these practices are outlined in the accompanying box, "Best Practices in Early Intervention."

EARLY INTERVENTION FOR CHILDREN WHO ARE VISUALLY IMPAIRED

The best practices that have been identified apply to all young children with disabilities, including those who are visually impaired. Early-intervention services are effective with children who are visually impaired as well (Ferrell, 2000). When providing early intervention to children with visual impairments, it is important to understand the unique ways that vision loss affects learning (see "Basic Principles of Early Intervention for Children Who Are Visually Impaired"). Understanding the significant impact of vision loss on learning helps early interventionists to plan programs that are relevant for children who are visually impaired, thus carrying out the required legislation in a meaningful way for each individual child. The next section provides a review of the federal legislation that affects early intervention services.

LEGISLATION AND SERVICE DELIVERY

The federal legislation supporting early intervention services to children from birth to age 5 has steadily improved each decade since the passage of P.L. 94–142, the Education for All Handicapped Children Act, in 1975, although there is no guarantee that this trend will continue. Amendments to this legislation, the name of which was changed in 1990 to the Individuals with Disabilities Education Act (IDEA) were signed into law in 1986. This legislation, P.L. 99–457, while addressing a variety of educational services, expanded special education services to children of preschool age (3–5) with disabilities and to those who are at risk for developmental delays and provided greater incentives for serving the birth to 3-year-old population.

During the following decade, P.L. 99–457 was strengthened further with the 1997 amendments under P.L. 105–17 to Part C of IDEA, which became law in July 1998. These amendments specified that services be delivered to infants with disabilities and those who are at

BASIC PRINCIPLES OF EARLY INTERVENTION FOR CHILDREN WHO ARE VISUALLY IMPAIRED

The following are basic principles about how children who are visually impaired learn. These principles are important to remember when providing early intervention services to this population.

➜ In general, children who are visually impaired will need more time than sighted peers to acquire developmental skills, especially those skills acquired primarily through vision.

➜ Young children who are visually impaired may demonstrate a different sequence of acquisition than sighted children in reaching certain developmental milestones (Ferrell, 2000).

➜ Incidental learning, the method by which sighted children achieve many of their developmental skills and learn about their world, is not as readily available for children who are visually impaired, especially for those who are totally blind.

➜ Children who are visually impaired do not have the benefit of vision as a unifying sense to assist in learning the meaning of sounds and the functions of objects and to help organize their world.

➜ Some concepts may be fragmented for children who are visually impaired, as touch and sound may provide only partial understanding without guided exploration and verbal explanations.

➜ Use of real objects and experiences during intervention increases tactile, auditory, and visual comprehension for children who are visually impaired.

➜ Active involvement and participation in exploring the world help to optimize the motor and cognitive development of young children who are visually impaired.

➜ Children who are visually impaired and their families need specialized instruction and educational guidance from professionals who have expertise in addressing their disability-specific needs. These educational vision specialists should be involved in all phases of the planning and implementation of the educational program of young children who are visually impaired.

Rona L. Pogrund

risk for developmental delay from birth through 36 months. Those eligible infants and their families are required to receive a multidisciplinary assessment and to have an Individualized Family Service Plan (IFSP) developed. The 1997 amendments also improved the provisions affecting services to young children who are visually impaired. For the first time, vision services were included in the list of early intervention services available for infants and toddlers. In addition, orientation and mobility (O&M) specialists were listed under the qualified personnel who may provide early intervention services. Having this language specified in the federal law under part C increases the possibility that vision services and O&M will be included in the assessment process and early intervention services provided to young children who are visually impaired. (See Chapter 11 for more information on the law and children who are visually impaired).

Because each state specifies its own lead agency to coordinate its early intervention services, these agencies vary from state to state. For example, a lead agency could be a state department of education, health, or social services or could be an early childhood intervention division of one of these departments. If there is no one knowledgeable of the unique needs of young children with visual impairments in the lead agency or on the state interagency coordinating council (as mandated in IDEA, a body appointed by each state governor to advise and assist the lead agency which must be representative of the state population and must include parents of young children with disabilities), it is not uncommon for vision services and orientation and mobility services to go unaddressed in the implementation of the federal laws and in the disbursement of funds, especially for children with multiple disabilities. It is therefore important that someone at the state level who has expertise in visual impairment works with the lead agency, or that a knowledgeable individual be appointed to the state interagency coordinating council, if at all possible, to ensure that the policies and procedures established address the needs of these young children who are visually impaired. Even though educational laws are created to improve the quality of children's lives, it is the implementation and monitoring that determine how effective the services will actually be. It is also important, therefore, that families and vision professionals act as advocates for appropriate services at the local level. (See Chapter 11 for information on advocacy strategies.)

CHILDREN AND FAMILIES SERVED

The numbers of young children who are visually impaired and their families being served are increasing (Dote-Kwan, Chen, & Hughes, 2001) and reflect the changing composition of the American family in general. The increase in numbers of various ethnic groups, teen births, and premature births are all factors affecting the makeup of the populations being served. Based on data from the National Center for Health Statistics (1998) and estimates from the Center for Disease Control and Prevention, several significant population changes have affected the type of children and families that professionals in the field of visual impairment are serving.

According to these data, there were 3,941,553 total live births in the United States in 1998. More than half these births were to women in their 20s, 12.5 percent were born to teen mothers, more than 2 percent to women over age 40, and less than 0.1 percent (158) to women ages 50–54. The increase in teenage pregnancy has also increased the incidence of premature births and lower birthweights. Teens are more likely to have poor eating habits, smoke, drink alcohol or take drugs, gain inadequate weight during pregnancy, have sexually transmitted diseases, and are less likely than pregnant women to get regular prenatal care. All of these factors increase risk for pregnancy complications and for having low birthweight babies, increasing risk of visual and other impairments (NCHS, 1999; Berenson, Wiemann, Rowe, & Rickert, 1997). Later maternal age increases complications of labor, toxemia, and the occurrence of Down syndrome—all of which increase the chance of visual impairment in the newborn.

There has been a steady increase in the birth of premature babies (less than 37 weeks of gestation) between 1988 and 1998. Premature births increased about 14 percent from 10.2 percent of live births to 11.6 percent. Approximately 200,000 premature infants born each year in the United States are kept alive. More premature infants than ever are surviving because of the extensive advances in neonatal technology. Many of them, however, have a variety of disabilities, and there is also a steady increase of retinopathy of prematurity (ROP) among these surviving infants.

A significant correlation to prematurity is low birthweight. Low birthweight is often associated with a variety of birth defects, including some visual impairments, such as ROP; the incidence of ROP increases as birthweight decreases (Trief, Duckman, Morse, & Silberman, 1989). Between 1988 and 1998, the number of low-birthweight infants (less than 2,500 grams [5.5 lbs.]) increased nearly 10 percent (from 6.9 percent to 7.6 percent of all live births) and the number of very-low-birthweight infants (less than 1,500 grams [3.3 lbs.]) also increased from 1.2 percent in 1988 to 1.49 percent of live births in 1998. Every year more than 4,200 babies are born weighing less than 1 pound. These low- and very-low-birthweight infants are often the children needing early intervention services, as they may have a variety of disabilities, including visual impairment.

The leading causes of birth defects in 2000, according to the March of Dimes Perinatal Data Center (2000), are structural and metabolic causes (such as nervous system disorders and Down syndrome), congenital infections (such as congenital syphilis, congenital HIV infection, and congenital rubella syndrome), and other causes (such as fetal alcohol syndrome). There is a higher prevalence of visual impairment among children with multiple disabilities (Orel-Bixler, Haeyerstrom-Portnoy, & Hall, 1989). Children with cerebral palsy, developmental disabilities, Down syndrome, fragile X syndrome, and hearing impairment have a higher frequency of severe vision problems than children without disabilities. In addition, the increase in drug use by pregnant women has further affected the number of infants being born with visual and other impairments. Approximately 11 percent of pregnant women use at least one of the following drugs: heroin, methadone, amphetamines, PCP, marijuana, and cocaine. A study conducted by the National Institute on Drug Abuse (NIDA) found that the average annual number of drug-exposed newborns more than doubled from 1982 to 1987. There were approximately 38,000 drug-exposed babies in the United States in 1987, with a steady increase since that time (Rosetti, 2001). These drug-exposed infants may show signs of neurological impairments, including cortical visual impairment (CVI), which has also increased as a diagnosed vision problem over the past decade (Russo & Self, 2001). CVI, in which lesions of the posterior visual pathways in the brain occur, resulting in impaired visual functioning in children, is now a leading cause of visual impairment in young children in the United States (Murphy, & Bernas-Pierce, 1995). CVI can be caused by a variety of insults to the brain and can be associated with different disabilities. (See Chapter 3 for more information on cortical visual impairment.)

In viewing the population of children who are visually impaired being served, it is important to look at the changing ethnic makeup of the American people. According to the 2000 United States Census, the Hispanic population grew nearly 60 percent in the 1990s. The Hispanic population has become equal in size with the African American population and soon will represent the largest ethnic minority group in the United States. Moreover, the census most likely underestimates the numbers of Hispanic individuals, since there are probably significantly more undocumented immigrants living in the United States who were not counted. The Census Bureau projects that Hispanics will more than triple in number by 2050, accounting for one fourth of the U. S. population. The Asian American population has increased significantly over the past decade as well. It is predicted that more than 50 percent of all families nationwide will be from non–European-American backgrounds by the year 2030 (Salend & Taylor, 1993). The need for cross-cultural competency and sensitivity toward the diverse ethnic groups in the United States by vision professionals cannot be overestimated (see Chapter 2 for more information on cultural competency).

Table 1.1 shows the numbers of births to teenagers and the infants that were low- or very-low-birthweight and preterm in the United States in 1998 among Hispanic, non-Hispanic white, and African American mothers. It is significant to note that the incidence in the United States of teen births, premature births, and low- and very-low-birthweight infants are higher among mothers of Hispanic and African American origin, resulting in a higher rate of visual impairment among their children. These families will constitute a significant number of those served by professionals in the field of visual impairment.

TABLE 1.1 **ETHNICITY OF MOTHER AND TYPE OF BIRTH**
(United States, 1998)

| TYPES OF BIRTHS | ETHNICITY OF MOTHER | | | | | |
| | HISPANIC | | NON-HISPANIC WHITE | | AFRICAN AMERICAN | |
	Number	Percentage	Number	Percentage	Number	Percentage
Total births	734,661	—	2,361,462	—	593,127	—
Births to teenagers	124,104	16.9	221,301	9.4	128,280	21.6
Low-birthweight infants (less than 2500 grams or 5.5 lbs)	47,295	6.4	154,596	6.6	78,012	13.2
Very-low-birthweight infants (less than 1500 grams or 3.3 lbs)	8,416	1.1	27,117	1.1	18,425	3.1
Preterm births (less than 37 weeks gestation)	82,282	11.4	240,300	10.2	103,588	17.6

Source: *Vital Statistics of the United States—Volume I, Natality.* (Hyattsville, MD: National Center for Health Statistics Vital Statistics. 1998).

NUMBERS OF CHILDREN WHO ARE VISUALLY IMPAIRED

It is difficult to accurately assess the exact number of children birth to 5 who are visually impaired in the United States, but it has been estimated that there are as many as 19,000 children under age 5 who have visual impairments (Dietz & Ferrell, 1993). The National Center for Health Statistics sponsored the National Health Interview Survey–Disability Supplement in 1994–1995. This survey is a cross-sectional household interview survey covering the civilian noninstitutionalized population of the United States. According to this parent survey, there were 46,294 children ages birth to 5 with serious difficulty seeing (measured by a question indicating serious difficulty seeing letters in regular print with best correction) and 9,072 children who are legally blind in this age group, according to the parents answering the survey. This survey relied on the parent's diagnosis rather than on medical or educational diagnoses. The 1998–1999 American Printing House for the Blind federal quota census identified 12,437 infants, toddlers, and preschoolers who were visually impaired. These figures only include those children registered who qualify under the definition of legal blindness. According to the U. S. Department of Education's Office of Special Education Programs for 1997, there were approximately 8,800 infants and toddlers (birth to 2) who received "vision services" under Part C of IDEA.

There are most likely young children with visual impairments who are not legally blind or who have multiple disabilities who are not identified in many of these child counts because their visual impairment may not be recognized at an early age or because they are included under a disability category other than visual impairment. Many young children in these two categories often go undiagnosed, unreferred, unassessed, and/or unserved. Based on the steady increase in the numbers who are served and the increased child-find efforts (specific plans to identify children with disabilities or those who are "at risk" in the community) in most states, the population of children who are identified as visually impaired will continue to grow in the years ahead.

Four possible factors placing a child at risk of developing a visual impairment are prematurity, a family history of visual defects, infection during pregnancy, and difficult or assisted labor. In addition, a newborn infant may be visually impaired because of congenital cataracts, glaucoma, retinoblastoma, retinitis pigmentosa, optic-nerve hypoplasia, or cortical visual impairment. According to Project PRISM (Ferrell, 1998), a longitudinal study of 202 young children with visual impairments and their families, the most frequent visual diagnoses were cortical visual impairment (20.6 percent), ROP (19.1 percent) and optic-nerve hypoplasia (16.6 percent). (See Chapter 3 for more information on causes of visual impairment.) In addition, as noted earlier, many children with other disabilities also have a higher incidence of visual impairments (for example, children with cerebral palsy, Down syndrome, and hearing impairment). Several studies (Ferrell, 1998; Robinson, Jan, & Kinnis, 1987; Walker, Tobin, & McKennell, 1991) have indicated that from 56 to 64 percent of young visually impaired children have additional disabilities. Ferrell (1998) found that optic nerve hypoplasia and albinism were the most frequent visual diagnoses in children who did not have additional disabilities, whereas those with severe multiple disabilities were most often diagnosed with ROP and CVI. Accurately identifying all of the children birth to 5 who are visually impaired is an ongoing challenge for statisticians and data collectors, and this task affects funding disbursement, knowledge of the need for adequate personnel, and the provision of quality services.

KEY ISSUES THAT FACE FAMILIES AND PROFESSIONALS

Even though laws and services for children who are visually impaired and their families have significantly improved over the past decade, professionals and families still face a number of key issues. It is important to be aware of some of the more philosophical, global, and logistical issues of service delivery.

Specialized versus Generalized Services

There are varying views within the field of early intervention about the importance of specialized services compared to more generalized services for young children with disabilities. Is expertise in generic special education and early childhood development more important than specialized knowledge of visual impairment when serving young children who are visually impaired? This question is raised most often when serving the infant and toddler population and when serving children with multiple disabilities. Some early childhood interventionists feel they can best meet the needs of these children. But do they really have an understanding of the impact of vision loss on development? Ensuring that appropriate and qualified personnel are serving children who are visually impaired should be a top priority.

Personnel Shortage

As the numbers of young children who are visually impaired increases, there continues to be a personnel shortage of teachers of students who are visually impaired and O&M specialists, especially those knowledgeable of early childhood development (Corn & Ferrell, 2000; Corn, Hatlen, Huebner, Ryan, & Siller, 1996; Corn & Silberman, 1999; Council for Exceptional Children, 2000; Dote-Kwan, Chen, & Hughes, 2001; Silberman, Corn, & Sowell, 1996; Wiener & Sifferman, 2000). There is an ongoing need to recruit, train, and retain teachers to serve this young population. Maintaining current university training programs and increasing the number of new programs to prepare teachers of students who are visually impaired and O&M specialists are more important than ever, as the majority of professionals in the field are over age 40, and most will be leaving the workforce within the next two decades (Dote-Kwan, Chen, & Hughes, 2001), creating an even more critical shortage.

Cultural Competence of Professionals

The issue of cultural competence among professionals is more significant than ever, as noted earlier in this chapter, because of the changing demographics of this country. An important finding in the study of teachers serving young children with visual impairments by Dote-Kwan, Chen, & Hughes (2001) was that the respondents' backgrounds did not reflect the cultural and linguistic diversity of the children they serve. It was suggested that preservice training programs emphasize cross-cultural competencies to increase the effectiveness of services when professionals work with families from diverse cultures (see Chapter 2 for more information on cross-cultural competency). It is also important to recruit new professionals into the field of visual impairment from a diversity of ethnic backgrounds.

Natural Environments

Since the federal law states that early intervention services be provided in natural environments to the maximum extent appropriate, there has been some confusion as to what educational settings are considered natural environments. Can a disability-specific early childhood program be a natural environment? Does the natural environment have to be one in which children without disabilities participate? According to Chen (1999a), a program designed to meet the unique needs of young children who are visually impaired may very well be the appropriate natural environment for a particular child. Services can be provided in a variety of settings and program models. These may include home-based, center-based, or combination programs and may be at a preschool or day-care center, a generic special education program, or a disability-specific program. (See Chapter 11 for more information on program options.) Maintaining an array of program options and models continues to be important in order to meet the individualized needs of all children who are visually impaired.

Caseload Size and Service Delivery Models

Two ongoing service delivery dilemmas for professionals serving young children with visual impairments involve caseload size and direct service versus a consultation model. There is much discussion as to the appropriate caseload for a teacher of students who are visually impaired or an O&M specialist when serving young children (see the section on caseload size in Chapter 11). Decisions regarding caseload size and the model of service delivery should always be based on the individual needs of the children. Too often, professionals perceive pressure to continue adding children to their caseload and to change from a direct service model to a consultation model in order to accommodate more students. Such decisions often result in increased stress on the service provider and poorer quality of service to the children and families involved. A consultation model may be appropriate in some transdisciplinary programs (programs in which service providers from different disciplines share specific roles and strategies without direct hands-on intervention by each of them), but there may be times in each child's development when more direct service by an educational vision specialist may be appropriate. The guiding light for all caseload and service delivery model decisions should always be the assessed needs identified in the IFSP or Individualized Education Program (IEP) for each child.

Children with Multiple Disabilities

Children with multiple disabilities continue to be the majority of young children who are visually impaired being served by professionals (Dote-Kwan, Chen, & Hughes, 2001; Hatton, 2001). Often the early childhood interventionists are the primary service providers for the children, and the vision professionals serve as related service providers. It is more important than ever that teachers of students who are visually impaired and O&M specialists learn strategies of collaboration and teaming with other professionals so that a more effective transdisciplinary model of service delivery can be implemented to meet the complex needs of children with multi-

ple disabilities. (See Chapter 11 for more information on transdisciplinary teaming.)

OVERVIEW OF *EARLY FOCUS*

The chapters that follow provide comprehensive resources on
young children who are blind or visually impaired for professionals
working with this unique population. The service providers who
would benefit from this book include, but are not limited to, preservice and inservice teachers of students who are visually impaired,
O&M specialists, early childhood interventionists, occupational
therapists, physical therapists, speech and language therapists, psychologists, social workers, classroom teachers, assistant teachers, administrators of early intervention programs, medical personnel, and
any other member of a child's educational team. The book also has
much valuable information for families and caregivers who wish to
understand more about the development of their children who are
visually impaired.

Each chapter has a specific focus, as indicated by its title. Chapter 2 starts with a focus on the family, including a section on cross-
cultural competence. It is followed by the chapter on vision, including the medical and functional implications of vision loss in young
children. Each succeeding chapter focuses on a specific developmental area of importance for young children: cognition, literacy,
social skills, independence, behavior, motor skills, and O&M skills.

Each chapter on development contrasts typical development
with development of the child who is visually impaired. Recent research (Ferrell, 1998) indicates that children who are visually impaired may not always follow the same sequence of development as
sighted children. The use of typical developmental progression is
provided only as a reference point for readers who are not familiar
with the typical development of young sighted children. Such familiarity also assists in communication and collaboration with other
providers of early intervention services. Assessment strategies and
strategies for promoting each area of development are also included.
References to children with multiple disabilities are integrated
throughout the book, with specific examples offered for this population in each chapter. The book ends with a chapter on teaming and
advocacy, supporting collaboration between all professionals and
families as the model which best maintains the focus on meeting the
unique needs of each child who is visually impaired. A comprehensive resources section can be found at the end of the book.

2 FAMILY FOCUS

Working Effectively with Families

CONTRIBUTORS

Diane L. Fazzi Supportive Communication

M. Diane Klein Cultural Considerations

Rona L. Pogrund Supportive Communication

Patricia Sacks Salcedo Emotional Reactions of Families, Supporting Families through Transitions

In the belief that the family is the most significant influence in the life of a child who is visually impaired, the content of this book starts with a focus on the family. The young child who is visually impaired cannot be viewed as an entity unto him- or herself, but must instead be seen as part of an interactive family system. Therefore, approaches that support and strengthen existing family resources and address family goals and priorities are most likely to positively impact the child. The professional's effectiveness in working with young children who are visually impaired is increased when working with a family-centered philosophy. Professionals working with visually impaired children will have a greater impact if they have an understanding of, sensitivity toward, and respect for the family.

The image of the two-parent family with the father as "breadwinner" and the mother who stays at home to care for the children and the house is no longer a true representation of American society (Thomas, Correa, & Morsink, 2001; Thorp & Brown, 1987). The American family portrait must be expanded to include working mothers; families separated by divorce; "blended" families or stepfamilies; same-sex partners; single parents; grandparents as primary caregivers; unwed teenage mothers; and adoptive, foster, migrant, and homeless families.

Early childhood specialists need to be increasingly sensitive to these current family structures when collaborating to design and implement early intervention programs. Professionals need to view the family as a system and realize that interventions with the child can affect all members of the family. Effective partnerships between professionals and families expand beyond mothers and their children with disabilities to include the fathers, siblings, and extended family members who are involved with the children on a daily basis (Thomas, Correa, & Morsink, 2001). Intervention strategies should reflect the individual family's values, concerns, priorities, and cultural background. Integrating an understanding of unique family structures and other family characteristics into the intervention process will, in all likelihood, result in a greater impact on the child's overall development.

This chapter outlines the cycles of grief and coping and family reactions associated with the birth of a child who is visually impaired. Professional responses, including supportive communication, active listening, and information sharing, are discussed. Families of visually impaired infants and preschoolers go through many difficult transitions, including their experience at the hospital, the transition from hospital to home, the transition from home to school, and the transition from school to school. Suggestions are made to assist professionals in supporting families through these transitions. Cultural considerations and differences in child-rearing practices are presented to help professionals understand other perspectives and be more effective when working with families from different backgrounds.

EMOTIONAL REACTIONS OF FAMILIES

Each family is a dynamic system that can experience many changes throughout the lifespan. Changes in family composition occur through marriages, births, deaths, and relocations. Changes in family resources (internal and external) may also occur through education, career changes, illnesses, spiritual involvement, prosperity, and economic hardship. Each of these types of changes can create stress for the family system. The birth of a child who has a disability can also be a source of stress for a family, but like all other changes it can be a positive influence on individual family members and can cause a positive outcome for the family unit (Thomas, Correa, & Morsink, 2001; Turnbull & Turnbull, 1997). For example, in a family in which both parents work full-time, the birth of a child with multiple disabilities can place stress on the family system if typical caretaking options (such as a neighborhood day-care facility) no longer seem most appropriate or are no longer the family's preference. The stress caused by this situation might result in a positive outcome for the entire family if, say, the father wanted to change to part-time work and stay at home to care for the child, and the family had the resources to do so. The father might then have more quality time to spend with siblings, and the mother might experience less stress at work knowing that everyone is well cared for while she is at the office. In the long term, this unanticipated life change could lessen stress on the entire family.

The birth of a child with a visual impairment can change the equilibrium of the family, bringing forth a multitude of emotions and reactions. For some parents, the birth of a child with a disability may symbolize the loss of the "imagined perfect child" and the parents' self-esteem. It has been suggested that families go through a specific sequence of feelings (Cohen, 1992) very similar to the grief cycle (typically including the stages of shock, denial, guilt, anger, depression, objectivity, and resolution) felt by people experiencing a major loss, as illustrated by the traditional model pictured in Figure 2.1. From this author's parental perspective (see also Herring, 1996), individual family members do not adhere to orderly, sequential, predictable reactions. Individuals may go through the stages of reaction countless times in varying orders, expending different amounts of time and energy at each stage, and they may skip some stages altogether. Indeed, many parents comment that specific events trigger all or parts of the cycle. The emotional responses of families are too complex to classify into absolute, rigid stages, as suggested by the revised and individualized models shown in Figure 2.1.

Mothers

The individuality of emotional reactions experienced by families is highlighted by Patricia Salcedo (1986) in her following comments on

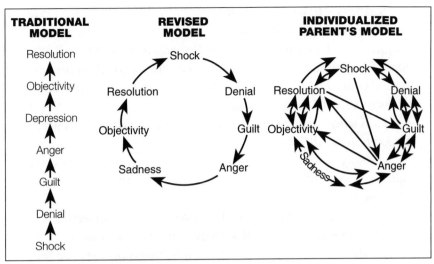

Figure 2.1. Three models of the sequence of feelings experienced after the birth of a child who is visually impaired.

her feelings as a mother of a child with a visual impairment and additional disabilities when her daughter was 3 years old:

> Shock *came first in my particular experience. I felt as if I were outside the window looking in. Surely this prevented my jumping through the window.*
>
> *I decided to skip* Denial *as previously arranged. This resulted in "over-handicapping" my child. I could not see her strengths because I was overwhelmed with her weaknesses. However, in dealing with those weaknesses, I set up a very comprehensive intervention program. The benefits of this program have been worth the emotional cost to me.*
>
> *"Let's skip* Guilt, *too," I thought. This has been a well-orchestrated pregnancy. Daily quarts of milk began two months before conception. We didn't even sit in the smoking section of restaurants. I know that I could not have prevented my child's birth defects. I also felt no guilt in choosing to bring her home from the hospital and raise her.*
>
> Anger, *however, consumed me. Anger against people in the supermarket. Anger against insensitive doctors. Anger against my elder daughter when she spilled milk. Anger against the neighbors with normal children. Anger against the President of the United States. It knew no bounds. Some anger lay outside of the coping process. (Some professionals blame all anger on the coping process, as if it were illegitimate or an alien feeling.) Slowly, it weakened. Occasionally, it stirs deep inside.*

Sadness *follows, theoretically. Sadness deserves its own circle in the coping diagram. It accompanies all the other stages. Sadness surfaces when we fail to reach developmental milestones. It surfaces when we do reach them, often because of the pain and extended effort our kids spent achieving them. It occurs on birthdays, at surgeries, with rude remarks, and with developmental testing. I feel pain when I realize my child will always be different in a world unaccepting of difference.*

Pushing sadness away requires continual effort. One positive outcome—bonding easily with other parents of impaired children. We understand each other's pain. This *is coping.*

Objectivity *should follow. We parents must be objective. We are the responsible party. Objectivity can be hard to define. Professionals and parents may disagree while both claiming to be "objective." In the coping process, however, such a stage is vital. After the tears, we need to assess what we must do: which services are necessary, what medical advice is valid.*

Resolution. *We felt it Day One: love, responsibility, acceptance. We had nowhere to go but up. Our family bonded tightly. Trauma came with other people's lack of "Resolution." On good days, I feel as I did at my child's birth. It's a "high" that is difficult to maintain. We walk a fine line—accepting our children's limitations yet pushing them toward an unknown potential.*

Guilt *caught up with me. When my child was two years old, she required emergency surgery. Why had I missed the symptoms (why had the doctors missed the symptoms)? The signs were unobservable, yet I punished myself for not finding them.*

Denial, *too, sneaks in. As my child grows, the finality of her limitations looms. I fight this. A little can't hurt—it allows me to try one more time.*

It is important to be sensitive to a family's current emotional state and equally important to avoid categorizing family members according to predetermined expectations that accompany more traditional models. At any given point, families need opportunities to express themselves, and they need acknowledgment of their feelings by others.

Individual family members may react differently to the birth of a child with a visual impairment (Herring, 1996). All family members can experience the complex and individualized range of emotions often attributed only to mothers. For example, a mother might take her child to countless doctors looking for a cure or a different diagnosis, while the father accepts the child's visual impairment and

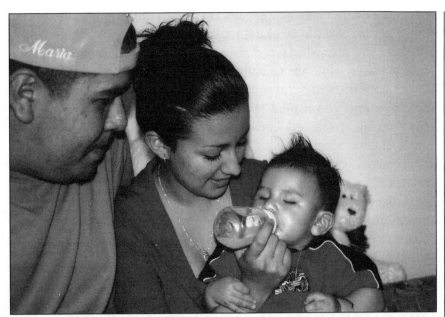

Family members may have different reactions to the birth of a child with a disability. It is important to be sensitive to their emotional states and avoid predetermined expectations based on traditional roles.

starts to explore ways to play with the young child that are enjoyable for both. Some siblings may be jealous of the "special attention" given to the child with a disability, while others may not initially form a bond, fearing that the child is too fragile to hold. There is a common assumption that the incidence of divorce is higher in families in which there is a child with a disability than in the general population. Giving birth to a child with a visual impairment produces stress, which can weaken an already threatened marriage bond. Some couples, however, are able to increase their communication and partnership skills and develop strategies to address the added stress and form a stronger marriage. (For suggestions on keeping marriages on an even keel when there is a child with a disability, see Holbrook, 1996.)

Fathers

Some fathers who assume a traditional "breadwinner" role may retreat into their work, justifiably feeling an increased economic burden when they think about the child's potentially expensive additional needs. Work may also provide an escape hatch where other concerns temporarily take the place of dwelling on the child's needs. The ability of fathers to continue to provide for the family in spite of overwhelming emotional upheaval should not be minimized.

Fathers contribute in more ways than providing food and shelter. Many fathers assume an equal partnership in the education of their children and are willing and able to be actively involved in raising their children who are visually impaired. These fathers may go to doctor appointments, attend Individual Family Service Plan (IFSP) meetings, and go on field trips. Their perspectives form important contributions to the educational team. Less formal activities in the home, such as roughhousing, may prove to be very beneficial to the child's sensory integration, body awareness, and motor development. Exploring outdoor activities (once considered "dad-type" activities), such as camping and fishing, may introduce the child with a visual impairment to a rich set of experiences that will contribute to concept development and the development of meaningful recreational and leisure activities within the family.

Siblings

Brothers and sisters also experience a range of emotions (Bolinger & Bolinger, 1996). Older siblings may be asked to participate in caretaking tasks—and some will enjoy the responsibility. Other children may feel left out as the child with the disability receives the majority of adult attention. Some children may act out; others may become more withdrawn. Professionals who provide home-based services can consider a variety of approaches for making visits a positive experience for other siblings who may be at home, such as:

Supporting Siblings

→ spending a brief period of time at the beginning or end of the session to converse with or play with the child's brothers and sisters;

→ bringing toys, books, videos, or activities for siblings to use during the visit (these can be done independently or alongside the specialist and the child); or

→ involving brothers and sisters in aspects of the session with the child (such as selecting or handing toys to the specialist or holding a mirror for the child with a visual impairment to look into).

Many brothers and sisters benefit from sibling groups, feeling safe to share their feelings about their sibling with a disability in a structured or facilitated setting. Such groups can decrease feelings of isolation felt by children who may not want to add additional stress to their parents by talking about their own feelings. One little girl, when arriving at such a sibling support group asked, "All these kids have babies like my sister?" Then she breathed an audible sigh of relief because for once she would not have to explain to others why her sister was different. Parents often remark that their sighted children grow up with a greater sensitivity to human difference and a greater acceptance of individuals with disabilities. Some siblings will choose to work in disability-related fields as a result of their experiences growing up with a sibling who has a disability. For additional suggestions for providing support to siblings of children with disabilities see Holbrook (1996).

Grandparents

Grandparents also share in the mix of emotions. They may respond to the birth of a grandchild with a visual impairment with grief on two levels: They feel many emotions surrounding the loss of the dreams they had for their grandchild, and they may experience these same emotions for the baby's parent—their own son or daughter (Herring, 1996). The entire family receives and requires a tremendous amount of new information about visual impairment in a short amount of time, and many family members feel they are in uncharted waters. This reality may alter the pattern of communication between adult children and their parents because the traditional parenting advice of the elder generation may not seem as relevant or appreciated. Some grandparents experience the same roller coaster of emotions as the baby's parents and cannot immediately be expected to provide wisdom, support, and guidance.

The nature of grandparents' participation in the grandchild's life may also change. Parents may need assistance with doctor and hospital visits or rely on grandparents for respite care "just to get something done around the house." Some grandparents take on the role of family supporter by assisting with gathering information, identifying resources, and becoming better listeners.

As each family member develops new dreams, goals, and priorities, his or her relationship with extended family, friends, and community members will also change. Parents report that they form new "families", composed of some of the members of the extended family, along with old and new friends who are accepting of the new baby. The process of emotional adjustment is lifelong and dynamic. Respecting the individual styles, needs, and strengths of each individual contributes to the family's ability to function as a unit and successfully raise a child with a visual impairment.

RESPONSES OUTSIDE THE IMMEDIATE FAMILY

Although the emotions of the family at the birth of a child who is visually impaired child may be tumultuous at times, it is not uncommon for friends, members of the extended family, and medical and other professional personnel to respond to families by denying their feelings in a variety of ways. Denial of their feelings can exacerbate parents' confusion and pain during the diagnosis period. Statements or questions such as, "You're never given more than you can handle," "I'm sure there's a specialist somewhere who can give you a second opinion," "You must be very special to be able to deal with this," or "What are you going to do now?" can be roadblocks to open and interactive communication.

When relatives, friends, and professionals acknowledge families' feelings, they can be more supportive by responding with such statements as:

- "It sounds like you're feeling a great deal of pain."

- "You must be feeling confused and overwhelmed now."

- "Not knowing what to expect must be scary."

Validating statements can be accompanied by sensitive listening and emotional support when the family wants it.

The following suggestions can provide professionals and others with concrete approaches to supporting families of young children who are blind or visually impaired:

Supporting Families

→ Professionals are perceived as supportive if they listen empathetically first and wait to provide information until they know what is needed and relevant to a particular family at a given time (for example, referral to a family support network or explanations of an eye report completed by an optometrist).

→ Active listening involves reflecting back or paraphrasing what a person says or what you think he or she feels to verify understanding. For example, "You are feeling frustrated with the amount of paperwork involved." This communication skill demonstrates empathy.

→ By listening actively in an attempt to understand family concerns, professionals allow families to utilize their own strengths to solve problems that are a priority for them.

➡ If unsolicited by the family, even well-intentioned professional advice may not lead to an acceptable resolution. More importantly, giving advice may communicate a lack of trust in the other person's capabilities to solve his or her own problems.

➡ Families are most likely to implement actions they have personally determined to be important.

➡ Professionals can help families to expand their existing resources by providing them with specific, relevant information regarding their child and support networks that help them to adjust positively to raising a child with a disability (Thomas, Correa, & Morsink, 2001).

SUPPORTIVE COMMUNICATION

Thomas, Correa, & Morsink (2001, p. 160) define communication as ". . . a dynamic and ongoing process in which people share ideas, information, and feelings." Professionals who work with families of young children who are visually impaired may need to consider both verbal and nonverbal communication styles when sharing information and interacting with families. Body language (such as leaning forward) can show readiness to listen to the person who is speaking. It is also important to observe the nonverbal signals exhibited by others. There are occasions in which an individual may communicate confusion or strong disagreement through body language (such as frowning or crossing arms) yet is not willing to express these emotions verbally. Professionals who are sensitive to these details can work to build team consensus and stronger partnerships with families and other professionals. In verbal communication, team members must concern themselves with what is being said and how it is being presented. It is important to understand how what a person says is understood by others. A certain amount of small talk can be helpful in easing tensions prior to the start of a formal meeting. Informal conversations can be helpful in finding commonalities between families and professionals—a starting place to make connections. Skillful communicators are able to lead discussions back to issues at hand and to summarize group thoughts and agreements reached.

Establishing a climate in which supportive communication can take place provides the foundation for improved understanding, increased problem solving, and collaborative partnerships. Turnbull and Turnbull (1997) noted three factors that are essential prerequisites to developing positive professional–family partnerships:

- self-understanding and the ability to appreciate the perspectives of others

- mutual trust and respect

- a willingness to collaborate and work together as equal partners

To facilitate a supportive environment, other factors also need to be present: (1) a genuine desire to communicate with others, for if the desire is not genuine, others can tell and will not feel free to communicate; (2) careful and attentive listening; and (3) a sharing of one's own perspective with others, *with a shift of thinking at times*. Listening and thoughtful consideration of family perspectives may leave professionals open to a change of opinion from time to time. In addition, Thomas, Correa, & Morsink (2001) stress the importance of maintaining confidentiality and being sensitive to cultural differences in developing a supportive climate for communication.

Supportive communication means moving from thinking in terms of preconceived answers to thinking in terms of the desired end results and seeking solutions to meet those ends. In other words, professionals must work together with families to set priorities among goals for example, independent toileting, and develop strategies to achieve them that work for a given family, rather than handing family members a generic list of toileting approaches. For additional tips that professionals working with families of young children can use to establish supportive communication and share information see "Communicating with Families in a Supportive Way."

SUPPORTING FAMILIES THROUGH TRANSITIONS

Certain predictable transitions in a child's life create changes for the entire family. Such times may be stressful for all families and may present additional challenges for the families of children who are visually impaired.

The Hospital Experience

Hospitalization can have a negative impact on anyone, but the often lengthy stays involving complicated medical procedures that may follow the birth of a child with a disability can exhaust parents

COMMUNICATING WITH FAMILIES IN A SUPPORTIVE WAY

The following suggestions will help professionals establish a supportive climate for families of children who are visually impaired and improve communication with them:

➜ Provide relevant information, not advice.

➜ Make sure that individuals are in the company of a trusted relative or friend when given a medical or developmental diagnosis.

➜ Provide more than one opportunity for sharing information and asking questions of families, especially those under stress.

➜ To increase understanding, present information clearly and without jargon, in a variety of ways.

➜ Share information in a sensitive and confidential manner.

➜ Provide information from a culturally relevant perspective (for example, information can be provided on the impact of a physical therapy exercise on the entire family rather than just on the individual when the culture emphasizes the importance of the family unit) and in language understandable to the family.

➜ In sharing information, encourage parents to use direct communication in expressing their concerns and priorities.

➜ Assist families in preparing questions and their observations about their child to present to medical personnel and other professionals.

➜ Give families time to process assessment results before beginning educational and program planning. For example, it would be important to give a family time to digest a diagnosis of cortical visual impairment and cerebral palsy before asking them to decide on which program option they would prefer for their child.

➜ Note taking or tape recording can help some families process technical or complicated information or share information with family members who are not present.

➜ Professionals must treat family members as individuals.

➜ Give brothers and sisters of visually impaired children accurate information, and encourage them to talk openly about their feelings.

Diane L. Fazzi & Rona L. Pogrund

and disrupt family life. For the premature infant with retinopathy of prematurity, the hospital experience can be prolonged for months due to associated neonatal care. Children with congenital cataracts and glaucoma may undergo many corrective surgeries very early in life (Harrell, 1992).

Families of infants who are visually impaired will often have to interact with numerous medical personnel whose involvement with them often changes on an hourly or daily basis. Some families may be dissatisfied with the amount of information and lack of emotional support provided by medical staff. Other families may simply be intimidated by the entire process, and they will never ask questions that might be important. Specialists may offer the following suggestions to families who are overwhelmed by interactions with medical professionals:

- Ask another family member or close friend to attend any scheduled medical consultations so that you have emotional support, a ride to and from the hospital or office, another individual to ask questions, and perhaps an additional perspective on the information obtained.

- Use a tape recorder to maintain an accurate record of diagnoses, medical procedures, and treatments.

- Maintain a list of questions as they come up, so that they are handy when doctors or nurses make rounds and are not forgotten.

- Schedule follow-up consultations as appropriate to discuss concerns or questions that may arise.

- Keep a list of doctors or specialists who will be involved in the child's medical care and each professional's area of expertise.

Medical professionals may have different perspectives and may vary greatly in interpersonal skills. During their child's hospitalization, family members may be trying to juggle their daily routines while spending long hours at the hospital. All these factors may contribute to increased emotional and financial strain on the family (Harrell, 1992).

Transition from Hospital to Home

Although the day when a family brings their child home from the hospital is usually a happy one, the new situation can also create new stresses for the family of an infant who is visually impaired. Issues associated with the transition from hospital to home may include the following:

➜ In the case of fragile infants with extensive medical needs, ongoing caretaking responsibilities (such as maintaining a heart-rate monitor for night sleeping or feeding an infant with a gastrointestinal feeding tube) may become the family's central focus.

➜ Family members' social contacts and activities may be reduced due to discomfort on the part of friends and relatives as a result of stereotypes about blindness.

➜ Increased isolation can result in reduced social supports for the family.

➜ Medical procedures, such as putting eyedrops in the infant's eyes, inserting contact lenses, patching, and suctioning, may be difficult for family members to implement at home.

➜ Parents may feel guilty when they do not follow procedures precisely because they make the child uncomfortable or the child protests.

➜ The family must adjust to caring for the baby's medical needs without the immediate support of the child's doctors and nurses.

➜ The family may have concerns regarding the balance between employment and child care. Child care can be complicated when considering the needs of an infant with a visual impairment, especially if the child has additional disabilities.

➜ The family will need to learn a whole new vocabulary of medical and educational jargon (terms such as *low vision, tracking,* or *inclusion*) in order to communicate effectively with professionals.

➜ The family will need to familiarize themselves with available community resources and will need to schedule additional medical and professional services within the family routine from such practitioners as ophthalmologists, physical therapists, teachers, and orientation and mobility (O&M) specialists.

➜ The family may need to develop advocacy strategies (such as being assertive when requesting services or preparing a list of questions to ask a doctor or specialist) to make sure that community services are provided for their child.

_____

Transition from Home to School

When the child with a visual impairment reaches preschool age, many new issues may become important, such as the following:

_____

Issues in Home-to-School Transition

→ If a home-based program has served the child, the family may face losing contact with a teacher whom they know and trust and with whom they feel comfortable.

→ If the child is to begin a school-based program, the family will have to deal with teachers and routines they do not know and possibly with teachers who are unfamiliar with their child's disability. They may feel that they have to "settle" for certain conditions because no one else can care for their child as much or as well as they do.

→ With the start of a school program, parents may lose control over many aspects of the child's life that were central to the home routine. If the child is nonverbal, parents may lose contact with portions of the child's activities during the day.

→ The family may also be forced to deal with the bureaucracies of both general and special education within the school system (such as paperwork, rules, and regulations).

→ Parents need to become familiar with the policies, procedures, and options available to them.

→ Transportation to and from school must be addressed. The family may be concerned about the child riding the school bus, the length of the ride, or the child's safe arrival at school or at home. Transportation issues may be especially difficult when the family has chosen a program that is not available in the young child's local home area.

_____

Transition from School to School

As the child with a visual impairment changes schools and moves from one classroom to another, many of the issues involved in the home-to-school transition remain relevant. In addition, parents must deal with new situations, such as the following:

→ If the child who is visually impaired is placed on an inclusive campus (in which children with and without disabilities learn together), the child and family must deal with the curiosity of other children and adults. Other children may be curious about the appearance of the child's eyes, why the eyes don't work the same as theirs, or the child's special equipment or materials (such as braille books, magnifiers, or the long cane).

→ The family may find themselves spending a great deal of energy educating the new teachers about their visually impaired child (for example, the child's preferred foods, learning styles, or special equipment and materials), obtaining necessary services for their child (such as O&M training or interpreter services), and ensuring continuity of services from one setting to another (for example making sure that the frequency of braille instruction is maintained if the child moves from a specialized to a generic preschool program).

Helping Strategies

Offering families effective support while they go through these early transitions also supports the development and well-being of the child who is visually impaired. Professionals working with families in transition can help in a variety of ways. See "Helping Families Through a Transition" on the next page for suggestions that may facilitate smoother transitions. It is important to remember that it is always the family's choice to act or not to act on the information provided by professionals. Family–professional relationships in which mutual respect exists are the most beneficial to all parties involved.

CULTURAL CONSIDERATIONS

Given the reality of increasing diversity in U.S. society, individuals working with young children with disabilities must ultimately deal with a wide range of families whose cultures are significantly different from their own—not just in terms of race, ethnicity, and language, but also in terms of socioeconomic status and lifestyle.

HELPING FAMILIES THROUGH A TRANSITION

The following suggestions can help professionals support families during a variety of difficult transitions:

➡ Encourage the family to have face-to-face meetings with the child's new teachers; the teacher and the family may feel more comfortable with each other if they meet before the first day of school.

➡ Provide in-service training to the school staff and information to classmates about the child who is visually impaired, the disability's implications, and available support and resources.

➡ Provide resource contacts, such as consultants, agencies, or social service entities, in writing to the family as well as to the staff; the name of a contact person is often helpful.

➡ Apprise the family of applicable laws, rights (such as due process), and available services. Although the family may not utilize all the information offered at the time, they may refer to it as needed in the future.

➡ Provide formal or informal advocacy training for the family, possibly by role-playing difficult situations and anticipating problems and responses to them.

➡ Encourage collaboration between families and professionals. Inform families about educational and support meetings where collaboration can occur.

➡ If possible, provide contact with other families of visually impaired children for support purposes.

Diane L. Fazzi, Patricia Sacks Salcedo, & Rona L. Pogrund

Professionals serving families and young children with visual impairments also come from diverse cultural backgrounds. Increasing awareness and skills for working in a multicultural society can help professionals to build stronger, more lasting partnerships with the families they serve.

Culture Defined

The word *culture* refers to the ways in which individuals perceive, evaluate, believe, and behave. One's culture provides a "blueprint that determines the way an individual thinks, feels, and behaves in society" (Gollnick & Chinn, 1994, p.4). Individuals may not even be aware of the most fundamental core of their own culture. Cultural norms are so much a part of daily thought and behavior in people's day-to-day lives that it is almost impossible for individuals to perceive them. Yet most people are very sensitive to the cultural characteristics of others that are different from their own.

Cultural characteristics are shared by a group of individuals, they are learned, and they are dynamic. There is great diversity even within large groups. Such umbrella terms as *Hispanic* or *Asian* comprise many subgroups that have distinct cultural differences. Although all members of a cultural group never have exactly the same values, beliefs, and behaviors, they tend to be similar. It is this tendency toward commonality that provides the members of a given group a sense of identity. Cultural identity is a complex phenomenon, and it is shaped by multiple influences. (For a detailed discussion, see Gollnick & Chinn, 1994; Lynch & Hanson, 1992; and Gollnick & Chinn, 2002.)

Culture is learned; it is not a biological phenomenon. Even though it is true that being born a member of a certain race or ethnicity increases the likelihood that you will assume the cultural features of that particular group, it is not guaranteed. For example, a Vietnamese child adopted by a white middle-class family in Minnesota may share few if any characteristics of Vietnamese culture.

Culture is dynamic; it develops and changes as groups adapt and accommodate to various realities. For example, war and political upheaval have forced some groups to undergo mass migrations and refugee status that can permanently alter their values, beliefs, and behaviors. The advent of technology into a society has a profound effect on people's daily lives. The cultural characteristics of successive generations of the offspring of immigrants will change over time. Although culture may have certain commonalities at a given point in time, it is by no means static.

The Importance of Culture in Early Intervention

A basic tenet of effective early intervention is that it requires strong partnerships between families and professionals and the ability to work together within any given family structure. With an emphasis on providing early intervention services within natural environments, services are increasingly being delivered within the home and home community. As the potential for what is referred to as "culture clash" increases, so, too, does the risk of communication failure and reduced intervention effectiveness. Culture clash occurs when values learned at home are not valued or supported at school or by professionals who serve the child and family (Milian, 2000). For example, differences in approaches to discipline based on cultural beliefs about child-rearing practices may occur between some families and professionals. Early interventionists and disability specialists must develop what Lynch and Hanson (1992, 1998) refer to as "cultural competence." Cultural competence is more than simply knowing about different cultures. Cultural competence includes:

- understanding your own culture and biases and how differences between your own values and someone else's may interfere with intervention effectiveness,

- understanding the range of ways in which families may differ from your own culture, particularly in the areas of child rearing practices, attitudes toward disability, and their views of early intervention, and

- developing ways of interacting and communicating with families that minimize the impact of cultural differences and take maximum advantage of the family's own cultural values and practices.

Specific suggestions for minimizing the impact of cultural differences while working in family homes are provided later in this chapter.

CULTURAL VARIATIONS IN CHILD-REARING ATTITUDES AND PRACTICES

Families' attitudes toward how children learn and the role of parents in their children's development are significantly affected by cultural background. Thomas, Correa, & Morsink (2001) state, "The belief system held by the family may actually be a strength for coping with and caring for the child with a disability." (p. 285) The following brief summary highlights the dimensions along which families may vary as they strive toward one universal goal—the healthy growth and well-being of their children.

It is important for early childhood professionals to understand that, with few exceptions, all parents want their children to be happy, healthy, and successful. Parents do their best within the context of their own values and beliefs and within the constraints of their resources. As Norton (1990, p. 3) states, "Human beings raise their children to fit into the society they know. Child-rearing practices reflect what parents know about life in their community, what they believe will be useful, and what they recognize as realistic aspirations for their children."

Attitudes and beliefs about what is best for children and specific child-rearing practices vary in many ways according to complex influences. Some of these influences include, but are not limited to:

- the parent's own previous role models for parenting,

- beliefs about parents' roles,

- beliefs about how children learn and the nature of child development,

- religious beliefs,

- availability of resources and environmental constraints,

- family structure and organization, and

- degree of isolation from other cultures and communities.

This list of influences reflects both the material resources and the cultural factors that are manifested in the day-to-day activities of families. Furthermore, these influences are constantly changing. Families are dynamic rather than static entities; they are always changing and must continuously accommodate to the materials and cultural influences around them. This adaptation is the essence of "ecocultural niche theory" as described by Gallimore, Weisner, Kaufman, and Bernheimer (1989). This theory helps provide a framework for an appreciation of the complex and dynamic nature of families.

There are several dimensions of child-rearing attitudes and practices along which families from different cultures may vary. Although it is important to be sensitive to and learn about the influences of a family's culture, it is equally important to observe the individuality of families within given cultural groups. Considering the impact of such variables may help professionals to work side by side with individual families to develop effective programs that support the growth and development of young children who are blind or visually impaired.

Independence versus Interdependence

According to Levine (in Klein & Chen, 2001), as societies become more affluent many families tend to develop a value for autonomy and independence. Working-class and poor families may be more likely to value obedience because the kinds of employment available to them require obedience for success (Kohn, 1977).

Certain Western industrialized societies—especially the United States—value the characteristics of independence and assertiveness, whereas many other cultures emphasize the values of interdependence, obedience, harmony, and respect. These differences result in very different child-rearing attitudes and practices. American middle-class children may be viewed by some other cultures as disrespectful, aggressive, and overindulged. For example, in mainstream U.S. culture, the abilities of the young child to initiate verbal interactions, to use language to make requests, and to carry on a conversation with adults are often seen as important and positive skills. They are often included in the early communication goals and objectives identified for young children with special needs.

In many other cultures, however, such behavior in children is viewed as inappropriate. Children are expected to be "seen and not heard." They are not supposed to initiate interactions with adults or to assert their preferences and desires. It may therfore cause conflict for a family with such values when the early intervention team indicates they should be helping their child initiate requests, for example. In such a situation, it would be very important for the professional to explore the family's degree of comfort with such a goal and to communicate why this goal might be important for success in the mainstream culture.

There may also be gender differences in expectations for independence from the family. Such social roles as breadwinner and homemaker may be emphasized more for boys or girls in different cultures. These types of differences may affect a family's priorities for setting and implementing educational goals.

Approaches to Discipline

Another area that varies widely across cultures, and which is often an area of cultural mismatch between families and early-childhood professionals, is discipline. The greatest variation between mainstream U.S. culture and many other cultures can be found regarding whether their parenting styles tend to be authoritarian or egalitarian (democratic). In authoritarian families, the parent is the absolute and final authority in the home. In such families, the use of physical punishment tends to be more common. The more democratic views of child rearing and discipline are less likely to use such punishment, and the rules are less fixed. Children are given the opportunity to give their side of the story and sometimes may even participate in the selection of rewards and punishments. Authoritarian families place great emphasis on obedience and respect and are likely to say things like, "Do it because I say so." Physical punishment or "shaming" are common disciplinary strategies (Harry, 1992). Although some families fit into one style or the other, many families fall along a continuum between these two discipline styles and may vary in approaches depending on the context of a given situation.

Variation can also be seen in the age at which discipline becomes appropriate. For example, in some Asian cultures an abrupt shift in discipline practices may occur around the age of 4 years (Chan, 1992; Chimm, 1989). Although parents may be indulgent and not utilize discipline at all in the early years, the 4-year-old is expected to begin to conform to adult expectations. Seemingly harsh consequences may be used to facilitate this learning.

There may also be significant gender differences in how young children are disciplined. Boys may be indulged whereas girls are punished more severely, or vice versa. In many cultures, boys are given a special status compared with girls.

Such differences in discipline approaches are important to consider when a behavior support plan needs to be developed. For example, providing a young child with a visual impairment with increased opportunities for making choices during play may be a strategy to support positive peer interactions. Such a strategy may be easier for a family to implement if they use a democratic style of discipline in the home, rather than in an authoritarian family in which children are expected to share toys because they are told to do so. In order to achieve consistency across environments and across significant people in the child's life, the discipline practices valued by the family must be respected and incorporated when possible.

The Influence of Racism

Racism is a very real phenomenon in American society. Racism and prejudice are experienced to some extent by all minority groups in the United States and in many other parts of the world. Racism can have a major impact on child-rearing practices. According to Peters (1985), African American parents must prepare their children to cope and survive in a racist society. Many parents express this as being their most important parenting responsibility. Milian (2000, p. 205) supports this notion by stating, "Racism and discrimination are still daily factors in the lives of African American children and adults and still hamper their ability to make use of available opportunities." According to Boykin and Toms (1985), African American parents must struggle to help their children reconcile three different influences in their lives: (1) the racism experienced by being a member of a minority culture; (2) the heritage and traditions passed down from their African roots, and (3) the values and behaviors dictated by U.S. mainstream culture.

African American children who have ocular albinism experience a unique phenomenon in developing their cultural identity. The combination of light skin, hair, and eye pigments together with other physical attributes of individuals who are African American may contribute to confusion in cultural identity and increased social isolation. Specialists working with these children need to be sensitive to these issues and listen carefully to how families talk about social interactions, expectations, and feelings.

Family Structure

Another area of cultural differences often encountered by early childhood professionals is family structure. As discussed previously, family structures vary greatly, and two-parent families are no longer the norm. Many families from minority groups include numerous extended family members: grandparents; great-grandparents; sometimes aunts, uncles, and cousins; and spouses and children of grown children living under one roof. Such large family units, particularly if they live in relatively small quarters, may seem chaotic to professionals who have grown up in smaller nuclear families. Professionals may be concerned about overstimulation of the young child with a visual impairment or inconsistent, unpredictable child-rearing practices when there are multiple caregivers. In many cases, however, extended family households provide important support for parents and their young children with disabilities. For example, in many Navajo families, grandmothers and aunts often help care for young children and older adults may be consulted on child-rearing issues (Milian, 2000). In some Hispanic families, older siblings may assume a caretaking role with younger children in the home. In many cultures parents are often uncomfortable leaving their children with people outside the family; other families may not be able to afford outside day care. Members of extended families provide trusted, culturally compatible care for children while parents work or attend school functions. In some cases the pooling of economic resources ensures the survival of the family unit. Extended family can also provide important opportunities for child interaction and nurturing.

Developing the complete picture of the family unit is important for developing goals on an IFSP or IEP that will address family priorities. Parette and Petch-Hogan, (2000, p. 8) caution professionals to ". . . carefully consider who the 'real' decision makers are in a particular family." Enlisting support from family members (whether it be a parent, sibling, or grandparent) who might be most available to help with follow-through activities (such as sound-localization activities) at home is essential to ensuring a successful intervention program.

Parents' Roles

There are interesting cultural differences in how parents see their own roles in their children's development. Most middle-class parents in the United States clearly view themselves as teachers of their children. They teach their children concepts and vocabulary and help them learn to solve problems. Parents in some other cultures may also see themselves as teachers of their children, but what they teach may be different. For example, in many cultures, such as some Hispanic families, it is the parents' responsibility to teach morality and proper behavior rather than linguistic and cognitive skills.

In some families, there is a strong focus on not spoiling the children. This practice often entails not being overly responsive or indulgent. For some the goal is to teach children—especially boys—to be tough and be able to defend themselves. Still other families may believe that all skills simply evolve as a normal course of development and view their roles as teachers or intervenors as minimal. Exploring families' perceptions regarding the roles of parents can help professionals to form realistic expectations of the ways in which families will be able to comfortably participate in the child's specialized education or home follow-up. It is important to value and emphasize the roles that families can play in their visually impaired child's education.

Communication between Caregiver and Child

Another area of great cultural variation that has major implications for early intervention is parent–child communication. Talking is highly valued in middle-class America. Mainstream U.S. culture values verbal assertiveness and competence. By the standards of other cultures, many Americans may be considered to be excessive talkers. This talking carries over into their interactions with young children. Parents typically respond verbally even to very young infants, long before they have any intentional communication. It is not unusual for a parent to respond to an infant's burp or sigh as though he or she just said something very profound! Very young children are expected to be able to label and explain and to initiate and maintain a conversation. Parents also believe that they can play an important role in helping children learn these skills.

In the United States, family interaction patterns are often fairly democratic. In many mainstream families, children even have the right to challenge the directives and decisions of adults. There is a belief that even young children should be allowed to explain and defend themselves, ask questions, and carry on conversations with adults. These skills, in turn, translate into the very skills that are important to school success and literacy achievement.

In some cultures that emphasize rank and hierarchy in family structures, verbal behaviors such as rationalizing, asking questions, and conversing with adults are likely to be considered inappropriate. In many families, children are supposed to listen while adults or older siblings talk. In some cultures, such as some Native American groups, adults may rarely talk to infants or very young children until they have learned to talk (Heath, 1983). Compare this with the typical U.S. attitude that children learn to talk best through adults' responsive interactions with them. This contrast presents a serious mismatch of values. Early childhood education programs, as well as early intervention programs, strongly value activities that help children develop verbal abilities. Often the kinds of activities modeled in these programs, such as adults expanding on children's utterances and following children's leads in conversations, are completely foreign to some parents, such as those in some Native American communities. It not only requires learning a new skill—a new way of interacting with their children—but a skill that is quite contrary to the norms of their culture. In such cases it will be important for the professional to explain to the parents that while these may be unfamiliar interactions, they can prove beneficial to the language development of their children who are blind or visually impaired. Professionals can work simultaneously to include many aspects of adult storytelling into the child's language development program. Whenever possible, professionals can include important elements of the family's language and cultural communication style within the existing intervention program. "Dealing with Cultural Differences in Early Intervention and Education" in this chapter provides additional suggestions for accommodating cultural differences.

Effects of Scarce Resources

Poverty rates are higher for children than any other age group (U.S. Census Bureau, 1999). Examples of the influence of poverty upon child-rearing practices are endless. As noted earlier, the practice of extended families and multiple caregivers living under one roof in some instances may be the result of scarce resources rather than cultural preference. Migrant and homeless families may deal with changes in temporary housing or shelters on a daily or weekly basis.

The provision of many appropriate toys and learning materials, such as books and crayons, and access to such experiences as movies, fairs, the zoo, concerts, and vacations, require financial resources.

DEALING WITH CULTURAL DIFFERENCES IN EARLY INTERVENTION AND EDUCATION

This approach may be helpful when working with families from diverse backgrounds:

➡ Listen to families' descriptions of why specific cultural practices are important to the family (for example, perhaps a family can explain a specific approach that they used to teach other children in the home to eat independently and use utensils and why they think it was most effective).

➡ Explain to families the professional reason for using a particular approach and how it may benefit the child and the family (for example, why it is all right if a young child who is blind wastes a bit more food while trying to feed him- or herself, and how this skill will help the child participate more fully in the neighborhood preschool program the following year).

➡ Explore new approaches that may represent a compromise between the perspectives of the family and the professional (for example, encouraging the child to learn self-feeding skills only with foods that are plentiful in the home initially).

➡ Integrate the family's values and beliefs into developmentally appropriate practice whenever possible (such as working with an older sibling to help the young child who is blind or visually impaired drink from a cup).

➡ Maintain an open mind and open lines of communication while exploring approaches that are acceptable to both family and professionals. Listen carefully, discuss concerns, clarify areas of confusion, and check back regularly.

Source: Adapted from B. Harry, M. Kalyanpur, & M. Day, *Building Cultural Reciprocity with Families: Case Studies in Special Education* (Baltimore, MD: Paul H. Brookes, 1999), p. 7.

Transportation can be another drain to limited resources. Frequent diaper changes in order to keep babies dry requires the money to buy diapers. Encouraging infants to develop self-feeding skills results in wasting food that is spilled or thrown on the floor or winds up in the child's hair. Poor families cannot afford such waste, regardless of how developmentally appropriate professionals may consider it to be.

Another reality of scarce resources is increased stress. Families living in poverty may experience disproportionate amounts of stress related to their fear of violence and the difficulty of coping with limited resources. These conditions are often present in low-income neighborhoods, particularly in urban housing projects.

Considerations regarding the priorities of families with limited resources may focus on maintaining basic necessities for survival. When working in the home, professionals can incorporate the use of available household items into activities, such as using a wooden spoon for tracking, rather than suggesting that the family purchase new toys for the same purposes. Assisting the family in obtaining resources and services may help them to be able to focus more intently on the child's developmental needs.

Influence of Religion on Child-Rearing Practices

Religion often plays a major role in families' attitudes toward child rearing and in child-rearing practices. Many Western religions are congruent with the major values of the dominant culture. They tend to emphasize individual control and self-responsibility. Other religions foster a more passive view, believing that all events can be explained by supernatural forces. These different views influence how families view the raising of children and children with disabilities.

One of the most familiar early Chinese traditions is: "Spare the rod; spoil the child." This philosophy suggests that children must be firmly disciplined for inappropriate behavior and that overindulgence of children is undesirable. This belief continues to be an important religious principle within many African American communities that results in a reliance on physical punishment as the primary disciplinary strategy (Franklin & Boyd-Franklin, 1985). In many Asian families, when a child brings serious shame upon himself and upon his family, use of physical punishment is considered appropriate (Chan, 1992).

Many religions, such as Christianity and Judaism and the philosophy of Confucianism place a strong emphasis on the importance of teaching. For example, a well-known Bible verse says, "And teach a child in the way he should go." In both Confucian and Buddhist traditions, one of the most important responsibilities of a parent is teaching his or her children how to behave properly and to live lives that honor the family and their resources.

Learning about a family's religious beliefs may help interventionists to understand perspectives on child rearing that may be different from their own. While it may be inappropriate or uncomfortable to directly ask families about their spiritual beliefs, professionals can learn a great deal from listening to families talk about things that are important to them. In addition, some families display religious articles (such as a menorah, crucifix, statue of Buddha, sand paintings, or totems) in the home that may inform the professional about religious beliefs.

Influence of Beliefs about How Children Learn

Families have very different beliefs about how children learn, and thus what teaching strategies are most effective. Some believe that children learn simply as a result of maturation and do not need to be specifically "taught." Others believe that children learn through observation of adults, or through responsive interaction with adults. Yet others believe that certain skills must be taught directly.

Mainstream European-American and European families emphasize "social mediation of the environment" (Anastasiow, 1986), as espoused in the theories of Bruner (1982), Vygotsky (1978), and Feuerstein, et al. (1980). In essence, this approach supports the notion that adults must be responsive to children's interests and to their attempts at communication by using language as well as physical assistance to help children expand their understanding of the surrounding world, to advance to the next level of development, and to refine language and reasoning skills. This approach is responsive and highly interactive. The theory also considers play to have an important value as a context in which to teach children.

Another important characteristic of the approach to child rearing used by many middle-class families in the United States has been a greater reliance on "experts" and research in such fields as developmental psychology, rather than on religious doctrine or family tradition. As a result, the specifics of child-rearing practices are constantly changing as the experts' theories change. Unfortunately, changes in trends often create confusion about the "best" way to raise children, especially for younger parents. Parents may lack self-confidence in their parenting abilities. They may seek assistance from parenting classes, books, magazines, the popular media, friends, and professionals.

Many families from non-mainstream backgrounds may place relatively greater emphasis on direct instruction and purposeful modeling to teach their children. In contrast, in many Native American families, children are expected to learn from the consequences of their actions rather than through overt teaching (Milian, 2000). A common strategy used in many Latino homes to teach language is a *triadic interaction,* in which the parent instructs the child to say something to someone else (for example, "Say 'I want to play' to your big cousin.") (Eisenberg, 1982). In many agrarian cultures, parents and older siblings may teach younger children to make tortillas or work in a garden by physically demonstrating the skills and encouraging the child to imitate.

In many traditional Asian families, adults may frequently use language to exhort and teach appropriate behaviors and to explain important traditions and principles. The child's role is to listen respectfully while the adult explains. In traditional Asian families, there can frequently be relatively little interaction between parents and children, especially between fathers and children. Communication is generally one way: "The parent speaks; the child listens" (Chan, 1992, p. 220). Learning through observation, memorization, and rote practice are considered to be highly effective approaches by many Asian American families (Milian, 2000).

Individuals in various other cultures believe that children learn not through direct instruction or responsive interaction but simply by being in the company of adults and observing. For example, in many African American communities (Heath, 1983), Native American communities (Joe & Malach, 1998), and in Western Samoa (Ochs, 1982), children are expected to learn primarily through observation. They are often present during adult social interactions or storytelling and thus have many opportunities to observe language and social customs. The process of learning language is quite different for these children when compared to children from other groups. It's as if these children must "break the code" on their own. Both Heath and Ochs report that children in these communities begin to use language by spontaneously imitating the final words of sentences and words that are highly stressed, such as expletives. In Laotian culture, according to Luangpraseut (1989), adults purposely avoid giving direct instruction to children. Yet, great importance is placed on children learning appropriate social behaviors. Thus, the primary method of teaching is through observation.

For children who are blind or visually impaired, incidental learning opportunities may be more limited. In such cases, the specialist must be creative in finding ways to incorporate family beliefs into intervention approaches yet help the family to understand when there are other approaches that may help children who are blind or visually impaired develop. For example, knowing that a family does not use direct instruction in teaching their children, the O&M specialist could explain to the family how their young blind child needs to observe by touching. The specialist could demonstrate by having the young child ride on the father's back to get the feeling of moving through space. Encouraging the family to expand their approaches, the O&M specialist could then suggest that the family use a few verbal descriptions (such as "walking forward," "bending down," or "swinging your arms to and fro") to help the child learn motor skills and spatial concepts. Similarly, if a family values "formal" education approaches such as memorization and drill and practice, the teacher could explain the importance of opportunities for young blind children to explore their surroundings for concept development. Although toddler exploration is typically done informally, a compromise approach of structuring the exploration in some way may make the process more comfortable for the family and become a valued part of the family routine. Most effective intervention programs incorporate highly valued approaches of both the family and knowledgeable specialists.

CULTURAL INFLUENCES ON ATTITUDES TOWARD DISABILITY AND EARLY INTERVENTION

Another area of cultural influence and variation is in the family's attitude toward disability. In many cases, families influenced by mainstream U.S. culture may view the causes of disability fairly "scientifically." They may believe that there are specific causes for disability, including genetic factors, toxins, injuries, specific diseases, prenatal conditions, and so on. Families from mainstream U.S. cultures often accept the recommendations and interventions of "experts" even though they do not know them personally, and often strongly believe that "more is better" when it comes to obtaining the wide spectrum of services that may be available to them. There is also a strong belief that through these efforts the effects of the child's disability can be minimized.

Religion may play an important role in how families view a child's disability, particularly in many non-mainstream cultures. Some Asian American and Pacific Islander families may feel that a disability such as visual impairment can be caused by fate or a curse (Cheng, 1993). In many cultures there is a belief that if a child is born with a disability or has a serious illness, God is punishing the family for some wrongdoing. It may be the mother whose behavior is believed to have brought about the punishment. Such a strong belief may continue even through generations of acculturation. Sometimes this belief that the child's condition is an act of God makes it very difficult for families to seek help from professionals. Parents may believe that trying to "fix" or intervene in any way with the child's disability is questioning God's authority. Such families may feel they must accept a child as he or she is and bear the burden of the child's disability as appropriate punishment for past sins. For these families, challenging God's authority would be the ultimate sin. Families from some cultures may place varying degrees of confidence in the use of healing or nontraditional medical practices (such as acupuncture, use of herbs, rubbing coins, and other various healing rituals) (Cheng, 1993). Families may or may not share these beliefs or practices with professionals who serve their children.

It is easy to see how parents whose religion influences them in this way would feel very conflicted about early education and intervention for their child. "The system"—mainstream health care and social services in the United States—expects them to aggressively seek out services and to follow through on the suggestions of various health and education professionals (such as a physician's recommendations about medications or surgery, the education vision specialist's recommendations for activities to strengthen the use of the child's vision, or the teacher's request that the parent attend parent-training sessions on a regular basis to learn how to carry over the activities of an intervention program). Most parents are well aware that "the system" believes these things are important to do. They may even be aware that professionals believe that parents are inadequate or unconcerned if they do not participate in these activities. At the same time, some parents may have strong gut-level emotions that tell them that such interventions are in some way wrong.

Some families may also feel shame related to a child with a disability. Some Asian parents who view their child's disability as retribution for their wrongdoing may be hesitant to place their child in a special program where all the world can see the evidence of their behavior. In addition, some Asian American families may be reticent to accept a diagnosis such as learning disability if they equate degree of effort to success in learning (Milian, 2000).

The emotional conflict that can result from these opposing influences of religious beliefs and societal expectations can be disturbing for families. This conflict often creates ambivalence toward the intervention program and may manifest itself in inconsistent attendance in center-based programs or in not being home when the early interventionist arrives for home visits. Yet when the parents interact with the teacher, they may be very positive about their intentions to follow through on the child's programming and to attend more regularly.

It may be difficult for early interventionists to realize that, in many cases, parents are probably not fully conscious of their own ambivalence and conflict. Some parents themselves may not understand why it is so difficult to follow through or to participate enthusiastically in their young child's intervention and therapies. In some cultures, such as some Native American cultures, it may be important to avoid disharmony, and contradicting professionals could create such a result (Milian, 2000). It is important that early interventionists avoid making families feel guilty for not participating fully. That does not mean that interventionists cannot explain the value of repetition and consistency in helping children learn. It simply means that it is important to avoid implying that parents are "bad" or that they are willfully harming their child by not following

HELPING FAMILIES FROM CULTURALLY AND LINGUISTICALLY DIVERSE BACKGROUNDS BECOME COMFORTABLE WITH EARLY INTERVENTION SERVICES

Families from some cultural backgrounds may tend to feel uncomfortable with early intervention services, regardless of whether the services take place in the home or in a professional setting. The following suggestions may help put families at ease:

HOME-BASED SERVICES

➜ Spend initial home visits developing a rapport with the family, including parents, child, siblings, and extended family and neighbors, as appropriate.

➜ Take time to talk with and listen to families.

➜ Find positive aspects of the family's childrearing practices and compliment them on those (for example, "It's terrific how you carry Adam with you in a baby sling while you do housework and gardening. He is really able to look and listen up close").

➜ Involve interested family members in learning activities (for example, reading books that have both print and braille on them and encouraging siblings to find real items that can be shown to the child in place of pictures, such as a rocking chair or bowl to illustrate "Goldilocks and the Three Bears").

➜ Avoid judging families if they are not totally supportive of a given intervention strategy, such as following through on having a toddler wear prescription glasses at home all day; it may be more difficult than the professional realizes to get a toddler to be compliant with wearing glasses, especially if the family does not notice any difference in visual functioning. Try to encourage small but meaningful steps, like having the toddler wear the glasses while looking at books or eating meals and searching for Cheerios on the high chair tray.

➜ Do not take it personally if a family misses or cancels a few home visit sessions.

CENTER-BASED SERVICES

➜ Make initial visits to a new center-based program with the family and encourage them to ask questions or voice concerns.

➜ Encourage the family to invite a respected elder, clergy member, or community leader to visit the center.

(continued)

> ➜ Provide the family with contacts or arrange a meeting with other families of similar cultural background whose children attend the same program.
>
> ➜ Overlap the start of a center-based program with the end of home-based services to make the transition easier.
>
> ➜ Once the child starts the program, maintain open communication to monitor his or her comfort level.
>
> ➜ Maintain an open-door policy for the family to visit the classroom or participate in activities at the center-based program as appropriate.
>
> *Diane L. Fazzi*

through or attending the program regularly. Adding guilt to someone's already existing uneasiness about the appropriateness of trying to change their child's condition may only decrease the likelihood that they will continue to participate at any level in the program.

In some cultures, while there may be a religious belief that the disability is God's will, it is not seen as a punishment. In such families, their religious belief may be a significant source of support. Sometimes the child is seen as "God's gift," or as a focal point that brings the family closer together. In these families, spirituality offers important emotional support for dealing with the child's disability or health problem. For example, in many Native American tribes all children, including children with disabilities, are accepted for who they are (Anderson & Fenichel, 1989). It is possible that these families may also tend to avoid early education and intervention. In some cultures the nature of young children is viewed as relatively impervious to efforts by adults to change it—not so much that it is wrong to try, but that efforts will simply be ineffective.

Even when religion does not influence families' attitudes toward early intervention services, there may be significant differences from mainstream values. Individuals in many cultures are wary of taking advice from "strangers" or allowing them into their home. They may be much more comfortable receiving help from a family elder, a good friend, or someone in the community who plays the role of "healer."

Awareness of and sensitivity toward the unique characteristics of a variety of cultures fosters more effective work with families of given cultures. Of course, there are many differences among individual families within groups. The first step in developing cultural competence is to become aware of the range of differences that characterize families' attitudes and practices related to child rearing, the nature of disability, and the role and value of early intervention.

STRATEGIES FOR PROVIDING CULTURALLY COMPETENT SERVICES TO FAMILIES

When working with young children who are blind or visually impaired and their families, service providers must develop and maintain relationships with a variety of individuals and family units from diverse backgrounds. Sensitivity to, and understanding of, the family's cultural values and context enhance the professional's effectiveness as a service provider. The accompanying box, "Developing Skills for Working with Families from Culturally Diverse Backgrounds," includes a number of cross-cultural strategies that may be particularly helpful. Such strategies may provide a general framework for cultural considerations. It is, however, important to deter-

---

FOCUS ON EFFECTIVENESS

DEVELOPING SKILLS FOR WORKING WITH FAMILIES FROM CULTURALLY DIVERSE BACKGROUNDS

Early intervention professionals need to develop skills and strategies for working with families from a variety of cultural backgrounds, such as the following:

➜ It is important that service providers examine their own feelings about members of different ethnic and cultural groups. Self-awareness is the first step to effective communication and developing cultural competence.

➜ Determine the family's degree of cultural assimilation by talking with, observing, and listening to families as they talk about their child and interact as a family. Second- or third-generation families may have adopted mainstream American values and lifestyle choices. Some families may have developed a combination of traditions that reflect multicultural influences.

➜ Take time to establish rapport and get to know the family and its traditions and values before getting into the details of a possible intervention plan for the child.

➜ Avoid relying on stereotypes and remember that each family is a unique and dynamic system that has to be defined in its own right.

(continued)

→ Take time to establish trust with the family. Interact with the family in a personal yet professional manner. Involve siblings and extended family members, as appropriate, who may provide caretaking for the child.

→ Work with the child in the presence of the family; ask key members to participate or share ideas and observations.

→ It may be helpful to identify a respected senior member of the family's community to serve as a liaison to the family initially.

→ Recognize family strengths and make positive comments about the family and child.

→ Accept courtesies, such as food and small gifts, from families as a sign of respect.

→ Call ahead before making home visits, as some families may adhere differently to time schedules and place differing degrees of importance on punctuality.

→ If appropriate, tell the family something about yourself to make interactions more personal and reciprocal in nature.

→ Limit the use of educational jargon and slang terms in written and oral communications when working with the family.

→ Be aware of differences in nonverbal communication styles and how your behaviors might be interpreted. When unsure of appropriate behavior in the family's home, simply ask.

→ Explore strategies for involving families in the decision-making process. It is equally important to help family members raise questions even when there is disagreement with professionals.

→ Whenever needed, use a bilingual service provider who speaks the same language as the family. When a bilingual professional is not available, use a trained interpreter to facilitate communication with the family. Clarify terms and expressions that may be unfamiliar to either the family or professionals.

→ Attend training workshops on developing cultural competence when working with young children and families. Such workshops may be available through school district professional development programs and local, regional, and national professional conferences.

> ➡ Printed materials made available in the family's primary language will also help to inform family members and build their confidence in participating in the intervention process.
>
> ➡ Spend time with families and children in natural environments, such as home or neighborhood cultural events, before IFSP or IEP meetings to support their involvement in making decisions for their child.
>
> ➡ Recognize that families may experience a variety of stressors. Take time to identify each family's priorities and try to ensure that intervention plans and strategies are not adding any undue stress to the family unit. Look for equally effective alternatives to replace interventions that may cause unnecessary stress to the family unit.
>
> ➡ Service providers often change throughout the child's educational experience. Help families to build on their strengths so that they can learn how to deal with the special education system, independent of a given service provider.
>
> *Diane L. Fazzi & Rona L. Pogrund*

mine to what extent each individual family has become assimilated into the American culture. Second- or third-generation families may be more likely to have adopted nontraditional values and life styles. Part of being culturally sensitive is avoiding the assumption that families maintain all traditional cultural values.

No one can be an expert on every cultural group. The challenge to individuals working with a variety of families of young children with visual impairments is to understand that serving the child within the context of the family cannot be fully met without developing a degree of cultural competence. Collaboration with families is a two-way process: learning to understand families and helping families to understand and participate in the educational system (Thomas, Correa, & Morsink, 2001). Approaching families with a nonjudgmental, open mind and taking time to observe and listen may be the most effective strategy of all.

3 VISION FOCUS

Understanding the Medical and Functional Implications of Vision Loss

CONTRIBUTORS

Jane N. Erin Functional Vision Assessment

Diane L. Fazzi Promoting Use of Vision

Robert L. Gordon Vision Rehabilitation Optometry

Sherwin J. Isenberg Pediatric Ophthalmology

Evelyn A. Paysse Pediatric Ophthalmology

U nderstanding the growth and development of the eye, the developmental landmarks in vision, and the process of visual learning is essential when working with young children who are visually impaired and their families. Knowledge of the components of vision forms the basis for interpreting visual behaviors. Familiarity with the critical stages of visual development helps early interventionists plan appropriate programming to promote use of vision in order to ensure that young children function to their fullest potential.

Common causes of visual impairment in young children will be reviewed in this chapter. The roles of the pediatric ophthalmologist, the optometrist specializing in vision rehabilitation, and educational vision specialists will be identified, and common assessment and intervention procedures will be detailed.

DEVELOPMENT OF THE EYE AND VISION

Growth and Development of the Eye

The eye is the most developed organ of the body at birth, and it develops more quickly than any other after birth. From birth to maturity, the body increases to 21 times its birth size. The eye, on the other hand, increases to three times its birth size and almost fully completes its growth at 3 years. The diameter of the eye is 16 mm at birth and 24 mm in adulthood. Of the 8 mm growth in diameter, one-third

FOCUS POINTS ON VISION

The following key ideas are addressed in this chapter.

→ Understanding the developmental landmarks in vision, the components of vision, and the sequence of visual learning assists professionals and families in developing appropriate programs for young children who are visually impaired.

→ Understanding the causes of visual impairment in young children provides professionals with an important tool in addressing the varied needs of individual children who are blind or visually impaired.

→ The roles of medical eye-care specialists (ophthalmologists and optometrists) and educational vision specialists (teachers of students who are visually impaired, and O&M specialists) are unique, and each specialist should work together with the others to best meet the individual assessment and intervention needs of each child who is visually impaired.

→ A thorough functional vision assessment by a teacher of students who are visually impaired and an O&M specialist provides the educational team with information on how much usable vision a young child has to perform visual tasks.

→ An intervention program which promotes the use of vision should be developed by the educational vision specialists so that the use of vision is encouraged by all team members when it would make participation in tasks that are relevant to daily life and learning easier and more enjoyable for the child.

occurs in the first year, and growth is totally completed by puberty. The diameter of the cornea, the transparent tissue covering the front of the eyeball, is approximately 9–10 mm at birth, although it is sometimes smaller in the premature infant. In the adult, the diameter is 11.75 mm. Measurement of the corneal diameter is an important diagnostic tool. A larger than normal corneal diameter may indicate glaucoma, whereas a smaller than normal diameter may indicate microphthalmia. Blood vessels from the optic nerve emerge at 16 weeks' gestation and grow into the retina around toward the front of the eye. By 8–9 months' gestation, the retina is fully developed as determined by ophthalmoscopy, and the retina completes histological maturation growth at 3 years of age (Duke-Elder & Cook, 1963; Isenberg, 1989; Taylor, 1997).

The sequence of normal eye development can help determine the age of a premature infant. The development of the macula in the center of the retina and the persistence of iris blood vessels that cross the pupil (persistent pupillary membrane) that normally occur only in utero can be used as landmarks for this purpose. The degree of development indicates the infant's gestational age.

The speed of the growth and development of the eye limits the time during which medical interventions can be effective for children with congenital visual anomalies. Early diagnosis and treatment are important for the prevention, rehabilitation, and stabilization of vision loss in the young child. A full discussion of congenital visual impairments is presented in section on "Causes of Visual Impairment in Young Children" in this chapter.

Developmental Landmarks in Vision

During the twelfth week of gestation, the globes (true eyeballs) form in the fetus. At birth, normal visual acuity is approximately 20/200, at 1 year 20/50, and at 2 years 20/20. That is, at birth a typical infant can see at 20 feet what an adult with unimpaired sight can see at 200 feet; at 1 year the infant can see at 20 feet what someone with unimpaired sight can see at 50 feet; and at 2 years the child has "normal" vision. This degree of visual acuity, however, is often not demonstrated by a child due to short attention span or other factors. This acuity has been proven by visual evoked potential, a visual cortex-specific electroencephalogram. All visual acuity figures for infants and young children, however, are estimates based on the testing modalities, including preferential forced looking and visual evoked potential responses to specific stimuli (see descriptions of these tests later in this chapter in "Tools for Assessing Visual Acuity"). Infants are usually born with moderate farsightedness (hyperopia) and astigmatism. By 1 year of age, mild farsightedness continues, and approximately 8 percent of children still have astigmatism. Accommodation, the ability to change the shape of the lens to focus objects from distance to near, is present at birth. By 3–6 months, it is adultlike in performance. Fixation, the ability to maintain a gaze on a light source or an object, becomes obvious at 6–8 weeks and is accurate by 6 months. Visual searching, which begins at 3 months, in combination with the development of fine motor abilities, forms the basis of eye–hand coordination. The ability to transfer objects from hand to hand typically emerges between 6 and 7 months, and the pincer grasp is refined at 10 months. Visual–form perception emerges at 12 months, when the child is able to see images and pictures and relate them to the real world.

Figure 3.1, Parent's Preschool Visual Development Checklist, was prepared by developmental optometrists and educators as a

PARENTS' PRESCHOOL VISUAL DEVELOPMENT CHECKLIST

Date: _____ Child's Name: _____ Age: _____

1. APPEARANCE OF EYES
- ❑ Unusual redness of eyes
- ❑ Unusual redness of lids
- ❑ Crusted eyelids
- ❑ Styes, or sores, on lids
- ❑ Excessive tearing
- ❑ Unusual lid droopiness
- ❑ One eye turns in or out with fatigue

2. EVIDENCE OF DISCOMFORT
- ❑ Excessive rubbing of eyes
- ❑ Avoids bright light
- ❑ Keeps eyes closed too much of the time

3. EXPECTED VISUAL PERFORMANCE

Birth to 6 weeks of age
- ❑ Stares at surroundings when awake
- ❑ Momentarily holds gaze on bright light or bright object
- ❑ Blinks at camera flash
- ❑ Eyes and head move together
- ❑ One eye may seem turned in at times

8 weeks to 24 weeks
- ❑ Eyes begin to move widely with less head movement
- ❑ Eyes begin to follow moving objects or people (8–12 weeks)
- ❑ Watches parent's face when being talked to (10–12 weeks)
- ❑ Begins to watch own hands (12–16 weeks)
- ❑ Eyes move in active inspection of surroundings (18–20 weeks)
- ❑ While sitting, looks at hands, food, bottle (18–24 weeks)
- ❑ Now looking for and watching more distant objects (20–28 weeks)

30 weeks to 48 weeks
- ❑ May turn eyes inward while inspecting hands or toy (28–32 weeks)
- ❑ Eyes more mobile and move with little head movement (30–36 weeks)

(continued)

Figure 3.1. Parent's Preschool Visual Development Checklist.

30 weeks to 48 weeks *(continued)*
- ❏ Watches activities around him for longer periods of time (30–36 weeks)
- ❏ Looks for toys he drops (32–38 weeks)
- ❏ Visually inspects toys when seen (40–44 weeks)
- ❏ Creeps after favorite toy when seen (40–44 weeks)
- ❏ Sweeps eyes around room to see what's happening (44–48 weeks)
- ❏ Visually responds to smiles and voice of others (40–48 weeks)
- ❏ More and more visual inspection of objects and persons (46–52 weeks)

12 months to 18 months
- ❏ Now using both hands and visually steering hand activity (12–14 months)
- ❏ Visually interested in simple pictures (14–16 months)
- ❏ Often holds objects very close to eyes to inspect (14–18 months)
- ❏ Points to objects or people using words "look" or "see" (14–18 months)
- ❏ Looks for and identifies pictures in books (16–18 months)

24 months to 36 months:
- ❏ Occasionally visually inspects without needing to touch (20–24 months)
- ❏ Smiles, facial brightening when views favorite objects and people (20–24 months)
- ❏ Likes to watch movement of wheels, egg beater, etc. (24–28 months)
- ❏ Watches own hand while scribbling (26–30 months)
- ❏ Visually explores and steers own walking and climbing (30–36 months)
- ❏ Watches and imitates other children (30–36 months)
- ❏ Can now begin to keep coloring on the paper (34–38 months)
- ❏ "Reads" pictures in books (34–38 months)

40 months to 48 months
- ❏ Brings head and eyes close to page of book while inspecting (40–44 months)
- ❏ Draws and names circle and cross on paper (40–44 months)
- ❏ Can close eyes on request, and may be able to wink one eye (46–50 months)

guideline for typical developmental sequence of vision. These expected visual performances are rough gauges by which vision professionals and families can determine a young child's general visual functioning. The guidelines are not to be used as strict standards for visual diagnosis, as all age ranges given are approximate. Sections 1 and 2 of the checklist highlight conditions and behaviors that need the attention of an eye care specialist, as they may indicate certain eye disorders that require treatment.

Vision: A Learned Process

The use of vision is a learned process from which emerges an understanding of what is seen, knowledge of the location of objects in the environment, and the development of necessary reactions to visual stimuli. Vision involves all the body's parts and senses and requires the integration of all sensory information.

It is important to intervene early in the development of an infant who is visually impaired to provide the building blocks for as efficient and complete a visual system as possible. Corrective procedures that could improve vision, such as surgery for congenital total cataracts or glaucoma, need to occur as soon as possible, usually within the first 2 months of life, in order to allow the brain to process visual input accurately. A clear visual axis with a properly focused image must be accomplished during these first 6–8 weeks or permanent visual impairment can result. If, for instance, cataract surgery for a total unilateral cataract is done beyond this critical period, the cataract may successfully be removed, but the child's visual acuity may not improve beyond 20/200 due to permanent immature visual processing, called *form-vision deprivation amblyopia*. Human beings, however, are very adaptable. Young children will develop compensations for vision loss (they may tilt the head if necessary for clear vision, shift attention from one eye to the other, or suppress information from one eye in order to assist the brain in processing information from the other). Understanding the components of vision and the sequence of visual learning helps formulate appropriate programming to promote the use of vision for the young child.

Components of Vision

According to Corn's (1983) model of visual functioning (see Figure 3.2), the components of vision include *visual abilities, stored and available individuality,* and *environmental cues*. *Visual abilities* are often assessed by an ophthalmologist and include visual acuity, visual field, ocular motility (movement of the eyes), fusion (the ability to use both eyes together at the same time), and stereopsis (vision in which two separate images from two eyes are successfully combined

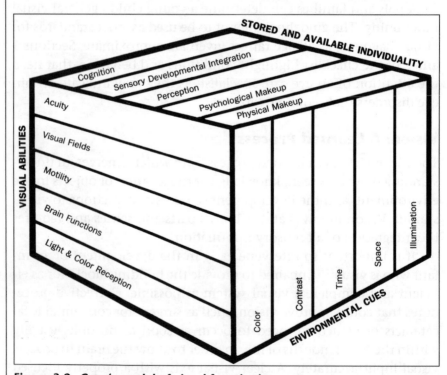

Figure 3.2. Corn's model of visual functioning.
Source: Reprinted with permission from A. Corn, "Visual Function: A Theoretical Model for Individuals with Low Vision," *Journal of Visual Impairment & Blindness, 77* (8) (October 1983), p. 374.

into one three-dimensional image in the brain), brain functions, and light and color perception.

Stored and available individuality includes past experiences and available functions an individual can call on to react to new stimuli or to use for creativity (Corn, 1983). The implications of stored and available individuality are reflected in the fact that two children with identical diagnoses and acuities may function differently because of their unique characteristics and abilities. Among the factors accounting for these individual differences are the following:

- cognition level,

- sensory integration and development (the integration of visual input with other sensory systems),

- perception,

- psychological makeup, and

- physical abilities.

Finally, *environmental cues* include characteristics of one's surroundings that provide information about the environment. Cues include the following:

- *color*, which involves hue, brightness, and saturation,

- *contrast*, which involves intensity in tone and color,

- *time*, which involves the need to anticipate events, plan motor activities, and make long-term decisions,

- *space*, which involves pattern, position, complexity, and clutter of visual stimuli, and

- *illumination*, which involves aspects of lighting, such as intensity, location on the spectrum, reflective qualities, and distance of light sources.

Different relationships exist between and among the various components and dimensions of Corn's model. Understanding these components allows the early interventionist to manipulate certain components to increase visual functioning. For example, increasing contrast and reducing background clutter may facilitate a child's visual abilities even though his or her acuity remains the same. All these factors can be varied to determine how a child functions visually under different conditions and to determine optimal environmental conditions for an individual child.

Sequence of Visual Learning

Children normally develop many visual abilities. It is important to become familiar with those abilities and to use them in setting goals for the individual. The older or more severely impaired a child is, the more important it is to be concerned with the developmental sequence rather than adhering to developmental charts established according to chronological age. Such charts may not take into account general developmental delays. The early interventionist needs to be aware of the developmental sequence in order to plan attainable and age-appropriate objectives and activities, especially for children with multiple impairments. Sidebar 3.1 shows the sequence of development for visual responses.

Familiarity with these developmental sequences should form part of the knowledge base needed for intervention. For example, if a child is unable to attend visually, that is fixate with the eyes, to his or her caretaker's face, it would be useless to spend large amounts of time trying to get the child to attend to a teddy bear. As a visual task, the latter would be developmentally more difficult for the child. Understanding the sequence of visual development can contribute to

---

SIDEBAR 3.1 SEQUENCE OF DEVELOPMENT OF VISION

The development of vision occurs in the following sequences:
→ First awareness, then attention, then understanding of stimuli,
→ First attention to light, then to people, then to objects,
→ First fixation, then tracking (visually following a moving object or light),
→ First interest in near objects, then interest in distant objects,
→ First peripheral (that is, side) vision, then central vision,
→ First preference for familiar stimuli, then preference for the novel,
→ First viewing part of an object, then viewing the whole object,
→ First interest in simple items, then interest in complex items and designs, and
→ First interest in large items, then interest in small items.

Source: K. A. Ferrell, *Reach Out and Teach: Meeting the Training Needs of Parents of Visually and Multiply Handicapped Young Children* (New York: American Foundation for the Blind, 1985) pp. 180–183.

the creation of a well-designed environment and effective intervention for the young child with a visual impairment.

CAUSES OF VISUAL IMPAIRMENT IN YOUNG CHILDREN

The most common causes of severe visual impairment in children in the United States are: cortical visual impairment (CVI), retinopathy of prematurity (ROP), optic-nerve hypoplasia, microphthalmia, anophthalmia, glaucoma, retinoblastoma, and congenital cataracts. Less frequently occurring etiologies include severe myopia, albinism, and nystagmus (Blind Babies Foundation, 1998; Foster & Gilbert, 1997). Two recent studies of young children with visual impairments found CVI, ROP, and optic nerve hypoplasia to be the three most frequent visual diagnoses identified (Ferrell, 1998; Hatton, 2001).

The following section provides a brief discussion of some of the more common early childhood eye diseases and conditions. More thorough information can be found in pediatric ophthalmology texts, such as those cited in the Resources section at the end of this book, or obtained from a medical or educational vision specialist.

Acquired Pediatric Eye Conditions

Pediatric eye conditions are categorized as acquired or congenital. Acquired conditions include ROP and a variety of conditions caused by trauma before or during birth or by infection.

INFECTION

Several infections may affect the neonate's visual system. Ophthalmia neonatorum (neonatal conjunctivitis) is caused by bacteria and other organisms present in the birth canal, such as gonorrhea and chlamydia. These infections are treated with antibiotics, usually with good outcome. It is also important to treat the parents of an infant who has a neonatal conjunctivitis caused by one of these infections.

There are several infections that may be contracted in utero or during birth. They are often known by the acronym TORCH, for *tox*oplasmosis, *r*ubella, *c*ytomegalovirus, and *h*erpes.

- Toxoplasmosis is a parasitic infection that the mother acquires from eating poorly cooked beef or lamb. The parasite is passed to the developing embryo or fetus and can cause retinal scarring and inflammation, nystagmus, necrosis (death or decay due to a loss of blood supply) of the optic nerve, brain calcifications, microcephaly, and developmental delay.

- Congenital rubella syndrome is rarely seen in the United States thanks to vaccination. It causes congenital cataract, glaucoma, pigmentary retinal abnormality, and microphthalmia, in addition to deafness, microcephaly, and cognitive impairments.

- Cytomegaloviral (CMV) infection is caused by a virus, cytomegalovirus. It is the most common of the TORCH infections. It is passed to the fetus during gestation. The mother contracts a viral illness with malaise and fever. Congenital cytomegaloviral infections can cause deafness, microcephaly, intracranial calcifications, cognitive impairments, cataracts, retinal pigmentary abnormalities, and optic nerve atrophy or hypoplasia.

- Herpes viruses are passed to the infant during passage in the birth canal. Herpes can cause infection of all tissues of the eye, skin, and mucous membranes. Additionally, herpes species can cause an infection of the brain and surrounding tissues.

Bacterial infections may also be caused by wearing contact lenses, which are more frequently being prescribed for infants than in the past, especially following the removal of congenital cataracts. These infections can be serious and can leave a large scar on the cornea which can cause form vision deprivation amblyopia.

RETINOPATHY OF PREMATURITY

Premature babies born with a birthweight of less than 4 pounds (1,600 grams or less) who were born at an estimated gestational age of less than 31 weeks, or who are exposed to oxygen are at significant risk of developing retinopathy of prematurity (ROP). ROP is a retinal disorder that causes changes in the retinal blood vessels and, in some cases, proliferation of the retinal blood vessels into the vitreous, the transparent gel-like substance between the lens and the retina. Fibrous tissues also develop through the retina and vitreous. The abundance of blood vessels and fibrous tissues causes traction on the retina, which may lead to eventual detachment of the retina and vision loss. Most ROP will resolve without treatment. Only approximately 10 percent of infants with ROP require intervention and treatment to prevent retinal detachment and vision loss. Approximately 2,100 infants annually in the United States experience severe loss of vision from ROP, and the number is rising as increasing numbers of smaller premature infants are surviving due to sophisticated neonatal technology (Trief, Duckman, Morse, & Silberman, 1989). The degree of prematurity correlates to the degree of severe visual impairment. Fifty percent of premature infants weighing less than 750 grams (1.65 pounds) have severe visual impairment or blindness, while 25 percent of those infants weighing 750–1000 grams (1.65–2.2 pounds) demonstrate a severe visual impairment, and only 5 percent of those premature infants weighing 1000–1250 grams (2.2–2.75 pounds) show signs of severe vision loss due to ROP (Holmstrom, el Azizim, Jacobson, & Lennerstrand, 1993; Palmer, Flynn, & Hardy, 1991).

The International Classification for ROP (Trief, Duckman, Morse, & Silberman, 1989) was developed to describe the progression of the disorder and to standardize classification of examiners. Infants will develop to a certain stage, and the disorder does not often regress without intervention.

- *Stage I.* Retinal blood vessels grow to a defined line in the retina, so part of the retina is supplied with retinal blood vessels and part is not.

- *Stage II.* The line at which blood vessel growth stops becomes a ridge extending into the vitreous.

- *Stage III.* New blood vessels (neovasculization) form in the ridge and may grow out of the retina into the vitreous.

- *Stage IV.* The retina is pulled off from its normal position in the back of the eye by the ridge (partial retinal detachment).

- *Stage V.* Complete retinal detachment.

If a child reaches a certain level of ROP called threshold (Stage III with other criteria) treatment is required. In the Cryo-ROP study (Cryotherapy for Retinopathy of Prematurity Cooperative Group, 1990), 50 percent of untreated eyes that reached threshold developed retinal detachment or retinal fold causing vision loss. This risk decreased to roughly 25 percent in the treated eyes. ROP that reaches threshold can be treated by a variety of methods. No effective method of prevention has yet been found. The most common treatments used are laser photocoagulation or freezing (cryotherapy) to the avascular retina. Both of these treatments are highly effective in causing regression of the ROP (Paysse et al, 1999). ROP can continue to progress to retinal detachment despite appropriate treatment, however, in approximately 15–22 percent of patients, resulting in impaired vision (Cryotherapy for Retinopathy of Prematurity Cooperative Group, 1990).

TRAUMA

Trauma may be incurred by amniocentesis (rarely) or by forceps delivery. Globe perforation can occur from amniocentesis, leading to corneal scarring, possible cataract, retinal detachment, and retinal or vitreous hemorrhage. Forceps, if placed over the eye, can cause rupture of Descemet's membrane in the cornea. Descemet's tear causes corneal edema transiently but can cause corneal scarring and severe astigmatism. Trauma, such as that resulting in severe retinal hemorrhaging, may also be nonaccidental. Shaken baby syndrome is unfortunately not uncommon and can cause cortical visual impairment.

Maternal drug abuse is another cause of trauma. Cocaine addiction, for instance, can cause infant addiction. An increase in the thickness and irregularity of the blood vessels of the iris has been reported. Clinical findings include: (1) visual inattentiveness; (2) abnormal results of a visual-evoked response (VER) test (a computerized recording of electrical activity of the visual part of the brain which is used to assess problems in the retina-to-brain nerve pathway); (3) a tendency toward delayed visual maturation; (4) higher incidence of strabismus, a deviation in the position of one or both eyes; and (5) refractive errors, which occur when light rays do not come to a point of focus on the retina and which are treated with corrective lenses. Cocaine and other drug intoxications can be treated with antagonists to the specific drug.

Congenital Pediatric Eye Conditions

Congenital pediatric eye abnormalities encompass a wide variety of conditions, ranging from albinism to optic nerve hypoplasia to congenital retinitis pigmentosa (Leber's congenital amaurosis), to coloboma. The following is a list of the most common congenital pediatric eye conditions.

ALBINISM

Albinism is a group of hereditary conditions that have an abnormality of pigment production in the eye alone (ocular albinism) or in the skin and the eye (ocular-cutaneous albinism). The deficiency of pigment occurs in the retina, iris, and choroid. In addition to being generally associated with photophobia (light sensitivity), albinism is also associated with nystagmus, strabismus, lack of depth perception, and poor macular development which leads to reduced levels of visual acuity. The use of sunglasses with ultraviolet filtration to shield the eyes from glare and sunscreen to protect the skin is important for the young child with albinism.

AMBLYOPIA

Amblyopia is also called "lazy eye." Amblyopia is defined as poor visual development caused by disease or misuse of an eye during the critical period of visual development (birth to approximately age 7–8 years). Some loss of depth perception and visual field can result, and legal blindness may occur if both eyes are affected and if the condition is not treated. Deprivation amblyopia occurs in the newborn when normal vision in one or both eyes is obstructed by a cataract, glaucoma, or other cause. Amblyopia can also result from strabismus (misalignment of the eyes), unequal refractive error (for example, one eye may be more nearsighted or have more astigmatism than the other), or other causes. Treatment for deprivation amblyopia is most effective in the first few months after birth. Amblyopia resulting from other causes may be responsive to treatment up to 9 years of age.

ANIRIDIA

In aniridia, the iris does not fully form, creating problems in controlling the amount of light entering the eye. Aniridia can be associated with kidney tumors (Wilm's tumor), cataracts, foveal hypoplasia (poor development of the central vision part of the retina), and nystagmus. It is the foveal hypoplasia and nystagmus that cause the poor vision.

ANOPHTHALMIA

Anophthalmia is the absence of the globe (true eyeball), usually occurring in both eyes. Anophthalmia is very rare. Eyelids and lashes are present but may be closed or partially fused. The eyelids may appear sunken because of the absence of the globe.

CATARACTS

A congenital cataract is a clouding of the lens that causes reduced visual acuity and increased glare due to the scattering of light entering the eye. Congenital cataracts can be caused by rubella or other congenital infection or galactosemia (a hereditary metabolic disorder in which an infant is unable to convert the galactose [a type of sugar] in milk into blood sugar, causing galactose to diffuse into the lens), or they may be of familial origin. Cataracts are treated surgically by lensectomy, or the removal of the clouded lens, followed by optical correction. If they are not treated early, the child may develop nystagmus and amblyopia. An artificial lens can be placed in selected cases. Otherwise, a contact lens or spectacles must be worn to see clearly.

CHARGE ASSOCIATION

CHARGE association is a congenital disorder. The acronym refers to *c*olobomas (see following section), *h*eart anomalies, *c*hoanel *a*tresia (congenital absence or closing of the choanae [the opening between the nasal cavity and the back of the throat], which results in breathing difficulties), mental *r*etardation, *g*enital abnormalities, and *e*ar anomalies. It occurs presumably because of a developmental insult during gestation (a problem of embryonic development) that affects all of these organs and is not hereditary.

COLOBOMA

A coloboma is a congenital cleft due to the failure of some portion of the eye to complete growth during development. Wherever the cleft is, there is missing tissue. Colobomas can affect the eyelid, iris, lens, retina, choroid, and optic nerve. If the coloboma affects the optic nerve or retina, significant visual impairment often results. The pupil may have a teardrop shape, which may cause photophobia. Contact lenses and sunglasses are used for cosmetic purposes and to reduce photophobia.

CORTICAL VISUAL IMPAIRMENT

Children with CVI appear to have normally formed eyes and a normal pupillary response. The vision loss is caused by damage to the visual cortex of the brain. The impairment varies from mildly affected to lack of light perception. The degree of neurological damage and visual impairment depends upon the time of onset as well as the location and intensity of the insult. A child's cognitive ability is not indicated by the presence of CVI. Visual abilities may improve with functional vision training, with peripheral vision usually increasing first. Incorporating tactile and kinesthetic modalities in vision training may enhance vision use in children with CVI. (See "Promoting Use of Vision in Children with Cortical Visual Impairment" later in this chapter for more suggestions on working with children with CVI.)

GLAUCOMA

Glaucoma, or increased pressure in the eye that causes damage to the optic nerve, can lead to loss of peripheral vision and eventual blindness if untreated. Symptoms of congenital glaucoma include megalocornea (a large cornea), corneal clouding, tearing, redness, pain, and frequent rubbing of the eyes. In some cases, however, there may be no symptoms at all. Early detection is important, and treatment with topical medication, laser therapy, or surgery may be indicated.

HEMIANOPIA

Hemianopia (or hemianopsia) is a visual field defect that affects both eyes. It is caused by damage to the brain anywhere from the optic chiasm (where the optic nerves come together and cross) to the visual cortex in the brain. Children with early-onset hemianopia often use an abnormal head posture in order to adapt to the visual field defect.

MICROPHTHALMIA

Microphthalmia is a condition marked by abnormal, poorly formed small eyes. It can occur with colobomas and is often associated with defects of the skull, vitreous anomalies, glaucoma, and cataracts. It is also present in many syndromes. Because of the malformation, these eyes usually see poorly.

MYOPIA

Myopia is a medical term for nearsightedness, characterized by good near vision and blurred distance vision. Myopia occurs when the image is focused in front of the retina. This phenomenon can occur when the eye is abnormally long, when the lens is abnormally spherical, or when the corneal curvature is too steep. It is correctable with lenses. The severe form is at risk for retinal detachment and retinal holes because the retina is stretched over a much larger than normal surface area.

NYSTAGMUS

Nystagmus is characterized by involuntary, rhythmic oscillating movement of one or both eyes from side to side, up and down, in a rotary pattern, or in some combination. Nystagmus may accompany other eye conditions, a neurologic abnormality, or may exist alone. Some children may turn or tilt their heads as they try to control the eye movements to improve focusing. Nystagmus can be due to a cortical (brain) problem, a retinal or optic nerve abnormality, or it can be merely a muscle problem. It often implies visual impairment.

OPTIC-NERVE HYPOPLASIA

Optic-nerve hypoplasia is manifested in the form of an underdeveloped optic nerve in one or both eyes. Vision loss varies from moderate to severe. Septo-optic dysplasia (deMorsier's syndrome) is a condition associated with optic-nerve hypoplasia. In this condition, there are absent or poorly formed parts of the brain, often associated with hormone deficiencies. Children with optic-nerve hypoplasia need to be evaluated by an endocrinologist in addition to an ophthalmologist and a low-vision specialist. Poor growth due to hormonal defects may be associated with this condition. This problem can occur in children of alcoholic mothers (fetal alcohol syndrome).

PETER'S ANOMALY

Peter's anomaly is a rare congenital ocular malformation in which the cornea may be scarred, and cataracts and glaucoma may be present due to failure or delay in the separation of the lens of the eye from the cornea in utero.

RETINITIS PIGMENTOSA

Retinitis pigmentosa is the name for a group of hereditary conditions that progressively affect peripheral and night vision and can lead to tunnel vision or blindness. Retinitis pigmentosa can be diagnosed in young children. However, the symptoms rarely manifest themselves to a significant degree until late childhood or early adulthood. Leber's congenital amaurosis is a congenital form of retinitis pigmentosa. Children with this condition have profound visual impairment. Initially, the retina in these patients may look normal, but over time a pigmentary abnormality of the retina occurs.

RETINOBLASTOMA

Retinoblastoma is the most common intra-ocular malignancy in children, affecting approximately 1 in 20,000 children. Depending on the location in the retina, vision can be detrimentally affected. This cancer can be treated in a myriad of ways. Different treatment options depend on the stage or severity of the tumor. Treatment options include laser or freezing (cryo) treatment, radiation, chemotherapy, and enucleation (surgical removal of the eye). Retinoblastoma can be hereditary. Its management is complex and requires a team approach including an ophthalmologist, an oncologist, a geneticist, and a social worker.

STRABISMUS

Strabismus is any deviation in the position of one or both eyes that results in the eyes having difficulty in working together for binocular vision. The "straight" eye is often favored while the image in the other eye is suppressed, resulting in amblyopia or "lazy eye." Difficulty with near visual tasks may result. A variety of treatment options are available, but the earlier the treatment the better, as the possibility of correcting strabismus decreases as the child gets older.

ROLES OF VISION SPECIALISTS

All the childhood eye conditions identified in the previous section can be treated or addressed, as appropriate, by a variety of specialists with expertise in the area of visual impairment. The specialists include, but are not limited to, the pediatric ophthalmologist, the optometrist specializing in vision rehabilitation, and the educational vision specialist.

A pediatric ophthalmologist is a medical doctor (M.D.) who diagnoses and treats eye diseases in children, performs surgery, and prescribes other types of treatment, including eyeglasses, other optical devices, or drugs, when necessary. An optometrist specializing in vision rehabilitation is a licensed, nonmedical doctor of optometry (O.D.) trained to work with the functioning rather than the pathology of the eye. This specialist performs the clinical low-vision assessment, measures refraction, and prescribes and fits corrective lenses and low-vision devices. The educational vision specialist is a teacher of students who are visually impaired or an orientation and mobility (O&M) specialist with expertise in working with children who are visually impaired in areas such as functional vision assessments and training, optical device training, and integration of visual functioning into daily routines at school, home, or in the community.

These professionals have the expertise to provide the necessary medical and functional information regarding each child's unique visual impairment so that an appropriate program can be developed. Without a proper medical diagnosis, an understanding of visual abilities, appropriate prescriptive optical and nonoptical devices, and a thorough functional vision assessment, it is not possible for other team members and family members to optimally promote use of the young child's vision. The ophthalmologist, the optometrist, the teacher of students who are visually impaired, and the O&M specialist, each with very specific roles, should all communicate their findings to one another and work together to better meet the needs of the young child who is visually impaired. (See Chapter 11 for more information on professional roles.)

There is no definite order in which each of these specialists may come into contact with any particular child. Typically, however, if a child is thought to have a vision problem at birth or in the early years, the child's pediatrician will often make the first referral to a pediatric ophthalmologist. Once a diagnosis is made and a thorough eye examination completed, it is beneficial if a child with any degree of usable vision is examined by an optometrist specializing in vision rehabilitation so that a complete clinical low-vision assessment can be done. Appropriate optical, electro-optical and/or nonoptical devices can be prescribed, if needed. Sometimes educational vision specialists may see the child prior to the optometrist's evaluation. In this case, it is often up to the teacher of students who are visually impaired or the O&M specialist to recommend the clinical low-vision assessment. It is important for the teacher and the O&M specialist to obtain copies of both the ophthalmological and optometric examination reports. It is then the role of the educational vision specialists to carry out functional low-vision assessments for both near and distance vision.

A compilation of the information from each of the specialist's reports will give the family, the educational vision specialists, and other team members valuable insight into how and what a particular child sees. It is this understanding of the child's vision that provides the data needed to develop an appropriate intervention plan. It is often the job of the educational vision specialist to synthesize the information from the various eye reports and assessments and to communicate with the eye doctors and the family on an ongoing basis.

Role of the Pediatric Ophthalmologist

Families of young children can help the ophthalmologist in several ways. Providing access to previous eye examination reports, evaluations of the child's functional vision, old photographs for visual comparison of eye appearance, and any eyeglasses or optical devices the child uses will be helpful to the examining physician. In addition, it is important to inform the ophthalmologist about any medications the child is using. Communication between the family and the pediatric ophthalmologist is an important element in the effective treatment of the child who is visually impaired. Sidebar 3.2 provides a list of questions that may be useful for families to ask when they visit their eye care specialist. "Fostering Communication Between Families and Eye Care Specialists" suggests some additional tips for developing a smooth relationship between families and professionals.

Pediatric ophthalmologists are specifically oriented toward early diagnosis and treatment of eye disease in children. They are concerned with the following areas:

- congenital anomalies,

- normal eye development,

- refractive errors,

- strabismus,

- amblyopia, and

- reading problems.

Although ophthalmologists who do not specialize in pediatrics may address the same concerns, they may not be oriented toward early intervention and may not be trained in the prevention of chronic conditions.

It is important for the ophthalmologist to first make friends with the child to put him or her at ease. After that, the rest of the

FOSTERING COMMUNICATION BETWEEN FAMILIES AND EYE CARE SPECIALISTS

The following suggestions may facilitate better communication and better service between families and the ophthalmologists or optometrists they are seeing:

➜ Consider geographical location when choosing an eye care specialist since on-going visits may be required as the child's vision is monitored.

➜ Talk with the doctor and express concerns and questions to see if he or she is receptive and respectful so that a comfort level exists initially.

➜ Observe how the doctor interacts with your child. Is the doctor comfortable in these interactions? How does your child respond? This issue is especially important for children with multiple disabilities.

➜ Fill out any forms ahead of time so that you are prepared to answer questions, and the amount of time you and your child spend at the doctor's office can be minimized.

➜ Be prepared for the doctor visit by observing your child's behavior and making notes so you can share what you notice about your child with the doctor, as this information is very valuable (for example, what things you think your child is seeing, how the child tilts his or her head, what colors the child seems to notice, and so on).

➜ Bring a written list of questions with you to the eye examination (see "Questions for Families to Ask the Eye Care Specialist" for suggestions).

➜ Ask the doctor the best way to contact him or her after the visit in case you have questions later.

➜ Keep good records of eye exams. Bring copies of all previous reports whenever you see an ophthalmologist or optometrist the first time.

➜ It is helpful to take someone else with you to the eye examinations. Taking an educational vision specialist along to ask relevant questions is ideal, if that is possible.

➜ Taking a tape recorder and getting the doctor's permission to tape his or her explanations can be useful later when trying to communicate the information to others.

Rona L. Pogrund

examination can proceed. The following techniques and areas are addressed during a clinical eye examination by a pediatric ophthalmologist:

→ Assessment of visual acuity by a variety of techniques, such as the use of an optokinetic nystagmus drum to induce nystagmus visually (rotating drum with alternating black and white bars presented before the child's eyes at varying distances, eliciting a pendular-type movement of the eyes while they attempt to fixate a target moving rapidly across the field of vision); fixation targets such as finger puppets; and a standardized visual acuity chart (for older children). Fixation preference for one eye or the other is determined.

→ Pupillary examination to insure normal function.

→ Evaluation of ocular alignment and motility.

→ Examination of the front of the eye using a penlight or portable biomicroscope.

→ If indicated, eye pressure is measured.

→ Refraction to determine refractive errors such as myopia or anisometropia (difference in refractive power in two eyes).

→ Examination of the back of the eye to diagnose optic nerve and retinal abnormalities. This test is done after giving eyedrops to dilate the pupil and temporarily paralyze the focusing muscle (ciliary body).

Although many of these techniques can be used in examining the eyes of young children with multiple disabilities, there are some unique issues to consider with this population. Children who are visually impaired with multiple disabilities are often difficult to assess because of difficulty understanding or responding to given tasks. Children who are autistic or hearing-impaired often cannot or will not verbalize, so the examiner must rely solely on the objective measurements made during the examination. Children with cerebral palsy and other developmental delays also often are unable to subjectively answer. An interpreter or a teacher who is familiar with the

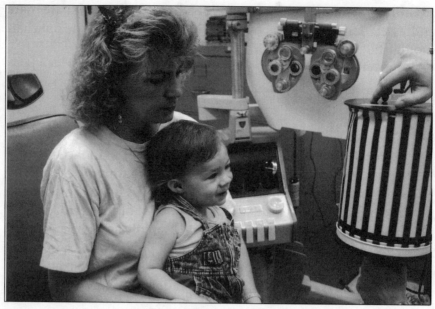

Visual acuity can be assessed using an optokinetic nystagmus drum.

child's communication method may be helpful in improving the communication between the child and the examining physician. Examination under anesthesia is sometimes necessary to completely evaluate a child with a retinal or optic nerve anomaly. Lastly, visual evoked potentials (VEP), electroretinograms (ERG), and electroculograms (EOG) are objective tests of brain and retinal function that can be employed with selected children.

Role of the Optometrist Specializing in Vision Rehabilitation

Evaluation of individuals who have a visual impairment but some degree of functional vision—impaired vision that is adequate to be used as a channel for learning or daily functioning—is commonly referred to as a low vision evaluation or clinical low vision assessment. Optometrists who perform this type of evaluation on young children should have specialized training and experience in the field of vision rehabilitation. It is also helpful if they have had experience working with young children. During the examination, the optometrist may address:

- the nature of the child's visual impairment,
- implications regarding visual functioning,

- prognosis of the visual impairment,

- measurement of any refractive error present,

- evaluation of the functional use of the child's vision,

- evaluation of any loss in field of vision,

- prescription of contact lenses and/or eyeglasses,

- prescription of specialized optical, electro-optical and non-optical assistive devices, and

- collaboration with the child's pediatric ophthalmologist and other members of the health care team to coordinate treatment protocols and share clinical findings.

The goal of the clinical low-vision assessment is to evaluate the visual functional abilities of the child to document any functional limitations that the child's health or visual condition has produced. Another goal is to make recommendations as to appropriate visual development activities, learning and reading media, low-vision devices, classroom seating and lighting requirements, and referral for additional evaluation and/or treatment. It is important to remember that, depending on the child's age and abilities, the results of this evaluation may range from an educated guess as to visual functioning level present to a very accurate measurement of visual function.

In performing a clinical low-vision evaluation, it is very important that the optometrist be provided with as much information as possible regarding how well the child functions visually. The optometrist will be interested in the child's developmental history, how independent the child is, if the child ambulates independently, how the child visually explores the environment, and the parents' and teachers' impressions as to how well the child functions visually. It is crucial to the successful outcome of this assessment that as much information as possible regarding what the child has accomplished and what visual activities the child can and/or cannot perform is related to the optometrist. As the everyday "eyes" of the optometrist, parents and other professionals are essential reporters of how well the child functions visually in daily activities.

The clinical low-vision assessment by the optometrist specializing in vision rehabilitation includes observations and evaluations of the child's functional vision as well as obtaining both objective and subjective data in the following areas, depending upon the age and functioning levels of the child:

Contents of a Clinical Low-Vision Evaluation

→ Collaboration with the child's pediatric ophthalmologist, neurologist, and other members of the health care team to coordinate treatment protocols and share clinical findings

→ General appearance and alignment of the eyes

→ The child's approach to investigating new objects

→ Presence of compensations for eye muscle difficulties such as head tilt, head turn, or squinting

→ Child's reaction to light and changes in illumination

→ Awareness and response to surroundings and visual stimuli

→ Eye muscle movement

→ Eye preference (if one eye has significantly better vision, the child will usually protest vigorously when this eye is covered)

→ Shape of the cornea

→ Measurement of visual acuity (see later note)

→ Presence of a refractive error; that is, objective and/or subjective determination of the presence of nearsightedness (myopia), farsightedness (hyperopia), and astigmatism

→ Testing for the presence of optokinetic nystagmus with an optokinetic nystagmus drum

→ Fixation ability—ability to aim the eyes at the object of regard

→ Tracking ability—ability to follow a moving target

→ Binocular vision—ability to simultaneously perceive the images from the two eyes and fuse them into a single image

→ Convergence—ability to rotate eyes inward towards each other accurately as a target approaches the eyes

→ Divergence—ability to rotate eyes outward away from each other as a target moves away from the eyes

→ Versions—ability to move eyes together to follow a target

→ Stereopsis—ability of the visual system to integrate information from the eyes and the environment to judge distance

→ Field of vision—extent of ability of the eye to see within a 180-degree semisphere without moving the eye

→ Form perception—ability to recognize visual sensations as shapes

→ Determination of best position of the eye and head to maximize the quality of the retinal image

→ Evaluation for low vision devices, including

> Telescopic lenses—devices that magnify the size of distant objects

> Microscopic lenses—lenses that provide magnification of near objects

→ Evaluation for contact lenses—lenses that are placed on the front of the eye (cornea) to correct large refractive errors, cover a scarred eye, selectively filter out light degrading the eye's image, provide for light control in eyes with an inability to adjust the amount of light entering the eye, or provide for better visual function than spectacle lenses

→ Evaluation for spectacle filters—tinted lenses that selectively filter out either harmful light radiation or light that degrades the eye's image

→ Evaluation for field expansion lenses—lenses that either move the image (prisms) or compress optical space (minimize visual space) to compensate for a loss in side vision

→ Evaluation for electro-optical devices—systems utilizing a combination of optics and electronics to enhance distant and/or near vision

---

Visual acuity is commonly measured at schools and motor vehicle departments, as well as during a formal eye examination. Although measuring visual acuity (the "sharpness" of vision, usually assessed by how well one can read an eye chart) is a rather simple and straightforward test when performed on an adult with "normal" vision, trying to estimate visual acuity of an infant who is noncommunicative with visual and multiple impairments is a much more difficult, less precise activity. Nevertheless, there are many ways to assess visual acuity, ranging from gross observation of a child's eyes to electrodiagnostic measurements. Some of the assessment tools used for children who can provide a subjective response include the following:

➜ Object recognition charts where the child either identifies orally a picture of a target or points to a matching picture

➜ Tumbling E chart where the child either points or describes the E as pointing up, down, right, or left. Variations of this test are the Landolt C test, hand position charts, and the Broken Wheel test where the child identifies the opening in the wheel. Increasingly smaller targets are a measure of visual acuity.

➜ Cheerio test where the child is asked to differentiate between a picture of a Cheerio and a similarly colored square

➜ Letter or number visual acuity chart where the child reads the letters or numbers

For children who are either too young or unable to communicate, the following tools can be used:

➜ Preferential viewing test, where the examiner watches the infant through a sighting hole to see whether the infant stares at a gray square or at a grating with varying contrast lines. If the infant can perceive the grating, he or she will prefer to view it to a no-contrast target.

➜ Observation of how well the infant or child scans the environment, reaches for toys, and is able to move and avoid objects.

➜ VEP testing where electrodes are taped to the back of a child's head while either a bright flash of light or alternating checkerboard patterns are presented to the eyes. A graph is created describing the quality of the image that is transported to the brain from the eyes.

This list is not all-inclusive but rather is just a sample of visual acuity tests, to familiarize the reader with some of the ways vision is assessed with young children. (For more information on ways to determine what young children can see, see Chen 1997a, 1997b; Orel-Bixler, 1999.) Generally, the older the child and the better the child is able to respond to verbal requests, the more reliable the information obtained will be.

The clinical low-vision assessment is a crucial step in the process of establishing a program to maximally utilize the visual input a child with a visual impairment receives. The results of this evaluation, in conjunction with the report of the pediatric ophthalmologist, provide important information for the educational vision specialists who will be performing the functional vision assessment.

Role of the Educational Vision Specialist

The educational vision specialist, who may be a certified teacher of students who are visually impaired or an O&M specialist, is primarily concerned with the following vision-related areas:

- functional vision assessment,

- functional vision training,

- optical device training,

- integration of visual functioning into daily routines, and

- coordination of all participants of the vision team, including eye care specialists and family members. (See Chapter 11 for more specific information on the roles of teachers of students who are visually impaired and O&M specialists.)

The following section describes in detail the functional vision asessment.

FUNCTIONAL VISION ASSESSMENT

A functional vision assessment determines how much usable vision a child has to perform visual tasks. It is typically conducted after the medical and the low-vision evaluations by an ophthalmologist and optometrist have been completed so that the professional who is conducting the functional vision assessment will have information about the etiology, the characteristics of the child's vision, and questions about vision that have not been answered through clinical evaluation. In some cases, a professional will recommend a clinical low-vision evaluation as a result of the findings of the functional vision assessment.

A new functional vision assessment must be conducted at least every three years as part of the ongoing educational evaluation process. Many teachers of visually impaired students conduct them annually; this is especially useful if the child is young or the vision is unstable, as with cortical visual impairment or glaucoma.

The resulting report should include the following:

- a summary of medical reports,

- observations of near and distance vision, visual field, and ocular motility as used in regular daily activity,

- description of procedures and activities used in assessment,

- statement of eligibility for vision services, based on visual functioning, and

- recommendations.

For an example of such a report, see the sample functional vision assessment report in Appendix 3A at the end of this chapter.

The functional vision assessment is an informal procedure. Formalized procedures are often inappropriate for the very young or severely disabled child because many require responses that these children are unable to produce. In addition, standard asessment devices may not be appropriate for this population because of the variety of factors affecting the child's visual functioning, such as medications that affect vision or state of consciousness, the child's limited attention span, and possible decreased activity level.

Screenings

A screening is a brief procedure that provides general information about a child's visual abilities. It helps the evaluator to identify children who might have a visual impairment and should undergo further assessment. The children who demonstrate unusual visual behaviors through screenings will then be referred for clinical and functional vision evaluations. Screenings commonly used are the Infant Vision Checklist and the Peabody Functional Vision Inventory for Multiply and Severely Handicapped Children.

The Infant Vision Checklist (*Vision Screening Project,* 1980) covers a wide variety of areas including:

- pupillary responses,

- the Hirschberg corneal reflex test, consisting of holding a light 12 inches from the eyes and looking for the reflection; if the eyes are aligned, the reflections are balanced,

- momentary regard of objects,

- momentary regard of a person,

- prolonged regard of objects,

- horizontal eye coordination,

- ability to follow a moving person visually,

- vertical and circular eye coordination,

- free inspection of surroundings (i.e., visual examination of the environment and exploration of objects),

- ability to turn the eyes to light and objects,

- ability to follow an object from central to peripheral areas,

- tendency to blink at the shadow of a hand,

- ability to follow a ball left to right visually,

- tendency to reach for objects (not the same as grasp),

- the cover test, used to detect strabismus and amblyopia, in which vision in one eye is occluded and the occluder is then quickly moved to the other eye; when the "good" eye is occluded, the amblyopic eye will align, and

- the two-light test for peripheral-field assessment, in which one light acts as a distracter while the other is moved to various points and the ability to shift gaze from center to peripheral points is observed.

The Peabody Inventory (Langley, 1980) includes both a screening inventory and a functional-vision inventory. Some of the items are similar to those of the Infant Vision Checklist, addressing such areas as:

- pupillary responses,

- tendency to blink at the shadow of a hand,

- ability to orient peripherally,

- tendency to fixate on four-inch objects,

- shifting gaze,

- tendency to reach in response to a visual cue,

- ability to track horizontally, vertically, and circularly,

- convergence, or the ability to follow an object as it approaches (the child's eyes should demonstrate esotropia [the eye turning inward] at about four inches; with a muscle imbalance there may be early convergence of one eye), and

- ability to track or pick up a small object; tested with 3 mm and 1 mm beads and thread by scattering larger beads first, then the smaller and the thread, and having the child locate each.

Screenings for acuity are generally designed for students functioning at the two-year level or above. Two screening devices that may be used with very young children are Lighthouse House, Apple, Umbrella Series Flashcard Test and the Parsons Visual Acuity Test (see the sources of these and other assessment tools in the Resource section).

Lighthouse flashcards are based on three basic symbols: house, umbrella, and apple. They have several advantages for use with young children:

- Children can be screened by selecting a matching card from a group of cards placed close to them. Each symbol is on a separate card, making it easier to identify the chosen card.

- The cards require only consistent, rather than accurate, labeling; for example, a child may call the umbrella a mushroom, as long as it is always identified as a mushroom throughout the test.

- The cards are plastic and easily cleaned.

The Parsons Visual Acuity Test (Parsons, 1979) was developed for individuals who are severely disabled and may be used with children from 18 months. The test does not depend on language for results, and a training component is included with the test. The Parsons test provides acuities only.

Assessment

After screening is completed, assessment is carried out. The Peabody Functional Vision Inventory for the Multiple and Severely Handicapped (Langley, 1980) can be used for both screening and assessment. The required materials are extensive, and activities for vision usage are provided. Some items included in the assessment, resulting in a vision profile, are

- observation of eye structure,

- the noting of behaviors incompatible with vision (such as hand flapping and eye poking),

- observation of the use of eyeglasses (for example, looking over or under the lenses, or otherwise avoiding their use),

- observation of the ability to deal with obstacles (difficulty descending stairs is noted, as is balking at stairs),

- observation of reflexive and voluntary eye movements,

- observation of near and distance vision (for instance, the distance at which the child will search for an item is noted, as is the size of the item),

- observation of the ability to locate dropped objects (the child must have developed object permanence—the understanding that objects exist even when they cannot be seen—to do this),

- observation of the ability to match pictures,

- estimations of acuity,

- testing for field assessment, and

- assessment of visual perceptual skills.

Individualized Systematic Assessment of Visual Efficiency (ISAVE), a more recent assessment and curriculum by Langley (1998), provides a comprehensive instrument for evaluating visual function in children with severe disabilities, including those with physical and motor disabilities. It is a valuable resource for teachers of students who are visually impaired and O&M specialists who want more information on the interaction of vision and motor development.

While the format of the assessment varies, a complete assessment describes visual abilities in the following areas:

Contents of a Functional Vision Assessment

→ *Observation of eyes:* The report should describe the appearance of the child's eyes, including any unusual characteristics such as pupils of different sizes, drooping eyelids, and so on.

→ *Ocular reflexes:* Evaluators should check for a brisk blink reflex and for pupillary responses to lighting changes.

→ *Near point vision:* The child's response to large and small objects within three feet provides information about acuity and visual field. Typical activities to be observed can include noticing small pieces of food and picking up small objects. Observers should notice whether the child tries to move closer to materials or whether he or she tilts or turns the head in trying to view objects.

→ *Distance vision:* Turning the head and eyes to look at objects at a distance will provide information about the child's ability to see detail when the object is not within touching distance. Activities to be observed may include smiling to another person's smile, walking toward a wanted object, and attention to an event outside the window or on the other side of the room.

→ *Visual field response:* Because it is difficult to evaluate an infant's visual field clinically, observation will play an important part in deciding whether the child has a normal visual field. Presenting a small object from behind is one way to observe whether the child notices an object with a typical range. Observations of head and eye movements when someone walks into the room or when a quiet rolling toy is moved past the learner will provide additional information.

→ *Eye movements:* The evaluator should observe whether the eyes move together when the child is tracking and scanning materials in the environment. If the child will tolerate having an eye covered briefly, eye movements should be observed with each eye.

→ *Special visual responses:* Some children with neurological difficulties show different responses to visual experiences. The functional vision assessment should describe responses such as photophobia (light sensitivity), selective responses to color (noticing red more than another color), intense attraction to light, difficulty with perceptual tasks that involve placing or moving objects, and responsiveness to specific types of materials (for example, moving objects).

Table 3.1 provides guidelines for estimating a child's visual acuity based on the size of an object the child is able to see and its distance from the child.

The following tests can also be used as part of a functional vision assessment with young children (see the Resources section for sources):

1. *The Holmgren Test for Color Blindness*—a test of color blindness that uses matching of 40 swatches of different color yarn to evaluate vision (Hyvarinen, 1995–1996).

2. *The LEA Near Test*—(developed by Lea Hyvarinen, a Swedish ophthalmologist) a "two-sided test of near vision acuity that uses Sloan letters (the standard letters on eye charts that are

TABLE 3.1 APPROXIMATE FUNCTIONAL VISUAL ACUITY FOR DIFFERENT SIZES OF OBJECTS AND DISTANCES

Functional visual acuity is measured in natural environments. The objects used as text targets should be familiar and motivating to the child; their size is measured at their widest point or will be equal on all sides. The objects are placed at sequentially greater distances, and the child's response is observed. This table assists the examiner in estimating the child's functional visual acuity, given the size of the object and the greatest distance at which the infant appears to see it.

SIZE OF OBJECT	DISTANCE FROM CHILD				
	2 FEET	4 FEET	6 FEET	8 FEET	20 FEET
1/4 inch	20/200	20/100	20/67	20/50	20/20
1/2 inch	20/400	20/200	20/133	20/100	20/40
3/4 inch	20/600	20/300	20/200	20/150	20/60
1 inch	20/800	20/400	20/267	20/200	20/80

Source: Reprinted with permission from I. Topor, "Functional Vision Assessments and Early Interventions," in D. Chen, Ed., *Essential Elements in Early Intervention: Visual Impairment and Multiple Disabilities* (New York: AFB Press, 1999), p. 177.

calibrated by width and height to acuity) around a different order on each side" (Hyvarinen, 1995–1996).

3. *The LEA Distance Test*—tests of distance acuity [also developed by Hyvarinen, (1995–1996)] using the circle, house, apple, and square as test symbols.

4. *The Hiding Heidi Low Contrast Test*—evaluates the child's ability to see differences between "Heidi's" facial expressions by matching pairs at six different levels of contrast (Hyvarinen, 1995–1996).

5. *The Diagnostics Assessment Procedure*—the assessment portion of Barraga's (1980) *Program to Develop Efficiency in Visual Functioning.*

Assessing Children with Multiple Disabilities

The functional vision assessment is an individualized procedure that should reflect both the child's best visual abilities and typical use of vision. When conducting a functional vision evaluation for a child with multiple disabilities, vision should be observed during several activities. Specific procedures might be followed to evaluate physical responses such as pupillary response and blink reflex, but vision should be observed during at least three of the following activities:

- daily routines (feeding, diapering, dressing)
- individual interaction with objects
- interaction with another person
- novel environments or situations
- gross motor activities or travel

"Factors to Consider When Conducting a Functional Low Vision Assessment with a Child Who Has Multiple Disabilities" presents additional considerations.

Assessing Infants

As noted earlier, when assessing infants, the evaluator should be knowledgeable about typical visual development. (Figure 3.1 presented age ranges for typical visual development). Infants who are younger than six months have not yet developed excellent detail or central acuity, and oculomotor skills such as convergence or tracking may still be developing. The child may not respond visually because he or she does not see objects as meaningful or interesting. Developmental milestones such as hand manipulation, reaching and grasping, and recognition of pictures will influence the types of materials that can be used in the assessment process, and evaluators should be aware of the child's developmental characteristics before attempting specific interactive tasks.

Some infants demonstrate delayed visual maturation (DVM), a lack of visual responsiveness in early infancy. This condition subsides after the infant's neurological system matures, and it is important that families encourage use of vision among children who seem to show no visual response, since the factors that improve vision in these infants are still unknown (Topor, 1999).

The child's family members should be active participants in the assessment to provide information about their knowledge of the child's vision. Their interactions with the child can elicit visual responses that may not be observed in interactions with unfamiliar people. Topor and Erin (2000, pp. 825–826) provide a list of questions that can be asked of parents to help gain specific information about a child's vision, including the following:

FACTORS TO CONSIDER WHEN CONDUCTING A FUNCTIONAL LOW VISION ASSESSMENT WITH A CHILD WHO HAS MULTIPLE DISABILITIES

To obtain a representative picture of a child's vision from a functional low vision assessment, especially if the child has multiple disabilities, the evaluator should consider the following factors:

➜ *Familiarity:* The child's visual behaviors should be observed in both familiar and unfamiliar settings, with both familiar and unfamiliar objects and people.

➜ *Motivation:* The evaluator should be aware of the child's interests (for example, food, bright colors, favorite toys), and these interests should be considered in observing visual behaviors across activities.

➜ *Medical Issues:* Vision can be influenced by the medications that a child takes. Light sensitivity, state of alertness, and muscle control can change as a result of medications. Children who have seizures may show visual changes before, after, and during seizures. When there are other medical conditions present, it is important to observe children at different times of day on different days to allow for these variations. If a deterioration in visual abilities is noticed, the child's doctor should be informed so that the effects of medication and physical changes can be considered.

➜ *Communication:* Because infants and young children with multiple disabilities communicate using nonsymbolic forms, evaluators should be aware of the child's major methods of communication. Vocal sounds, movement toward and away from objects or light sources, reaching, head turning, and eye movements will be important behaviors to notice in drawing conclusions about what the child can see.

➜ *Positioning and movement:* Children may use vision differently when their position varies. These visual differences may be due to changes in their ability to control eye movements as well as different perceptions of the world based on position. In some positions, children can more easily reach for objects and move through space, enabling the evaluator to observe more visually related behaviors. The functional vision assessment should include observations when the child is in different positions: lying and sitting, supine and prone, moving and stationary.

➜ *Temperament and state of alertness:* While any group of people shows variations in temperament, the presence of disabilities can influence a wider range of differences among young children. Some children have difficulty adapting to changes or new people; others dislike extreme sensations such as texture or light; and still others seem unresponsive to any stimuli except the most intense. When evaluating a child's vision, team members should be aware of the child's preferences and dislikes, and they should introduce materials that will not be unpleasant to the child. Extreme responses to visual stimuli such as photophobia or moving stimuli should be noted as part of the functional visual assessment.

Jane N. Erin

- *What is your impression of your child's ability to use vision in activities? What does your child like to look at? . . .*

- *What does your child do when you are about 8 to 12 inches away and look at her? . . . Is the child using both eyes to look at you? What is the child's head position when looking at you? . . .*

- *Does your child use both eyes to look at objects or at your face when close to him or her (about four inches away)? . . .*

- *Does your child use both eyes to follow a moving object that crosses from one side of his or her body to the other? . . .*

- *Does your infant swipe at, reach for, and grasp colorful objects that are close to him or her? . . .*

- *Does your infant seem to respond to your face or brightly colored toys? If so, how far away, how close, and in what positions are they noticed? . . .*

- *How does your child visually respond if many toys are presented at the same time? . . .*

- *What toys does your child prefer? . . .*

- *Does your child seem to squint in bright sunlight or turn away from bright lights coming from windows or lamps? . . .*

If students cannot respond to a test by speaking or pointing, a preferential looking procedure may be used to determine an approximate acuity. These procedures are based on the assumption that the child will prefer to look at a pattern rather than a plain target or stimulus. The Teller Acuity Cards are one version of this procedure. These cards each display two squares on a rectangular background. One square is gray and the other contains black and white stripes of different widths. An infant's acuity can be estimated by presenting the cards and noting the width of the stripes that are too small to attract his or her attention (Topor, 1999). This procedure can provide information about the visual acuity of a young child or a child with multiple disabilities who cannot respond to a standardized procedure, which requires a developmental age of about 2 years.

Functional Vision Assessment Kit

Materials for conducting a functional vision assessment are not standardized. Some suggestions for basic materials to include in an assessment kit are occluders, measuring tape, penlights, colored light bulbs, an extension cord, and objects for the child to look at, such as styrofoam balls, balloons, matching cards, cause-and-effect toys, toys that light up, toys that make sounds, reflective toys, foil balls, rolling toys, bubble-making toys, pom-poms, and scarves. It may be helpful to package items according to size for easy reference. It also may be helpful to include stickers for marking specific distances in a room (two feet, four feet, six feet, and so on) at which to place the target objects.

When assembling materials to use, it is important to include items that will be motivating for the child to look at. It may be helpful to make a list of all materials with which a particular child has regular contact and use these items to start. Next, making a list of items that may be unfamiliar but that seem to be motivating to the child and noting their common characteristics may be useful. On the basis of these listings, it is possible to construct a set of materials that incorporates the characteristics of the preferred materials with those of the unfamiliar items.

The most difficult aspect of assessing functional vision is deciding whether a child's lack of response is due to an inability to see, a lack of motivation to see, or an inability to respond. Care should be taken when assessing functional vision to use objects with no auditory clues, to ensure that the child is truly responding visually and not just reacting to the sound stimuli. It is important to be aware that motivations can vary and not to make assumptions regarding the child's motivation. In terms of planning materials and programming, it is essential to be aware of both motivation and functioning.

INTERVENTION: PROMOTING USE OF VISION

The results of the clinical and functional vision assessments, together with an analysis of the visual demands of given environments, form the starting point from which teachers, specialists, and family members can design an appropriate program for promoting the use of vision. The use of vision should be encouraged when it would make participation in tasks that are relevant to daily life easier or more enjoyable (Topor, 1999). The process of learning to use vision is sequential (moving from simple to complex processes) and includes understanding of visual information and coordination of vision with motor activities.

Functional Vision Training

The goals of functional vision training for young children who have low vision are:

- to create an increased awareness of visual stimuli,

- to develop understanding of what the stimuli mean, and

- to coordinate the use of vision with other skills and actions.

Children who have multiple disabilities may experience the added physical and/or cognitive challenges of responding to visual stimuli and clearly communicating understanding and visual abilities to others. Functional vision training can help these children participate more fully in a range of meaningful activities.

Families play a vital role in promoting their young children's use of vision. Together with professionals, they can prioritize meaningful opportunities, activities, and approaches to encourage vision use. Young children who have low vision need abundant experiences and continual encouragement to utilize their sensory abilities and eventually to become comfortable and competent in doing so. To fully assist families in supporting their children's use of functional vision, teachers and specialists should be knowledgeable about and help families to understand:

- the specific etiology of each child's visual impairment and its functional implications (for example, a child with albinism may have photophobia, and this sensitivity to light can be addressed through control of illumination),

- the factors that may affect a child's use of vision (for example, age, motivation, time of day, posture, and activity level), and

- the developmental sequence of visual skills (for example, a child must be able to fixate on an object before he or she can "track" or follow a moving target).

Finding creative ways to incorporate functional vision training within naturally occurring contexts for young children with visual impairments helps to ensure that use of vision will transfer to appropriate skills. If the functional approach to promoting vision use provides the *"how"* of promoting use of vision, knowledge of the developmental sequence of vision skills provides the *"what,"* or the content of the curriculum to be addressed. In discussing the use of functional vision, Utley, Roman, & Nelson (1998) stress:

> . . . *the importance of adhering to developmental sequences when appropriate. To ignore the importance of developmental sequences is to risk the potential success of the student. A failure to adhere to a common-sense application of the progression of [typical] de-*

velopment may result in the selection of instructional objectives that simply are too far beyond the physical or cognitive capabilities of a student." [p. 374]

Topor (1999) has identified six visual skills that can be addressed as part of the functional vision training program:

- localizing

- fixating

- scanning

- tracking

- shifting gaze

- eye–hand coordination

Visual-skill development can be supported in home, day care, and school environments with relatively simple modifications. For children who have multiple disabilities, proper positioning, such as supporting a child's neck if he or she has poor head control, can make it easier for a child to use vision more effectively when engaged with toys or people. The accompanying box, "Encouraging the Use of Functional Vision in Young Children," provides some other strategies for helping visually impaired children make use of functional vision.

Through a range of experiences, young children learn the natural consequences of using vision across a variety of environmental contexts. Some children will be able to better use their vision when a few simple adjustments in lighting, color, contrast, or positioning are made. Other children may benefit from specific instruction in how to use their vision (Topor & Erin, 2000). External reinforcement may be used to encourage children to use their vision (for example, playing enjoyable music when a child is looking in the mirror while his or her face is being washed). Such reinforcement strategies may be most useful when a child uses vision for some tasks but not for others or for children who have additional neurological impairments and may respond positively to appropriate visual experiences (Topor & Erin, 2000). Even in instances in which reinforcement strategies are embedded within the vision-training program, it will still be important to maintain a functional context for activities that young children and their families may enjoy. In this way, children who have low vision can benefit from frequent and consistent opportunities to use their vision. Functional vision activities have endless possibilities and can be incorporated across social, cognitive, lan-

ENCOURAGING THE USE OF FUNCTIONAL VISION IN YOUNG CHILDREN

The following are some activities and modifications that support the use of functional vision for young children who are visually impaired:

→ increasing the amount of illumination in a room to increase an infant's *awareness* of available toys on the floor

→ placing a high-contrast color bar of soap at the edge of the bath to facilitate *localizing* during bath time

→ singing a soft tune to encourage *fixating* on a mother's face during breast-feeding,

→ seating the child in an optimum position (such as in front of or to the side of the teacher, depending on the child's best viewing angle) to encourage *fixating* on the teacher's face during circle time,

→ placing favorite foods at a child's height to enable *scanning* in the pantry to locate a box of cereal,

→ storing interesting books and toys at the child's height to encourage visual *scanning* for free play,

→ using a consistent word or phrase, such as "See it coming," to help a child with successfully *tracking* a moving spoon full of food in order to open one's mouth at the appropriate time,

→ counting how long it takes each child to slide down the slide to encourage *tracking* on the playground,

→ providing a choice between two toys of contrasting color to encourage *shifting gaze,*

→ playing circle games that require children *shifting gaze* as children pass things from one to another,

→ allowing children to feed themselves to develop *eye–hand coordination* in a motivating activity, and

→ encouraging a child to wear a hat or visor while outdoors to reduce glare and make it easier to be successful at games that require *eye–hand coordination,* such as "Duck, Duck, Goose."

Diane L. Fazzi

guage, and motor domains. Functional activities can promote vision use by encouraging young children to participate in activities that will ultimately be enhanced through the use of vision.

For infants, the first functional use of vision takes place during the infant–caregiver interaction. With a keen interest in round shapes and optimum focal distance of 12–18 inches, infants are predisposed to direct visual attention to caregivers' faces as they are fed, held, diapered, cuddled, and talked to. Care can be taken to position the child so that natural lighting is maximized to enhance the caregiver's face. In some cases brightly colored lipstick, hair pulled back from the face, or a dark beard may improve contrast and attract the child's visual focus. In most instances, pairing the infant's glance with a pleasing sensation (for example, soft words or singing from the mother or a warm embrace from the father) may be all the encouragement needed.

These early days are an important time to assist families of children who have low vision in promoting visual attention during caregiving routines. Developing the social skill of establishing and maintaining eye contact can enhance the quality and satisfaction of family interactions and prove to be a beneficial skill throughout the visually impaired child's life. Social interactions with siblings and peers will also provide an opportunity to promote vision use. The following are examples of how use of vision can be easily embedded within family activities:

- Diaper changes can be a fun time to encourage the young child to spot and track the diaper in anticipation of the change from wet to dry.

- Young children seem to have a natural interest in older siblings and can be encouraged to look as their older brother or sister plays a game of tickle or peek-a-boo.

- Feeding, whether breast-, bottle-, or spoon-feeding, is another early opportunity for functional vision training that involves many visual skills and high levels of motivation for both caregiver and child. In order to participate in feeding, a child will have to spot and fixate on the breast or bottle. Scanning may be used to locate a bottle or spoonful of food as it is brought to the mouth.

- Simple games with boldly colored hand puppets can be used to encourage visual skills during play.

In each case, the use of vision can be incorporated into functional tasks and social activities within the home. (See Chapter 7 for additional ideas on promoting vision use in daily routines.)

When professionals and families are working on vision-related tasks, it is important that no value judgments be expressed in response to a child's visual functioning. It is easy to communicate subtly that it is "better" if the child sees more. Many times the child is using vision to the best of his or her ability, and a child's self-esteem should not be tied to praise for visual performance. Families and professionals may encourage the young child with a visual impairment to "tell me what you see on the shelf" or "describe what the doll looks like" rather than asking "Can you see this?" and "Can you see that?" By accepting a child's response and moving on from there, adults encourage the use of vision as well as honest responses. Vision simply *is,* and while it is beneficial to encourage children to use their vision to the greatest degree possible, words of praise should be used with care during functional vision assessment and training.

Functional use of vision may be optimized when auditory, tactile, kinesthetic, and motor-skill components are integrated into the training process. In many cases, multisensory experiences provide the most accurate and complete input for young children who are visually impaired. Young children who have multiple disabilities can also benefit when appropriate sensory cues are paired to encourage skills such as visual attention, fixation, or tracking. For example, a young child with cortical visual impairment may increase his or her ability to maintain visual fixation to pick up a drinking cup when he or she has first had a chance to explore the cup tactually. A child who sees a jack-in-the-box will understand the concept more fully if he or she is able to touch and activate the toy and listen to the many sounds it makes. This involvement provides the young child with the necessary verification to assist in the development of needed concepts and may also motivate the young child with a visual impairment to investigate places and objects within the environment, thus encouraging further use of vision.

The ultimate goal of functional vision training is to coordinate purposeful use of vision with activity. Integrating other sensory modalities into the training process is key in promoting this development. Sensory integration can begin with the earliest infant–caregiver interactions, such as stroking the infant's face before breast- or bottle-feeding, gentle rocking in conjunction with a father's soft singing, or encouraging the young child to look at the caregiver's face during cuddling and playing. Opportunities to incorporate other sensory systems in functional vision development may also include:

Opportunities for Sensory Integration

→ encouraging young children to look at and listen to events in the surrounding environment (for example, watching an older sibling wash dishes while listening to the running water and the clinking dishes),

→ letting young children hold items that they may see on a daily basis (for example, holding onto a diaper in anticipation that a diaper is going to be changed),

→ giving children time to smell and compare the various olfactory cues associated with activities of daily living that they observe (for example, choosing from two different types of lotion by their fragrance and noting which color bottle the preferred one comes in),

→ allowing young children to touch objects that they may usually only see from a distance (for example, exploring the gas pump and nozzle that may be seen from the car), and

→ helping children to engage in visual tasks while moving or being moved (for example, crawling in pursuit of a wind-up toy).

These same activities and approaches can be equally appropriate to use with young children who have multiple disabilities. Some children will require additional physical assistance to fully participate in activities or more wait time for indication of a visual response. Other children may benefit from careful attention to positioning of materials. For example, in some instances presenting a visual target on the child's side rather than directly in front is beneficial. Postural supports can enable some children to more effectively use their vision when they do not have to concentrate so much on a specific motor control. For example, some children may more easily see their food when they are in a "standing chair" in which the food tray is set at head level.

Promoting Use of Vision in Children with Cortical Visual Impairment

As noted earlier, CVI has become one of the most common diagnoses of visual impairment in young children in the United States. It is one of the three categories of neurological visual impairment (California Deaf–Blind Services, 2001). Children with cortical visual impairment are unique in the ways they use their vision (Morse, 1999). Therefore, the strategies for promoting functional use of the their vision may need to vary, and families and professionals who work with young children with CVI may often feel perplexed as to the best strategies to use.

Children with CVI appear to receive clear visual images (unless there is an additional visual problem or refractive error present) but apparently have trouble processing and interpreting visual information due to neurological impairment (Crossman, 1992; Steendam, 1989, Blind Babies Foundation, 1998). There is often inconsistency from day to day, and sometimes moment to moment, as to what can be seen and how the child with CVI interprets visual input. This inconsistency is seen more often in children with seizure disorders or in children on such medications as Tegretol, Dilantin, or Phenobarbital (California Deaf–Blind Services, 2002). Spatial confusion is common in children with CVI due to the close proximity of the occipital and parietal lobes of the brain. Many children with CVI are photophobic (light sensitive), while some seem to enjoy gazing at lights. The children may exhibit poor depth perception, so the children may have difficulty reaching for a desired target. The accompanying "Working with Children Who Have Cortical Visual Impairment" presents some suggestions that may be helpful when working with children in this group.

Environmental Considerations for Enhancing the Use of Vision

In addition to incorporating functional vision activities within daily routines, there are ways that families and professionals can modify the young child's living and playing environments to enhance their use of vision. Aspects of the physical environment can either hinder or enhance the use of vision for the young child who is visually impaired. According to Corn's model of visual functioning presented earlier, environmental cues to consider when designing or modifying an environment for the young child who has low vision may include illumination, space, time, contrast, and color. These environmental cues are discussed in the following sections.

ILLUMINATION

Proper illumination can increase the visibility of objects, tasks, and activities within the child's environment. Vision professionals should work together with families to determine the young child's sensitivity to and preference for the following:

- intensity of light (strong, bright lights vs. diffuse lighting),
- position of light source (angle of projection over head vs. over shoulder), and

WORKING WITH CHILDREN WHO HAVE CORTICAL VISUAL IMPAIRMENT

There is no clear-cut formula for interventions that works for all children with cortical visual impairment, but the following strategies may be useful to try. Similar strategies can also be effective for children with visual impairments who have other etiologies.

➜ Red or yellow items may be perceived more easily since color vision is usually intact.

➜ Items should be presented in a simple, uncluttered manner, as foreground/background perception may be a problem.

➜ Items should be presented at a close distance as there may be a preference for close viewing even though the child's visual acuity is normal.

➜ Try various positions in order to find one that is most comfortable and one in which the child is able to see the best.

➜ Excess visual stimulation may be distracting, so do not overload the child's senses at one time.

➜ Tactile exploration or pairing auditory cues while looking at an object may increase recognition and understanding.

➜ Use of familiar and real objects (for example, yellow sippycup) helps children to successfully interpret what is seen.

➜ Bright lighting may help a child see and attend to visual materials more readily. Controlled incandescent lighting may be better than florescent lighting.

➜ Fatigue may affect visual performance, so working in short blocks of time and taking frequent breaks during longer tasks may help.

➜ If central viewing is difficult, it may help to present objects to the side where the child has the best peripheral vision.

➜ Allow sufficient time for children to interpret and respond to visual stimuli.

➜ Moving the visual stimuli or moving the child may enhance visual processing.

Sources: California Deaf-Blind Services, "Neurological Visual Impairment," Fact Sheet #022, retrieved March 20, 2002, from sfsu.edu/!cadbs/Eng022.html; Pediatric Visual Diagnosis Fact Sheets (San Francisco: Blind Babies Foundation, 1998); M. Smith & N. Levak, Teaching Students with Visual and Multiple Impairments: A Resource Guide *(Austin: Texas School for the Blind and Visually Impaired, 1997).*

• type of light (natural vs. fluorescent or incandescent).

The intensity or amount of light may be increased or decreased according to the individual child's functioning. Teachers can use a hand-held light meter (like those used by professional photographers) to determine the actual lighting in various areas. Needs for illumination are highly individualized, and the quantity, type, and position of lighting sources should all be considered (Utley, Roman, & Nelson, 1998). Teachers and specialists can discuss home lighting options (natural lighting vs. fluorescent and incandescent lighting) with families to help them make the best choices for their children. In general, the closer the lighting source is to the visual target the better the contrast will be, but this belief must be balanced with the individual needs of the young child. Some children do not function well under increased illumination. Lighting sources are often positioned to shine over the individual's shoulder, but the best position again depends on the child's specific visual functioning (Utley, Roman, & Nelson, 1998).

Glare is a constant consideration for all individuals who have low vision. Glare can create discomfort or inhibit visual functioning depending on the source or type of glare experienced. Highly reflective surfaces—including flooring, walls, ceilings, work and play surfaces, and instructional and play materials—can all be sources of glare for young children who have low vision. The following suggestions can be helpful in minimizing glare for children with low vision:

Minimizing Glare

→ When selecting positioning for the young child or for portable lighting sources, avoid creating shadows and reflecting light directly into the child's eyes.

→ Care should be taken to select materials that maximize light absorption (for example, matte-finish rather than glossy-finish photos).

→ Be sensitive to changing lighting conditions outdoors as well. Visors or hats with a minimum three-inch brim can help to eliminate some of the glare experienced outdoors.

→ Help to select for children who are sensitive to glare appropriate sunglasses or filters that will minimize glare without minimizing visual functioning.

SPACE

For the child who has low vision, space is an important organizer of visual perceptions. The following considerations will help in planning positive visual experiences:

→ Simple and regular patterns are more easily viewed than complex ones.

→ Objects placed too close together may be difficult for the young child with a visual impairment to distinguish from one another.

→ Provide appropriate and regular spacing between items to avoid visual clutter and overwhelming sensory input for the child with limited vision.

These considerations are relevant when making room-decorating decisions and when arranging toys or eating utensils for the young child.

TIME

Individuals who are visually impaired may require additional time to complete tasks that require the use of vision or when adjusting to changes in lighting. Young children may need additional time to complete tasks that depend on the use of vision. Activities that require a degree of anticipation (such as playing with switch-activated toys and jack-in-the-boxes) may initially be difficult for a child who is being asked to retain visual information. With regard to time, the following approaches may help young children feel more confident and complete tasks more successfully:

→ Young children with visual impairments should be given extra time to complete visual tasks.

→ Children with low vision will likely be more successful in tracking a slow-moving target than a fast-moving target because they will have more time to do so.

→ If a child seems disinterested in toys whose use involves a sig-

Organizing Space

Allowing Enough Time

nificant element of time, try toys that prompt more immediate interplay until the child develops stronger visual retention abilities.

➔ Allow the child adequate time to adjust to changes in lighting prior to asking him or her to negotiate obstacles or stairs
or complete part of a daily routine.

_____

CONTRAST

Maximizing contrast between objects and work and play surfaces can
help children who have low vision maintain a greater sense of control over the items that they manipulate. Utley, Roman, & Nelson
(1998) contend that "integration of enhanced contrast into daily
routines is one of the most necessary, fundamental, and effective
techniques to increase visual efficiency" (p. 382). Contrast can be enhanced through the use of increased illumination, careful choice of
colors, or selection of black and white materials. Higher-contrast
items are easier to locate, distinguish, and keep track of.

The following approaches can be used at home or school to enhance contrast:

_____

**Enhancing
Contrast**

➔ Cookie sheets with white contact paper on one side and dark
on the other (the same effect can be achieved with spray
paint) make playing with small items easier for children with
visual impairments to locate and handle.

➔ Contrasting placemats on the tabletop help children to define their eating space and to locate their food more efficiently.

➔ Placing a light-colored bath soap in a dark-colored soap dish
makes it easier for young children to find it and helps them
begin to assume a degree of independence during bathtime.

_____

Wherever possible in the home or at school, contrast should be maximized to facilitate greater independence and increased use of vision.

COLOR

Color selection is an important environmental consideration for
young children who are visually impaired. The following general

ideas may be helpful to vision professionals and families of young children who have low vision:

Using Color

→ Infants (birth to 3 months of age) prefer to look at black-and-white geometric patterns, with lines being approximately 3/4 inch in width, and by 3 to 4 months of age prefer primary colors.

→ Primary (or bold) colors are more easily seen than pastels, with red attracting the most attention.

→ As noted earlier in this chapter, children with cortical visual impairment have been found to respond positively to the colors yellow and red.

Color preference and visibility are highly individualized and must be explored with young children who are visually impaired to determine which colors are easiest to distinguish.

Making environmental modifications in the home and at school may encourage environmental exploration, independence, and functional use of vision for young children who have low vision. Facilitating increased participation in activities of daily living, preacademic activities, recreation, and socialization through environmental sensitivity can help the young child to acquire positive, enriching experiences that may form the basis for future life successes.

CONCLUSION

Young children with visual impairments function at varied levels and have varied prognoses for visual development. Understanding the medical and functional implications of visual impairment helps professionals plan appropriate intervention strategies with families. Eye care specialists, teachers of students who are visually impaired, O&M specialists, and family members need to work together to formulate an accurate picture of the young child's visual functioning. As a team, families and professionals can develop and implement an individualized plan that will minimize the frustrations associated with vision loss and maximize the successes associated with increased visual efficiency.

APPENDIX 3A **SAMPLE FUNCTIONAL VISION ASSESSMENT**

Name of Child: Tyler Martin
Date of Birth: 12/19/97
Date of Assessment: 2/16/01

Assessment results compiled by: Sharon Price, orientation and mobility specialist and teacher of students who are visually impaired.

Persons attending assessment: Mr. and Mrs. Martin, Charles (brother); Sharon Price, certified orientation and mobility specialist and teacher of students who are visually impaired; Hannah Ford, preschool teacher; Kathryn Morris, teacher of students who are visually impaired and low vision specialist.

Reason for referral: Tyler's early childhood teacher referred him for this functional assessment to determine if the effects of using monocular vision are interfering with his learning. Mr. and Mrs. Martin want to know if Tyler needs any educational adaptations because he is using just one eye and because he has some acuity loss in that eye.

Background information: According to Mrs. Martin, Tyler did not like to have his picture taken when he was one and a half years old. Tyler's right eye began to "flutter and glow" when he was two years of age. On April 28, 2000, it was removed due to the detection of retinoblastoma (cancerous tumor). Dr. Abbott, Tyler's pediatric ophthalmologist, also noted that there was stage 5 retinal detachment of the right eye. Tyler has had three surgeries, and the skin on his right eye orbit is not growing out to allow Tyler to wear his prosthetic eye. According to the parents, Tyler's left eye is cancerfree; however, he has a high degree of myopia in that eye from what the doctor describes as secondary effects from the surgery.

Tyler is using a computer and mouse and can visually locate the cursor to play Reader Rabbit. He views the computer screen from 8–10 inches when the images are small. Mrs. Martin stated that Tyler has some difficultly catching objects that are in the air. Mr. Martin reported that Tyler does not enjoy swinging as much as climbing. He is cautious when climbing, but is improving in this skill. Tyler has asked his parents, "When will I have two brown eyes?" This statement may be a reaction to the insensitive comments that other children made when he is attending toddler tumbling classes. Mrs. Martin said that Tyler is responding with less anxiety to the comments, but she is anxious to have him wear his prosthetic so that he looks like the other children.

Assessment environment: The assessments occurred in the preschool classroom and within the outdoor playground areas. The day was overcast, with cloud cover. The preschool "play area" was lit with artificial illumination (fluorescent light banks). The outside sunshine was not available due to the overcast conditions.

Tests used: The LEA symbol near and far distance visual acuity tests, Holmgren color type vision test, low contrast sensitivity test, and some items from the Diagnostic Assessment Procedure to Assess Efficiency in Visual Function were administered. Tyler also looked at pictures in a book, colored with crayons on white paper, played ball indoors, and climbed on playground equipment outdoors.

RESULTS OF THE ASSESSMENTS

NEAR

Informal: Tyler wore glasses and demonstrated how he cleans them with his shirt. No prescription for the glasses was available during this assessment. Tyler moves his left eye to fixate and follow a two-inch red bear at 12-16 inches to the right, left, below and above eye level. He used his head and eye to follow its movement. He followed the movement of a three-inch car across a small flat surface at the same distance. Tyler enjoyed coloring (by report he can stay within lines) and reproduced vertical, horizontal, and diagonal lines. He made a circle with a fluorescent orange pen and was pleased with his success, stating, "That's my best circle!" He reproduced a face with eyes and mouth in reverse so that the evaluator was viewing the face right side up! Tyler successfully identified images as small as one-inch in books and manipulated two blocks to match the evaluator's position of the blocks.

Formal: LEA SYMBOLS: OS (left eye): 2.5M (20/125).
Since Tyler is just three years of age, the discrimination ability is adequate for the kinds and sizes of images that he will access. Also, it is a minimal estimate of his functioning.

HOLMGREN COLOR TYPE MATCHING TEST: Using a systematic approach, Tyler successfully matched 22 of 24 color yarn swatches. His errors were those of saturation of color, e.g., a lighter blue was matched with a different shade of blue, etc. Interestingly, his quick matching ability of same color for so many colors suggests typical color perception of the left eye. He demonstrated problem solving ability to correct some of his original matches.

HIDING HEIDI LOW CONTRAST TEST: The LEA Low Contrast Symbol Test was not available, so we used the Hiding Heidi Low Contrast Version. A gaze in the direction of the face that gets a lighter gray as the contrast decreases is the way that the sensitivity is measured. The evaluator asked that Tyler look at the "lighter" face, changing the test procedure. Despite this change, Tyler responded to the 1.2 percent contrast, indicating no difficulty in detecting contrast. Mrs. Martin has not noticed Tyler having any visual problems in low contrast situations.

DISTANCE VISION

Informal: Sharon Price assessed Tyler's vision during travel and motor activities. During the assessment, Tyler was observed in the motor room of the preschool and on the playground. The room was filled with exercise mats, balls, a hanging swing, and a slide. Tyler readily walked through the room without holding his mother's hand, using vision to guide his moves. He negotiated obstacles in the room with little trouble. He stumbled over the edge of a mat one time but had no difficulty anywhere else in the room. He observed his brother's activity from about eight feet away. Tyler climbed onto a small trampoline in the room, then felt his way back down. He easily climbed onto a moving swing. He then climbed up the steps in a plastic play box but required help finding the rungs to back down. He did not try to descend the steps either visually or tactually.

When using his vision for near tasks, Tyler moved his head to orient so that his left eye was central. This adjustment was not noticed when Tyler moved throughout the room. Outside, Tyler adapted quickly. He traveled up the slide stairs with both feet on a stair, using the rail. He investigated other equipment, trying to shoot baskets into a low hoop and playing with sand in a kitchen. He was unsure how to negotiate a jungle gym (a pattern of metal bars in a dome shape), so he climbed through an opening and stood under the dome. He did not want to climb on the outside of the gym, even after being shown how to move. Tyler's parents report that Tyler negotiates terrain changes with some caution but maneuvers well once he interprets the change.

At an eight-foot distance, Tyler rolled and received two-inch yellow, red, and blue balls on a blue mat. He offered a "ready" position by extending both hands and arms outward. He sometimes used one hand to receive the balls and slid toward a ball if it rolled to his right or left sides. He demonstrated a direct reach to all the different colored balls. Mrs. Martin stated that she used a bigger ball at home for catching practice.

Formal: *LEA DISTANCE LINE CHART AT 10 FEET:* With correction: OS (left eye): 20/80, which indicates a moderate difficulty in seeing materials clearly at a distance.

Tyler used the puzzle pieces to demonstrate his naming ability. He readily named the symbols on the chart.

SUMMARY

Tyler uses his vision to discriminate detail well at near and far distances. He participates in age-appropriate visual motor activities. He looks at, and negotiates familiar and unfamiliar environments without experiencing difficulties in movement. He alters his head and body position when needed to use his vision to his best advantage.

RECOMMENDATIONS

OPHTHALMOLOGIC/OPTOMETRIC

1. Tyler should wear his glasses as protection for his left eye at all times. Tyler's regular visits to Dr. Abbott are necessary to monitor the health of his left eye and the progress of the skin growth in the right orbit. A website called "A Parent's Guide to Understanding Retinoblastoma" is available at *http://www.retinoblastoma.com/guide/guide9.html* if Tyler's parents would like more information about the condition.

EDUCATIONAL

1. Continue to encourage activity that requires interpretation of a variety of terrain textures and depths.
2. Continue to encourage bike riding when possible.
3. Tyler is learning to use his left eye to use cues in the environment (color, contrast, differences in lighting, time) that allow him to detect depth. If he appears to ever be wary in an unfamiliar environment, look at the environmental conditions and describe them (for example, the shadows that are created by different lighting, color/contrast differences). To teach catch, continue to use a bigger ball that is brightly colored, giving Tyler the ability to determine time and distance cues more readily because of the size and color of the ball.
4. The evaluators did not identify any significant effects of decreased visual functioning on Tyler's ability to learn. Provide him with enrichment in the areas of literacy (Mrs. Martin checked out *On the Way to Literacy: Early Experiences for Visually Impaired Children* by Josephine Stratton and Suzette Wright, published by the American Printing House for the Blind, 1991.) Give him opportunities to play with puzzles of increasing difficulty so that he practices his visual closure skills/figure ground perception skills. If he does these puzzles regularly, his part-to-whole relationships skills (visual perception) will improve along with his thinking skills and increase commensurate with his age.
5. Allow him to position books and visual materials as he prefers, and if he prefers a closer viewing distance, offer him the use of an easel or bookstand as he begins to read printed materials.

6. Schedule another follow-up evaluation in eight months to a year to check Tyler's progress in visual development and functioning.

The family and school are providing an appropriate and rich educational environment for Tyler. The evaluators encourage the family to contact them if there are additional concerns about visual behaviors.

Contributed by Dr. Irene Topor

COGNITIVE FOCUS

Developing Cognition, Concepts, and Language

CONTRIBUTORS

Diane L. Fazzi Concept Development, Language Development

M. Diane Klein Cognitive Development

Vision is the primary system of sensory input for human beings; it is the basis for the majority of human learning. When it is reduced or eliminated, there is a major impact on the individual as a whole. When vision loss occurs during early childhood, the development of cognition, concepts, and language is altered during sensitive stages of the child's development. In order to compensate for lack of vision, it is important for the child who is blind or visually impaired to maintain activity in and involvement with the environment.

Ferrell (2000) writes, "All children are unique, and children with visual impairments are no different in their uniqueness and need for loving home environments that are both stimulating and supportive" (p. 111). Learning environments will be most supportive of cognitive development in young children who are blind or visually impaired when they are individualized to reflect curricula that are both developmentally appropriate for young children and unique for children who are visually impaired. To provide developmentally appropriate services, professionals trained in visual impairment must also have an understanding of child development (Ferrell, 2000).

Cognition, concept development, and language development cannot easily be separated. They are presented together in this chapter under the umbrella of cognitive development for consideration when working with young children and their families. Familiarity with theories of the development of cognition, concepts, and language in young children who are sighted can provide a basis from which professionals in the field of visual impairment can more fully understand the development of young children who are blind or visually impaired and more effectively collaborate with other professionals in the field of early childhood education. The impact of visual impairment upon each area of development is highlighted and related to intervention strategies that can be implemented by families, early childhood educators, and specialized professionals.

EARLY COGNITIVE DEVELOPMENT IN INFANTS AND YOUNG CHILDREN

The term *cognition* refers to a number of different processes and phenomena that are related to human learning and thinking. Warren (2000) suggests that the literature on cognition reflects two somewhat different areas of functioning. One is related to children's understanding of the properties of the world, including the development of logical thought and problem solving. The other includes "executive functions," such as memory, attention, and information processing. This discussion of cognitive development will focus on how young children develop an understanding of reality and their ability to utilize mental processes to learn and solve problems. This section will also consider those aspects of cognitive development which may be most affected by congenital blindness and provide strategies for promoting the development of cognitive skills.

Piaget's Theory of Early Cognitive Development

Jean Piaget is one of the world's most renowned theorists in the area of cognitive development. Piaget's (1952) theory of infant and early childhood cognitive development suggests that cognitive development is not simply a gradual continuum of increasing complexity of thought, but rather a series of fairly distinct stages. His theory that cognition develops in stages is widely accepted and provides a good framework from which to examine cognitive development of both children who are sighted and children who are visually impaired.

THE STAGES OF COGNITIVE DEVELOPMENT

Piaget divides the progression of cognitive development in infants and young children into four stages:

- In the *sensorimotor stage,* from birth to approximately 2 years of age, the child makes sense of the world primarily by physically reacting to and interacting with the world that he or she experiences through his or her senses. Important achievements during this stage include the development of intentionality, trial-and-error exploration, and eventually object permanence.

- In the *preoperational stage,* from approximately 2 to 7 years of age, the child develops the ability to represent his or her experiences mentally (to "think"), to represent the world symbolically through language and pretend play, and to begin the processes of problem solving. While the child is now able to represent the world mentally, his or her thought patterns are fairly inflexible: the child has difficulty taking a perspective other than his or her own, and cannot consider more than one variable at a time.

- In the *concrete operational stage,* from approximately age 7 to 12 years, the child's thinking becomes much more flexible and logical. The child is able to consider more than one variable at a time (referred to as *conservation*), take others' perspectives, and engage in reversible thinking as long at it linked to concrete (tangible) objects.

- In the final stage of *formal operations,* from approximately 12 to adulthood, the individual can engage in hypothetical reasoning and abstract thought.

THE CONSTRUCTION OF KNOWLEDGE

An important tenet of Piaget's theory is the notion that the child *constructs* knowledge through the processes of acting upon and interacting with the world around him or her. In infancy this action is physical. Later this constructive process is also mental. In the fields of education and child development this theory of learning is referred to as *constructivism*. "From a constructivist perspective, delays in active exploration or variations in concrete experiences will affect the rate at which an infant's intellectual capacity develops" (Recchia, 1997, p. 402). For this reason, early intervention efforts need to focus on encouraging children who are visually impaired to be active explorers of their environments.

The pattern into which related behaviors or thoughts become organized is called a *schema* or scheme. For example, during the earliest sensorimotor period infants first suck the breast or bottle nipple as a reflex. Thus, the infant's initial sucking scheme is reflexive. Quickly, however, infants adapt this reflex to develop additional sucking patterns: a pacifier, a thumb, a hand, a favorite rattle. In this way the sucking scheme becomes much more complex and differentiated. The infant has indeed become "smarter" about sucking.

As the child makes the transition from the sensorimotor period to the preoperational stage, the processes of learning about and understanding the world around him or her become "internally represented" (the child can now *think* about things). The processes of constructing new schemes may be mental. For example, even very young children develop an internal representation or scheme for the concept of "mother". By the age of 2, a typical toddler has an organized scheme that connects the behaviors, images, odors, and sounds of mothering. Thoughts about what mothers do, how they talk and move, and what they look like are organized into a complex system. While the child's own mother clearly contributes important things to this scheme, the scheme is not like a simple videotaped representation or simple compilation of memories of her. Rather, the scheme for mothering is actively constructed into a complex pattern that can be drawn upon to engage in pretend play with dolls, to understand the behavior of a mother dog and her puppies, or, eventually in adulthood, to drive one's own female parenting behavior and feelings.

Schemes are dynamic and changing, and new schemes are constantly emerging. According to Piaget, new knowledge is organized and constructed into schemes via two complementary processes: *assimilation* and *accommodation*. When a child is first confronted with a new experience or task, he or she attempts to incorporate it into existing schemes (existing knowledge or ways of doing something). For example, a child may have learned the word "doggie." The child sees a cow for the first time and says, "That's a doggie." In another example, an infant attempts to pick up a small piece of a cookie by using the existing "raking" grasp he or she has learned previously. In these examples, the child takes in the information and applies existing schemes to react to the cow and the piece of cookie. These are examples of assimilation. However, in both cases a slight conflict arises if, for example, the child's father says "No, that's not a dog, that's a *cow*," or if the child in the second example cannot pick up the cookie piece with the usual grasping strategy. Piaget refers to this cognitive conflict as *disequilibrium*. The child must now accommodate or change his existing scheme. Thus, the child learns that there are animals that have four legs and bark that are "dogs," and there are bigger animals that have four legs and horns and moo that are "cows." The child is developing a more complex scheme for "animals" as well as refining his or her scheme for "dog." Similarly, in the second example, (assuming a sufficient level of motor maturation) the child may accommodate the existing scheme for grasping objects with different characteristics. The child learns that the raking grasp works best for picking up large, soft objects, like a blanket (or mashed potatoes!), and a pincer grasp is more effective for picking up a piece of cookie or a button. He or she begins to incorporate this new knowledge into his or her "grasping scheme." He or she can know, simply by looking at an object, which type of grasp will work best. The child does not have to use trial and error to figure out which works best each time. He or she knows which will work best because of his or her newly elaborated (or adapted) scheme.

The Role of Vision in Early Cognitive Development

A wide range of differences in cognitive development exists among young children who are blind or visually impaired (Warren, 1994). Degree of vision loss and age at onset of visual impairment can be factors contributing to the development of cognition, as well as co-ocurring disabilities such as developmental delay (Hatton, Bailey, Burchinal, & Ferrell, 1997). The following sections discuss the role of vision during the first two stages of cognitive development, sensorimotor and early preoperational, that occur during infancy and toddlerhood. Suggestions are also offered here for providing meaningful learning experiences for children who are visually impaired.

THE SENSORIMOTOR STAGE

During the sensorimotor stage of development the infant's behaviors begin as reflexive and become more purposeful as development progresses.

Reflexes. The infant enters the world with no real control over his or her behavior. For the first month, infants' behaviors are primarily reflexive. Hunger sensations cause the infant to cry; placement of a nipple in the infant's mouth causes the infant to suck; touching the infant on the cheek causes the infant to turn his or her head toward that side in search of a nipple; loss of physical support causes the infant to extend his or her legs and arms, and so on. Visually, the most important stimulus is the caregiver's face, particularly the eyes. At birth, the sighted infant is capable of and automatically interested in the caregiver's face.

Primary and Secondary Circular Reactions. During the first 6 to 8 months, the infant does not engage in truly *intentional* behavior. By two months, the infant does begin to engage in *primary circular reactions,* actions involving the child's own body. These actions are discovered accidentally, and the infant may sustain pleasurable sensations by repeating them several times. For example, the infant may begin to flail his or her arms and legs and, because he or she enjoys the sensation, may repeat the action several times. Later, between four and eight months, the infant will accidentally discover and maintain interesting effects outside his or her body, often by using objects. These are called *secondary circular reactions.* For example, the infant may discover that banging a rattle on a high chair tray creates interesting auditory (and social) effects. He or she will continue the behavior over some length of time if not stopped. Trawick-Smith (1997, p.168) refers to this humorously as the "period of incessant pounding."

During the period of secondary circular reactions, the infant becomes more aware of the "distal sensations" (stimuli away from the child's own body) of sounds and sights, begins to develop neural connections between hearing and vision, and can make associations between familiar sights and other sensory input. However, the infant still cannot intentionally initiate actions. The infant is not sure what causes what; he or she does not have a sense of cause and effect.

Development of Intentionality. Somewhere between 8 and 12 months, infants begin to engage in truly intentional behavior. They intentionally engage in a behavior and bring about a certain effect. They can pull, push, whine, bang, and cause intriguing effects. Moreover, they do not have to stumble upon these actions accidentally, because they can initiate them intentionally. During this stage, infants can also coordinate circular reactions by combining several behaviors they practiced earlier. For example, an infant may purposely bang a cup and squeal at the same time, knowing the auditory effect this behavior will have.

Obviously, vision plays an important role during this period. Certain sights create interest and motivation to act upon the environment. For example, the infant sees his or her bottle just out of reach and intentionally reaches for it and then may even crawl toward it. Hearing an interesting sound does not seem to provide the same sort of motivation or guide toward specific, intentional behavior at this early stage. Also, when an interesting visual event follows an intentional action, that action can be strongly reinforced. For example, if the infant whines or hollers and the caregiver immediately appears, or if the infant bangs a cup full of milk and the milk flies into the air, these visual events can serve as powerful reinforcers of the behavior and also serve to validate the infant's efficacy and control over the environment.

For the infant who is congenitally blind, it is important to keep in mind the importance of finding ways to strengthen the salience of nonvisual sensations. These approaches should include all sensations: not just auditory stimuli, but olfactory, tactile, and kinesthetic stimuli as well. Consistently presenting certain sensory cues to alert the child's interest and attention and then following up with clear nonvisual sensations as consequences may strengthen the infant's development of intentionality and his sense of efficacy. For example, if a young child loves ice cream, heighten anticipation not only by saying "Let's have some ice cream" but also by letting the child feel the cold container. Then wait for him or her to engage in some intentional behavior, such as vocalizing or perhaps patting the container. In addition to immediately giving the child a bite of the ice cream, let him or her smell it and touch it; then say, "That's ice cream."

Trial-and-Error Behavior. During the period from 12 to 18 months, the toddler begins to develop novel behaviors through the important process of trial and error. Because toddlers can now intentionally engage in behavior that brings about interesting effects, they become motivated to bring about new effects. They begin to systematically vary their actions and observe the results. For example, children often enjoy banging spoons on high chair trays and then will switch to banging cups, dishes, pieces of food and so on to observe the different sounds that may make and the reactions they may cause with adults. In this way infants begin to take more responsibility for their own learning. They engage in "exploration" of their environment and experimentation with various causes and effects. The challenge during this stage for the professional working with toddlers who are visually impaired is to encourage this trial-and-error activity, again being mindful of the importance of interesting nonvisual consequences. Eating utensils can be very helpful, since they serve a useful function and create interesting sounds on various objects. This type of exploration should be encouraged when possible and practical.

Also important during this stage is what is referred to as *means–end behavior:* the discovery that one action can be used to obtain a desired object or effect that cannot be obtained directly. This behavior is also related to *tool use*—using an object as a tool to obtain something or bring about a desired effect. A few common examples of tool use in young children are:

- using a spoon to bring food to the mouth,

- banging a toy hammer to pound balls through a hole,

- tugging on a tablecloth to pull an interesting-looking glass closer that was just beyond reach, or

- using a stick to knock a bag of cookies off a high counter and onto the floor.

Another type of means–end behavior is the child's discovery that he or she can use a variety of communicative behaviors to encourage another person to do something or give something he or she wants. For example the 14-month-old may vocalize and point to the cookie jar while looking first at the adult and then at the cookies. For congenitally blind children, who do not have access to the visual input that often motivates means–end behavior, the professional may need to create motivation and teach tool-usage strategies. The professional can devise situations in which the child who is blind is motivated to obtain a given object and then help him or her do so with the use of an available tool, for example, showing a child how to push a chair over to a kitchen counter in order to reach some crackers. Children who are blind may also need specific instruction in how to point to items of interest. For example, when an adult notices that the child is interested in playing with a toy across the room, he or she might physically help the child point to the toy and say, "Do you want the toy next to the couch?"

The Development of Object Permanence. The period from approximately 18 to 24 months marks the end of the sensorimotor stage. The major accomplishment during this period is the mastery of the complete concept of *object permanence*. While it progresses in stages during the first two years, its full achievement is a very important cognitive milestone. The concept of object permanence is the realization that objects and people continue to exist even if you cannot directly experience them. An infant does not search for an object that is taken away, even if he or she watches it disappear. "Out of sight, out of mind" describes this early lack of understanding. A bit later the child will search for the object if he or she sees it disappear. Gradually the child develops internal (mental) representation of important objects, people, and events. The child no longer has to watch its disappearance in order to know that an object continues to exist, and he or she knows how to search for it.

Understanding object permanence is an important cognitive achievement. It enables the child to develop mental representation of reality and to significantly expand the process of thought. No longer must the child perform an action in order to "know" it, nor must an object be immediately present for the child to know it exists.

Much has been written in the literature related to the development of object permanence in children with visual impairment. There is general consensus that there is some developmental lag, but the nature of this lag is not clear. Ferrell (1998) found that infants with visual impairments were delayed in learning to search for a removed object, commencing this behavior at a median age of 15 months, in comparision to infants with sight who typically looked for dropped objects at around 6 months of age. Not only was this cognitive milestone delayed, but the infants in the study who were visually impaired achieved the milestone in an atypical sequence. Research conducted by Hatton, Bailey, Burchinal, & Ferrell (1997) supported the notion that there was a strong relationship between the attainment of object permanence and motor development (for example, reaching and locomotion). Warren (2000) suggests that until about a year and a half infants who are blind show evidence that their developing concept of object permanence is as developed as that of sighted infants. However, when the tasks used to demonstrate the infant's knowledge of the concept require complex spatial displacements (such as "next to" the child and "underneath the blanket"), the disparity between blind and sighted infants emerges. He suggests that the differences noted are less reflective of problems with object permanence and more related to difficulty in understanding spatial structure.

THE PREOPERATIONAL STAGE

By 2 years of age (earlier in many children), the development of the ability to represent reality internally (mentally) marks the end of the sensorimotor period and the beginning of true thought. The child is no longer tied to the here and now, which is experienced through immediate sensation and action patterns. Now the child can begin to think about the past and contemplate the future. Despite this newly developing mental ability, however, the child's thought is illogical, and higher-level thinking, such as problem solving, is influenced by immediate perceptions rather than logic and reasoning.

Another important development during this stage is symbolic thought. While the emergence of symbolic behavior begins at the end of the sensorimotor period, with the development of the child's first words, symbolic thought becomes greatly elaborated in the preoperational stage. The greatest early symbolic achievement is language. (The development of language in young children is discussed in more detail later in this chapter.) Another area of symbolic development is pretend play (see Chapter 6). Later, in the concrete operations stage, children master another important symbolic skill, literacy (see Chapter 5).

Understanding the stages of cognitive development for children provides a framework from which early interventionists and family members can gain insight into the growth and development patterns of young children who are blind or visually impaired and set appropriate goals for early intervention. Additional learning theories, such as that propounded by Vygotsky (1962), provide a framework for intervention strategies that can be useful in optimizing cognitive development for all young children.

Vygotsky's Theory of Cognition and Learning

Vygotsky's (1962) theory of cognition and learning has greatly influenced an understanding of how children learn as well as ideas about how to facilitate children's learning. Vygotsky discusses the role of social mediation of a child's experience in enhancing learning. The most important aspect of this theory for early interventionists is the concept of the *zone of proximal development*. This zone is described as the nexus, or link, between what the child can do without assistance and what the child can do when assisted by a more competent peer or adult (Tharp & Gallimore, 1988). It is within this zone or range of task demands that learning takes place most efficiently. If a task is too simple, the child can already perform it independently. If the task is too difficult, the task will probably not be learned even with adult support. The kind of support that is most helpful when provided within this zone of proximal development is referred to as *scaffolding* (Bruner, 1982). Adults can provide just the right amount and type of support necessary for a young child to perform a task, similar to a painter's scaffold that supports him while he or she performs the task of painting. Gradually, this scaffolding can be reduced until the child can perform the task without assistance.

One example of scaffolding might be helping a child feed with a spoon. The child's independence level is that he or she can hold the spoon and bang it on the tray but does not attempt to scoop or bring the spoon to mouth. A skill that would fall within the zone of proximal development might be learning that food can be obtained by bringing the spoon to mouth. The adult assists the child with the scooping, then carefully *scaffolds* by helping the child bring the spoon toward his or her mouth, rotate the wrist, deliver the food to his or her mouth, and remove the spoon. Once the child can perform this part of the task independently (via the adult's gradual reduction of scaffolding), the adult moves on to assist the child in learning to independently scoop the food.

Exactly *how* the adult scaffolds each of these learning tasks is part of the art and the science of early intervention. Assistance can take many forms, including:

- physical and motor prompts (such as physically helping a child pull a shirt over his or her head),

- verbal instructions (such as "Head first, then arms"),

- tactile cues (such as letting the child feel the shirt to anticipate the dressing activity), and/or

- simple encouragement (such as "Good job putting that shirt on by yourself").

When working with infants and young children with visual impairments, practitioners must consider both Piaget's "constructivist" approach to understanding children's development through successive stages and Vygotsky's "social mediation" view of assisting children's performance in moving from simpler to more complex levels of understanding.

FACILITATING THE DEVELOPMENT OF COGNITIVE SKILLS

Several cognitive milestones are particularly important targets for early intervention. Visual impairment—particularly if accompanied by other disabilities such as motor disability or hearing loss—will impact children's achievement of these important early cognitive skills. For example, the blind child may have particular difficulty with the achievement of object concepts and object permanence. The child with a motor impairment may have difficulty discovering means–end strategies, and opportunities to practice trial and error exploration may be limited. Children who are visually impaired and have additional disabilities may have a harder time making connections between an action and its result and may need significant assistance in achieving these milestones (Erin, 2000). The sections that follow suggest specific strategies for facilitating the development of key cognitive skills described earlier with infants, toddlers, and preschool age children who are blind or visually impaired.

Intentionality

During the first 6 to 8 months of age, one of the most important sensorimotor achievements is the development of intentionality. The infant can now initiate or perform an action on purpose. Intentionality is a requisite behavior to almost every other skill. The ability to deliberately act upon the environment is an important key to continued development.

Children who are blind or visually impaired may need assistance in the development of intentionality, particularly if they have other disabilities. Intentional reaching, touching objects, and transferring objects from one hand to another may be significantly delayed, even in those infants who do not have other disabilities (Ferrell, 1998). Learning to produce a behavior volitionally that has a clear and immediate effect on the surrounding world is a major accomplishment. "Strategies for Developing Intentionality" in this chapter gives examples of ways to facilitate this important cognitive milestone.

Trial-and-Error Exploration

For some children, trial-and-error exploration may need to be taught directly. The systematic manipulation of objects and modification of one's own actions lead to self-directed learning and the discovery of new behaviors and solutions. For the child with significant visual impairment, the exploration of space will be particularly challenging.

STRATEGIES FOR DEVELOPING INTENTIONALITY

The following suggestions will help young children who are blind or visually impaired develop their ability to act purposefully:

→ *Increase the child's motivation to interact with surroundings through use of high-interest objects and activities.* Begin by carefully taking inventory of high- and low-preference objects, people, and activities. It will be necessary to interview care-givers to obtain a good understanding of the infant's likes and dislikes. One easy way to assist caregivers in thinking carefully about this is to conduct a simple 24-hour inventory, asking the parent to describe typical daily activities and to indicate whether the child enjoys particular activities. Caregivers can also be asked how they know the infant likes or dislikes a particular activity, food, or object. (See Klein, Chen, & Haney, 2000 for more detailed strategies.)

→ *Create the desire or need to perform intentional acts.* Once the infant's pref-erences have been identified, several strategies can be used to increase his or her intentionality:

- Begin a pleasurable activity, then abruptly stop it. Wait for the child to do something in an attempt to continue the activity. For example, push the child in the swing, then stop the swing. Or begin feeding the child a favorite food and then stop. Wait for some kind of signal from the child (such as leaning forward or vocalizing) that he or she wants to continue, then resume the activity.

- Engage in an unpleasant activity, such as washing the infant's face, then discontinue the activity if the child indicates rejection, (for example, pushing your hand away).

- Interpret even unintentional cues, such as head-turning or arm-waving, as intentional; respond as though the child did it purposely. For example, if the child inadvertently moves his arm toward a favorite toy or food, respond quickly by handing the child the toy or saying, "Oh, you want more avacado!"

- Use physical prompts to teach the child to reach for a highly desired object. Gradually fade the prompt.

→ *Allow ample time for the child to initiate a purposeful behavior.* Some children appear not to demonstrate intentional behavior simply because they have learned that there will not be enough *time* to organize a response. For example, a child may not react to food placed on a tray because someone has always fed him or her in the past. Adults may frequently anticipate the child's needs or perform actions for him or her, interfering with the child's initiation of intentional acts.

→ *Target the child's understanding of cause and effect.* In addition to understanding that he or she can initiate an action, the infant must also learn that a particular

(continued)

action can bring about a certain effect. Thus the infant moves from being a passive receiver of stimuli to an active agent—one who can make things happen. An all too common "intervention" activity in the field of visual impairment for infants who have some vision is to present a variety of stimuli into the infant's visual field. Examples might be pom-poms, light boxes, flashlights, highly reflective materials such as foil, and so on. The goal of such an activity might be to encourage the infant to visually search, focus, fixate or track the visual event. If the visual event is determined to be of some interest to the child, such an activity can easily be transformed into a functional opportunity to teach cause and effect using the following steps:

1. Determine the visual event that is most preferred by the child.

2. Identify a behavior that the child can use to signal a request, for example, reaching forward.

3. Initially provide a motor prompt for the child to move his or her hand forward.

4. As soon as the hand is forward, move the interesting visual object or event into the child's visual field, saying, "Oh you want the flashlight, don't you!" In this way, the child learns that he or she can control the delivery of the light by reaching out for it.

→ Depending on the child's visual skill, it might be possible to further shape a specific visual response, such as tracking or fixating, by *increasing the intensity or variety of the visual stimulus* when the desired visual response occurs. For example, if the stimulus is bringing a flashlight into the child's visual field and then moving it to the side, if the child tracks the movement, then the intensity of the light can be increased or the light can be turned on and off.

M. Diane Klein

In attempting to assist children in learning these exploratory strategies, caregivers must realize that they are teaching a process, rather than a specific behavior. For example, to stimulate exploratory behavior in a toddler with significant visual impairment who loves graham crackers, he or she would first be given a small piece of cracker. When the child finishes eating that piece of cracker, the caregiver places a second piece on the highchair tray, perhaps in the corner of the tray where the child will not easily contact it by accident. Using physical prompts, such as tapping the child's hand, the caregiver encourages the child to systematically search different areas of the tray. The child is also learning an important element of task persistence here. The point is to teach the child to keep modifying his or her reaching movements until he or she contacts the cracker. Eating the cracker thus becomes a reinforcer for both systematic exploration and persistence.

It is important to understand the difference between teaching the *process* of exploration and teaching a specific motor behavior. For example a child may be interested in learning to operate a specific toy, such as a jack-in-the-box. The caregiver could choose to teach the child directly how to operate the jack-in-the-box, by careful task analysis of the specific actions needed and then prompting the child step by step through the sequence. If the goal is to develop cognitive skills, however, the caregiver may choose to teach the child to use trial-and-error exploration and persistence. In this case, the caregiver would encourage the child to try different ways of holding the jack-in-the-box and turning the crank and then, before the child reaches the point of frustration, scaffolding the rewarding "pop" of the jack-in-the-box.

Means–End Behavior and Tool Use

As toddlers learn to act intentionally and to explore their environment systematically, they discover that these actions have certain effects upon objects and people. Now they engage in specific acts to bring about a certain result. They also learn to use both people and objects as tools to achieve their desired "end." They are then able to create "new means" of accomplishing a goal and begin to enter into problem solving. For typical children this process often involves obtaining something "out there": that is, the motivation is often "distal" (things seen at a distance, such as a colorful box of cereal to retrieve from a shelf) rather than "proximal" (things close by, such as a toy within arm's reach). For the child who is blind, however, it may be necessary to begin with more proximal ends to encourage means–end behavior and tool use. Examples of activities that offer proximal motivation and might be effective in encouraging means–end behavior and tool use include:

Encouraging Means–End Behavior

→ using simply constructed toys and interactive materials that produce an interesting tactile or auditory response to a specific type of manipulation,

→ using infant toys, such as "busy boxes" (a series of buttons, switches, knobs, and so forth that can be manipulated to produce interesting results) and jack-in-the-boxes that can be easily activated or musical toys that may be enjoyable for infants who are visually impaired,

→ teaching the child who is having great difficulty opening a container to hand it to the caregiver,

→ teaching the child, with careful prompts and repetition, to activate a favorite music tape by discriminating and pushing a certain button on a tape player.

The concept of tool use is possibly more difficult for children who are blind or visually impaired to learn. Pushing a stool up to the counter in order to climb and reach cookies is an example of tool use. In this example, climbing and reaching are the means, the cookies are the end, and the stool is the tool. Vision (seeing the cookies) provides the motivation; vision (scanning the environment for an available tool) also provides quick access to a tool and supports the planned action (getting to the cookies). This type of tool use clearly requires concerted orientation and mobility training. For children with significant visual impairment, an important "tool" is the long cane. Using the cane to find a desired object and then moving toward it and accessing it is another example of tool use.

A less obvious example of tool use occurs in the development of communication skills. Initially, such nonverbal behaviors as pointing and vocalizing are the tools used to "activate" the means—in this case the caregiver—to provide a desired object or activity. As mentioned earlier, children who are blind may exhibit difficulty with nonverbal behaviors such as pointing. Eventually the child will learn the ultimate tool: speech. Thus, an important contribution to the development of means–end behavior and tool use is a responsive social environment in which caregivers do not anticipate and immediately provide for all children's desires, but are responsive to children's attempts to use them—the caregivers—as means to an end.

Object Permanence

The achievement of the concept of object permanence is critical to the child's development of mental processes, including memory and mental representation. As mentioned earlier, the research on the extent to which the concept of object permanence is delayed in children who are blind is not conclusive.

There are many simple ways that the permanence of objects and people can be demonstrated for young children. Perhaps one of the first such activities introduced to sighted infants is the game of peek-a-boo. This is a simple way to demonstrate that a person continues to exist even when the infant cannot see the person's face. Sighted infants learn the concept of object permanence gradually first by watching something disappear and reappear, then gradually learning strategies for searching for an object that was observed to disappear, and eventually generalizing the knowledge that an object still exists even when they do not see it disappear. A wide variety of commercially available "lift-the-flap" books incorporate covers that conceal an object, character, or scene from the story and can be raised to reveal the hidden picture. Reading such books with young children is another way to support the development of understanding of object permanence and is a motivating way to involve them in stories that are being read to them.

Similar games and activities can be used with young children who have low vision. For the child who is blind, however, learning that objects continue to exist even when you cannot hear or touch them or see them disappear may be more difficult. "Helping Young Children Who Are Blind Learn about the Permanence of Objects" on the next page offers suggestions on promoting the achievement of this important cognitive milestone.

Deferred Imitation

The ability to re-create an action observed at a previous time generally follows the development of the concept of object permanence and is another important cognitive skill. Along with an understanding of object permanence, deferred imitation requires the beginning development of memory skills and the ability to mentally represent a sequence of events. Deferred imitation eventually plays an important role in the development of pretend play and language development.

The development of imitation skills, both immediate and deferred, may be challenging for children with visual impairments. In trying to facilitate the development of these skills in this group of children, the selection of the model to be imitated is important. The modeled action must be tactile or auditory, for example, making a certain sound, banging on a surface, or touching a part of the body. The accompanying box, "Encouraging Imitation" presents a sequence of activities to teach both immediate and deferred imitation.

Symbolic Representation

As 2- to 3-year-olds make the transition from toddlerhood to preschool age, an important developmental cognitive achievement is

HELPING YOUNG CHILDREN WHO ARE BLIND LEARN ABOUT THE PERMANENCE OF OBJECTS

The following strategies are helpful in teaching children who have little or no vision learn that objects continue to exist even when they cannot be immediately sensed:

➜ Routinely search for something the child hasn't experienced since the day before. For example, when the child wakes up, rather than simply giving him or her a favorite stuffed animal, develop a search routine. Say "Oh, where is Teddy? We'd better go look for him." Pick up the infant and carry him or her to several different locations saying, "Is Teddy in the bathroom? No. He's not in the bathroom. Let's go to the porch. Is Teddy on the porch? No, Teddy's not on the porch," and so on, until Teddy is finally found.

➜ Place toys and other items of interest in consistent locations to help the child anticipate the existence and location of items that are beyond arm's reach.

➜ Teach systematic search patterns to help the child who is visually impaired be more successful when looking for objects that are either dropped or taken from his or her grasp. This skill can help the child deal with the spatial aspects of understanding object permanence.

➜ Give young children who are blind the opportunity to search for or retrieve toys and other objects of interest independently or semi-independently rather than bringing them to the young child.

➜ Encourage young children who are blind to independently or semi-independently put away their own toys in familiar locations or storage bins.

M. Diane Klein & Diane L. Fazzi

that of symbolic representation. Evidence of symbolic skills can be observed first in the child's use of words and pretend play to represent things that are not immediately present. Symbolic representation is also reflected in children's mental images of objects and events that are not immediately accessible to them in their pretend play. The ability to allow one thing to stand for something else, such as a block representing a car or a tissue representing a blanket, is evidence of the child's developing symbolic representation skills.

It is important for professionals to be aware of the significance of facilitating play skills in general, and particularly pretend play to support cognitive development. Initially, teachers, family members, and peers can model pretend play activities that are familiar to the child, such as:

- pretending to eat,

- preparing to go to sleep,

- using materials that are real (such as a pillow) in pretend play, or

- using materials that closely resemble real objects (such as a small plastic spoon or tiny cup from a tea set) in pretend play.

For some children, the notion of "pretending" may be cognitively challenging. For the child with limited or no vision, pretending may not emerge spontaneously. Play routines at home, such as pretending to talk on the phone or the familiar tea party, may need to be repeated frequently to assist the child in understanding that

---

FOCUS ON EFFECTIVENESS

ENCOURAGING IMITATION

The following sequence of strategies will encourage young chidren who are blind or visually impaired to develop imitative behavior and eventually to learn deferred imitation:

1. Begin by imitating the child's behavior, encouraging turn-taking, and then encouraging the child to continue the game. For example, if a toddler is holding a block and begins tapping the mother's arm with the block, the mother then does the same thing to the toddler. Children will happily see this as a sort of Simon Says game.

2. Next, introduce a variation of the behavior to see if the child will attempt to follow suit. For example, tap the block on the table.

3. Once the child can easily imitate a variation of his or her own behavior, the teacher or caregiver can be the initiator of the imitation game, rather than imitating the child's behavior first. Older siblings may also enjoy participating in this game.

4. When the child has acquired a generalized imitative response (attempting to imitate novel behaviors in addition to those that have been trained) and has developed the concept of object permanence, it may be possible to teach *deferred* imitation. The length of time between presentation of a model and imitation of the model can be gradually increased. For example, a 3-year-old can be taught to pretend to "walk like a duck," or, if the child is not mobile, to "talk like a duck," making quacking sounds. Later in the day, the teacher or caregiver can say, "Can you remember what we learned this morning?" This task requires the child to use both memory and imitation skills.

M. Diane Klein

the materials and actions are not the "real" ones but rather are *representing* real events.

This simple level of pretending can also be encouraged in group activities. For example the teacher can say, "Let's pretend to be a cat" or "Let's pretend to swim." For the child who is visually impaired, it will be important to select pretend activities that represent very familiar activities or concepts. Children cannot pretend to do or be something they have never experienced. Providing children with visual impairments with a wide range of meaningful real-life experiences (such as playing with animals, preparing food in the kitchen, or talking on the telephone) will support such opportunities for pretend play.

Gradually, the teacher can introduce pretend play scenarios that involve other actors, such as dolls and stuffed animals, as well as other children acting out familiar roles, in relationship to one another. Classrooms and home toy boxes should include dramatic play materials. These include materials that encourage pretending, such as Daddy's shoes, toy cups and dishes, brooms, telephones, dolls and doll beds, blankets, baby bottles, and so on.

Also, the teacher can gradually encourage the use of objects that are more and more abstract. For example, a wooden block can be a car or a phone. The ability to use the same block for two different things represents the emergence of the kind of mental flexibility (such as reversibility and understanding of transformations); such flexible thinking is a hallmark of the next stage of cognitive development—the stage of concrete operations.

The following example demonstrates the facilitation of symbolic play skills in a child with severe disabilities.

Andrea is blind and displays some autistic-like behaviors. She loves to sit in the rocking chair and rock. The teacher decides to move the rocking chair into the dramatic play area, where Jason and Monique love to play house. The teacher suggests to Jason and Monique that maybe Andrea could be the mother today, and she could help put the baby to sleep by rocking her. After rocking for a while, while Jason and Monique are "cooking," Andrea is encouraged to put the doll in the doll bed, saying, "Night-night dolly." Now it is time for everyone to go to sleep. Jason and Monique lie down with their pillows, and the teacher helps Andrea do the same. The baby then wakes up crying; since Andrea is the mother, she must rock her back to sleep. Andrea becomes intrigued with this play sequence because there are many things that are familiar:

rocking, saying "night-night," and lying down with a pillow. However, it is not a "real" situation.

Such a scenario as the one just described could also be worked into a play script which is repeated several times. In this way, a child like Andrea could be assisted not only with pretending but with language development and cooperative play as well.

CONCEPT DEVELOPMENT*

The strategies suggested in the previous section to promote cognitive development require the young child who is visually impaired to become increasingly involved in the immediate and expanding environments. With active involvement, the child will experience many opportunities for the development of relevant concepts. Many concepts, which may be learned incidentally by children who are sighted, may need to be introduced to young children who are blind or visually impaired in a systematic and thoughtful manner.

Professionals and families can work together to introduce young children who are blind or visually impaired to a myriad of concepts that they will need to learn. In many instances, these concepts will emerge naturally from family routines and play experiences. In other cases, plans may need to be made to systematically expose young children to concepts that may be more difficult for them to experience directly, such as farm animals or leaves on the branches of a tall tree. Understanding how concepts are developed and how this process might be challenging for young children who are blind or visually impaired will help families and professionals develop successful approaches to teaching important concepts to their children.

Development of Concepts

Concepts are mental representations or understandings of people, places, things, physical properties, events, actions, and reactions. Specific concepts develop through a process of classifying or grouping things that are similar that proceeds through the following stages:

1. an awareness that something (for example, a chair) exists,

2. an opportunity and desire to interact with it (for example, touch, explore, read about it, sit on it, or climb on it) (Skellenger & Hill, 1997),

---

*This section adapted in part from D. L. Fazzi & B. A. Petersmeyer, *Imagining the Possibilities: Creative Approaches to Orientation and Mobility Instruction for Persons with Visual Impairments* (New York: AFB Press, 2001).

3. other people supplying labels for it (for example, "Mamma is sitting in her chair and you are sitting in your highchair;" "There were three little bears sitting on chairs;" "Would you like to rock with Daddy in the wooden rocking chair?"),

4. multiple experiences with different types within that classification (different types of chairs), and

5. the ability to appropriately classify different examples of the concept (objects of different shapes, sizes, and materials that fit within the concept of "chair").

For infants, the repetition of simple sensory–motor patterns (such as reaching, kicking, and grasping) facilitate interactions with the environment. Touching a mother's face, kicking at the foot of the crib, or reaching for a musical mobile provides young children with contact with the surrounding environment. Each contact has the potential to result in initial ideas about things in the young child's immediate world. For example, kicking at the foot of the crib feels a certain way and makes a certain sound; kicking while on the floor would feel and sound different to the child. These experiences help to create initial ideas about concepts like hard and soft or rough and smooth.

Understanding concepts increases and becomes refined with increased exposure. Learners are able to more accurately discriminate between categories of concepts (such as dog versus cat or chair versus table) with experience. Language provides the labels for concepts that are commonly used. Parents seem to provide those labels naturally to their children who are sighted when they do everyday things, such as look at picture books ("See the brown doggie!") or take a trip to the market ("Look at all the fruits and vegetables"). As the child develops a generalized understanding of a concept, language is expanded so that labels are used to include all of the appropriate exemplars of the concept.

Concept Development for Children Who Are Visually Impaired

Vision plays a major role in the formation of concepts for children without visual impairments. Children with visual impairments must find alternate or supplemental means for learning about the world.

Young children constantly use vision to understand the world around them (Ferrell, 1996). Ferrell states, "According to some researchers, vision is usually involved in 90 percent of the learning that takes place in early development" (p. 89). Children with visual impairments, including those children who have multiple disabilities, must rely more heavily on other forms of sensory input. For example, a young child who sits in his or her highchair can look around to see how Dad prepares breakfast. The child may see him put bread in the toaster and then see it pop up when it is toasted. This visual information will help the child learn about certain food and cooking concepts. A child with a visual impairment in a similar situation would receive a lot less sensory information from which to draw conclusions about the breakfast preparation. The child might only hear the bread bag crinkling, the toaster handle being pushed down, and then the sound of the toaster popping up the bread. For the child with an additional hearing loss, auditory feedback would also be limited. For this child, toast might seem to be something that magically appears on the table. The auditory information alone would not be as helpful as visual information could be in creating a connection between the noises heard and the idea of how toast is made for the child who is visually impaired.

Typical vision enables children to experience and learn about many new concepts by starting with the whole picture. Children with visual impairments must often learn concepts from part to whole. For example, young children who are sighted see a dog (the whole picture) and then discover its many parts (such as, tail, teeth, and nose). Learning about concepts in this manner is very effective and often occurs with very little formal teaching. In contrast, children who are congenitally blind use tactile, auditory, olfactory, and kinesthetic senses to develop concepts part by part (wagging tail, wet nose, sharp paws, four legs, pointy ears, loud barking, and smelly breath) until these impressions are fully integrated into a complete *concept* (dog!). In some instances, they may never experience certain aspects of the concept and thus they end up with incomplete or slightly inaccurate ideas. For example, if the blind child's first experience with a dog is an unpleasant one, he or she may not feel comfortable enough to explore further and may never feel a dog's tongue or soft fur. The *wholeness* of the concept of "dog" is thus dependent upon the child's ability to integrate many pieces of sensory information without the advantage of seeing the whole entity. It is likely that the accuracy and completeness of understanding will depend on the quality and quantity of sensory experiences provided by teachers, specialists, and family members.

While children without visual impairments develop many life concepts incidentally (by simply observing others and the world around them), congenitally visually impaired children often need well-thought out interventions to achieve similar results. For example, preschool children with typical sight learn many aspects of the concepts of walking, running, jumping, or riding a bike from watching others as they move about the house, yard, or playground. Children with severe visual impairments may need opportunities to feel the leg or arm movements and the balance involved in those activities to understand fully the same concept. They will also need support from families who allow them to try and sometimes fail while attempting to learn these skills.

Assessing Concept Development

As with any assessment of young children, it is helpful for the assessor to follow some general principles, including:

- Talk with families and listen to their descriptions of their child's strengths and family concerns.

- Observe the child function and play in natural environments.

- Use an understanding of ranges of typical development (for example, within what age range children who are sighted might be expected to learn a given set of concepts) as a framework or organizer for collecting assessment data (Greenspan & Meisels, 1996).

Time should be spent talking with and listening to family members as they describe their child's abilities and areas of concern within the context of family routines and priorities. This information is especially valuable when the child is nonverbal and cannot provide answers to given assessment questions. Additional time must be spent observing the child function and play in natural environments. If family members are at ease with the assessor and fully understand the purpose of the assessment, they may be willing to have their own interactions with the child observed in the home or at the center-based facility as appropriate. This interaction often yields the most relevant information for the assessment. If the young child is familiar with the assessor, the assessor may also interact with the child to determine the child's attainment of specific skills. For preverbal children who have necessary receptive language to follow simple requests, the assessor will have to rely on the child's ability to point, show, or complete a given task rather than relying on the child's ability to label or verbalize specific information.

In order to know what to look for during observations of family and child, it is imperative that the assessor be knowledgeable about ranges of typical development. Familiarity with typical development can be gained through observations of children who are sighted who are of a similar age group or by referring to developmental charts prior to the assessment. It will be the assessor's knowledge of typical development and sensitivity to the significance of the interactive family system that gives meaning to the information gleaned from observations and family reports and serves as an organizer for assessment results.

When specifically assessing the conceptual development of a young child with a visual impairment, the assessor may look at concepts such as:

- body awareness—parts, functions, and movements,

- shapes—circle, square, and triangle,

- sizes—big, little, tall, short, wide, and narrow,

- textures—rough, smooth, hard, soft, and bumpy,

- positional concepts—top, down, middle, and under, and

- object concepts—ball, house, doll, table, driveway, and mailbox.

These concepts can form an important foundation for more complex concepts and abstract reasoning. In each case, talking with the family, observing the child's use of household implements (such as, spoons, containers, toothbrush, comb, and so on), listening to the child's use of language or gestures, watching family interactions in daily routines, and noting how the child plays with familiar and unfamiliar age-appropriate toys will help to provide a fuller picture of the young child's overall conceptual development.

Body awareness is a good starting place to look at conceptual development since it is the most familiar set of concepts to young children and is relevant to many daily tasks. For example, between 12 and 18 months of age, most young children who are given the opportunity to learn the labels for facial features and major body parts will be able to point with some consistency to them when asked. In order to assess body awareness in a 14-month-old who has low vision, the assessor could do the following:

Assessing Body Awareness

1. First talk with the family about whether they considered this an important area of development.

2. Have families describe instances in which their sons or daughters may have shown that they know where certain body parts are located.

3. Talk about bath time and dressing routines to determine the context in which the child has had opportunities to learn about various body parts.

4. Ask families if they have favorite sing-song games or activities that emphasize body parts (for example, "tickle, tickle on the belly, tickle, tickle on the toes," and so on or "if you're happy and you know it clap your hands, stomp your feet") that may easily be observed.

5. Certain feeding, dressing, or face-washing routines may also be observed in the home.

6. Older children can be observed playing in the yard or on play equipment at the family's home or child care facility to see the range of body movements that they engage in.

If the child and specialist have good rapport, the specialist may come prepared with a variety of fun, age-appropriate activities and props to help assess the child's body awareness, such as:

- high-contrast feather duster or magic wand to tap or point to various body parts,

- hypoallergenic lotion for the child to apply to various body parts,

- realistic dolls or large teddy bears to dress, pat, bathe or play with, and

- music tapes with songs that require children to move various body parts (such as, Hokey-Pokey).

Similar approaches can be utilized in assessing positional and object concepts. It may be slightly more challenging to know where to start and what to cover in assessing these concepts, because there is less information available regarding developmental norms for object concepts and the infinite list of possible concepts can be a bit unwieldy. In general, however, when assessing positional or directional concepts, start with the child's body and extend outward to objects in the near and distant space. Similarly, it would be expected that most children would be exposed to and master object concepts in the home first, then neighborhood, and then the larger community. Concepts that may help young children with visual impairments more fully participate in and enjoy family activities can also be prioritized for assessment.

The results of the assessment provides information for the intervention program by creating a picture of the child's development, the priorities of the family, and the context for learning. The assessment will hopefully reveal intervention strategies that can be easily integrated within family routines.

Promoting Concept Development

Intervention strategies for successful concept development should encompass a variety of integrated approaches based on the learner's age and abilities. Intervention must begin early to address the concept needs of young children who are blind or visually impaired, including those who have additional disabilities. By working together with families, teachers and specialists can greatly increase the effectiveness of an early concept development program. Family involvement will help to ensure that concepts that are learned incidentally by sighted children will be introduced and experienced in a meaningful way for visually impaired children.

In order to develop conceptual understanding of the world, children must be actively engaged with people and things in a wide variety of meaningful environments. Very young sighted children interact with their surroundings primarily through play and exploration, and these forms of interactions are equally important for children who are visually impaired. However, in some instances families and teachers may be overly protective—fearful that children with visual impairments may injure themselves if they are active and moving about. It is not uncommon for sighted toddlers and preschoolers to get bumps and bruises as a part of their active learning. Families of children with visual impairments can be reassured that the same is true for their young ones, and that safe exploration should be encouraged and even expected as part of healthy development. Providing accessible play environments can help encourage active exploration and concept development in young children who are visually impaired.

Each early experience in home and at school begins to form the foundation for future learning and exploration. Family members, teachers, and specialists can further facilitate conceptual development by giving labels to objects, providing descriptions of their properties and functions, and including narration for their actions and their consequent reactions. The following example illustrates a manner in which family members can provide narration to facilitate concept development,

---

"Kathryn, Mamma is opening the refrigerator. Feel the cool air? The refrigerator keeps our food cold, like milk and juice and eggs and butter. Can you help Mamma put the milk in the refrigerator? That's right—it goes on the top shelf. Ok, let's close the door of the refrigerator to keep the cold air inside of it."

It may be challenging to find ways to address concepts that are based primarily on visual perceptions with young children who are blind. For example, young children who are sighted learn to label the colors of objects that they see in the environment. Colors play a major theme in preschool books, crayons, and fingerpaints. However, there is no strategy in which a blind child can truly experience the concept of color in an alternate sensory format. Similar challenges are inherent in learning about things like clouds and rainbows.

When children's curiosity is piqued about visual images, adults can try their best to relate such constructs to other concepts that are familiar or to those that can be represented tactilely or auditorally. For example, colors can be compared to temperatures (for example, blue is cool like water and orange is warm like the sunshine) or clouds can be represented tactilely with cotton ball puffs. In neither case is the strategy sufficient to develop a true understanding of the abstract concept, but it may adequately satisfy a blind child's questions and provide him or her with a reference for what others are talking about.

Teachers, specialists, and family members can assist young children who are visually impaired, including those with additional disabilities, in developing awareness of body concepts, positions, size, shape, objects, and textures by using consistent and appropriate terms in everyday routines. Situations in which such concepts can be introduced and reinforced include the following:

Reinforcing Concepts

→ Family members can reinforce concepts of size by using three sizes of chairs, bowls, and blankets to act out the story of *Goldilocks and the Three Bears*.

→ Family members can reinforce the concepts of *right, left,* and *next to* at the dinner table during meals by using the terms to describe the location of items on the table.

→ Family members can identify body parts during bath time and encourage their children to explore how body parts move, such as using hands to play a splashing game or making a game of "where's the sponge?" so that body parts can be identified.

→ Preschool teachers can reinforce the concepts of *in front* and *behind* by making a game of "who's in front and behind?" when children are lining up for playground time.

→ Teachers can use *top, middle,* and *bottom* when referring to the location of children's cubbies or storage shelves.

→ Orientation and mobility (O&M) specialists can use consistent terminology for moving the cane tip from side to side when teaching beginning cane skills to preschool-age children.

→ O&M specialists can take the time to fully describe environmental features discovered in the home, neighborhood, or yard while encouraging the child to tactilely explore relevant items.

Children who are blind or visually impaired will benefit from concrete, hands-on, multisensory experiences in developing conceptual understanding. It takes both time and creativity to provide children who are visually impaired with the many meaningful experiences necessary to support the development of concrete, functional, and abstract concepts. For example, many young children like to have pretend birthday parties, complete with cake baking and a chance to blow out the pretend candles. So how does a child who is blind or visually impaired develop all the concepts related to baking a cake? Before being able to bake a pretend cake, the child will need real-life opportunities to:

- touch, taste, see, and smell ingredients for making the cake,
- feel the ingredients mixed in a bowl and poured into a cake pan,
- feel the heat from the oven,
- look as the cake rises,
- listen to the ticking of the timer,
- watch and help put the chocolate icing on the white cake, and
- taste and smell the yummy results.

In addition, children who are blind benefit from being shown how to systematically explore their surroundings. In the kitchen, for example, a child can be assisted in exploring the counter systematically to discover the arrangement of bowls, pans, and mixing spoons. If a child is given similar cooking implements to play with in a sandbox and provided with some creative modeling and expansion, he or she may begin to demonstrate some aspects of functional play that show understanding of concepts related to cake baking.

Quality experiences that are clear and thorough will be most beneficial when they do not create sensory overload for the young child. Sensory overload occurs when there is too much stimulation at one time. For example, trying to teach a child who is deaf-blind how to scan the highchair tray for pieces of cereal while Dad is washing dishes and siblings are running back and forth from the kitchen to the living room may be ineffective. The child is likely to experience sensory overload because of the amount of visual and auditory stimuli distracting the child from the task. All individuals have their own tolerance for the level and variety of stimuli that can be processed. Children who are sighted frequently use vision to figure out the sources or context for the many sounds and sensations around them. Visually impaired children may "overload" more quickly if they have a limited context for the sounds they hear and the things they feel. When on overload, children may simply "tune out" (or not process) certain stimuli.

A combination of clear verbal descriptions and meaningful hands-on learning activities will assist learners who are visually impaired with concept acquisition. (For example, describing how the water comes out of the faucet while the child helps to wash dishes is a meaningful combination.) Learning activities for young children may include the thoughtful use of:

Activities for Learning Concepts

→ *functional tasks* to utilize conceptual knowledge in daily routines, such as learning body concepts while dressing,

→ *games* to practice concepts in a social context for example, playing a game of red light–green light for positional concepts,

→ *play* to explore the physical properties of toys and objects, for example, shaking and mouthing a rattle,

→ *pretend play* to exercise imagination in exploring conceptual applications, like having a tea party to experiment with concepts like *full* and *empty*,

→ *models* to illustrate things that are too large or inaccessible to explore tactilely, such as examining a model of a bus,

→ *manipulatives* to provide hands-on materials for learning concepts, for example, stacking blocks to learn about height and balance,

→ *field trips* to experience concepts first hand, for example, visiting the petting zoo to learn about different animals.

Activities that will be most meaningful are those that provide concrete, hands-on experiences and those that promote positive interactions with the physical and social environments.

Some additional creativity may be needed to assure that young children who have additional physical disabilities are given opportunities to actively explore home, school, and community environments and have access to materials and hands-on activities that facilitate their understanding of important concepts. For specific suggestions, see "Promoting Concept Development for Young Children Who Have Multiple Disabilities."

Each fully formed concept provides the learner with a foundation for future understanding and expanded possibilities for learning. Cognitive growth, including the development of new concepts, enables the young child to experience meaningful interactions in more aspects of life, which, in turn, provides the child with more motivation and opportunity to communicate with others. As children move through the stages of cognitive development, their level of understanding of objects, people, and actions supports the use of language for communication. Similarly, attainment of language supports complex thought and reasoning. In this way, cognition, concepts, and communication are closely intertwined.

COMMUNICATION

The foundation for communication is formed long before early words are formed and phrases are used (Warren, 2000). Reciprocal interactions between children and their caregivers (for example, eye contact, smiles, and touches) signal the beginning of nonverbal communication and lead to later mastery of speaking, reading, and writing. Language acquisition—the active construction of language by children—occurs through interaction with the environment.

PROMOTING CONCEPT DEVELOPMENT FOR YOUNG CHILDREN WHO HAVE MULTIPLE DISABILITIES

The following suggestions for working with children who have disabilities in addition to visual impairment will be helpful in ensuring that they have appropriate opportunities to learn important concepts.

➜ Concepts that will help children to actively participate in family routines or play with peers should be given priorty when planning activities for children with multiple disabilities.

➜ Some children who are nonambulatory may benefit from exposure to a smaller, contrived environment, such as Nielsen's "Little Room," (Dunnett, 1997) in which they can interact with a variety of sensory materials within arm's reach.

➜ Other children may need some assistance moving about in order to explore an entire room or play area.

➜ Additional postural support may help some children concentrate on using their vision to examine novel and other interesting objects.

➜ Children with dual sensory impairments will need carefully selected toys and materials that will provide meaningful interactions through tactile exploration. Thoughtful use of color, contrast, or amplification (as appropriate) will help children who are deaf-blind to experience more of their surroundings.

➜ Use of repetition and incorporating learning opportunities within natural routines help children who have multiple disabilities to make connections between experiences and concepts and actions and reactions.

Diane L. Fazzi

Language Development

While humans have a predisposition to acquire language, as evidenced by the regularity of certain aspects of language acquisition (Rogow, 2000), cognitive and social development are closely intertwined. Interactions with the physical world help children to develop concepts for which they can use language to label, describe, categorize, and complete complex reasoning tasks. Social exchanges provide the means for learning language and the end of satisfying communication with others.

Theorists have focused on these different aspects of language learning. Chomsky (1965) theorized that children were innately programmed to learn and use language. Bruner (1974) connected language development to a set of behaviors that can be used to communicate meaning in various social contexts. Language, indeed, meets many social functions. Cognitive theorists have emphasized the relationship between formal language acquisition and cognition (Rogow, 2000). Parallels to Piagetian stage theory (for example prelinguistic and linguistic stages of communication) provide a useful framework for explaining many of the intricacies of the attainment of language structure and rules. While these theories each maintain a contrasting perspective, together they help to explain the complexity of language development.

The development of communication involves two distinct stages that occur during the first five years: prelinguistic and linguistic.

PRELINGUISTIC COMMUNICATION

During the first year of life the interactions in which children engage lay the groundwork for language acquisition. Behaviors such as fussing, crying, and smiling may initially not be intended for specific communication, but caregivers quickly interpret them as communicative in attempts to respond to the newborn's needs (Lueck, Chen, & Kekelis, 1997). Eye contact with significant persons reinforces caregivers' efforts to interact with a preverbal partner. Initially, children smile at any human face; they then learn to discriminate and smile selectively at familiar family members and close friends. Smiling reinforces interactions between caregivers and children and strengthens the emotional bond. Infants begin to use various preverbal signals as they initiate purposeful communication (Leuck, Chen, & Kekelis, 1997). At this stage, children may use and interpret a variety of communicative tools such as:

- eye contact,

- pointing and reaching,

- laughing and crying,

- smiling and other facial expressions, and

- babbling sounds and voice tone.

These individual or combinations of communicative behaviors can be used to accomplish a variety of objectives (Rogow, 2000; Leuck, Chen, & Kekelis, 1997), including:

- getting someone else to start or stop a given activity,

- requesting an object,

- attracting or maintaining another person's attention,

- sharing attention for items of interest,

- greeting a familiar person,

- seeking comfort or satisfying personal needs,

- anticipating routines or events, and

- modeling or imitating language use.

Parents commonly begin to notice and look for objects and activities that seem to interest the child and add words to label and describe them. The use of *motherese* (caregiver use of higher-pitched voice tone, slower rate of speech, and exaggerated intonation while expanding on the baby's vocalizations or utterances) is believed to increase an infant's interest in listening to spoken language (Klein, 2001). Motherese should not be confused with the use of baby talk that is beneath the young child's language ability.

Communicative partners frequently misunderstand children's initial attempts to express themselves, but children are quick to develop strategies to repair these misunderstandings. For instance, a child may squeal during a pleasurable activity and if a parent mistakes that squeal for a request to end the activity, the child may quickly reach for the toy that was being played with to communicate an interest in continuing. The caregiver's ability to interpret these nonverbal communications provides the infant with a satisfying means for enjoying and developing further communication skills.

LINGUISTIC COMMUNICATION

During the first year, infants begin to make sounds. Caregivers reinforce babbling attempts as they respond positively to their infant's early exploration with sounds. Responsive parents share in the child's joy in these early sounds and may recognize some initial communicative intent on the part of the baby and respond accordingly. For example, an infant might smile and laugh while making a "d-d" sound and the mother might say, "Oh, you want your Daddy."

Between the ages of 10 and 18 months, many young children acquire their first words. Common early words in many cultures in the United States are labels for familiar people or objects. In other countries or cultures in which the language emphasizes the action words in sentences, verbs may be more common first words for young children (Cowley, 2000). The words may be similar to adult words (bottle may be "ba-ba") or very different (blanket may be "deedle"). Visual information (for example, reaching or pointing) is often used to make sense of these early utterances. Young children may also label things by the sounds that they make ("meow" for cat) or by the functions they fill (such as, "nursees" for breasts or "pop" for a jack-in-the-box). The key at this early stage is to recognize words that are used in a consistent way and to reinforce these early attempts to communicate. For example, if a child seems to consistently use the sound "u-u" along with outstretched arms, the caregiver can reinforce these communicative attempts by picking him or her up and expanding on the utterance by saying "Up. You want Mamma to pick you up?"

As vocabulary grows, young children extend words to represent categories, such as "dog" for all pets (Rogow, 2000), based on their experiences and/or interests. Children expand one- word utterances to two-, three-, and four-word complex phrases (for example, "Baby go bye-bye"). Language skills are refined to form sentences with nouns, verbs, and objects. Pronouns, such as "I" and "you," are commonly used incorrectly at this point. Questions are used to acquire information such as names for objects of interest or location of familiar people. At this stage, children may enjoy the repetition of books and songs with rhyming and nonsense words. Conversational skills enable children to more fully participate in a variety of social contexts (Timmins, 1997).

Language Development for Children with Visual Impairments

While there are certain commonalities in language acquisition for young children, there are also variations across individuals, languages, and cultures (Rogow, 2000). Vision facilitates both prelinguistic and linguistic communication development (Warren, 2000). While early eye contact is typically used to elicit caregiver attention or to perceive meaning from facial expressions and gestures, other forms of early social interaction, such as a child lying very still to let Mommy know that the child is listening to her talk, can be developed in the absence of visual information. Nonvisual interactions may contribute to significant differences in early reciprocal communications for child–caregiver dyads when the infant is visually impaired (Warren, 2000). However, while there may ultimately be subtle differences in the semantics (meaning of words used) and pragmatics (uses of language in social context) of language use (Timmins, 1997), there is little evidence that these differences will necessarily contribute to delays in language acquisition for children with visual impairments (Rogow, 2000). The severity of visual impairment, presence of additional disabilities, and quality and quantity of interactions with the social and physical environment may each impact language development (Timmins, 1997).

EARLY COMMUNICATION WITH CHILDREN
WHO ARE VISUALLY IMPAIRED

Perhaps vision is most important during the earliest caregiver–child interactions. The inability to share visual attention may lead to differences in the way children and caregivers interact. Without visual cues, it is harder to initiate and maintain social interactions. Limited visual information makes it difficult for children with visual impairments to create changes in activity or interactions within their environment (Munoz, 1998). For example, a child who is blind who is bored with a given toy would have more difficulty communicating a desire to play with something else since he or she might not be aware of the choices available in the immediate area. Children who are sighted can more easily point to other items of interest in order to communicate their needs or wants. Before young children have words to make their needs known, visual impairment may pose the greatest limitations to effective communication with caregivers (Lueck, Chen, & Kekelis, 1997).

The visual cues given by their children provide most parents with reinforcement to continue interacting with children and vice versa. Parents of blind children may need assistance in finding cues to which they can respond and alternative means for establishing reciprocal interactions. As Timmins (1997) notes, the "intent of subtle or unconventional behaviors of infants with visual impairments may not be recognized or may be misinterpreted" (p. 49). For example, babies who are blind may clench their fists and assume a quiet

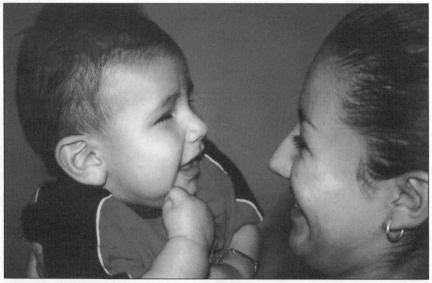

Parents can establish reciprocal interactions such as encouraging babbling using nonvisual cues.

position when they are interested in an activity, as opposed to sighted infants who commonly move their hands and feet excitedly. Parents may misinterpret this less familiar behavior as lack of interest and stop interacting with the infant. Similarly, children who are blind may smile with less frequency and less selectively than children who are sighted. Caregivers of children who are blind may misinterpret this behavior and believe that their children have not adequately bonded to them, which may lead them to attempt less frequently to interact with their children.

The parents of a child with a visual impairment cannot rely on visual cues such as eye gaze and gestures to communicate to them their child's interests. In addition, the infant who is blind does not have the same strategies for attracting attention or correcting communicative misunderstandings as do sighted infants. As a result, some children who are blind may tend to be fussy or have tantrums if they are not understood. Interpreting babbles may also be more challenging as the infant who is visually impaired may have more limited use of eye gaze and a more limited repertoire of gestures. In a number of ways, it is more challenging for caregivers to interact with an infant who is visually impaired, but with patience and creativity, alternative pathways for interacting can lead to equally satisfying relationships. For specific approaches, see "Creating Alternative Pathways for Caregiver Interactions." (For additional suggested activities for supporting positive early caregiver interactions see Klein, Chen, & Haney, 2000.)

LINGUISTIC COMMUNICATION OF CHILDREN WITH VISUAL IMPAIRMENTS

Children with visual impairments appear to develop first words around the same time that children who are sighted do, but how they use the words may be somewhat different (Lueck, Chen, & Kekelis, 1997). Some of those differences may include:

- more use of labels (the words for objects such as "airplane") than functional words (describing the function of objects such as "flying"),

- less overextension of words to categorize related concepts (for example, less likely to use the word "doggie" for all four-legged animals),

- more talk about their own experiences rather than actions of others, and

- prolonged confusion with pronouns (such as *me, she* or *he*) and difficulty changing perspectives.

CREATING ALTERNATIVE PATHWAYS FOR CAREGIVER INTERACTIONS

Infants who are blind or visually impaired do not have access to the visual cues for communicating with their caregivers that are commonly used by sighted infants. The following suggestions will help caregivers establish alternative ways to develop communication with visually impaired infants:

➜ Take time to observe the child's communicative behaviors, such as changes in body movements, alertness, fussiness, or vocalizations in order to understand how she or he might be trying to communicate likes, dislikes, needs, and interests.

➜ Establish predictable daily routines, such as going for a walk in the stroller after breakfast everyday, and use consistent cues, such as jingling the house keys, to help the child anticipate the event. Eventually the child may be given the keys to jingle when he or she is ready to initiate the activity.

➜ Engage in nonvisual forms of turn-taking such as adapting traditional games like peek-a-boo to include a gentle blow of air onto the baby's face after helping the child remove his or her hands. Eventually a child might place her hands on her face to initiate a game of peek-a-boo and remove them when ready for the puff of air.

➜ Allow time for the child to respond to communicative cues (such as saying "Hello") and time to initiate his or her own communication. For example, the caregiver might stop the swing until the child signals "more" through kicking his or her feet, squealing, signing "more", or using the word more, depending on the child's level of communication.

Diane L. Fazzi

In particular, children who are blind may show differences in the number of questions that they ask, the frequency of echolalia, their ability to sustain conversations, and the meanings that they associate with words.

Use of Questions. Children who are blind tend to ask many questions, sometimes inappropriately, such as questions not related to the topic of conversation. (Kekelis & Sacks, 1988; Kekelis, 1992). It is important to determine the underlying function of the questions, such as:

- gathering information,
- attracting attention,

- initiating an interaction,

- maintaining an interaction, or

- responding to fear or confusion.

It is important that children learn socially appropriate and effective means for achieving these ends. For example, even though questioning may be one effective means of gathering information, independent or assisted exploration of a novel object or concept can be encouraged in conjunction with questioning. A question may be initially effective in initiating a conversation, but follow-up strategies (such as moving closer to the person and talking about something of interest to them) are necessary to maintain those interactions. Questions may be used to obtain reassurance about someone's presence or of activities in surrounding areas. Adults can be sensitive to this need and give verbal information about people's movements and other events that might be unexpected. Children with visual impairments can be encouraged to express their feelings directly rather than through an overreliance on questioning.

Echolalia. As part of typical language development, children often use imitation to practice spoken words and phrases. Echolalia—the repetition of statements used by other people—is commonly used with greater frequency and for a longer period of time by children who are blind or visually impaired (Segal, 1993). As with questions, it is important to determine the function of the child's use of echolalia, such as:

- using imitation as a strategy to practice language (for example, a child repeats the phrase "go potty" to improve his or her ability to say it clearly),

- rehearsing verbal input in order to more fully process it (for example, a child repeats the phrase "go potty" while thinking about what will happen when he or she gets there),

- trying to initiate and/or maintain an interaction (for example, a child repeats the phrase "go potty" to keep an adult's attention), or

- providing a form of self-stimulation (for example, a child repeats the phrase "go potty" to him- or herself for personal gratification) .

Imitation is an important strategy for language acquisition for children with visual impairments (Rogow, 2000). While echolalia is a natural part of early communication, it is a concern if the child is repeating many statements that he or she does not have the ability to understand, or if it becomes the child's primary form of communication. Modeling appropriate interaction strategies and helping children to expand upon their language usage can be effective strategies to eliminate such repetitive language. In more intense cases, the educational team may need to develop a plan for reducing or extinguishing the behavior.

Sustaining Conversations. Without the advantage of visual and social cues, it is challenging for many children with visual impairments to listen to and stay on track with conversations. They may make comments that are not related to the topic at hand. Since it is more difficult to keep track of the activities and interests of others through auditory input alone, some children who are blind may seem to focus solely on their own interests in conversations. Although it is natural for all children to stray from conversations at times, children with visual impairments may need explicit instruction in the nuances of participating in give-and-take conversations. These skills can be modeled and practiced during play sessions and daily routines with adults and then later with siblings and playmates when the child is more skilled and confident. (See Chapter 6 for more information on developing social skills in children who are blind or visually impaired.)

Meanings of Words. Children who are blind or visually impaired may have different meanings for words. Children with visual impairments are likely to develop vocabularies that are comparable to children who are sighted, but may have meanings that demonstrate a slightly different focus (Munoz, 1998). For example, young children who are sighted and those who are visually impaired would both likely know what flowers are, but when asked to describe them, visually impaired children might focus on properties that are olfactory (such as fragrances) and tactile (for example, silky petals and prickly thorns) rather than visual (like color). A child who is blind may know what a mirror and a window are, but have a difficult time describing what the differences are since tactilely they are similar.

Children with visual impairments may have more difficulty grasping abstract or large-scale concepts (such as streets) because, as noted earlier, they experience them in part-to-whole segments that are difficult to piece together. Spatial concepts (such as *between*) that rely heavily on visual referencing are also difficult to comprehend. These conceptual challenges may present themselves in language usage. *Verbalisms,* use of words for which the child has no understanding, may also be prevalent in the young child's developing language.

COMMUNICATION DEVELOPMENT
FOR CHILDREN WITH MULTIPLE DISABILITIES

It is important to strive to help the young child who is visually impaired to develop communicative competence. For children who have multiple disabilities who are not demonstrating expressive language, alternative communication techniques can be discussed with a speech and language specialist. For example, *communication boards,* with which children can communicate their needs by pointing to specific pictures, can be adapted for use with children who are visually impaired. Children who have low vision can use boards with enlarged and/or high-contrast pictures. *Calendar boards* or *boxes* have places to put actual objects or pictures (like an empty cup to signify snack time) in a sequence to represent the daily routine. A child may be required to move an object to the appropriate box to initiate the next activity. These types of organizers can help children to anticipate events in preparation for communicating with others verbally or nonverbally.

Touch cues are signals made on a child's body to communicate an upcoming event, such as a touch on the shoulder to signal circle time. This type of communication can be used with young children who have dual sensory impairments to let them know that someone is there and that something is about to happen (Chen & Schachter, 1997). For example, three strokes to an infant's cheek can be a touch cue to signify that nursing is about to begin. Similarly, *objects* can be used as communication cues. For example, a clean diaper can be pressed against a deaf-blind infant's hand to signal a diaper change. When the touch cue or object is used consistently, it helps to give the child an opportunity to anticipate daily activities and establish the beginnings of an interactive communication system.

Electronic communication devices, such as those that utilize synthesized speech phrases (such as "yes," "no," or "I need help,") can assist in communication and facilitate the development of expressive language. The introduction of a few basic *sign-language* words for communication purposes is another strategy that can be employed when working with children who have expressive language delays. Children who are visually impaired and are limited in their English proficiency may need the services of both programs in visual impairment and bilingual or English-immersion programs (Munoz, 1998).

Assessing Communication Skills in Children with Visual Impairments

As with assessing concept development, time should be spent talking with and listening to family members as they describe their child's abilities and areas of concern for communicating within the context of family routines and priorities. Time must also be spent observing the child interact and communicate in natural environments.

In order to know what to look for during observations of family and child, it is imperative that the assessor be knowledgeable of ranges of typical language development. Familiarity with typical development can be gained through observations, reading, and taking language samples of sighted children who are of a similar age group, or by referring to developmental charts prior to the assessment. A language sample can be taken by tape or video recording (with permission) of a young child's expressive language for a set length of time and then transcribing the verbal exchange to examine the child's use of language. It will be the assessor's knowledge of typical development and his or her sensitivity to the significance of the interactive family system that gives meaning to the information gleaned from observations and family reports and serves as an organizer for assessment results.

When specifically assessing the communication skills of a young child with a visual impairment, the assessor may look at:

- interactions with familiar caregivers (such as, initiation of interactions, ease at which caregivers interpret communicative attempts, and ability of child to regulate caregiver's behavior),

- opportunities for making needs known through preverbal or verbal communication (for example, objects of interest available for request, choice-making opportunities, or time given to communicate that the child wants "more" of an enjoyable activity), or

- samples of language usage (including comprehension of vocabulary and use of language in functional contexts).

In each case, talking with the family, observing the child in natural environments, listening to the child's use of language, and noting how the child communicates with familiar adults and children will help to provide a fuller picture of the young child's overall language development.

Having the family describe instances in which their son or daughter typically initiates interactions will help the assessor note the family's comfort level with recognizing and interpreting the child's nonverbal cues. Talking about favorite family routines can provide the context in which the child has had opportunities to communicate needs and interests. Some families may have favorite sing-song games or activities that emphasize taking turns and vocalizations (such as singing a familiar song, stopping to let the child say the last part of a line or verse, and then continuing) that may easily be observed. Certain feeding and dressing routines may be rich in communicative intents and may also be observed in the home. Older children can be observed talking with teachers or peers in the classroom or playground.

Communication skills that may help young children with visual impairments more fully participate and enjoy school and family activities can also be prioritized for assessment. The results of the assessment should provide information for the intervention program, by creating a picture of the child's language development, the priorities of the family, and the context for communication. The assessment will hopefully reveal intervention strategies that can be easily integrated within family and school routines. For example, if it was noted that a child who had multiple disabilities was initiating communication only on a limited basis, then family members could be encouraged to "delay" certain expected, highly motivating events (such as waiting to put the child in the warm bathtub until he or she responds in some way to request it) or asking preschool teachers to allow additional time for a child to communicate a preference for a food choice at snack time. In both instances, the strategy can easily be used, and as long as the activity is of high interest to the child, the approach is likely to result in some noticeable improvement. Standardized assessment tools, such as the Battelle Developmental Inventory (Newborg, Stock, Wnek, Guidubaldi, & Svinicki, 1984), Oregon Project (Brown, Simmons, Methuin, Anderson, Boigon & Davis, 1991) or Brigance Diagnostic Inventory of Early Development-Revised (Brigance, 1991), provide another means for assessing the development of communication skills in young children, including those who are visually impaired. (See the Resources section at the back of this book for sources of these and additional assessment tools.)

In some instances a child with a visual impairment may need to be referred for a formal language assessment from a speech and language specialist. The teacher of students with visual impairments can work together with the specialist, other teachers (as appropriate), and the family to plan and conduct the assessment. However, standardized language assessment instruments rely heavily on visual materials and tasks. When use of these tools or subtests cannot be avoided, adaptations can be made, for example, substituting an actual quarter for the picture of one. Norms should not be used on adapted tests, but the results can be used to develop a descriptive summary that may be helpful in developing a full picture of the child's communication abilities. Informal measures, including language samples, observations, and interviews, can add to the data collected and provide a natural context from which to assess the child's language development (Munoz, 1998).

Promoting the Development of Communication Skills in Young Children Who Are Visually Impaired

When all members of the young child's early educational team have an understanding of the impact of vision loss upon language development, they are better equipped to address the issues facing children who are blind or visually impaired and their families in a positive way. Families and early intervention professionals will be the first to support the development of prelinguistic communication skills in young children, and linguistic communication will continue to develop as children attend preschool and have increasing interactions with peers.

PROMOTING THE DEVELOPMENT OF PRELINGUISTIC COMMUNICATION

Establishing an environment with the proper conditions for facilitating communication is an important step toward developing the basis for communication skills. As Erin (2000) notes, "Creating an environment that has consistent routines and that allows the student to anticipate events and make choices will build a foundation for later communication, whether or not it includes language" (p. 735). Predictable routines help children anticipate events and feel in more control over their environment (Klein, Chen, & Haney, 2000). Turn-taking is one of the earliest communication routines established between infants and caregivers and forms the basis for engaging in conversations. Both elements are essential to supporting prelinguistic communication. For other strategies that can be used to promote prelinguistic communication in children with visual impairments see "Promoting Prelinguistic Communication."

PROMOTING THE DEVELOPMENT OF LINGUISTIC COMMUNICATION

Professionals can work together with families to promote the development of linguistic communication in children who are blind or vi-

PROMOTING PRELINGUISTIC COMMUNICATION

Predictable routines that allow children to anticipate events and reinforce the child's early communication efforts, as in the following activities, are crucial to supporting the development of prelinguistic communication in young children with visual impairments.

➜ Establish prelinguistic turn-taking routines (Lueck, Chen, & Kekelis, 1997) that are playful and fun. Simple babbling exchanges or games like pat-a-cake can be used to establish and practice turn taking with infants.

➜ Establish routines for everyday interactions (such as greetings). For example, when coming home from work Mommy can always call her child's name and clap three times before picking up the child.

➜ Interrupt favorite activities to give the child a chance to communicate a desire for "more." This technique can be very effective when used during a rhythmic activity like pushing a child in a swing.

➜ Teach family members alternate routes for reciprocal interactions. Pairing physical contact (massage of infant's legs) and verbal input ("soft skin"), for instance, may help reinforce the infant's smiling and babbling. Consistent use of changes in voice tone can also be used during interactions.

➜ Listen and watch the child to notice nonvisual cues of interest or distress (such as changes in body movements or skin tone color) and find consistent ways to respond to them (like talking about the object or event the infant was interested in or comforting the distressed child by cuddling him or her with a favorite blanket).

➜ Encourage the young child to make his or her needs known (such as requesting "more" or signaling "enough") rather than always anticipating and providing for things ahead of time.

➜ Acknowledge the young child's efforts to communicate by responding in a positive way. A child's early attempts to communicate need to be encouraged. When families and professionals repeat and expand on children's language (for example, "Book. You like that book. You are turning the pages in the book."), children are encouraged to continue talking.

Diane L. Fazzi

sually impaired. The use of words to communicate with others provides a powerful tool for a multitude of social interactions. Simple labels such as "bottle" may represent many children's first formal use of language to communicate needs to others. The ability of young children to describe to others the functions of objects, the actions of people, and their own interests will become important in

PROMOTING LINGUISTIC COMMUNICATION

The following strategies will help professionals and family members support the development of verbal communication in young children who are visually impaired.

→ Make playful games out of vocal imitation and turn taking (Lueck, Chen, & Kekelis, 1997). Repeating, rephrasing, and using pauses can encourage vocal turn taking and have positive effects on language development (Dote-Kwan, 1995).

→ Model appropriate ways to initiate and maintain social interactions. Good social skills can be modeled and practiced during symbolic play routines (for example, pretend kitchen and food preparation or talking on a play telephone).

→ Support the child's participation in a variety of everyday activities. Hands-on experiences will support language development and provide topics of interest to talk about.

→ Provide extra information about things that are discussed. Instead of merely labeling objects, events, and actions, describe the things that are of interest to the child. Also talk about and describe other's actions so that the child with a visual impairment does not become too self-involved in his or her own experiences and language use.

→ Avoid bombarding children with questions. Since children with visual impairments often rely on imitation to learn language strategies and may also have a tendency to become overreliant on questioning, modeling an overuse of questions could be counterproductive.

→ Respond to the ideas and feelings in the child's speech. By paying careful attention to the child's actions and the events taking place around him or her, others will be able to respond to the child's underlying communicative intent. For example, a child saying, "I don't want to do it" may actually mean, "I'm afraid to try it."

→ Express your own feelings verbally and help put the child's feelings into words. Children with visual impairments cannot easily read frowns, smiles, and expressions of others. Other person's feelings need to be explained, and the child needs to be taught how to express his or her own feelings appropriately.

→ "Try to expand on the child's existing language. The child's attempts to communicate can be used as the basis for further communication. For instance, if a child says 'ba-ba,' the father can respond with, 'Yes, that is your bottle' and go on to describe it or its function."

→ Assist the child in developing socially appropriate responses. Attention to social communication skills can assist children in maintaining conversations and participating in play with peers. For example, the child may be taught to listen to and identify what other children are doing and to imitate their behavior if he or she wants to join in their play.

→ Encourage children to talk about and dictate stories about recent individual or group activities. By doing so, children can be assisted in relating actual experiences to linguistic concepts and structures (Munoz, 1998).

→ Help children act out videos, stories, and songs to increase their understanding of embedded concepts (Munoz, 1998). For example, preschool children commonly act out the events in the song "The Wheels on the Bus." Doing so helps children understand concepts such as windows going up and down.

Adapted in part from "Promoting Language Development: Intervention Strategies," by Linda S. Kekelis, pp. 48–49 in the 1992 edition of this book.

negotiating play situations with peers. For specific strategies that can be used to promote linguistic communication in children with visual impairments, see the accompanying box on "Promoting Linguistic Communication".

CONCLUSION

Maintaining high expectations for the young child with a visual impairment can be the first step toward the child's attainment of communicative competence. Both families and professionals must expect and encourage young children who are blind or visually impaired to communicate their needs, likes, and dislikes rather than anticipating and providing for their needs before they have an opportunity to express them. The ability to use language in a socially appropriate way has long-term implications for the child with a visual impairment in the areas of socialization, academics, self-esteem, and independence.

Visual impairment can have a profound impact on the development of cognition, concepts, and language. These developmental areas are essential building blocks in the formation of more complex skills and levels of learning. With appropriate individualized intervention, young children who are blind or visually impaired can develop competencies that will enable them to parallel more closely the growth and development of their peers who are sighted.

5 LITERACY FOCUS

Developing Skills and Motivation for
Reading and Writing

CONTRIBUTORS

Alan J. Koenig

M. Cay Holbrook

The foundation for literacy is developed during the early years of a child's life. While the definition of *literacy* has many components, it is commonly agreed that literacy involves reading and writing as well as basic computation skills. The reading and writing skills that eventually will be used to study in school, complete duties at work, and enjoy books and magazines during leisure time begin to grow in infancy, toddlerhood, and preschool years. Family members and early childhood educators have a vital role in providing a wide range of quality experiences that will help ensure early development of literacy skills. For a child who is blind or visually impaired, including those with additional disabilities, the role of families and educators is heightened, since the activities and events that are essential for early literacy development must be provided in a planned and direct, not incidental, manner.

This chapter will present information on how young children develop literacy skills and the implications for those with visual impairments. Special strategies will be presented on arranging a rich environment, teaching related skills that support literacy development, and providing opportunities for reading and writing experiences to ensure that the early years are optimal for developing literacy skills. Also, this chapter will address the process for selecting appropriate literacy media (print and braille) for each child.

DEVELOPMENT OF LITERACY SKILLS

During the first five years of their lives, children who are sighted have exposure to an enormous number and wide variety of symbols and words that eventually will have meaning. They are also in contact with many models of mature, knowledgeable readers and writers. These early experiences with written language are referred to as *emergent literacy.* Children who are blind or who have low vision frequently do not have the same types or degree of exposure. In some cases, children who are blind receive their first literacy experiences when they are provided literacy instruction for the first time, perhaps as late as the age of 4 or 5. Family members and early childhood educators who understand the need for early literacy experiences and the importance of providing an environment rich with accessible words and symbols can help children who are blind or visually impaired develop an early understanding of language and literacy.

Children who are visually impaired and have additional disabilities also have unique challenges during the early years. These challenges generally are related to cognitive level, physical limitations, and/or communication. Their early experiences with symbols may provide a foundation for using literacy skills in functional ways during their school years and beyond. "Providing Literacy Activities for Children Who Have Additional Disabilities" discusses issues and provides strategies for parents and educational teams in providing appropriate early literacy instruction to students with visual impairments and additional disabilities.

PROVIDING LITERACY ACTIVITIES FOR CHILDREN WHO HAVE ADDITIONAL DISABILITIES

Children whose visual impairment is accompanied by other disabilities face unique challenges related to literacy, especially in the early years. Additional disabilities that occur with visual impairments range from mild to severe and might include cognitive, physical, emotional or behavioral, and other sensory disabilities. The range and type of possible additional disabilities make it difficult to develop firm rules for providing literacy instruction for these children. Following are some general suggestions for providing literacy instruction for children who have additional disabilities in addition to visual impairment.

➜ Keep all options open. It is often difficult to determine the potential level of literacy for young children with visual impairments and additional disabilities. A child's ability to use tactile or visual symbols in a meaningful way may develop over a long period of time and should be encouraged throughout his or her entire life.

➜ Examine the meaning of functional literacy for each child. Many children who have disabilities in addition to their visual impairment will use literacy for functional purposes, such as using labels or object cues for personal items, items in the child's environment (cereal boxes), and symbols on a communication device.

➜ Use typical literacy strategies. Many techniques used by parents and teachers for supporting literacy development for children without additional disabilities can be useful for all children. Examine the child's unique needs and modify the technique as appropriate. For example, reading aloud to a child is always important. Children with additional disabilities benefit from listening to a story being read aloud just like children without disabilities. Some modifications might be needed, such as positioning a child who has a physical disability so he or she can be involved in the experience by examining and turning the pages of the book.

➜ Work with all members of the child's educational team. Children with visual impairments and additional disabilities have a variety of needs that can best be met through a team approach to make sure that cognitive, sensory, and physical needs are being met.

➜ Use meaningful activities. Combining opportunities to use tactile or visual symbols or object cues with meaningful activities will help make literacy useful in a child's life. One common use of symbols involves representing daily events in a sequential manner through the use of a calendar box. Visual or tactile symbols that represent activities in the child's day can provide a motivating and functional way to incorporate literacy in a child's life.

➜ Be consistent in literacy activities. Follow a predictable routine. For example, make sure to read to the child every night before bedtime or to examine the day's calendar as soon as the child arrives in the preschool classroom.

Alan J. Koenig & M. Cay Holbrook

Cambourne's Conditions of Learning

Cambourne (1988) studied the development of literacy skills for children who are sighted and identified seven conditions that are essential for acquisition of language skills, including written language skills: immersion, demonstration, expectation, responsibility, use, approximation, and response. The following discussion of Cambourne's conditions of learning will set the stage for the later discussion of providing a balanced literacy program. An understanding of the underlying reasons behind the strategies used to assist children who are blind or visually impaired can help family members and early childhood educators provide effective literacy experiences for young children.

IMMERSION

Children who are sighted see many examples of written text before they are ready to begin to interpret letters and words. In addition to early books, children who are sighted see printed words on household items (such as diaper boxes and cereal boxes), books and magazines, birthday cards, toy boxes, and environmental signs (such as McDonald's™, Coca-Cola™, and candy wrappers). They see big print and little print, different colors of print, different styles of print, and words written left to right and top to bottom. Cambourne believes that this immersion in a variety of texts is important to the development of literacy skills for children who are sighted. Children who are blind or who have low vision do not have the same access to similar literacy experiences from birth. Children who are blind may not have regular, frequent, or any experiences with braille or tactile symbols prior to formal instruction. Children with low vision may be able to take advantage of some environmental print, but their access may be limited.

DEMONSTRATION

Children who are sighted almost constantly watch experienced readers and writers interact with print. Examples of these demonstrations include watching siblings complete homework assignments, parents read the daily newspaper, store clerks read price tags, and grandparents write letters. All these experiences are valuable because the child observes a knowledgeable person "demonstrating" literacy tasks in the medium that the child will use for reading and writing. These experiences with print will also be valuable for the child with low vision, but the child's awareness of the demonstrations may be limited by his or her visual impairment. Children who are blind typically have very limited opportunities to observe mature readers and writers of braille. Because of this, teachers of students with visual impairments must make plans for persons who are blind to engage in shared reading and other literacy activities with young children who are blind.

EXPECTATION

The expectations of others are extremely important in the development of literacy skills. Children who are sighted are expected to achieve a level of literacy in part because those around them understand print literacy through personal experiences. Children who are blind or visually impaired, on the other hand, are often given the message that they are not expected to develop the same level of literacy skills. This message is given through statements such as:

- "I don't understand how anyone could ever learn braille. I can't feel the dots at all."

- "Braille reading will always be much slower than print reading."

- "This child can't see very well, so he won't be able to read very well."

Family members and early childhood educators must carefully monitor and check their own attitudes and perceptions about literacy for children who are blind or visually impaired so that they do not lower their expectations for literacy development.

Parents and educators face special difficulties in this area when children have disabilities in addition to their visual impairments. It is often difficult to predict the level of literacy attainment that will be possible for these children. For this reason, expectations for the development of literacy for children with visual impairment and other disabilities are often either unrealistically high or unrealistically low. Parents and educators address children's individual needs by providing options for all children to grow in literacy development while keeping a sound perspective on each child's learning and on established priorities in learning objectives.

RESPONSIBILITY

When children begin to participate independently in literacy activities (such as scribbling with a crayon and drawing on a piece of paper), they are beginning to take responsibility for their learning by choosing to spend time engaged in literacy experiences. However, in order for children to begin taking responsibility for their learning, they must have the tools and experiences necessary to allow them to independently choose reading and writing activities. This means that paper, pencils, crayons, and braillewriters should be available for visually impaired children to use at any time throughout the day. Setting up the environment to encourage independent choice is critical. Some children will require the assistance of a physical therapist, occupational therapist, or speech and language therapist to make sure that their environment meets their unique skills and challenges.

USE

Children need to be able to practice their developing literacy skills in a variety of activities. Scribbling notes and cards to parents and siblings and "reading" a favorite storybook over and over again are examples of ways that children practice their newly found reading and writing abilities. For these experiences to be valuable, children should be able to use their literacy skills throughout the day, whenever they wish. Children who are learning to read and write in braille or to use visual or tactual symbol systems often use these skills only when they are involved in direct instructional activities. Family members and early childhood educators who find ways to encourage children to be involved in literacy activities at other times throughout the day support the development of literacy skills.

APPROXIMATION

Cambourne points out the importance of allowing children to make mistakes as they develop literacy skills. Children who are blind or who have low vision should also be allowed to approximate reading and writing without being told that their responses are incorrect. Sometimes, when adults concentrate on emerging literacy skills, the right answer or correct word becomes more important than the child's ongoing development of early reading and writing skills. While perhaps well intentioned, this practice actually hampers literacy development and therefore should be avoided, especially during the emergent literacy phase. As a child begins to be more confident in his or her literacy skills, the parents and teachers can use modeling techniques to encourage more correct responses. It eventually will be important to make sure that the child moves from approximation to accuracy.

RESPONSE

Finally, Cambourne believes that it is important for children to receive feedback from "knowledgeable others" (p. 33). For children who are sighted, almost anyone can serve as a "knowledgeable other," since most adults know the skills (reading and writing print) that the child is learning. However, the idea of a "knowledgeable other" is somewhat more complicated for the child who is blind. It is likely that most adults in the child's environment will not know and use braille. Therefore, it is important to create a supportive environment with as much expertise and knowledge as possible. Family members and early childhood educators who learn the braille alphabet are able to participate more fully as knowledgeable others in the literacy development of these children. Also, providing interactions between the child and proficient braille readers who can serve as role models offers another dimension to the feedback from knowledgeable others.

Principles for Providing a Balanced Literacy Program

While many of the conditions for learning described by Cambourne occur naturally in the lives of children who are sighted, they may not be as consistently available in the lives of children who are blind or visually impaired. For this reason, it is important for family members and early childhood educators to work together to create a supportive environment and to provide access to a variety of direct experiences that will provide the foundation for developing literacy skills. Of greatest importance is balancing attention on a variety of experiences, including those that relate to general development and those related specifically to development of literacy skills. Four interrelated principles for providing a balanced literacy program will be addressed next, while specific strategies for promoting early literacy skills will be discussed later in the chapter.

FOCUS ON QUALITY EXPERIENCES AND MEANINGFUL LANGUAGE

The meaningfulness of reading and writing events relates directly to the quality of a child's experiences and his or her understanding and use of language. For example, a child who has background experiences in camping outdoors will develop a rich understanding of words, such as *campfire, forest,* and *tent.* The child can then use these words meaningfully when talking with others. These same experiences and vocabulary are also used to bring meaning to reading and writing activities. If a letter is "written" to a friend about camping or if a book is read aloud on this subject, then the child will have the background needed to understand, enjoy, and benefit from these literacy experiences.

Children with visual impairments and other disabilities often benefit from using symbols to represent people or events in their daily life. Visual or tactile symbols that can be connected to a child's daily schedule or calendar can provide a functional use of literacy skills. Some children benefit from use of photographs or tactile objects used in communication boards or notebooks. For example, parents might prepare the child for a visit from his or her grandmother by showing a photograph of her.

Young children gain rich background experiences by engaging in the typical activities of childhood such as playing in the backyard, visiting grandparents, going to stores, and enjoying family outings. They also extend their direct experiences by watching television or observing others engaged in various activities of which they are not directly a part. Such vicarious experiences are not as available or beneficial for children who are blind or visually impaired. Direct and active engagement in a variety of experiences is needed to assure that a child's language is rich and meaningful. This practice, in turn, will assure that literacy events are similarly meaningful. Some suggestions for providing a wide range of experiences are presented in the accompanying box on "Providing Rich Experiences."

FOCUS ON BOTH READING AND WRITING ACTIVITIES

In providing early literacy experiences for children with visual impairments, family members and teachers should address both reading and writing. "Reading" for a young child may take many forms, such as pretend reading, reading with an adult, and telling a story based on pictures in a book. Similarly, "writing" may take a variety of forms, such as scribbling, drawing, and use of invented spellings. These early attempts at reading and writing are typically referred to as emergent literacy skills. These emergent literacy skills are meaningful to young children and serve a key role in linking abstract symbols with meaning, a link that is essential for development of formal literacy skills.

There may be some tendency to focus only on reading because the primary strategy that is used to promote early reading awareness (that is, reading aloud) is easily understood and applied. However, the strategies for fostering an early understanding of writing are not so easily understood, though with some guidance are easy to use. Because writing, by nature, actively engages the child through pencil strokes or braillewriter movements to produce abstract symbols, a balanced focus on writing will help assure that a direct link is made systematically between the abstract symbols that make up words and meaning.

Including writing activities for children who are visually impaired and have additional disabilities may be more difficult, but

PROVIDING RICH EXPERIENCES

➜ Provide a wide range of experiences at home, such as:
- helping prepare a snack or bake cookies;
- picking up the morning paper;
- helping stack dishes in the dishwasher;
- helping rake leaves or plant flowers;
- picking up clothes or toys;
- getting the mail from the mail carrier;
- playing with siblings or friends in the backyard;
- calling Grandma and Grandpa on the telephone.

➜ Expand experiences into the community by providing such activities as:
- playing in the city park with siblings and friends;
- splashing in the baby pool at the public swimming pool;
- exploring the grocery store and stores at the mall;
- visiting a farm with animals and machinery;
- eating at a fast-food hamburger stand and a sit-down restaurant;
- visiting a petting zoo;
- visiting public places such as the post office, fire station, and library.

➜ Make sure the child is an active participant in any experience. He or she should use all the senses, since the more information that is received, the more accurately he or she will understand and be able to use this information as part of literacy experiences.

➜ If your child has vision, visual information should be paired with other types of sensory information during experiences. Again, the more senses that can be used to learn things, the better.

➜ If the experience includes several steps, make sure your child participates in all steps from the beginning to the end of the process. If you child only completes one or a few of the steps, then he or she may be unaware of all of the other steps that someone else completed.

➜ Throughout the experience, be sure to provide your child with the vocabulary associated with it. Then later, when your child hears you read these words, or reads them for him- or herself, the previous experience will provide a basis for understanding the story.

➜ Take advantage of special experiences that come up. While your primary interest is to provide a rich array of common experiences, take advantages of special opportunities. Such experiences will be a valuable enrichment to your child's life and yours.

Adapted from A. J. Koenig, "Growing into Literacy," in M. C. Holbrook (Ed.), Children with Visual Impairments: A Parents' Guide *(Bethesda, MD: Woodbine House, 1996), pp. 227–257.*

such activities are still important. When possible, the teacher and others on the educational team should work with the child to determine appropriate symbols to represent people, places, and events for use in communication devices. Children who are involved in the selection of tactile or visual symbols will use them more effectively.

FOCUS ON READING ALOUD AND "ENGAGED" LITERACY ACTIVITIES

Reading aloud to children, especially young children, is widely accepted as one of the most important factors in overall literacy development (Trelease, 1995). Reading aloud is also important for children who are visually impaired, with or without additional disabilities. While some may consider reading aloud to be a passive activity (that is, an adult reads and the child listens), there are strategies that can and should be used to assure that the child is actively engaged (as described later). A basic principle is to balance reading aloud with other types of literacy events in which the child must be more engaged. For example, acting out a story after it has been read aloud (Miller, 1985) or any form of writing activity requires active engagement on the part of the child. It is important at this point to ensure that literacy activities are extended beyond reading aloud to include other important experiences in which the child is directly engaged in receiving or conveying meaning through reading and writing.

FOCUS ON ACCESS TO LITERACY MATERIALS AND EVENTS

Young children begin to understand reading and writing by having literacy materials, such as books, magazines, greeting cards, and posters, readily available and by having access to models who use those materials in meaningful ways. For children who are blind or visually impaired, steps must be taken to create an environment in which an ample supply of literacy materials is available in accessible media, especially for those who may or will use braille as a primary literacy medium. (Sources for obtaining books in braille and print-braille are listed in the Resources section.) Gaining access to literacy events will require that children with visual impairments are actively engaged in reading and writing activities by adult role models, since observation and imitation of those models typically will not be effective. Children with additional disabilities must have access to functional uses of symbols throughout their day. The key principle is to provide an environment that is rich in both literacy materials and literacy events, which will ensure that the child has ongoing, active, and interesting opportunities to learn about reading and writing.

ENCOURAGING LITERACY DEVELOPMENT

The preceding section offered basic principles as a framework for arranging and providing early literacy experiences. This section discusses specific strategies for putting these principles into practice. These strategies focus on:

- providing a rich literacy environment,
- teaching specific basic or supporting skills,
- providing opportunities for early reading and writing experiences, and
- teaching early "formal" literacy skills.

Providing a Rich Environment

GENERAL APPROACH

A rich environment is one that provides ready access to literacy materials (books, magazines, letters, and notes) and tools (pencils, crayons, writing paper, braillewriters, and braille slates) in appropriate forms, that has a wide variety of literacy tasks occurring throughout the day and evening, that directly engages the child in literacy experiences, and that places a high value on and respect for literacy. To achieve this richness, the literacy environment for children with visual impairments will need to be modified both in the home and in other environments that are important to children, such as center-based preschool programs. Because it will not always be clear during the preschool years whether a child will use a visual system (print) or a tactile system (braille) as their primary literacy medium, it is recommended that literacy materials in both media be made readily available in their environment. Observing young children interact with and respond to visual and tactile learning and literacy materials is a valuable part of the assessment process that will eventually determine the student's literacy medium or media. More information on this process, called *learning media assessment,* is presented later in this chapter.

Providing a rich literacy environment calls for an extensive array of accessible materials to be readily available to the child at home and in preschool programs. It will be important for family members and general early childhood educators to work closely with a teacher of students with visual impairments, since he or she will know a variety of strategies for making print and braille adaptations. See "Creating a Rich Literacy Environment" in this chapter for suggestions about infusing literacy into the environment for children who are blind or visually impaired.

As indicated by these suggestions, careful attention must be paid to adapting books for young children, especially, the pictures that are presented in books. In regard to the adaptation of pictures, a word of caution is appropriate. The use of raised-line drawings or other forms of one-dimensional tactile rendering (such as puff paint or glue) generally should be avoided. Beyond simple geometric shapes, raised-line drawings will not convey the same information to a child who is blind as pictures will for sighted children. Even a simple raised-line drawing of a barn, for example, is not readily identifiable to a child who is exploring it tactilely without extensive prompting and guidance from an adult. The elements of dimension and perspective that are easily understood through visual interpretation will be a confusing array of seemingly random lines when examined tactilely. For a child with a visual impairment, the concept of "barn" will be developed by visiting a barn and actively and tactilely exploring it. Then a three-dimensional model of a barn can be used as a meaningful substitute during a literacy experience. At some point later in a child's education, the efficient interpretation of tactile graphics will be important. When charts, graphs, and maps are introduced in school subjects, specialized instruction in interpreting such displays will be provided by a qualified teacher of students with visual impairments.

FOCUS ON EFFECTIVENESS

CREATING A RICH LITERACY ENVIRONMENT

The following suggestions describe strategies and materials for making print, braille, and/or symbols easily available in the environments of young children who are blind or visually impaired.

➜ Label common items in the child's environment. Use print, braille, and other visual and/or tactile symbols. Focus first on items that are of importance to the child, such as his or her water glass in the bathroom or a nameplate on the bedroom door. It may be useful to first label personal items with the child's name, as this is an important, motivating, and very identifiable word for the child. Later, the specific word that identifies the item (such as *toy box, milk,* and *cereal*) can be used. Braille labeling sheets are available from the American Thermoform

(continued)

Corporation or Exceptional Teaching Aids. Another option is to use braille or large print-labeling guns, which are available from vendors such as MaxiAids.

➔ For a child who is using tactual or visual symbols instead of words in print or braille, make sure that the symbols are clear and consistent. For example, use a specific symbol (such as a texture, color, or picture) to represent the child's name. Then use the symbol whenever a label for identification is necessary. Allowing the child to participate in selecting symbols can help involve the child in the labeling.

➔ Be sure to place labels in positions that will facilitate visual and/or tactile reading. For example, a print label on the silverware drawer should be placed on the front of the drawer. However, depending on the child's height, it may be easier for him or her to read the braille if the label is placed inside the front panel of the drawer and in an upside-down position.

➔ Purchase a variety of print-braille books (see the Resources section for sources) that are of interest to the child and within his or her range of experiences. These books contain both print and braille versions of the same book. Typically, the binding of the original print book is cut off, the pages of the story are brailled onto plastic sheets, the print and braille sheets are reassembled, and the book is rebound. Print-braille books allow both print and braille readers to enjoy the same book at the same time. In this way, sighted parents can read the print words of the book as their child explores the braille words. The key is to have a wide variety of such books from which the child may select those of interest.

➔ Create print-braille versions of existing print books. The method described above for interleafing print pages with braille pages on clear plastic sheets can be followed by someone who is skilled in the braille code. For books with few words on each page, as is typical of early board books, a braille labeler or braille lables may be used to create a print-braille book. However, after the page contains more than a few words or a short sentence, this method becomes less useful since the braille begins to take more room than one page. Since print-braille books are not widely available in Spanish or other foreign languages, family members should work with the teachers of students with visual impairments to create print-braille versions of original books in the child's native language.

➔ Modify the cover of books with a tactile marker or object. For example, a button could be glued onto the cover of *Corduroy* (Freeman, 1972), since a missing button is a key element in this children's classic. Then, just as a sighted child could identify this book from the picture of a stuffed bear on the cover, a child with a visual impairment could identify the book from the button glued to the cover.

➔ Make meaningful modifications of pictures in books and stories. For young children, real objects are the best substitute for pictures. Miller (1985) suggests developing "book bags" to accompany books for young children. Book bags contain important objects that are part of the story. For example, a book bag for *Corduroy* might include a small stuffed bear, a pair of doll-sized overalls, and a detached button. Another option is to include objects within the book itself, either by gluing them onto the page or by placing them into clear plastic sandwich bags and binding the bags into the book. As the book is read aloud, the child can then hold and manipulate the objects that correspond to various parts of the story. When it is not possible to use life-sized objects, scale models may be substituted provided appropriate real-life experiences have taken place prior to or as part of the literacy experience.

➜ Make sure that modified books are durable. Tactile manipulation will place more demands on print–braille books than visual interactions alone. Be certain that books are bound with sturdy bindings, that pages are thick and durable, and that objects included in or accompanying the book are similarly durable. Also, it is preferable for objects that are not glued to the book to be washable.

➜ Place print-braille books in a convenient storage space that can be easily reached and explored by the child. Some books can be placed on the lower shelves of a bookcase if they will stand upright and next to other books. Books with objects in them or accompanied by a book bag may be better placed in a box, hung on a rod, or laid flat on the bookshelf. The important point is to place them in an organized manner than will allow for efficient searching and browsing by a child with a visual impairment. In this regard, a consistent and familiar place for storing books will be most helpful.

➜ Make sure that other sources of literacy materials in the environment are available in accessible media. For example, braille blocks (containing both print and braille letters) can be purchased through specialty companies, such as Exceptional Teaching Aids. Also, in center-based programs, information on bulletin boards, signs that are at child level, number lines on desks, and other similar materials should be modified in accessible visual and tactile formats.

➜ Work with the physical therapist, occupational therapist, and others to create appropriate visual or tactile symbols that are meaningful and functional, for children whose additional disabilities necessitate communication devices.

Alan J. Koenig & M. Cay Holbrook

USE OF BRAILLE BY FAMILY MEMBERS AND EARLY CHILDHOOD TEACHERS

Children who will or may learn to read and write braille need to have adults in their lives who know and use braille. A teacher of students with visual impairments will have braille skills, but this teacher may not be as involved in the child's early preschool education on a daily basis as family members and general early childhood educators are. Therefore, team members who do not know braille should learn at least the alphabet and, perhaps, the entire braille code. The 26 configurations that represent the letters of the alphabet (shown in Figure 5.1), common punctuation marks, and the convention for capitalizing words can be learned easily in a few hours. Also, writing with a braillewriter or with a slate and stylus (a portable device for writing braille in which the dots are punched individually) can be learned within this same time frame. A teacher of students with visual impairments or an adult who is blind can provide this instruction.

The complete braille code contains the alphabet as well 189 contractions and short-form words. For example, when the letter "c" stands alone in a sentence (that is, it has a space before and after it or is written in conjunction with only the capital sign or a punctuation mark), it is read as the word "can." There are similar contractions for 23 of the 26 letters of the alphabet. As another example, the letters "abv" stand for the word "above" when written in braille. There are a variety of other kinds of contractions in braille as well. Learning the contracted braille code and the rules that govern the code may take several months.

There are several key resources that are available for learning the contracted braille code. *Just Enough to Know Better* (Curran, 1988) was written specifically for parents and includes a friendly introduction to braille, along with reading exercises and flashcards for practicing braille skills. *New Programmed Instruction in Braille* (Ashcroft, Sanford, & Koenig, 2001) and *Instruction Manual for Braille Transcribing* (Risjord, Wilkinson, & Stark, 2000) are comprehensive textbooks on the braille code that discuss the rules that govern the code and contain extensive exercises for practicing braille skills.

The standard practice among teachers of students with visual impairments has been to use contracted braille from the initial stages of learning to read braille, even for toddlers and preschoolers. This practice is being challenged now, and some teachers are considering whether the use of uncontracted braille (that is, the alphabet only) would be more appropriate for younger children. While this issue is being addressed through professional dialog and research, it would be safe to say that consistent instruction in uncontracted braille would be more beneficial than no, little, or inconsistent instruction in contracted braille. Therefore, learning at least the basic elements of the code (that is, alphabet, key punctuation marks, and capital sign) would be valuable for parents, early childhood teachers, and others who work with young children who are blind. Such knowl-

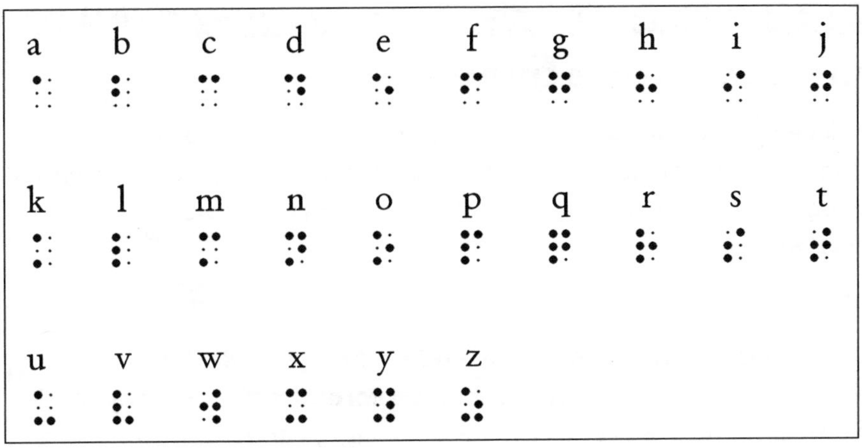

Figure 5.1. The alphabet in braille.

edge will be helpful in reading aloud to a child with a visual impairment and will be increasingly important as the child continues to develop early literacy skills. The reader is referred to Troughton (1992) for a comprehensive discussion of research and issues related to teaching uncontracted braille.

Teaching Specific Skills

Children who are blind or visually impaired must develop strong skills in specific areas to support their literacy activities. Specifically, it is important during the early years to provide support for the development of tactile skills, visual skills, and listening abilities. Throughout their lives, children with visual impairments will use their sense of touch to gather information and explore their environment, so the development of tactile skills is important for all children with visual impairments. Most children who are visually impaired have some level of vision that they can use meaningfully and therefore require support in increasing their visual skills. In addition, effective use of listening to gather information from the environment is one of the most important skills for children who are blind or visually impaired. The accompanying box on "Teaching Skills for Developing Literacy" provides suggestions for helping visually impaired children develop their skills in each of these areas. Children with disabilities in addition to a visual impairment have individual, unique issues relating to all three areas. Educational teams, consisting of parents, educators, and therapists, need to determine the best way to facilitate the development of tactile, visual, and auditory skills for each child.

TEACHING SKILLS FOR DEVELOPING LITERACY

As part of their development of literacy skills, children who are visually impaired need a foundation of strong tactile, visual (if they have some vision), and listening skills. The following suggestions and activities will help children develop their skills in each of these areas.

TACTILE SKILLS

➜ Provide opportunities for the child to develop fine motor skills by choosing tactilely interesting toys and objects. As the child explores the different toys and objects, provide descriptive words such as "soft," "rough," and "smooth."

➜ Increase strength of fingers by encouraging the child to play with Playdough, squeeze clothespins and place them on a piece of cardboard, climb, play the piano, and so forth.

➜ Be careful to allow the child to have control of his or her own tactile exploration of objects and toys. While some gentle prompting is sometimes important to encourage exploration, such prompting should be used only minimally. Sometimes, allowing additional time before intervening will allow the child the amount of time needed to initiate the exploration on his or her own.

➜ Warn the child when new tactile experiences are going to be introduced. For example, let the child know when you are going to pick him or her up. When handing the child something (such as a toothbrush), make sure to say "Here is your toothbrush," rather than just placing it in his or her hand.

➜ Use durable books with heavy pages to allow the child to easily explore books and turn pages. (See the suggestions for creating print-braille books in "Creating a Rich Literacy Environment" earlier in this chapter).

➜ Use hand-over-hand guidance (placing your hand on top of the child's hand and physically guiding the child to accomplish a task) and hand-under-hand guidance (placing your hand underneath the child's hand or wrist and allowing the child to have more control of the activity) to support the child's tactile efforts.

➜ Use daily living skills to encourage tactile exploration. For example, allow the child to snap and button his or her clothes independently. Encourage the child to sort and put toys in their storage area.

➜ Make sure that braille is available around the child's environment, and encourage the child to explore it. Using braille labels in the home and preschool can help the child to begin to use symbols to recognize personal items. (See "Creating a Rich Literacy Environment.")

VISUAL SKILLS

➜ Be comfortable with the use of words such as "see" and "look."

➜ Provide a wide variety of visual experiences for children. Use pictures, posters, and other materials with high contrast and bright colors throughout the child's home and preschool environment.

➜ Use environmental modifications (such as lighting or glare control) to provide a comfortable and pleasant visual environment for the child.

➜ Pair visual information with other sources of sensory information, which will promote a deeper and more accurate understanding of new experiences. For example, when guiding the child through a trip to the grocery store, allow the child the time to visually examine items such as fruits and vegetables, while also pointing out the way that different fruits and vegetables feel and smell. Later at home, tastes can be added to this sensory examination.

LISTENING SKILLS

➜ Play word games (such as "Old MacDonald" and "This Old Man") or rhyming games (such as "One, Two, Buckle My Shoe" and "A-tisket, A-tasket"). Use turn-taking strategies so that the child has to wait for someone else to finish a turn before the child can take his or her turn.

➜ Sing songs that have words that require the child to perform an action (such as "The Itsy Bitsy Spider" or "The Wheels on the Bus").

➜ Play listening games such as Simon Says, in which the child must follow directions from a leader.

➜ Use naturally occurring sounds in the environment to promote listening skills. For example, when walking in the neighborhood, point out sounds that can help the child orient to the environment, such as a wind chime on the neighbor's porch. Be sure to let the child explore the object that is making the sound whenever possible (for example, asking the neighbor to let your child explore the wind chime).

Alan J. Koenig & M. Cay Holbrook

Providing Opportunities for Reading and Writing Experiences

READING ALOUD

Reading aloud to young children, starting in infancy, provides the initial model of proficient reading and contributes to the process of connecting meaning with the abstract symbols (that is, letters and words) presented in books. For a young child, reading aloud may be a relatively passive activity or one in which he or she is actively engaged. When a child has a visual impairment, the importance of active engagement is heightened, since the incidental advantages of reading aloud (for example, identifying a book by its cover, seeing pictures and text in books, or watching an adult turn the pages) may be or will be missed. Using print-braille books and bookbags with objects from the story, and having the child interact with the person who is reading aloud provide a basis for meaningful involvement in a reading aloud episode. The accompanying box, "Suggestions for Reading Aloud," offers some strategies for ensuring that reading aloud is meaningful for a child who is blind or visually impaired.

EARLY READING EXPERIENCES

In addition to active involvement while listening to someone read aloud, there are other early reading experiences that will be helpful for young children with visual impairments in preparing for formal literacy instruction. The key is to move the focus of and responsibility for the literacy experience from the adult (as in the case of reading aloud) to the child. In a sense, these early reading experiences are similar to reading aloud, but with a higher level of engagement on the part of the child. This practice alters the experience for the child from listening to someone read aloud to sharing a reading experience with another person. Each participant shares the literacy experience and the ultimate enjoyment, but the child is never pressured to contribute any more than he or she chooses. Later formal literacy instruction will place increased demands on the child, but at the early stages, the focus is on learning what reading is all about and enjoying the experience.

Young children who have opportunities to interact with proficient readers, have a variety of literacy materials in accessible forms, and have guidance and support from family members or early childhood educators will begin to experiment with reading (and writing, as addressed in the following section). When a child makes such attempts, the role of adults is to support and encourage these behaviors by focusing on the meaning that the *child* generates, even when this is not at first apparent to others. For example, when a child scribbles something on a birthday card to Grandma, it may mean to the child: "Dear Grandma, I love you. Alex." Having the *child* read his or her message will confirm the meaning that was intended. The strategies suggested in "Promoting Early Reading Experiences" later in this chapter may be helpful in encouraging early reading development.

SUGGESTIONS FOR READING ALOUD

➜ Begin reading aloud at an early age, even in infancy. Reading nursery rhymes or short stories that have repeated patterns with expression and enthusiasm will hold the interest of infants and toddlers. As the child is able to hold and manipulate objects, provide him or her with an object that is appropriate to the story. Also, let the child explore the book as you read, so he or she will begin to understand that books are associated with the stories that are being read aloud. Infants and toddlers will learn early that book reading is different from regular speaking.

➜ Use finger plays early as part of reading aloud for infants and toddlers. Finger plays combine familiar rhymes, poems, and songs with hand and finger movements, such as "Patty Cake" and "Itsy Bitsy Spider." The benefit of using finger plays is that the child is directly engaged in the literacy experience, which is also a valuable social time between the parent or early educator and the child.

➜ Gather a wide variety of books for reading aloud, especially as the child becomes a toddler. Using books in accessible media, such as print-braille books, when reading aloud will help the child to make the connection between the symbols on pages of books and meaning.

➜ Choose books for reading aloud that are within the child's range of experiences. This practice will help assure that the literacy experience is meaningful. For books that center on new experiences, provide opportunities for gaining those experiences prior to or as part of reading the book. For example, a family outing to a train station to explore or take a ride in a passenger train could precede the reading of *The Little Engine that Could*. A model train could serve as the substitute for pictures as part of a book box once the actual experience has occurred. Another key experience for *The Little Engine that Could* would be walking up a steep hill to feel the natural exhaustion that occurs as one reaches the top (as was experienced by the Little Engine). This experience could be easily incorporated into an orientation and mobility lesson or any family outing.

➜ Let the child help select books for reading aloud. After reading a book several times, the child will begin to associate a picture on the cover or an object glued on the cover with the particular content when selecting a favorite book to read. Repeated readings of favorite books will allow the child to become very familiar with sentences and phrases, so he or she can help "read" later on. While pretending to read a book based on one's memory of the sentences is not conventional reading, this process is a valuable part of emergent literacy. With repeated experiences with books, children will eventually begin to pick up familiar or high-frequency words from their print or braille configurations.

(continued)

➡ Have the child turn the pages while reading aloud. This can be a fun and important activity for the child to maintain interest and engagement in the story, as well as serving a valuable instructional role. Through this process, the child will gain the understanding that pages contain a certain amount of information, and in order to get more of the story, the page must be turned. For young children, cardboard books may be the easiest to turn, since the pages are composed of thick cardboard. Placing braille in books makes the pages separate a bit, thereby making them easier to turn.

➡ Encourage a child who will read braille to keep his or her fingers on the braille lines and, as the child grows older, to move the fingers along the lines from left to right. At this stage, it is not important that a child's fingers are on the words that are being read. The key here is to make the link between hand and finger movements on the braille lines with the meaningful story that is being read by the adult. As the child becomes more proficient at tracking the braille lines while an adult reads aloud, Miller (1985) suggests that the adult should stop reading when the child stops tracking. This is a powerful means of having the child understand that one's fingers must be moving in order to read braille.

➡ Encourage a child with low vision to take time to explore the pictures in books. Begin with simple pictures with bold lines and colorful objects, and then progress to pictures with increasing amounts of visual information on the page. Adults can help a child with low vision learn systematic scanning techniques by pointing to specific elements of pictures in an organized manner. Distinguishing critical elements in pictures from unimportant or less important elements is part of the process of learning to use vision to gather information. For example, in a picture that depicts a crowded beach during the summer, the critical elements may be the character in the story and a mischievous dog; other elements, such as the other swimmers, the lifeguard, and beach umbrellas, may not be as critical. When a family member or teacher points to the central, critical elements and focuses the child's attention, he or she will learn that some items in pictures are more important than others.

➡ Take time to arrange the visual environment (such as adjusting lighting, eliminating glare, or increasing contrast) to best meet the individual needs of students with low vision. A teacher of students with visual impairments can share with family members and early childhood educators the results from a functional vision assessment and learning media assessment, which should address appropriate environmental modifications for each child. (See Chapter 3 for more information on arranging the visual environment; also see the section at the end of this chapter on the process of learning media assessment.)

Alan J. Koenig & M. Cay Holbrook

PROMOTING EARLY READING EXPERIENCES

Family members and educators can support the early experiments with reading of children who are visually impaired by focusing on the meaning that the child is attempting to create and trying some of the following strategies:

→ Make "object books" based on the child's recent experiences. For example, if the child helped to clean up the back yard, a parent and the child might gather together several things that were encountered during the experience. If the child helped to pick up sticks and trash, rake the leaves, and weed the flowerbed, then a stick, scrap of paper, leaf, and a weed might be glued to separate sheets of heavy paper or cardboard and bound into a book. The cover page might include one of these objects or another object that would represent the entire experience. Then the adult and child can "read" the book together. As each object is examined, the child would tell the story about that part of the experience. In this way, the leaf cues the child's memory about the event, which is the same as using picture cues. As the child turns from page to page, the objects will cue the next part of the story. Such books can be enjoyed over and over again. Object books are equally as effective for students who are blind as for students with low vision.

→ Add print and/or braille to object books. While object books may have no text whatsoever (like early picture books), either single words or short sentences can be added at any time. It is best to start with single words written in bold print and/or in braille. Then the child will know the one word on the page by identifying the object. If family members or early childhood educators are unfamiliar with braille, they will need to learn to read and write the code or work in collaboration with a specialist in visual impairment. For a child with low vision, the adult can point to the word on each page. For a child who is blind, the adult can guide the child's fingers to the words. This process will only be necessary a few times; thereafter, the child probably will find the words spontaneously.

→ Adapt conventional picture books using similar strategies, such as creating print-braille books, gluing an object on the cover, and using real objects in a book bag. Books that are based on a child's actual experiences typically are more interesting and motivating, however, since they relate directly to the child's life. Picture books with single objects on each page are a good option for toddlers with low vision, since the extraneous background information is minimized. As children grow older, and as pictures in books become more complex, family members or early childhood educators may need to help them with systematically examining and interpreting the pictures.

(continued)

➔ Write down stories that the child dictates and create books based on the child's experiences. This technique is known as the *language experience approach.* While this can be a primary strategy for teaching formal literacy skills (as discussed later in this chapter), it can also be used as part of early home literacy experiences. It is important to write the book in the appropriate medium for the individual child. If in doubt, both braille and print should be used. These books can be "read" primarily by the child, who will tell the story largely from memory, or jointly read by an adult and the child. After reading the book several times, the child typically will begin to contribute more and more to the reading experience by relying on memory and eventually by picking up key words in print and braille. For the latter to occur, though, someone who is skilled in braille must be available to help guide the child's finger and hand movements to match the story as it is being read aloud. This time is ideal to have an adult who uses braille as a primary medium read with the child.

➔ Provide opportunities for the child to contribute more and more during shared reading experiences, especially after books have been read several times. In rhymes and books with repeated patterns, the adult reader may pause at the point that the pattern appears in the story and let the child fill in the words. For example, while jointly reading "The Three Little Pigs," the adult (with appropriately animated expression) can read ". . . and the wolf said . . ." and the child will fill in "I'll huff, and I'll puff, and I'll blow your house down." In a similar manner, predictable words in other stories or the ends of sentences can be left for the child to fill in during shared reading. Words or phrases that make sense in the context of the story should be encouraged and reinforced, even when the words do not match the text.

Alan J. Koenig & M. Cay Holbrook

EARLY WRITING EXPERIENCES

Providing opportunities for young children with visual impairments to explore writing is as important as early reading experiences. Children typically begin this process by observing adults in the environment engage in writing activities and then scribbling or drawing as a way to imitate writing. Such scribbles or pictures will not conform to standard written language, but the meaning they hold for the child is the key to forming the foundation that will later lead to conventional writing and spelling in kindergarten and the early primary grades. For children who are blind or visually impaired, overt modeling of writing will be needed, along with more directed opportunities to engage in early writing experiences. "Promoting Early Writing Experiences" in this chapter provides suggestions for activities

PROMOTING EARLY WRITING EXPERIENCES

The following suggestions will give young children who are visually impaired a variety of opportunities to become involved in writing activities:

→ Use *writing aloud* to model writing activities. This technique may seem awkward at first to family members and to some early childhood educators, but it provides a powerful and effective way to let children with visual impairments know about the purpose of writing. The basic strategy is simple: the adult verbalizes the steps in the writing process as he or she completes the task. For example, the parent might engage the child in preparing a list, saying out loud each item as it is written, perhaps even spelling the words.

→ Use writing materials and implements that match the child's potential medium (paper and pencil for a child with low vision and braillewriter or slate and stylus for a child who is blind) when writing aloud. If the child's primary literacy medium has yet to be selected, then the family members and teachers should alternate between print and braille in modeling writing. For a child with low vision, the adult should make sure that he or she is positioned near enough to observe the writing process. For a child who is blind, the parent or teacher should make sure that the child has had prior experiences with a braillewriter or slate and stylus, so he or she will associate the sound with the act of writing. Another option is to allow the child's fingers to rest on the brailler keys, so he or she knows when the adult is pressing the keys. When writing with the slate and stylus, the adult and child can hold the stylus together, and the adult will actually do the writing.

→ Focus on meaningful activities that are of importance to the child when using writing aloud, such as making lists, writing messages or letters to relatives, signing greeting cards, writing down the address for a friend's birthday party, writing a note to the child's teacher, labeling personal items, and signing forms for school.

→ Provide appropriate writing materials, utensils, and equipment in convenient places for the child. Children with low vision should have access to materials like drawing paper, blank writing paper, crayons, pencils, and markers. A screen board (a writing and drawing surface made of a heavy piece of cardboard covered with window screen) might be helpful for providing tactile feedback while writing or drawing. A child who is blind should have access to a brailler and/or slate and stylus and braille paper. Young children probably will not be able to load the paper independently, so the parent and child might do this together and then leave the paper in the brailler or braille slate so it is always ready. Also, children who are blind may want to write or draw with crayons, since they know their friends or preschool classmates are doing so. Therefore, crayons, drawing paper, and a

(continued)

screen board should be available. Children who are blind will need to have hand-over-hand modeling in using the brailler and braille slate. After several modeling sessions, the child will then be able to "scribble" in braille as others scribble in print.

→ Encourage the child to use scribbling, drawing, or invented spellings to communicate ideas and thoughts. For example, when sending a greeting card to a friend, the child should be encouraged to sign the card in either print or braille. Depending on the age of the child, this might take the form of print scribbles, several braille dots, or invented spellings. After the child has written something, have him or her read back to you what was written.

→ Encourage the child to keep a journal or diary. This book might include pictures that the child draws or sentences that are written with scribbles or invented spellings that tell what happened in a given day. Another option is for the child to dictate some thoughts and for the parent or teacher to write them down or for the child to record the thoughts on a tape recorder (Miller, 1985). All of these provide ways to store ideas and then read them back later to relive previous experiences. Also, journal writing provides a natural way to pair the reading and writing processes.

Alan J. Koenig & M. Cay Holbrook

that encourage young visually impaired children to experiment with writing.

Teaching Early Formal Reading and Writing Skills

During the infant and toddler years, the focus of early literacy experiences centers on providing models of proficient literacy users, providing exposure to literacy materials and events, engaging young children directly in literacy activities, and supporting them as they make initial attempts at reading and writing. Beginning around the developmental age of 3 years, a child who is blind or visually impaired will need to start a systematic instructional program in literacy skills. This timing is especially true for students who are blind and will use braille as a primary medium. Also, for students whose literacy medium has not been determined, the same type of instructional program is needed. Because of the focus on developing the unique skills related to braille reading and writing, a teacher of students with visual impairments must be available to deliver this instruction. Additionally, students with low vision have unique needs related to their effective use of vision for reading and writing, and they also require the consistent involvement of a specialist in visual impairment. Since the early literacy needs of young children who are blind and those with low vision are often different, they will be discussed separately in this section.

PREBRAILLE SKILLS

For students who will or may use braille as a primary literacy medium, the teacher of students with visual impairments will begin a formal sequence of instruction that has been traditionally referred to as "prebraille" skills. This set of skills focuses on tactile perception, finger and hand movements, and identification of braille characters. The early sensory skills developed during the infant and toddler years will now be expanded and refined to allow a young child to perceive braille characters and words and to use hand and finger movements efficiently to read connected text as he or she progresses through preschool and kindergarten and into first grade.

As a general starting point, the teacher of students with visual impairments should provide direct instruction in prebraille skills for about a half hour up to one hour, five days per week (Koenig & Holbrook, 2000). This period of instruction typically lasts from the beginning of the preschool years through kindergarten. During this time, the teacher of students with visual impairments will provide direct instruction in areas such as the following:

Prebraille Skills

→ teaching hand and finger skills,

→ teaching tactile discrimination, perception skills, and hand movements,

→ fostering early letter and simple word recognition skills,

→ increasing conceptual knowledge and vocabulary skills,

→ increasing listening skills,

→ expanding the student's experiential base,

→ fostering early reading and writing skills,

→ fostering motivation for, and enjoyment of, reading,

→ applying braille in authentic contexts, and

→ bridging early literacy and beginning braille literacy (Koenig & Holbrook, 2000a).

Early formal instruction in reading braille for a preschool-age student from the teacher of students who are visually impaired may include "hand-under-hand" support for reading each line.

Since much of the uniqueness of instruction at this stage relates to braille, it is important for the teacher of students with visual impairments to use strategies to provide integration of mechanical skills with meaningful literacy skills. Lamb (1996) presented a creative way to foster tactile perception and hand movement skills within a meaningful context. As described more fully in Figure 5.2, a braille cell is given a certain meaning, related to a recent experience of the child, and then used for teaching tactile perception skills. For example, a child who had just been to a pumpkin patch to pick a pumpkin for Halloween could be told that a full braille cell (⠿) represents pumpkins. This symbol could then be placed two or three times in a row of cells with single dots (⠄) representing the field. The child would then be directed to search down the field and find the "pumpkins." Later, as the child learns alphabet letters, the configuration for the letter *p* (⠏) could be substituted in place of the full cell and, eventually, the word *pumpkin*. The possibilities with this approach are endless when used by a skilled and creative teacher.

There are other approaches as well to fostering early literacy skills during this developmental period, and one additional strategy will be mentioned here. The *language experience approach* uses the child's actual experiences as a basis for writing stories and making books. The child dictates to the teacher a story about a recent experience, and the teacher transcribes it in braille. This story is then used for teaching early word-recognition skills, primarily through associations formed by reading the story together with the teacher over a period of days. A direct match between the words under the child's fingers and the words being spoken is essential for this technique to have instructional value. Therefore, the teacher must be highly skilled and fluent in reading braille. A more complete discussion of the language experience approach with young braille readers is presented in Koenig & Holbrook (2000b). (See also Castellano and Kosman, 1997; Wormsley and D'Andrea, 1997; Swenson, 1999; Olson, 1981 for key resources on teaching braille literacy skills.)

While the teacher of students with visual impairments will take the lead in providing early formal literacy instruction, all members of the team will have a role in the process. Parents should continue to read aloud to their child at home, as well as to engage in shared reading and writing activities. The teacher may send stories or books home with the child, and these should be read to the child during the evening. During the school day, early childhood specialists will work to integrate braille into the child's daily activities. Both the parents and the early childhood specialist should coordinate their efforts closely with the teacher of students with visual impairments to assure that appropriate and meaningful literacy experiences are being reinforced.

DIRECT INSTRUCTION IN LITERACY
FOR STUDENTS WITH LOW VISION

For students with low vision, the teacher of students with visual impairments will work closely with family members and early childhood educators, as well as providing direct instruction during the preschool years. This instruction typically will take place less frequently than for students who are blind, since others on the educational team and family members will be able to assist with teaching literacy skills. The focus of this instruction generally will be on integrating the child's use of visual skills into typical activities, teaching use of optical and nonoptical devices in near and distant environments, and teaching listening and technology skills. Some children will need direct instruction in print literacy skills because of the nature of their visual impairment or because they are not making adequate progress in a general-education literacy program. Also, some children with low vision will also learn to read braille; if so, they will require a greater intensity of instruction as described above. The reader is referred to D'Andrea and Farrenkopf (2000) for more information and guidance on teaching students with low vision.

Exercise 1 demonstrates different levels of representation of key elements (e.g., gold)

1. **Child's Language:** "We went to Sovereign Hill and I found some gold."

   (a) distinctive pattern to represent *gold*

   ⠿⠿ ⠿⠿ ⠿⠿ ⠿⠿ ⠄⠄⠄⠄ ⠿⠿ ⠿⠿ ⠿⠿ ⠿⠿ ⠄⠄⠄⠄ ⠿⠿ ⠿⠿ ⠿⠿ ⠿⠿

   (b) initial letter or contraction

   ⠄ ⠄ ⠄ ⠄ ⠿ ⠄ ⠄ ⠄ ⠄ ⠄ ⠿ ⠄ ⠄ ⠄ ⠿

   (c) whole word

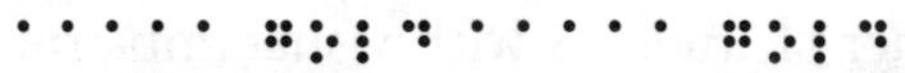

   ⠄ ⠄ ⠄ ⠄ ⠿⠢⠇⠞ ⠄ ⠄ ⠄ ⠄ ⠿⠢⠇⠞

Exercise 2 demonstrates how the task of discriminating the *eggs* can be made more difficult by increasing tactual complexity.

2. **Context: Easter theme.**
   The Easter bunny hops through the grass leaving eggs for children to find. The eggs are increasingly difficult to find as the grass gets thicker and longer, requiring finer discrimination.

   Activity: Look for the eggs. Go carefully (lightly) so you don't step on them. Can you count the eggs? (Establish *grass* before looking for *eggs*.)

   grass

   ⠇⠇⠇⠇⠇⠇⠇⠇⠇⠇⠇⠇⠇⠇⠇⠇⠇⠇⠇⠇⠇⠇⠇⠇

   egg

   ⠇ ⠇ ⠇ ⠇ ⠇ ⠇ ⠈⠿⠿ ⠇ ⠇ ⠇ ⠇

   ⠇⠇⠇⠇⠇ ⠈⠿⠿ ⠇⠇⠇⠇⠇ ⠈⠿⠿ ⠇⠇

   ⠿⠿ ⠈⠿⠿ ⠿⠿ ⠿⠿ ⠈⠿⠿ ⠿⠿ ⠿⠿ ⠈⠿⠿

Exercise 3 illustrates how the same patterns could be used to represent different text or elements within text.

3. **Child's Language:** "We found some mushrooms in the schoolground."

   Activity: Child is asked to look in the grass to find the mushrooms. Step lightly so as not to squash them. Count the mushrooms. (Establish *grass* before asking child to locate *mushrooms*.)

Figure 5.2. Activities for early braille instruction.
Source: Reprinted from G. Lamb, "Beginning Braille: A Whole Language-Based Strategy, *Journal of Visual Impairment & Blindness, 90* (3) (May–June 1996), p. 188.

. . . .
. . . . . ⠶ . . . . ⠶ . . . . . ⠶ . . .
. . ⠶ . . . . . . ⠶ . . . . ⠶ . . .
. . . . . ⠶ . . . . ⠶ . . . . . ⠶

The same pattern could be used to represent the following text:

People standing on the platform at the station.
Houses on the street.
Rocks in the water.

Sequential elements can be added to maintain story line as in Exercise 4.

4. We found some mushrooms growing in the school ground.

. . ⠶ . . . . ⠶ . . . . . . ⠶ . . . . . ⠶

We picked all the mushrooms.

. . . .

OR People standing on the platform at the station.
The people caught the train.
OR Rocks in the water.
The tide has covered them up.

5. **Child's Language:** "We went to the beach and I swam in the waves."

Activity: See how far out you can swim. See how fast you can swim.

sand   waves
. . . . . . ⠄ ' ' . . ' . . ' . . ' . .

child
. . . . ⠶ . . . . . ' ' . .

. . . . . . ⠶ . ' ' . . ' ' . .

. ' ' . . ' ' . . ' ' . . ⠶ . ' '

The same pattern could be used to represent the following text:

A beach ball washed away by the waves.
A car on a bumpy road.
Sailing in a yacht.

LEARNING MEDIA ASSESSMENT

One of many important decisions that must be made for a young child with a visual impairment during the first several years of life is determining how he or she will read and write. This is known as his or her *literacy medium or media.* The decision on whether a child will read in print, braille, or both is based on a systematic assessment process commonly called *learning media assessment.* Such a process is required by the Individuals with Disabilities Education Act (IDEA), which assumes that educational teams will provide for instruction in braille literacy skills for children who are blind or visually impaired unless a learning media assessment shows that braille is not appropriate for the child. It can take as long as several years to make this determination, so instruction in early tactile skills, hand and finger use, and possibly braille skills will typically be provided to all children with visual impairments until a sound decision is possible.

Over a period of time (generally several years in the case of an infant, toddler, or preschooler), the teacher of students with visual impairments and others on the educational team will gather objective information in key areas, such as:

Contents of a Learning Media Assessment

➜ the child's natural use of visual, tactile, auditory, and other sensory cues for gathering information during routine activities;

➜ the child's use of sensory information to complete tasks that relate to near academic and literacy tasks;

➜ the child's visual working distance from the page and the size of objects that he or she can readily and accurately identify using vision;

➜ the implication of the child's visual impairment in regard to whether its status is stable, progressive, or uncertain; and

➜ the implication of any additional disabilities that the child may have, especially related to the appropriateness of a conventional versus an alternate literacy medium (Koenig & Holbrook, 1995).

Data in these and other areas are gathered through observation of the child during routine activities or during instructional sessions.

SIDEBAR 5.1 **QUESTIONS TO GUIDE THE INITIAL LEARNING MEDIA ASSESSMENT PROCESS**

➜ When people enter the room, does your child recognize them by listening to them talk, touching them, or seeing them?

➜ When reaching for a toy, is your child attracted to it visually, or does he or she use other clues such as bumping into it or hearing a sound from it?

➜ When exploring toys or other objects, does your child use touch or vision?

➜ Does your child tell likenesses and differences in toys or other objects by touch or by sight? For example, does your child tell her shoes from someone else's shoes by looking at both pairs or by touching them?

➜ Does your child accurately identify objects at near distances (within 12 to 16 inches of the eyes) using vision or using other clues such as touch or sound? At intermediate distances (between 16 and 24 inches)? At far distances (beyond 24 inches)?

➜ Does your child accurately identify, visually or tactilely large objects (like a teddy bear or toy)? Small objects (like a paper clip, coins, or marbles)?

➜ When your child uses fine motor skills (such as stacking blocks or cutting with scissors), does he or she use vision or touch?

➜ When reading from a print book, does your child show interest in the pictures, or does he or she prefer to examine some real object that is associated with the story?

➜ When reading from a print-braille book, does your child attend more to the braille or to the print?

➜ Does your child scribble, write, and draw using his or her touch or vision?

➜ If your child is recognizing his or her name or other simple words, is he or she doing this in print or in braille?

Source: Adapted with permission from A. J. Koenig, "Growing into Literacy," in M. C. Holbrook (Ed.), *Children with Visual Impairments: A Parents' Guide* (Bethesda, MD: Woodbine House, 1996) pp. 252–253.

Specific questions that may help to guide this process are presented in Sidebar 5.1.

The early years of a child's life provide an ideal time for exploring the child's use of sensory information and responses to instruction and for documenting observations. Educational teams should not feel rushed to make a decision on the primary literacy medium or media. Having the time to increase the use of all senses, even if a particular sense will not be used for reading and writing, is a luxury that exists only during the early years. All children with visual impairments should have opportunities to learn to use their tactile sense efficiently. This may include early fun experiences with braille (such as those suggested by Lamb in Figure 5.2) and concurrent teaching of the print and braille alphabets and simple words. Placing similar levels of emphasis on print and braille in the early years will provide quality, objective information, which will help to inform the selection of the child's literacy medium or media. Also, this practice addresses the spirit of the IDEA requirements on braille.

At the point when multiple sources of data are confirming the child's preferences and needs, the educational team will meet to discuss the findings, consider the implications, and to select the child's initial medium or media. Generally, students who prefer to use visual information for learning (both in structured or unstructured settings), show potential for increasing the use of vision, and have stable eye conditions may be likely users of print. Students who prefer to use tactile and auditory information for learning, show potential for increasing the use of these senses, and/or have unstable or deteriorating eye conditions may be likely users of braille. However, these decisions are quite complex and should not be assumed to be as simple as these two statements suggest. Other factors, such as the child's psychological mindset and the parents' wishes, must be considered in making a decision. While there is no required time frame, typically the decision on a child's literacy medium will be made prior to the beginning of a formal literacy program in kindergarten or first grade.

After the initial decision is made on a child's literacy medium, the learning media assessment process will continue. The focus of the assessment is then placed on whether the initial decision continues to be appropriate, or whether a change is needed in the literacy medium. This may involve changing to a new medium or adding a secondary or supplementary medium. Also, the continuing phase of learning media assessment focuses on adding additional communication and literacy skills to the student's repertoire of literacy tools (such as learning new technology skills, use of low vision devices, and slate and stylus).

CONCLUSION

The development of literacy skills begins very early in life. Children who are blind or visually impaired must be provided opportunities to have experiences parallel to their sighted age mates which will encourage the establishment of literacy skills. Children with visual impairments face some unique challenges during the preschool years that may have an impact on learning to read and write and gaining meaning from their literacy experiences. Because of these unique challenges, it is critically important that they be provided with rich and varied literacy experiences and the direct support of a knowledgeable teacher of students with visual impairments. An early focus on literacy skills can help young children with visual impairments build a foundation for a life of using and enjoying reading and writing.

6 SOCIAL FOCUS

Developing Social Skills and Promoting
Positive Interactions

CONTRIBUTOR

Diane L. Fazzi

D eveloping a positive self-image is part of a continual emotional and social growth process and is a significant area of development for all young children. Meaningful relationships with others form the basis from which children perceive their social environment and gain confidence to explore and learn about the world. Most social skills are learned incidentally by young children who are sighted as they observe those around them modeling appropriate social behaviors and interactions. The process of acquiring social competence is quite different for young children who are blind or visually impaired. Sacks and Silberman (2000b) suggest, "Perhaps of all the developmental processes, socialization is most strongly affected by vision" (p. 377).

This chapter provides an overview of the development of social skills in young children. Early social interactions with both caregivers and peers are examined, and challenges for young children who are blind or visually impaired are identified. Considerations for assessing social skill development are discussed, and strategies for supporting caregiver–child interactions, interactions with peers, and the appropriate use of social skills are provided.

DEVELOPMENT OF SOCIAL SKILLS IN YOUNG CHILDREN

Social competence in young children—the ability to use a variety of appropriate behaviors to initiate and maintain positive social interactions—develops through opportunities for observation and imitation of others, as well as through positive experiential learning from social situations (Sacks & Silberman, 2000a&b). The ability to engage in relationships with others is a fundamental developmental skill (Greenspan & Wieder, 1997) that forms the basis upon which a sense of self develops.

Early Caregiver Interactions

Early social interactions play an important role in the development of children. The first important social relationship is formed between the infant and the primary caregiver or caregivers. Face-to-face interactions, emphasizing facial expressions, gestures, and vocalizations, create a means for infants and adults to regulate attention and provide responsive caregiving (Brazelton & Cramer, 1990). Visual cues (such as making eye contact or seeing someone smile) are often important to successful initiation of and response to a range of social interactions. From very early on, parents watch their newborns for signs of contentment or distress. Prior to the development of language, infants can use facial expressions, body posture, and crying to express their needs and emotions. Similarly, infants learn to interpret visual cues from their caregivers before they are able to understand the spoken language (Brazelton & Cramer, 1990). Important concepts to understand when considering the complexity of caregiver–child interactions include:

- the child's temperament,
- the responsiveness of the caregiver,

- attachment, and

- autonomy.

These variables have a dynamic and profound effect on the relationship between child and caregiver, and in turn, on the child's social development.

CHILD TEMPERAMENT

Thomas and Chess (1977) and (see also Lieberman, 1993) documented the varying behavioral styles or temperaments of infants and young children. Children are born with dispositions that may be considered "easy" or "difficult" for caregivers to manage. Infant temperament includes the child's:

- activity level,

- regularity in eating and sleeping schedules,

- length of attention span and persistence in completing tasks,

- relative ease in adapting to changes in routines, and

- overall degree of fussiness.

Each child varies along such variables, and the ultimate goal of caregiving should be to create a loving environment that is responsive to the baby's unique behavioral style and creates a sense of comfort for the child within his or her environment.

CAREGIVER RESPONSIVENESS

In the infant's first year of life, the caregiver's overall responsiveness and consistency is key to the child's development of self-esteem and expectations for later social interactions. In fact, Klein, Chen, & Haney (2000) support the belief that "Responsive interaction with primary caregivers is the most significant factor in a child's development" (p. 2). Responsiveness includes the ability to interpret an infant's cues and provide what the baby needs in a somewhat timely and consistent fashion. For example, a highly active and energetic mother may be available and interested in engaging her young child in turn-taking games such as peek-a-boo. In order to be truly responsive, however, she must be able to recognize when the child signals that he or she is overstimulated or tired of the interaction and then give the child time to regroup or rest. When the caregiver's style of parenting matches the baby's temperament, it is relatively easy to be responsive and consistent. However, when there is a mismatch between the caregiver's style and the baby's behavioral style, developing and maintaining a consistent and responsive environment can be challenging. For example, a parent who requires regular sleep in order to function clearly may be challenged to provide a responsive caregiving environment for an infant who does not seem to maintain regular sleep patterns and awakens frequently throughout the night and day.

ATTACHMENT

When infants are provided with responsive caregiving, they begin to develop attachments to their primary caregivers in the early months of their first year of life. Attachment behaviors can readily be observed, such as:

- recognition of caregiver,
- different reactions to people other than the primary caregivers,
- separation anxiety and reactions to strangers, and
- social referencing (the periodic "checking in" that children do with their parents as they begin to explore their surroundings, new objects, and people).

Depending on the situation and the child's comfort level, checking-in may be visual or a physical return to the caregiver's side or a hand placed on the caregiver's knee. For children who are verbal, a vocal exchange can also be used to verify that the caregiver is nearby and monitoring the child's safety and well-being. As Pearce (1992) notes, "Vision plays an important role in the development of attachment. The sighted child continually uses visual cues to draw the caregiver closer and to stay connected during brief physical separation" (p. 51).

AUTONOMY

While bonds with caregivers are vitally important to a child's social-emotional development, so too is the development of a sense of autonomy. Autonomy is based upon the child's understanding that he or she is separate from objects and others in the environment and from a motivation to manipulate those objects and people (Pearce, 1992). Autonomy, a desire to do things independently, is an important aspect of early childhood development. The early years can be a confusing mix of "I want Mommy!" and "I wanna do it myself!" Early social interactions with caregivers and other family members form a springboard for early social interactions with peers.

Early Peer Interactions

As infants grow, their desire and need to develop social connections extends beyond the family. Early peer relationships are thought to serve several functions for young children, including companionship, recreation, and general emotional support. Fazzi (1993) writes, "Expectations for attentiveness and responsiveness from peers are based on prior interaction experiences with the primary caregiver" (p. 8). For example, children who are raised in a responsive caregiving environment will likely expect generally positive treatment and interactions from peers.

ACCEPTANCE BY PEERS

In order to have positive social interactions and play experiences, children must be able to gain acceptance from peers. "Interactions with peers give children unique opportunities to develop and refine skills that are important for social development and acceptance by peers" (Kekelis, 1992, p.13). During interactions with peers, young children practice and learn how to:

- talk with peers,

- initiate play with peers,

- develop reciprocal friendships, and

- resolve conflicts with others.

These social learning opportunities are quite different from similar interactions with family members.

Young children grow up with an understanding of the social roles in their family. Depending on the family's culture, there may or may not be much room for negotiation of these social roles with parents, siblings or extended family members. For example, a given family may assert that older siblings must always relinquish toys to the youngest child when requested versus a negotiation for toys among peers.

In contrast, children may have to demonstrate their social interaction and play skills to other children to gain acceptance from peers. In other words, children often have to prove to one another that they will make good playmates. In addition, children have to be prepared for the possibility of rejection by peers within some social and play situations. This potential rejection by peers is very different from the unconditional acceptance of a parent who will likely be more available to the child regardless of social skills demonstrated. Young children who are socially competent with peer interactions are often consistent in their ability to initiate actions with peers, sustain relationships over time, and resolve conflict without aggression (Asher, Renshaw, & Hymel, 1982). Accepted peers are generally friendly and respond positively to other children when they initiate interactions (Dodge, 1983), often showing genuine interest in others, expressing appropriate degrees of affection, and offering compliments to others.

Young children are usually able to manage group-play situations when there are two or three children to share toys and space with, but larger numbers may present more challenges (Kekelis, 1992). Vision is used to monitor each other's actions and movements and can assist young children in quickly transitioning between rapidly changing play scenarios. Vision is especially helpful to toddlers at play, as they cannot readily rely upon clear verbal exchanges to inform each other of their intentions.

FORMS OF PLAY

As children develop, they are interested in and able to engage in increasingly complex forms of play. Types of play are commonly described according to two separate variables—whether or not the child is playing alone or with others, and how the child is using toys and objects in play. The following terms are used to describe how children play with one another or by themselves (Rettig, 1994):

Types of Play

→ *Solitary play*—also called "solo" play, when children play alone, show little interest in other children at play, and do not attempt to play with others

→ *Parallel play*—when children play alongside or near other children with either similar or different toys or items; some interest in what the other children are doing is noted

→ *Cooperative play*—when children are actively playing with others in an organized, give-and-take fashion

The following terms describe how children interact with and use toys and objects in their play:

→ *Manipulative play*—when children are engaged with toys or objects primarily through exploration such as mouthing or banging (for example, banging a spoon on the floor to hear the noise it makes or pushing buttons on a battery-operated toy to make lights flash or music play)

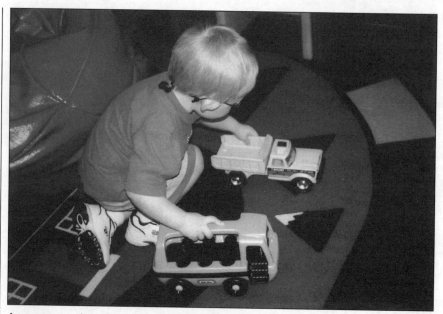

Age-appropriate functional play with toy trucks.

→ *Functional play*—when children use toys or objects in the way in which they are intended during playtime (for example, pretending to drive a toy car or cook with a toy saucepan)

→ *Symbolic play*—when children pretend that an object is another object in their play scenario (for example, pretending that cotton balls are scoops of ice cream or that a laundry basket is a boat)

→ *Dramatic play*—when children assume pretend roles in their play scenarios (for example, pretending to be a doctor or a cat)

Children can be engaged in combinations of both of these categories of play. For example, a young child can be engaged in functional play with toys alongside another child who is operating a jack-in-the-box. Similarly, a child can be engaged in solitary dramatic play (pretending to be a superhero) or cooperative symbolic play in which a small group of children organize a tea party.

Play, and specifically play with others, requires children to combine their language, cognitive, and motor abilities in an active way. Children who are visually impaired and children who have multiple disabilities may exhibit delays in one or more of these developmental areas, which can have a significant effect upon their play skills and social interactions (Rettig, 1994).

DEVELOPMENT OF SOCIAL SKILLS IN YOUNG CHILDREN WHO ARE BLIND OR VISUALLY IMPAIRED

As stated earlier, social competence in young children occurs through observation and imitation of others (Sacks & Silberman, 2000b). Social skill development is highly contingent upon visual cues and visual feedback. In order to support the development of social skills for young children who are visually impaired, families and professionals must work together to create meaningful opportunities for children to practice and learn these skills in natural environments. Each of the aspects of social skills development that were previously discussed will be revisited to examine the implications for young children who are blind or visually impaired.

Early Caregiver Interactions

The primary caregiver(s) provides the young child who is blind or visually impaired with the first opportunity for social learning. Family members can help very young children to learn social skills "through physical modeling, verbal feedback, and tactile cues and by teaching their children to explore the environment through coactive movement and through manipulation of materials and objects during activities" (Sacks & Silberman, 2000a, p. 630). Family members can be encouraged to find creative ways to establish emotional bonds without dependence on visual cues. (For specific suggestions, see the section "Supporting Early Caregiver Interactions" later in this chapter.) Positive social relationships with caregivers can serve as a pattern for success in future social relationships with family, friends, and co-workers.

CHILD TEMPERAMENT

Just as children who are sighted are born with individual temperaments or behavioral styles, so too are young children who are blind or visually impaired. However, blindness does seem to present a potential challenge to the ability to establish regular sleep routines, referred to as "sleep-wake-cycle" disorders in the medical community. Light input through the visual system can impact the secretion of the hormone melatonin. Sack, Blood, Hughes, and Lewy (1998, p. 145) describe the problem in this way:

> *Because they lack photic input to the circadian time keeping sys-*
> *tem, people who are totally blind have body rhythms that are not*
> *necessarily synchronized to the 24-hour solar and social day. As a*
> *result, they commonly experience recurrent episodes of insomnia*
> *and daytime sleepiness that may last days or weeks.*

The secretion of melatonin in blind babies is different than for sighted children, and it is common for some of these children to get their day and night times reversed for a period of time (Espezel & Jan, 1996; Sack, Blood, Hughes, & Lewy, 1998). Families of children who have sleep difficulties may report that their children are awake most of the night, and preschool teachers report that these children want to sleep all morning long. Irregular sleep patterns can lead to an increase in a baby's overall fussiness, which may make it more difficult to care for and be responsive to the child (Espezel & Jan, 1996). Medical treatment with synthetic melatonin in combination with the use of structured sleep routines has been found to have a positive effect on the sleep-wake-cycles of children with visual impairments, including those children with cortical visual impairment and children who have additional disabilities (Espezel & Jan, 1996).

Some young children who are visually impaired may show some difficulty adapting to changes in their immediate environment. For example, children who are visually impaired may be more likely to be fussy when initially picked up. While this lack of adaptability can be a result of a child's individual temperament, it may also be a result of a child with a visual impairment not being able to fully anticipate changes. Providing young children with consistent auditory or tactile cues that changes are about to occur (for example, parents leaving a room) may help children adjust to changes with less irritability and more confidence, knowing that they will get a signal before the next change is going to occur. Sample auditory cues can include the use of a specific phrase, such as "Daddy be right back" or the use of a jingle bell placed on a door handle to announce that someone is about to enter or exit a room. In addition, young children who have dual sensory impairments can be given tactile cues (such as a spoon to hold before breakfast is about to be served).

The smiling behaviors of newborns who are blind are similar to newborns who are sighted. Smiles can be elicited through pleasant touch or tickling and through interesting changes in voice pitch, music, or sounds. Reflexive smiling is visually reinforced through returned smiles, and soon infants who are sighted begin to try to imitate facial expressions. Infants who are blind do not receive the same reciprocal smiling reinforcement, which may diminish the amount of smiling exhibited unless replaced by adequate substitute reinforcement (Fraiberg, 1977). Fraiberg (1977) found that the social smiles of young children who are blind were less frequent and less intense. This difference in social smiling can reduce the satisfaction experienced by others when interacting with the young child and could ultimately lead to interactions that are characterized as less warm or responsive or to fewer interactions, which might hold lasting negative consequences for social development. Professionals can assist families in finding alternative ways to encourage smiling (such as using an expressive voice tone to reinforce smiling) and other important nonverbal, social communication behaviors in young children who are blind or visually impaired. In doing so, important early emotional bonds, social interactions, and overall social development are being supported.

CAREGIVER RESPONSIVENESS

When parenting a child who is blind or visually impaired, family members may need extra support in establishing responsive caregiving routines. Perhaps the biggest challenge is to learn to recognize the nonverbal cues offered by the visually impaired infant as signals to express need, comfort, and discomfort. Without the advantage of visual cues, the infant with a visual impairment may use cues that are different from those expected by parents. For example, a baby who is blind may continually fuss during each diaper change, not because he or she doesn't like to have the diaper changed, but because the feeling of the cool washcloth on the bottom is startling. If the caregiver can learn to interpret that cue, then he or she can help the baby anticipate the cold wipe or warm up the washcloth.

Consistency in caregiving routines is important and helps the young child to anticipate activity transitions. For example, a father can consistently signal the end of bath time with a funny song about diapering, helping the child to anticipate the change in activities. A caregiver's responsiveness to a child's needs helps to support the overall development of positive self-esteem for the child because it lets the child know that he or she is valued by others and that he or she is therefore valuable as a human being.

ATTACHMENT

When primary caregivers can be responsive to their child's needs, they are able to support the development of their child's attachment to them. In some children who are blind, there may be delays in forming attachments as caregivers struggle to interpret the infant's cues and adapt to using nonvisual cues (such as massage, cuddling, whispering, or singing) to communicate love and affection to their visually impaired infant. It is also possible that many infants who are visually impaired are securely attached to their caregivers, yet simply do not exhibit typical attachment behaviors. For example, blind infants who are securely attached to their caregivers may not fuss when less familiar people hold them—a common sign of stranger anxiety—or cry when parents leave the room—a common sign of separation anxiety.

AUTONOMY

Some young children who are visually impaired may rely on actual physical contact with their caregivers rather than the visual form of social referencing that sighted children use while exploring and trying new things. This need to remain close to a caregiver in order to maintain a feeling of security, coupled with the more limited incentives for moving and exploring the environment, may make it challenging for some visually impaired children to experiment with trying things on their own. Children who have additional physical disabilities and limited mobility may need to rely on caregivers to provide them with opportunities to spend some time doing things independently and to do some checking in by saying things like "Mommy is fixing lunch in the kitchen." Some family members may be fearful that young children who are blind will injure themselves if allowed to explore independently. Professionals and family members will need to encourage even the smallest steps towards independence. Even though it may mean slightly more risk of bumps or spills or taking a little extra time to get ready in the morning, families must encourage and praise children for attempts to do things independently. (For more detailed strategies on encouraging independence in young children who are visually impaired, see Chapter 7.)

Early Peer Interactions

In young children who are visually impaired, the absence of visual stimuli may be associated with decreased motivation to move through and explore the environment, to discover and manipulate toys, and to initiate and maintain play with peers. Vision loss makes it more difficult for children to understand and organize objects and sequence the events in the environment that are commonly incorporated within the play patterns of peers who are sighted.

For example, preschool-age children may use play cars to race around a pretend track. A child with a visual impairment might need to be familiarized to the various parts of the car (such as front and back) and shown how to move the car in a racing fashion about the room. Even with these skills in hand, the child with a visual impairment will need to be able to keep track of sighted peers as they move their cars about the room in order to fully participate in the play. Perhaps the child who is visually impaired can sit in the center of the racetrack oval in order to keep pace with the other kids.

Thoughtfully chosen toys, materials, and activities can also have a positive impact on the development of play skills and participation with peers. For specific suggestions on choosing play materials, see the guidelines for making play material selections in the section "Supporting Early Peer Interactions" later in this chapter.

ACCEPTANCE BY PEERS

Preschoolers who are visually impaired—especially those children with severe vision loss who lack the ability to use visual and imitation cues—do not necessarily adopt interactive play styles. Warren (1994) noted that children who are visually impaired do less than children who are sighted to try to promote social interactions with their peers. Kekelis (1992) observed that young children with visual impairments are less likely to state preferences for playing with specific children, respond to peer interests, imitate peer actions, offer compliments to other children, and share toys and ideas in a reciprocal manner. McCuspie (1992) found that children with visual impairments were likely to have fewer friends and sometimes confuse "assigned school buddies" or helpers as true friends.

It is often difficult for young children who are blind or visually impaired to interact appropriately with their peers. In play situations involving sighted peers, the visually impaired child may not be able to keep track of the activities in which the sighted children are involved. Attempts made by sighted children to engage the visually impaired child may be met with behaviors that may be interpreted as demonstrating a lack of interest, responsiveness, and enthusiasm (such as a dropped head, rocking, echolaic response, and the like). Sighted children may quickly lose interest in playing with a child who is perceived as unusual or different.

When children who are visually impaired play with one another, their interactions often appear to lack synchronization. In fact, two visually impaired children who appear to be playing together may actually be engaged in a form of parallel play. As children miss cues from each other (such as when one child has switched toys), they may lose interest in maintaining peer interactions, which often results in increased isolated play patterns for children who are visually impaired.

In trying to support the inclusion of young children with visual impairments in preschool programs with children who are sighted, it is common practice to assign a teaching assistant to facilitate children's adjustment and participation in classroom activities. As adults try to mediate social interactions between children who are visually impaired and those who are sighted, they may inadvertently create a barrier to more appropriate natural social interactions (Kekelis, 1992). The teaching assistant may unwittingly become the go-between in verbal communications. For example, sighted children may ask the adult, "Does Elijah want to play ball?" rather than asking the visually impaired child. The child with a visual impairment may grow dependent upon the adult to manage social situations (such as, suggesting play activities, initiating play with other children, adapting games to make them accessible, and keeping the other children interested in the activity). In such instances, the children who are sighted may increasingly interact with the adult rather than the child with a visual impairment. Careful thought must go into planning how an assistant can best facilitate social interactions for children with visual impairments in inclusive and specialized settings, such as:

_____

Facilitation of Peer Interactions Teaching Assistants

→ insisting that children interact directly with one another,

→ finding time separate from free playtime to orient the child to play areas and play equipment,

→ describing the play activities of other children and giving the child choices as to what to engage in,

→ avoiding hovering over the visually impaired child,

→ allowing the visually impaired child to play alone occasionally in order to provide opportunities for the child and other children to initiate interactions, and

→ giving honest feedback and praise for attempts to initiate and maintain interactions with peers.

_____

Working with families and other professionals, training staff, and providing age-appropriate classroom in-services are essential components of successful inclusion opportunities. For more details on providing responsive in-service training, please see the section on "Supporting Early Peer Interactions" later in this chapter.

FORMS OF PLAY

The types of play that children who are visually impaired engage in may be somewhat different from those of their sighted peers. Warren (1994) noted both qualitative (such as less imaginative use of toys) and quantitative differences (such as less frequency of engaging peers in play) in the play patterns of children with visual impairments. Young visually impaired children exhibit a tendency towards greater frequency of manipulative and fantasy play, while exhibiting fewer instances of functional and dramatic play (Parsons, 1986a&b). An example of functional play is using a child-size model kitchen set to simulate cooking and cleaning activities. Dramatic play is exemplified by acting out a familiar role or event, such as playing doctor and nurse. Rettig (1994) also noted a delay in symbolic play in children who are blind and suggested a link to language development and the delay in consistently using the "I" pronoun.

For children who are blind or visually impaired to develop socially, they need opportunities to interact with peers and strategies that will help them gain acceptance by peers and enjoy playing with others. Ideas for developing social opportunities that will have positive outcomes can be gleaned from an assessment of a child's social skills and interests. A team approach to assessing social skills can provide important information for starting a comprehensive program to support social development.

ASSESSMENT OF SOCIAL SKILLS IN YOUNG CHILDREN WHO ARE BLIND OR VISUALLY IMPAIRED

As with other developmental areas, the assessment of social skills in young children who are blind or visually impaired requires professionals to work in collaboration with families. Developmental checklists in the area of social skills can be used to assist the professional in acquiring an understanding of the typical sequence in which a given set of social skills may be expected to develop. However, relying solely on the completion of such a checklist would be limiting, in that social competence is more than a set of given skills. Social competence must be examined within natural contexts at home and school. After establishing a strong rapport with the family and determining what the family's priorities for social development (such as toileting, interactions with siblings, and using manners with oth-

ers) are, the professional will need to observe the young child's social interactions with family members and peers in natural environments.

Early Caregiver Interactions

Professionals can utilize a variety of strategies to assess the quality of
infant–caregiver interactions. Home observations are an important
part of this assessment process. In as unobtrusive manner as possible,
professionals will want to observe blind infants with their primary
caregivers (and other family members as well, when possible) during
natural routines. If the caregiver is comfortable, the professional can
observe the pair during feeding, bathing, diapering, and play time as
appropriate. In addition to looking for specific developmental skills
(such as recognizing the caregiver) the professional will also want to
consider the overall quality of the interactions and the general comfort level that each has with the other. Such observations can then be
sensitively discussed with the caregiver in order to determine if the
perceptions from the observation are similar to those of the caregiver.
For example, the professional might say, "I notice how content Dylan seems to be in the playpen, but that you both seem anxious when
you pick him up. It seems like your singing really calms him down
when he gets upset after being picked up. How does it seem to you?"
The caregiver may wish to talk about the observation and offer additional information. (For example, a mother might add, "And this was
a particularly fussy day for Dylan. I think he is teething."). Such information will be helpful in generating a complete and unbiased assessment report. Chen & Dote-Kwan (1998) have suggested the use
of videotape as an additional approach for learning about infant–
caregiver interactions. With caregiver permission, interactions could
be videotaped and then watched together.

Assessments may also include scripted or open-ended interviews
or surveys for caregivers to complete. Once again, an open-ended format, in which the caregiver is given an opportunity to describe a
child's favorite activities, most fussy moments and so on, provides a
fuller and more realistic picture of the child's overall social competence. In some instances in which it is difficult to determine the reason for or sequence of a given social behavior, a caregiver might be
asked to keep a log of specific social interaction patterns. For example, each time that the child naps could be recorded in order to determine if the child was developing a regular sleeping schedule. Caution must be taken, however, to ensure that caregivers are not asked
to spend inordinate amounts of time doing record-keeping when
they could be spending time enjoying parenting. Families lead full

and busy lives, and assessment activities used must be both meaningful and unobtrusive.

Early Peer Interactions

Conducting naturalistic observations of peer interactions can be challenging, to say the least. Young children will want to know why a new person is observing in their classroom or playground, and playgroups may be inhibited by the presence of a stranger. It may take some time before the presence of a new professional becomes familiar and accepted by the children so that their interactions become natural. For individuals who are unfamiliar with the play patterns of young children in general, it will be beneficial to spend time observing sighted children interacting at a given preschool prior to starting the assessment.

Kekelis (1992) suggests, "Examine both the rate and quality of interactions over time. It is desirable for peer interactions to increase in frequency and for roles played by both visually impaired and sighted children to be appropriate. To obtain an accurate picture of the visually impaired child's social experiences, careful, unobtrusive observation of interactions is required" (p. 49). In observing interactions with peers, professionals will want to note the following regarding the visually impaired child's social interactions and play:

Assessing Early Peer Interactions

→ the frequency with which the child attempts to initiate interactions with other children,

→ the effectiveness of the strategy that the child uses to interact with other children (such as calling out another child's name),

→ the length of time that the child remains engaged with another child,

→ the frequency and forms of play (such as manipulative or functional play or parallel or cooperative play) that the child engages in,

→ the types of toys and play equipment that the child selects,

→ the ease or confidence in movement that the child exhibits in the play area(s),

→ the manner in which the child maintains contact with toys or objects of interest (such as visually watching an object, mouthing an object to explore it, or by holding on to a toy tightly so that other children do not take it),

→ the willingness of the child to share toys and play materials with others,

→ the manner in which the child expresses preferences and emotions to others (such as by using words, throwing toys, biting others, or holding other children's hands),

→ the manner in which the child deals with conflicts with other children (such as passively withdrawing, negotiating, or hitting),

→ the amount of time the child spends engaging adults in conversations or play versus the amount of time spent engaging other children, and

→ the settings in which the child enjoys playing most.

As professionals spend time observing social interactions among peers, they will develop additional questions that are most relevant for the individual child being assessed or the priorities expressed by family members or teachers.

STRATEGIES FOR SUPPORTING SOCIAL SKILL DEVELOPMENT IN YOUNG CHILDREN WHO ARE BLIND OR VISUALLY IMPAIRED

In developing strategies for supporting social skill development (interaction with caregivers, interactions with peers, and other social skills such as appropriate use of manners) for young children who are blind or visually impaired, it is important to consider cultural and family preferences for establishing goals in these crucial areas. Professionals may ask questions such as:

• "Which caregiving activity is most enjoyable for you? And for your baby?"

• "In what way would you like to see your child interacting with peers from the neighborhood or playgroup?"

• "What table manners would be most helpful to you to make taking your child out to restaurants more comfortable?"

Questions like these provide an important starting point for determining family priorities. When social skills that are important to the family are addressed, the likelihood of follow-through at home is increased.

Supporting Early Caregiver Interactions

Professionals who work in the home with families of infants who are blind or visually impaired can provide invaluable assistance by supporting early infant–caregiver interactions. Leuck, Chen, & Kekelis (1997) suggest that by "emphasizing the endearing qualities of the infant" (p. 36) the early interventionist can help to support the emotional bond between parent and child. Acknowledging positive interactions and responsive caregiving can also support the development of attachments and parental confidence (Leuck, Chen, & Kekelis, 1997). Helping family members to recognize infant cues (especially those that may be different from signals typically used by children who are sighted) and respond accordingly can help set the stage for responsive caregiving. For example, it is common for an infant to respond to the approach of his or her mother by kicking legs and reaching with arms. This nonverbal cue signals to the mother that the baby is happy to see her and wants to be picked up or played with. A child who is blind may offer a different cue and clench fists and maintain a very still body when he or she hears the mother's voice. While this cue is different from what might typically be expected, it can be a clear signal that the baby is happy that Mommy is near. Videotaping can be done (with the caregiver's permission) of particular interactions and then watched together (Chen & Dote-Kwan, 1998). Caregivers can give narrative descriptions and professionals can provide feedback and encouragement regarding the many positive aspects of the session.

Families can incorporate nonvisual forms of play when spending time with their child who is visually impaired. Providing sound cues for tickling games, for example, can help the child anticipate actions and reactions. For example, saying "Tickle, tickle on the belly" before tickling allows the young child to get ready for the game. Using changes in inflection, pitch, and vocal pacing may provide motivation for young children to participate more fully in reciprocal play. For example, a mother might sing a song while bouncing a baby on her knee, and her pitch may rise as she holds her knee higher and higher while bouncing the baby. After doing it consistently, the baby may begin to demonstrate his or her anticipation of the rising knee by raising hands in the air. In this way, the child is participating in the play routine rather than simply acting as a passive recipient of the activity. Such reciprocal routines are very beneficial to the young child's development and can be a rewarding interaction for both infant and caregiver.

Providing a patented list of activities to implement in the home (one that might work for most children) can be helpful, but it places the impetus on families to decide which are most important and how they will incorporate so many things within their daily routine. Such a strategy may be overwhelming to some families. If professionals can take the time to discover the types of typical activities that caregivers and infants enjoy doing together, then approaches can be individually tailored to fit within the family's daily routine and build upon existing strengths. For example, if both infant and caregiver enjoy time spent nursing, the interventionist might suggest using that time to encourage the child who has low vision to initiate and maintain eye contact by having the mother sing a soft, pleasurable song. Similarly, if a father enjoys diapering his young child who has low vision and multiple disabilities, then that might be the perfect time to initiate some simple turn-taking routines like "peek-a-boo behind the diaper." The father could interrupt the game until the young child gives a nonverbal cue (such as kicking feet) that he or she wants more. Tailoring the intervention to the individual family and then making it fun are important for successful goal achievement. For additional suggestions for encouraging such reciprocal activities, see the accompanying box "Strategies for Supporting Early Interactions between Caregivers and Children."

Supporting Early Peer Interactions

An organized social skills intervention strategy is often an essential component of a successful preschool program for children with visual impairments. Early interventionists may help to expand the play repertoire of young children who are visually impaired in several ways. The selection of appropriate and stimulating toys and play materials can help to encourage young children with visual impairments to become actively engaged in exploring and acting upon the environment. For a resource on selecting toys for children who are blind or visually impaired see *Guide to Toys for Children Who Are Blind or Visually Impaired* (2002). Many good toys that are designed for children who are sighted will also be beneficial for children who are visually impaired (for example, wooden blocks, stackable rings, easy-grip balls, dolls, and trucks). Young children may also enjoy playing with the boxes that toys come in, plastic containers, kitchen utensils, pots and pans, and old clothes for dress-up. Such playthings lend themselves readily to engaging in functional play routines like

STRATEGIES FOR SUPPORTING EARLY INTERACTIONS BETWEEN CAREGIVERS AND CHILDREN

Caregivers may find it more difficult to know how to respond to and interact with an infant who is visually impaired. The following suggestions may help families interact positively with their young children and thus stimulate their early social development:

➔ Discover the preferences of caregivers and infants for activities (such as bath time together, rides in the car on freeways or highways, or the infant lying on the diaper changing table while Mom rubs lotion on feet and legs) to use as a foundation for positive and fun interactions.

➔ When working in the home, emphasize to caregivers the baby's lovable traits (such as cute babbling sounds or sweet pouting bottom lip) to support the emotional bond between parent and child. (Leuck, Chen & Kekelis, 1997).

➔ Observe caregiver–infant interactions and help family members recognize the infant's cues (such as clenched fists in anticipation of being picked up) and respond accordingly (for example, say "Are you waiting for Mamma to pick you up?").

➔ Help families understand the impact that visual impairment may have upon interactions with caregivers, siblings, extended family members, and peers and generate some simple strategies to use to alleviate these differences, such as giving an infant time to adjust to changes in caregiver by having the new person talk to the child softly while the first caregiver is still holding the child.

➔ Help families to establish caregiving routines in which the infant can anticipate events (such as always taking a bath before bed) and feel secure about his or her surroundings.

➔ Suggest sound cues that caregivers can use when playing common turn-taking games such as peek-a-boo. For example, while the sighted child is able to visually anticipate the uncovering of Daddy's face and simultaneous "peek-a-boo," a sound cue such as "one-two" can be used to help the blind child anticipate the upcoming "peek-a-boo."

➔ Notice what the child is interested in or paying attention to and model ways for drawing others' attention to the same object or event. For example, "Oh, you like the feel of the water. Let's call Daddy to come join us in the pool." *Joint attention,* simultaneous attention of both adult and child to an object or event, is an important social and communication skill.

➔ Use verbal descriptions to call the baby's attention to things that may be of interest to the adult. For example, while on a stroll the Daddy says to his daughter who has low vision "Oh, Kathryn, Daddy sees a pretty kitty. The kitty is on top of this brick wall. Let me bring you closer to see it, too. The kitty is black and white." Establishing joint attention will help the child learn to engage in reciprocal conversations with others.

Diane L. Fazzi

making cookies. The following guidelines may also be helpful in making play material selections:

Choosing Play Materials

→ Materials should be stimulating (interesting to look at, touch, listen to, or play with—such as a brightly colored jack-in-the-box for one child or a metal whisk that makes interesting noises in bowls and on wooden tables for another).

→ Materials should be easy to handle or operate, age appropriate, and developmentally challenging (require the child to practice an emerging skill, such as stringing beads for a child who is developing fine motor and eye–hand coordination).

→ Materials should provide opportunities for functional play (such as pretending to dial and talk on the phone).

→ Patterned objects, especially black-and-white concentric circles, are interesting to look at for infants who have low vision.

→ Mobiles should contain visually, tactilely, and aurally stimulating items and should be placed at nose level, within the child's reach but tied securely to encourage reaching, but ensure that the young child does not become wrapped in the mobile strings or cords.

→ The environment should be organized so that toys and stimulating objects are close enough to encourage the child to independently retrieve and replace toys.

→ Smaller toys (such as beads or Legos™) can more easily be kept track of by the child when placed in a shallow container or on a tray. However, small objects that may cause choking should not be given to young children who are still placing objects in the mouth.

→ Secured suction toys that can be temporarily attached to a table or highchair tray are helpful for children with motor control challenges.

→ Soft, cuddly plush toys may be tactilely unpleasant for some children who may be sensitive to tactile sensations.

→ Ordinary household items (such as, spoons, containers, hairbrushes, and sponges) can be motivating, manipulative toys that possess functional qualities.

While toy selection is important, it is also imperative that orientation and mobility (O&M) specialists familiarize young children with visual impairments to play settings, indoors and out, including some of the toys and playground equipment in the setting. If visually impaired children are able to competently manipulate or use much of the available play equipment, it may help to increase their play options and overall acceptance by peers. Young children need not have mastery of all of the toys and equipment; it is important that they begin to develop a systematic approach to the exploration of new objects of interest.

Smaller, well-defined play areas may be more manageable for some children who are visually impaired (Skellenger, Hill, & Hill, 1992; Kekelis, 1992); after the child who is visually impaired becomes familiar with the area and toys, a playmate can be invited to join the child. When the child who is visually impaired develops confidence with one playmate, then inviting a second playmate can be considered.

Mediating the play experiences between children who are visually impaired and sighted may be helpful initially. For example, the teacher can encourage other children to describe their activities verbally as an alternative to pointing or use of other nonverbal gestures. The adult can encourage visually impaired children to express their inability to understand visually what is happening by saying, "I can't see that—tell me what you're doing." They can also encourage participation in activities in which both sighted and visually impaired children are interested and feel competent (for example, movement-to-music games, such as the Hokey-Pokey, in a well-defined area; games requiring sighted children to wear blindfolds, such as Pin-the-Tail-on-the-Donkey; and climbing activities for children who have good motor coordination). Without being directive, adults can help bridge the gaps in social interaction often inherent in young visually impaired children's play. As mentioned earlier, adults may unintentionally become the go-between for children who are visually impaired and sighted. The specialist must be careful to avoid becoming the central focus of the child's play, because engaging in verbal interactions with adults may become preferred over socializing with peers. For more suggestions on promoting positive interactions with peers, see the accompanying box on "Supporting Peer Interactions."

Families can help their young children with visual impairments by involving them in household activities, thus fostering a better understanding of the functional uses of common household items. For example, a child who has been involved in making pudding with the family from start to finish may be more likely to engage in

SUPPORTING PEER INTERACTIONS

The following strategies can be used to promote positive peer interactions:

➜ Provide informal, responsive training to peers who are nondisabled. By responding to children's immediate and ongoing concerns and questions about visual impairment, specialists can address issues that are most meaningful to the children. The process should be ongoing in order to maximize the children's learning potential (Kekelis, 1992, p. 49).

➜ Discuss visual impairments with the visually impaired child and with peers. It is important to provide children with visual impairments with the means to explain their impairment to others and to take responsibility for their special needs. Children who are sighted also need to understand the similarities and differences between themselves and their visually impaired peer. Help the child's peers to understand and accommodate appropriately, without focusing solely on the disability (Kekelis, 1992, p. 49). For example, a description of how Rachel's eyes work differently can be followed up by noting the things that she likes to do that are similar to her peers, such as swing on the swing.

➜ Encourage the child who is visually impaired to display preferences. Children with visual impairments do not always provide the same reinforcing messages to peers as do children who are sighted. Specialists may need to prompt visually impaired children to verbalize their preferences, share toys, save a place for a friend, and put their feelings about other children into words (Kekelis, 1992, p. 49).

➜ Create smaller play areas for play with one or two peers (Skellenger, Hill, & Hill, 1992; Kekelis, 1992). Small play areas that are contained, like a sandbox, playhouse, workbench, or water table, make it easier for children who are visually impaired to keep track of toys and the play movements of other children.

➜ Suggest activities and games that can be played at a table or on a tray for children who use wheelchairs. Encouraging individuals or small groups of peers to participate in activities, like play with felt board dolls or miniature cars, will allow children who use wheelchairs to have opportunities to interact with peers.

➜ Orient children with visual impairments to indoor and outdoor play areas, toys, and equipment. Taking time to explicitly teach visually impaired children to operate or activate popular toys and to swing and climb on play equipment will help to keep them on a par with peers who learn to do these activities by watching others.

Compiled by Diane L. Fazzi

functional play involving "pretend" stirring, pouring, and eating. With lots of hands-on experience, young children can develop competencies that can extend into more complex forms of play.

Play is an important component of learning for all children. Children who are visually impaired can extend their choices of play and enjoy satisfying social interactions with their peers if they are supported at home and in school to experience a variety of activities and to initiate appropriate peer relationships in their lives.

Young children who are visually impaired have opportunities for play in the home, in playgroups, at day care, and in preschool programs. If family members, extended family, friends, and professionals are sensitive in providing play opportunities that foster reciprocity and active participation on the part of the visually impaired child, they may help create a foundation for future social interactions.

Supporting the Development and Use of Social Skills and Manners

An important part of interacting with others is the appropriate use of social skills such as waving, shaking hands, and saying "please" and "thank you." Families commonly assume the primary role for instructing their children in the social graces that are important to them culturally and/or personally. There may be instances when families and professionals lower their expectations for appropriate social use by children who have disabilities—possibly due to perceived limited abilities or because they believe that these skills would be less important for children with visual impairments or multiple disabilities. In fact, developing appropriate social skills at an early age forms an important foundation for social acceptance by peers and later success in school, work, and recreational social situations. Families and professionals can work together to help young children who are blind or visually impaired develop emerging social skills that will be a lifelong asset. Social skills that may be of particular importance to address for young children who are blind or visually impaired may include:

- manners, including saying "please" and "thank you," and appropriate behavior during meals;

- turn-taking and sharing, including taking turns in conversation, waiting in lines, playing games, and sharing toys; and

- gestures, facial expressions, eye contact, and social distances, including using them appropriately in a variety of social situations and maintaining appropriate distances when talking or interacting with others.

MANNERS

At a relatively early age, infants, toddlers and preschoolers can be taught to say or sign "please" and "thank you" when making or receiving requests. Similarly, learning to say "excuse me" when bumping into someone will be a useful skill for children who are blind or visually impaired. Young children with visual impairments, including children with additional disabilities, can be taught and expected to do the same within their own ability levels. The following suggestions provide some basic strategies for encouraging good manners:

Teaching Manners

→ As within all families, modeling good manners (whether at the dinner table or in a store) is possibly the simplest and most effective strategy for teaching young children.

→ Some children will need more explicit instruction such as learning when to say "excuse me" or how to say "no" in a nice but firm way.

→ Children who are blind or visually impaired can be shown how to sign "please" or "thank you" if they are preverbal or nonverbal.

→ Good manners can be reinforced through verbal praise or by consistently providing positive consequences (such as longer playtime or an extra portion of yummy fruit) as a result of using good manners.

TURN-TAKING AND SHARING

Turn-taking and sharing can be difficult for all children, especially those between the ages of 2 and 5. These social skills can be modeled by adults and encouraged through positive praise and gentle reminders. Reciprocal interactions with adults (such as peek-a-boo or pretending to talk on the telephone) provide early practice for turn taking with peers. For example, some younger children do well when an adult counts to 20 before they give a toy to the next child. The counting provides the child with an opportunity to anticipate giving up the toy and the realization that the next child has a limited amount of time with the toy before giving it back. Similarly, a timer can be used to set an agreed-upon time to give a toy to another child. Young children can also be encouraged to offer another child a trade

A child who is visually impaired takes turns with her peer.

of items (such as "You can use this car while I have a turn with that one").

Children with visual impairments face these same personal struggles with turn taking and sharing at an early age. Adults and children should expect the same level of turn taking and sharing when playing with children who have disabilities, with support provided as needed. Turn taking may be a bit more challenging for children with visual impairments, however. People frequently use visual cues to keep track of whose turn is next or when to move up in a line. Young children who are blind or visually impaired can be encouraged to listen to keep track of turns and to ask whose turn is it next. Children may need practice in keeping their place in line without stepping on the person in front of them. Sharing toys may be a scary proposition for a child who is blind or for a child who has limited mobility to retrieve toys that are lent to other children. The following suggestions for promoting sharing may assist families and professionals when working with young visually impaired children:

Promoting Sharing

➜ Providing visually impaired children with assurances that shared toys will be returned and encouraging other children to return borrowed materials can help children be more willing to share.

→ Letting children play in contained areas, such as a playhouse or train table, may make sharing more manageable for small groups of children.

→ Giving children similar toys or toy sets (such as crayons and tablets or building blocks) can also help to encourage active sharing between small groups of children (Sacks & Silberman, 2000a).

_____

GESTURES, FACIAL EXPRESSIONS, EYE CONTACT, AND SOCIAL DISTANCE

Children learn to use gestures, facial expressions, and eye contact at an early age through interactions with caregivers and imitation and modeling. Toddlers and preschool-age children commonly include the use of gestures and varied facial expressions in their play routines. Play provides an avenue to practice these important social skills.

Young children who are blind or visually impaired can also be taught to use gestures, facial expressions, and eye contact appropriately in social interactions, but they may need specific instruction, modeling, and lots of feedback to develop these skills. At an early age, infants can be encouraged to make eye contact with adults who are speaking by simply holding the infant facing the person who is speaking (Sacks & Silberman, 2000a). As they get older, they may need additional encouragement to look in the direction of people to whom they are talking or who are talking to them (communicating interest and attention to the conversation partner). It is not unusual for a child who is blind to turn his or her ear towards the person speaking or to hold the head down while listening. Facial expressions may be challenging to learn when children are unable to see others' facial expressions clearly. The following suggestions may help children who have low vision and children who are blind learn more about facial expressions.

_____

Learning about Facial Expressions

→ Young children who have low vision may need to get closer to see the subtle differences between a smile and a frown.

→ High-contrast picture cards of people's faces matched with the word for the feeling (which are commercially available) can also be used.

→ Books with baby faces in different expressions can be read to children.

→ Children who have low vision may enjoy practicing making faces into a mirror.

→ Family members and friends can be encouraged to express their feelings with words as well as facial expressions to help children learn about feelings.

→ Children who are blind may need opportunities to tactilely explore Mom's or Dad's face to feel what a scowl feels like at both the mouth and eyebrow and then to practice doing the same and feeling it on their own faces to compare. Of course, they will need feedback.

→ There are also dolls whose facial features children are able to feel; children can explore these and try to guess the feeling that matches the doll's expression.

→ Decorating cookies or tactile paper dolls can provide another fun opportunity to practice creating various facial expressions.

Maintaining appropriate distance from others is another aspect of social behavior that children must learn. While physical distances between people considered to be appropriate for various social interactions may vary by culture, young children who are blind or visually impaired often need specific feedback regarding accepted social distances to help them experience positive peer interactions. It is common for children with visual impairments to get very close to peers and adults or use physical contact (such as touching) when interacting socially. Maintaining close proximity may be an adaptive strategy for monitoring the location of a conversation or play partner, but honest feedback regarding the social acceptance of the child's close position or inappropriate touching (such as patting other children on the head during snack time) should be given, especially if the behavior makes others uncomfortable and less inclined to interact with the child.

For additional suggestions on helping children who are blind or visually impaired learn how to use gestures and expressions and accepted social distance, see "Supporting the Appropriate Use of Social Skills and Manners" on the next page.

SUPPORTING THE APPROPRIATE USE OF SOCIAL SKILLS AND MANNERS

The development of social skills and manners begins at an early age and is an important aspect of success in many areas of life. The following suggestions may be helpful in supporting young children who are blind or visually impaired to practice and develop these skills.

➔ Learn which social skills (such as shaking hands, saying "please" and "thank you," or taking turns) are a cultural, religious, or personal priority for the family, and work as a team to focus on these skills first.

➔ Help families and other professionals to establish high but realistic expectations for the use of appropriate social skills by their young visually impaired children.

➔ Reinforce good social skills while encouraging improvements as needed. For example, the child could be praised for saying "please" when ordering a sandwich at a restaurant and also reminded to face the food server when talking to him or her.

➔ Pair verbal descriptions with physical modeling to teach children who are blind how to use gestures appropriately in social situations. For example, tell the child to move his or her hand from side to side to wave goodbye while letting the child feel the teacher's hand as he or she models the waving gesture.

➔ Use carpet squares or cushions for all children during circle time to assist young children who are blind or visually impaired in determining appropriate social distances for group learning environments.

➔ Encourage the establishment of consistent routines for practicing and using social skills at home and at school. Consistent routines help children anticipate social events (such as good morning greetings or saying please when requesting an object or food item) and provide necessary repetition for children who have multiple disabilities to practice and master important skills.

Diane L. Fazzi

CONCLUSION

While children who are sighted seem to learn the social skills necessary for bonding with caregivers naturally, playing with peers, and interacting appropriately in a variety of social situations, young children who are blind or visually impaired, including those who have additional disabilities, may need more support and explicit instruction in acquiring similar skills. The most important role that professionals can assume when working in the home with caregivers and their visually impaired infants is to support the development of responsive and enjoyable caregiving environments. Families and professionals can work together to create opportunities for positive interactions with peers and help visually impaired children expand their play repertoires. High expectations for the appropriate use of social behaviors in a variety of social situations help the young child who is visually impaired to develop greater social competence and a more positive self-image.

7 INDEPENDENCE FOCUS

Promoting Independence in Daily Living and Recreational Skills

CONTRIBUTOR

Rona L. Pogrund

Mastering the necessary skills of daily living and having enjoyable recreation and leisure activities are two of the most significant areas that lead to a self-sufficient and fulfilling life as an individual develops toward independence. For the child with a visual impairment, professionals and caregivers need to provide adequate attention and specialized instruction in these two areas, especially during the early years when the foundations of independence are being laid. It is important that both professionals and families understand the significance of these curricular areas and provide instruction, adaptations, and opportunities for success in skills of daily living and recreational activities.

BASIC PRINCIPLES IN TEACHING INDEPENDENCE SKILLS

Instruction in daily living skills and recreational skills naturally lends itself to a functional teaching approach. A functional teaching model is based on the belief that there are certain skills that are practical and critical for children to learn regardless of their developmental or mental age. This approach teaches the skills a child needs to function in daily life without, in many instances, requiring "prerequisite" skills to be mastered. A good way to prioritize skills and objectives is to determine the functionality of a skill. "Does someone

---

The sections in this chapter on daily living skills were adapted in part from the section on "Development of Self-Help Skills," by Shirley A. Kirk, pp. 61–65, in the 1992 edition of this book.

have to do it (perform the activity) for the student?" (Falvey, 1986, p. 41). If the answer is yes, the skill should probably be made a priority. Some basic principles to consider when teaching daily living skills and recreational skills include:

- Use a family inventory to set priorities for skills to be taught.
- Teach skills in the context of functional activities.
- Consider the skills needed in future environments.
- Use chronologically age-appropriate materials and activities.
- Use natural contexts to teach skills.
- Teach skills in a natural environment.
- Start vocational training early.
- Consider adaptations that allow children to accomplish a task or participate partially in an activity.

These principles are elaborated on in the following sections.

Family Inventories

It is critical to ask family members and caregivers of infants and preschoolers who are visually impaired what they feel is important and what they want for their child. If the inventory of their concerns is constructed carefully, functional priorities can be identified, such as toileting, independent eating, or playing ball with a sibling. Educational objectives in the areas of recreation and daily living skills can be built around this information.

During a family inventory that assesses a child's needs in the area of daily living and recreational skills, the professional makes observations of the child's environment and notes family dynamics, as well as asking such open-ended questions as:

Family Inventory Focus

---

1. Can you tell me what daily life with your child is like?

2. What kinds of things do you enjoy doing as a family?

3. What activities does your child enjoy doing alone? With other children?

4. How does mealtime go? Are there any concerns you have about eating?

5. How does bathtime go? Are there any concerns about bathing or other grooming skills?

6. How does dressing go? Are there any concerns about dressing?

7. Are there any toileting concerns that you have?

8. Does your child help with any chores around the house (if age-appropriate)? Is that something you would like to see him or her doing?

9. What things do you think are important to work on first?

Based on the answers to such questions in a family inventory, the professional might identify family priorities, such as eating, that may be a particularly stressful time for a given family.

Functional Activities

It is helpful to analyze the environment and each skill on a developmental checklist and then find ways to functionalize the skill to the task in which the child needs to use it. This objective is accomplished by teaching the skill in a relevant and meaningful context of daily living instead of simply as part of an isolated task. For example, teaching the child to use a zipper as he or she puts on his or her jacket before going outside is more functional than having a time set aside to work on using the zipper in the preschool classroom.

Future Environments

The teacher always needs to be working toward the child functioning more independently in future environments. When working with an infant in the home, it is important to determine what activities will enhance the child's ability to function more independently in the preschool classroom. If the child is in preschool, it is important to look at skills needed for kindergarten survival, such as taking turns and standing in line. The best way to find out what may be needed in the child's next environment is to observe it ahead of time to see what expectations the child's teacher may have or what peers of a similar age are doing independently in the areas of recreation and daily living skills.

Chronologically Age-Appropriate Materials and Activities

Age-appropriate materials and activities can be determined by observing nondisabled children of the same age as the child with a disability. Just because a 4-year-old child tests at the 20-month level does not mean he or she will not enjoy activities for 4-year-olds. Age-appropriateness is particularly significant in teaching recreational and daily living skills, because the activities in which a child engages contribute to others' perception of the child. If preschool peers, for example, are eating independently, self-feeding might be a priority for the child who is visually impaired with multiple disabilities so that he or she would be able to eat with his or her peers.

Natural Times to Teach Skills

Eating, dressing, and other daily living skills are best taught at natural times in natural contexts, rather than at nonrelevant times. Learning to put toothpaste on the toothbrush while brushing teeth after meals or before bedtime is more relevant to the child than practicing the skill at a specified time during the day.

Natural Environments

Working with young children in their natural home, school, and community environments as much as possible increases chances of integration of skills into daily routines. For example, practicing early cane skills en route from the preschool classroom to the playground makes more sense to a young child who is blind than going to an unfamiliar, artificial environment to practice. There is a higher likelihood the child will use the cane on that daily route on a regular basis, thus integrating its use into his or her life in a meaningful context.

It should be noted, however, that the concept of natural environments does not always refer to just a place, but may be defined by what is occurring within the environment. It is more important to focus on desired learning outcomes for a child than on the environment, since if learning is not taking place, the environment is not appropriate for the child (Bruder, 2001). The most natural environment in the early years for some children who are visually impaired may be a setting focusing on specialized skills, rather than a totally inclusive setting (Chen, 1999a).

Vocational Training

It is important to begin thinking about the vocational area early. Vocational education at the preschool level, which ultimately leads to independence, includes training in attending to a task, understanding concepts of time, following rules, and beginning simple jobs at home and in the classroom.

Partial Participation

Partial participation and adaptations can be used on a variety of levels. For instance, using Velcro closures on shoes is an example of an adaptation that may allow a young child to participate partially in dressing him- or herself. Young children who are visually impaired can also participate in many sports and games partially, even if a vision loss prevents full participation. For example, a blind child can be the caller in the game "Red Rover" or run with a partner initially until he or she becomes more familiar with the procedures and layout of the area. Partial participation in all activities, however, may not always be in the best interest of the self-esteem of the child who is visually impaired. It is equally important that the child be able to participate fully and compete with others in some activities.

Keeping the basic principles of teaching independence in mind during the assessment and instruction of daily living skills and recreational skills will assist in the development of a meaningful and individualized program for each child. It is also important to recognize the need for the child to have fun when learning these valuable life skills so that they will be well received by and make sense to the child who is visually impaired.

DEVELOPING INDEPENDENCE SKILLS
FOR DAILY LIVING

One of the most significant issues facing many children who are visually impaired is the concept of *learned helplessness* (Seligman, 1975; Pogrund & Strauss, 1992; Marks, 1998). The more control a person has over the environment, the greater the chance for success. Learned helplessness is a perception of the lack of control, whether or not that perception is accurate. If many things are done for the child who is visually impaired by family members and teachers, this child may grow up feeling incompetent and helpless. He or she will begin to feel ineffective and become passive, allowing others to control his or her life as he or she grows older. The best way to foster a feeling of competence is by giving responsibilities to the child who is visually impaired.

There is no area that develops competence and responsibility in a child more than the area of independence skills for daily living. The activities of daily living that are part of the routine life of everyone offer rich opportunities to counteract the learned helplessness which so many children who are visually impaired experience. Each small step that the young child is able to master in his or her daily living skills adds to these feelings of success and independence. It is extremely important that families and professionals begin allowing and encouraging the young child who is visually impaired to try these skills on his or her own whenever it is age-appropriate and the child is physically capable. Helping with daily chores at home and in the classroom increases the child's feeling of belonging and of being a contributor rather than a taker. These are attitudes that form early and can carry on into adult life as to how individuals perceive themselves and their role in the world.

Daily living skills include a variety of areas such as personal hygiene, toileting, eating, dressing, organizational skills, household chores, and so on. Without instruction and encouragement, many young children who are visually impaired exhibit delays in moving toward independence in these areas. The motivation for sighted children to do many of these tasks independently evolves from observing what others do and wanting to imitate them. If they see older siblings sitting on the toilet, they may want to "go potty" like their siblings. The child who is visually impaired may need verbal descriptions and hands-on assistance to increase motivation for toileting. Sometimes, in the case of the child with multiple disabilities, the child may not have the motor or cognitive skills to be able to perform certain tasks at an age-appropriate time. Adaptations or partial participation may need to be considered in such cases so that each child can be as independent as possible. For example, the child with motor delays may need low rails by the toilet in order to be able to "go potty" independently.

According to the 1997 amendments to IDEA-Part C, early intervention services are to be provided in natural environments to the maximum extent appropriate. Indeed, the ideal place for instruction and practice in daily living skills is in the child's natural environments, if possible. The home is the young child's most natural environment, and many daily living skills are part of the daily routines at home. There are also many that can be taught within the natural context of the daily routines at school. It is much better, for example, if dressing skills are taught at naturally occurring times when the child would be changing clothes (for example, at toileting, in the morning, at bathtime, before going outdoors to play), rather than providing separate instruction on dressing in the middle of class time. As noted earlier, using naturally occurring opportunities on a daily basis to teach such skills increases the likelihood of these skills being integrated into regular routines independently.

Part of the role of professionals is to make families aware of what kinds of independent daily living skills are age-appropriate at various stages (this is especially important for first-time parents). Table 7.1 provides examples of some of the independent daily living skills that sighted children typically perform at different ages. These have been extrapolated from a chart of typical development. Remember that such charts are only guidelines of age-appropriate expectations and should never be used strictly, as each child develops individually at his or her own pace.

Professionals also provide strategies for instruction and practice and suggestions for adaptations. "Promoting the Development of Daily Living Skills in the Home" offers some ways families can facilitate the learning of daily living skills at home. The sections that follow discuss specific areas of daily living skills. Readers can refer to Table 7.1 for rough guidelines on when to begin to introduce various skills.

It is likewise very important that professionals be patient and understanding if parents do not always work on daily living skills at naturally occurring times on a regular basis because of the realities and time constraints of family life. For example, it is a major effort for some families with two working parents just to get everyone dressed and fed and out the door on time each morning. To expect that lots of extra time be spent on independent dressing skills on weekday mornings is not a realistic expectation for some families. Professionals need to be sensitive to individual family needs and lifestyles as

TABLE 7.1 EXAMPLES OF INDEPENDENT DAILY LIVING SKILLS FOR SIGHTED CHILDREN

AGE RANGE	SKILL	AGE RANGE	SKILL
6–12 months	Feeds self cracker. Holds cup with two hands. Drinks with assistance. Holds out arms and legs while being dressed.	12–24 months	Uses spoon, spilling little. Drinks from cup, one hand, unassisted. Chews food. Removes socks, shoes, pants, sweater. Unzips large zipper.
24–36 months	Uses spoon, spilling little. Gets drink from fountain or faucet unassisted. Opens door by turning handle. Takes off coat. Puts on coat with assistance. Washes and dries hands with assistance.	36–48 months	Pours well from small pitcher. Spreads soft butter with knife. Buttons and unbuttons large buttons. Washes hands unassisted. Blows nose when reminded. Uses toilet independently.
48–60 months	Cuts easy foods with a knife (e.g., hamburger patty, tomato slice). Laces shoes.	60–72 months	Dresses self completely. Ties bow. Brushes teeth unassisted.

Source: Adapted from "Chart of Normal Development," *Mainstreaming Preschoolers: Children with Visual Handicaps* (Washington, D.C.: U.S. Department of Health, Education, and Welfare, 1978).

well as to cultural differences in independence beliefs. Some Asian cultures, for example, do not have the same timeline for expectations of independent feeding, dressing, and toileting as traditional Western cultures. Some traditional Asian cultures are more relaxed in the early years and do not encourage independence and responsibility

PROMOTING THE DEVELOPMENT OF DAILY LIVING SKILLS IN THE HOME

The following principles and suggestions will help families encourage their children who are visually impaired while learning daily living skills:

→ Pick one or two priorities, based on family and child assessments, on which to focus at one time.

→ Choose skills that are needed the most for independence and that can be practiced and reinforced daily.

→ Have the child perform skills in natural environments and at natural times of the day whenever possible.

→ Have the sighted adult do the skill blindfolded to see for him- or herself what the steps are to accomplish the task and where the difficulties lie.

→ Use adaptations as needed and appropriate to encourage more independence.

→ Have similar expectations of a child with a visual impairment in terms of self care, participation in family chores, and so on, as would be expected of a sighted child.

→ Be consistent in cues, words, and gestures used while working on a daily living skill.

→ Follow a consistent routine.

→ Be patient in teaching and practicing a skill while the child is learning.

→ Label items with pictures or tactile markings.

→ Leave adequate time for the child to do tasks alone.

→ Do some of the steps in a task so that the child can complete it independently.

→ Try to make daily routines as much fun as possible (for example, singing songs or using a timer for a race when picking up toys).

Rona L. Pogrund

until the child is much older. (See Chapter 2 for more detail on culture and child rearing practices.) Being aware of different family values and expectations helps in setting more realistic goals for the young child who is visually impaired.

Personal Hygiene

Personal hygiene skills can be taught early, and these skills develop into lifelong habits that affect the child's health and social appearance. The skills addressed under the category of personal hygiene include: washing and drying the hands and face, brushing teeth,

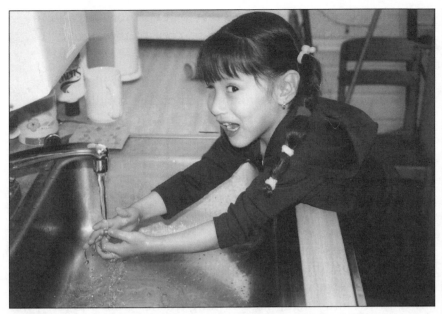

A preschool age child uses the classroom sink independently to wash hands before snack.

combing and/or brushing hair, blowing the nose, and bathing (Silberman, 1986). Providing grooming supplies with contrasting colors for children with low vision and organizing items in a separate container in the drawer help the child locate items needed independently. Teaching good basic hygiene skills early on (such as frequent handwashing) leads to a healthier lifestyle. Many young children have trouble with nose blowing and need to be reminded to throw used tissue away and wash their hands afterward.

Bathtime can be traumatic for some infants, but it is a favorite activity for others. If it is not an enjoyable activity, keeping the body partly covered and providing a lot of physical support during bathtime may help. As the child gets older, privacy issues, appropriate to individual family cultures, should be discussed and respected during bathtime. Standard safety precautions of careful water temperature adjustment, covering faucets with foam covers to avoid bumping, and using rubber mats to reduce slippage can be followed to prevent injuries and keep bathtime a positive experience. No young child should ever be left alone in the tub, even for a minute. Minor adaptations, such as the following, may make many personal hygiene skills easier to master:

- Liquid soap is sometimes easier to manage than hunting for the soap bar.

- A pump toothpaste dispenser may be easier for the child to manipulate and make it easier to control the amount of toothpaste coming out.

- For children with a poor grasp, an electric toothbrush or a regular toothbrush with foam taped on the handle may be easier to hold and control when brushing independently.

- Marking the hot and cold faucets with a tactile or brightly colored differentiation can help with independent temperature control (Chen & Dote-Kwan, 1995).

It is important to remember that a variety of other developmental areas can be incorporated into personal hygiene practice. Many concepts can be taught within the context of learning these skills. For example, bathtime is a great time to teach the concepts of wet and dry, hot and cold, and in and out; toothbrushing teaches up and down, gentle and rough; handwashing teaches clean and dirty, wet and dry, and slippery. Visual skills can be incorporated into personal hygiene skills as well, for example, by practicing spotting the shampoo bottle, tracing the edge of the tub to the faucet, and tracking a floating toy. Body parts and body concepts can be taught here, too, within the natural conversations of each activity (such as, "Blow your nose with the tissue," or "You still have dirt on your fingers.") Language development and orientation and mobility skills can also be enhanced during personal hygiene routines (for example, "Can you find the sink at the back of the classroom to wash your hands?" or "The trash can to throw away your tissue is next to the stove in the kitchen. Can you tell me how you would get there?").

Eating

For the infant, breast- or bottle-feeding occupies a significant portion of at least the first several months of life. If a parent is having problems with feeding, it is best to consult a doctor, nurse, occupational therapist, or lactation specialist who can make suggestions on making breast- or bottle-feeding a more enjoyable experience for both caregiver and infant.

Keeping the infant who is visually impaired upright, with head tipped slightly forward and well supported (almost facing the mother), may facilitate easier breast-feeding. When the infant is between 4 and 6 months old, the positioning of the child is a primary consideration. Traditional, semi-reclined positioning may not be the most effective breast- or bottle-feeding position for infants who are visually or multiply impaired and who have sucking, swallowing, or head-control problems. Placing the infant upright in a special seat or corner of a chair or couch may offer added support and free the care-taker's hands for bottle-feeding. Although the technique just mentioned may facilitate easier feeding for infants who have difficulties, holding and cuddling the infant before and after feeding is important for the bonding process and should not be overlooked (Kirk, 1992).

It may be helpful to use fingers to support the baby's mouth if the infant has difficulty mouthing the nipple or spoon. Sucking can be encouraged by gently rubbing the baby's cheeks or by gently stimulating the inside of the infant's mouth with a finger.

Feeding problems begin with games of control, in which the parent and child fight over when, how, what, and how much the child should eat. A control struggle can be avoided by learning to read the child's cues (such as the signal for when he or she has had enough food) and responding simply and clearly to him or her. It is sometimes helpful, if there is concern about the amount the child is eating, to consider the amount consumed within the last 72 hours rather than focusing on one meal (Kirk, 1992).

To help the older infant who is starting solid foods and the young toddler who is visually impaired make connections between events, it is useful to give specific auditory and tactile cues about what is happening prior to and during feeding, such as tapping the spoon on the bowl or gently touching the child's cheek or chin before a bite. Providing information about size and texture and waiting until the child is ready to take a bite facilitate calmer eating times. If the child is continually surprised with what is coming next or feels too rushed at eating times, his or her stress level may increase. If the young child has some functional vision, position the food in the child's field of vision, and use color-contrasting plates and bowls to help the child use his or her vision and anticipate what is going to happen. Body awareness can be enhanced during feeding with a focus on stimulating the mouth and facial area.

For an older child who is able to use a highchair, feeding activities can incorporate exploration, tactile experiences, and cause-and-effect experiments. He or she may tip over a bowl or throw utensils on the floor to see what happens; the child may also put his or her hands in the food. This time can be used for concept development in a variety of areas including those relating to texture of various foods, liquids, napkins, and trays; receptive language such as descriptions of events and foods; and body awareness. For the preschool-aged child, it is easy to develop extended activities around eating, including cooking (which incorporates fine motor and social skills), going to the supermarket, science (measuring and comparing items), and taste or sensory awareness activities.

Choice of foods is important. Commercially available "junior foods" often precipitate feeding problems because children become confused by their texture, which is neither solid nor liquid. It may be better to grind regular table food for the child. This method helps the child make the transition to the table and to regular family food because the texture of food is more uniform and predictable, and the child will be accustomed to the flavors in the family's food (Kirk, 1992).

Some children will eat slightly mashed table food rather than entirely solid food. Young children may have sophisticated tastes, which should be respected. For the child who is visually impaired, a wide variety of tastes, smells, and textures of healthy foods adds to the inducement to eat. The introduction of different flavors and textures during the first year of life will encourage the infant to eat more of a variety later on. Because some young children who are visually impaired can be tactilely defensive, it may be necessary to carefully introduce a new food. Naming the food, putting the child's hand on the caregiver's when taking food to the mouth, or letting the child taste a little on the finger or on the lips first may help the child receive new foods more favorably. Repeating new foods in small portions over several days may reduce anxiety over new textures and tastes.

An adapted spoon, bowl, and cup make it easier for a young child who is visually impaired to feed herself.

For the toddler and preschooler, the primary goals in feeding are independence and competence. Competence comes with instruction and practice. Independence comes with confidence and trust in the child's abilities to carry out the task. It is important to provide an environment for working on eating that allows for "safe failure." If it seems that the world is ending because the child made a mess, the child will not try the task again. Messes are part of learning to eat independently for all children (Kirk, 1992).

Other strategies for facilitating a positive eating experience include the following:

Mealtime Strategies

→ Using a consistent pattern when setting the table and presenting food helps the child who is visually impaired to be more independent.

→ Good lighting at the highchair or table assists the child with low vision see better.

→ Child-sized utensils make for easier control.

→ Using plates or bowls that suction to the table or placing a damp paper towel or cloth under the bowl or plate helps keep them stable as the child tries to scoop or fork the food, increasing chances of success. Use of divided plates keeps food separated for the young child.

→ Teaching the child who is blind to use a piece of bread or a butter knife edge as a "pusher" to help him or her get food onto a spoon or fork is a useful skill for independent eating as the child gets older and is more pleasant for others to watch than allowing fingers in the food.

→ Pouring can be taught successfully by using a small pitcher and teaching the child to place a finger inside the cup so he or she can feel when the liquid reaches the top.

All of these methods facilitate success in eating so it is a less stressful and a more enjoyable time for the child and the family (Chen & Dote-Kwan, 1995).

Toileting

Toileting is a very individual process, and early toilet training is not imperative. It is not unusual for sighted children and children who are visually impaired not to be trained by 3 years of age. It is important to communicate this information to families and to encourage them to relax about toilet training. Many children with multiple disabilities will take much longer to become independent in toileting, and many need repeated and consistent systematic instruction to succeed. Parents sometimes feel pressure to get children out of diapers too soon because of a desire to get into a particular preschool program that requires that children be toilet trained or because of the high cost of diapers. When children are ready to be trained, they will indicate in some way (for instance, pulling at diapers) that they are uncomfortable with wet or soiled diapers. It is important to be alert to such signals.

It is sometimes helpful for parents to begin training by taking the child with them to the toilet. The child should also be checked to determine when he or she is wet and dry to estimate the time when a visit to the toilet will most likely next be needed. It is important for the parents to maintain a relaxed, positive, nonchalant attitude toward toileting. If the child senses that toileting provokes stress, a power struggle may ensue. Toileting and eating are two of the few things children can control in their lives. The greater the reaction that a child with little power receives from the parent regarding these two activities, the more stubborn and determined to gain control he or she may become (Kirk, 1992).

As the child reaches preschool age, additional toileting considerations need to be addressed.

Toileting Strategies

→ Boys who are blind may need practice in order to learn to urinate into the toilet.

→ For boys with low vision, providing a contrasting color ring around the toilet will help with better aim.

→ Utilizing the base of the toilet or edge of the urinal as guidelines for the placement of the feet may help the young boy line up to prevent accidents.

→ Orientation to soap, toilet paper, paper towels, sinks, and trash cans in preschool or day-care center bathrooms should be given if independent toileting is to occur.

→ Wearing easy "pull up" and "pull down" clothing (such as elastic-waist pants) leads to more success in independent toileting.

For children with physical disabilities who may have trouble balancing on a toilet, consultation with a physical or occupational therapist is important. If the child feels unstable and insecure on the toilet, he or she will not be able to relax and attend to toileting.

Dressing

Dressing encompasses both putting on and removing clothes. Undressing is usually easier than dressing, and most children learn undressing first. For the infant, it is important to give cues prior to and during the removal of clothing. Body awareness can be developed by playing body-part-naming games. A Mylar mirror near the changing area may be useful to help create an interest in surroundings for the child with some vision.

As soon as the child can sit up alone, activities related to dressing should be carried out while the child is sitting to give him or her vestibular stimulation (movement of the fluid in the inner ear) and a new orientation to pulling clothes on or off. It is important to use words and directional terms that are literally accurate when talking with the child. For example, "your socks are on the bed" is more accurate than "your socks are over here." Broader extensions of getting dressed and undressed include experience with putting clothes away or hanging them up; putting dirty clothes in the hamper; understanding concepts of clean and dirty; and separating, washing, and folding clothes.

Choices are important, and the child's decision-making skills can be developed by presenting him or her with simple choices, such as which of two shirts will be worn. Decisions about clothing can be made on the basis of texture, design, sleeve length, style, and color. For the child who is blind, developing a system for marking and storing clothes is important (see the following section, "Organizational Skills"), and strategies that can be formulated at a very young age can be used for a lifetime. Using pictures or tactile markers on drawers and clothes can help with organization.

Dressing skills require a variety of cognitive and motor skills, many of which may seem very difficult for the young child who is visually impaired to master. As mentioned earlier, families may not have the time to work on these skills in the rushed morning routine. If mornings are not realistic practice times, then families can make an effort to practice dressing and undressing at bedtime in the evenings. Finding appropriate and natural times during the school day (for example, before or after going outside to zip or unzip a coat, at toileting to pull pants up and down, and before or after nap time)

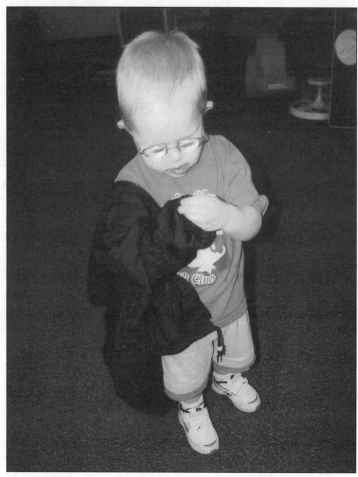

A preschooler works independently to get his hand through his jacket sleeve so he can go out to play at recess.

may be more realistic. Once a child has learned a particular skill, he or she can then practice more quickly at home.

Other techniques that facilitate independent dressing skills include:

Dressing Strategies

→ It is best to teach dressing skills using the child's own body as opposed to using dolls or lacing boards, as the motor patterns are reversed on such artificial tools (Silberman, 1986).

→ Using larger buttons and zippers initially helps with success.

→ Finger dexterity, pincer grasp, and body imagery and orientation (front and back, body parts, and body planes) are all needed for successful independent dressing. These concepts and motor skills can, however, be developed through dressing skills.

➡ Adaptations that lead to more independent dressing sooner include use of pull-over shirts instead of button-down shirts; use of Velcro shoes rather then laces; use of Velcro fasteners for zippers, buttons, or snaps; and use of a key chain on a coat zipper for easier grasp.

It is important, however, to continue working on more difficult dressing skills at the same time that adaptations are used so the child who is visually impaired does not become dependent on such adaptations as he or she gets older. Some children with multiple disabilities may continue to use adaptations into adulthood if they do not develop the motor or cognitive skills necessary for more complex dressing skills.

Organizational Skills

Being well-organized is an important ability for all people, especially those who are successful at home and at work. Having good organizational skills is essential for a person who is blind or visually impaired if he or she is to become an independent individual at home, at school, and in the work place. Without vision, it is often necessary to rely on others to help locate needed items if a person is not well organized.

Most people who are blind or visually impaired can benefit from some amount of systematic instruction in more effective ways to stay organized. This instruction should start in the early years, as age-appropriate, so that efficient lifelong organizational skills can be incorporated into daily routines.

Infants do not need to be organized, as most tasks are done for them at this stage of development. Strategies for assisting in organizational skill development include the following:

Tips for Staying Organized

➡ As the child who is visually impaired becomes a toddler, teaching skills such as systematic search patterns, putting toys back on the shelf or in the basket, and putting dirty clothes in an easily accessible hamper is appropriate.

→ Providing divided trays or separate containers for grooming items rather than leaving them loose on the counter facilitates independence in personal hygiene as the child gets older.

→ Using trays as a work surface or placemats at the table assists the child in keeping items in front of him or her as he or she works, plays, or eats.

→ Using a consistent pattern of utensils and dishes at mealtime also helps promote independence and prevent messes.

Organizational skills can be taught and reinforced in the preschool classroom as well by encouraging the child who is visually impaired to put art supplies, toys, and personal belongings away when done with a task or activity. Well-defined spaces in the classroom for his or her things (for example, clearly marked cubbies, coat hooks, toy shelves, table trays, chairs and carpet squares) assist with organization. An item can be taped on the edge of a shelf with a braille and print word next to it for the prereader. Teaching young children early on the concept that after you take something out (such as a puzzle, a game, CDs, trucks, or dolls), it is important to put it back before the next activity is basic to staying well-organized. Instead of family members, classmates, or teachers always being the ones to clean up after an activity and put it away, the child who is visually impaired needs to clean up and put the item back where it goes so that next time he or she will be able to locate it on his or her own. This habit prevents the child from tripping on items left out as well. Of course instruction and assistance initially will be needed. It is often easier for others to do the task for the child who is visually impaired, as it may take longer for him or her to do it independently. The extra time when the child is learning pays off with feelings of competence later on as the task is completed. It also saves time for others in the long run once an organizational task is mastered independently.

Young children who are visually impaired may also need assistance organizing their clothes. As mentioned previously in the section on dressing, it is important for a visually impaired child to be able to understand and use a system of marking and organizing clothing so eventually he or she can make independent dressing choices. The following are some methods of organizing and labeling clothing:

• Sock sorters can be used to keep pairs of socks together in the wash and the drawer.

- Some families decide to buy socks in one color and style for daily wear so that matching is not an issue.

- Some also decide to buy shorts, pants, and t-shirts that can all be mixed and matched interchangeably to simplify the dressing procedure and allow the child to pick any top and bottom out of the appropriate drawer.

- Special clothing that is not distinguishable by texture can be marked with a tactile symbol or French knot on the tag or elsewhere so the child can recognize the various outfits.

- Labeling drawers or closet sections with visual or tactile markers and using drawer dividers or cardboard between closet sections helps the child know where to look for a particular item.

- There are many commercially made devices and systems that can be purchased at a store that specializes in organizational merchandise or in special catalogs (see Resources) that can be useful in helping a child become better organized.

Household Chores

It is important for all children to participate in household chores, as age-appropriate, in order to feel like they belong to their family. For example, helping with the laundry is a chore in which all children can assist, regardless of age. A one-year-old can put dirty clothes in the hamper if the child is given an appropriately sized hamper. A two-year-old can match socks by color or texture if the parent provides a small number of easily distinguished socks at first. A three-year-old can put wet clothes in the dryer when the adult sets the wet clothes on the dryer door. A four-year-old can help with the folding by starting with easy items such as a washcloth or pillowcase. A five-year-old can measure detergent with a scooper made to hold the exact amount of detergent; can set dials marked by nail polish, tape, or puff paint; and can put clothes away by memorizing where they go or marking drawers. Helping other family members by doing a portion of the daily chores makes children feel less helpless, as opposed to when everything is done for them. Each small task a child masters becomes part of his or her repertoire as he or she heads toward becoming an independent adult.

It is very beneficial if families include their children who are visually impaired in household chores. It may take longer for the child who is visually impaired to learn how to do a chore independently, but the value of participation cannot be overemphasized. Professionals can help here by suggesting chores that may be manageable and showing the child how to do tasks prioritized by the family. Once family members see the child showing competence in a specific chore, they will be more likely to allow the child to participate. Sometimes participating partially is a good way to be involved in family routines and learn new skills at the same time, adding more steps each time. For example, a young child with a visual impairment would probably not wash the family car by him- or herself but could certainly participate by soaping up the sides or cleaning the wheels.

There are a variety of household chores in which a young child who is visually impaired could participate. As noted earlier, very young toddlers can put their dirty clothes in the hamper, put their diapers in the diaper pail and get a clean one, hang their coats on a hook, and put their toys away after use. As toddlers become preschoolers, they can give the family pet food and water, unload and sort silverware from the dishwasher, set the family table, empty the trash can, carefully take dirty dishes to the sink after meals, and sort the recycling and put it in the proper containers. Outdoor activities in which a child who is visually impaired could help include gardening, weeding, bathing the dog, or watering the plants.

The kitchen is a wonderful place to involve young children who are visually impaired during food preparation, as in the following activities:

_____

Food Preparation Activities

→ Teaching basic spreading skills (frozen bread helps keep bread from tearing), how to use a knife safely, stirring skills, pouring a drink, getting a bowl of cereal, and tearing lettuce for salad are all relatively simple tasks that can be learned at an early age.

→ Making slice-and-bake cookies together and going through the steps of making a cake from cake mix are good beginning cooking activities.

→ For the child with low vision, it may be helpful to use a light-colored cutting board when working with dark foods and vice versa for light foods to provide contrast.

→ The microwave is a good, safe cooking appliance to teach preschoolers to use. It may be helpful to mark the dials with puff paint, colored tape, or colored glue to help with independent tactile settings.

→ Marking kitchen timers and oven dials is also useful.

→ Learning to wipe the work area systematically (in back and forth or circular patterns) after cooking and to help with washing and drying dishes are also important.

It is useful if children experience all of the steps in the process of a household chore, even if they cannot participate in every step. That way a task does not seem so fragmented. There is more to making a cake than mixing and eating it. There are many concepts (such as, dry/wet, hot/cold, and soft/hard) and fine motor skills (such as opening jars and stirring) that can be reinforced in food preparation activities as well.

Children who are visually impaired can also participate in other household chores. They can help with vacuuming (a lightweight cordless vacuum is easier to manage for the young child), dusting (reinforce systematic patterns to cover a surface thoroughly), laundry (sorting, pouring detergent, and putting clothes in the washer and dryer), and cleaning the bathrooms.

Techniques for Teaching Activities of Daily Living

In teaching activities of daily living, the emphasis is too often on task completion, making it difficult to maintain an emphasis on the process involved in acquiring the abilities for the task. Useful techniques for teaching daily living activities include:

- task analysis,

- backward chaining,

- modeling,

- motoring,

- demonstration,

- use of routines, and

- reinforcement.

TASK ANALYSIS

Task analysis is useful as a method of approaching problem solving and provides a strategic approach if the child has difficulties with an activity. Task analysis involves breaking down a task, such as tying shoelaces, into small sequential steps and teaching one step at a time. For example, the steps involved in tying shoes (using the "bunny ear" method) may be broken down as follows:

1. Place the shoe on the foot.

2. Pull the laces tightly with the index fingers and thumbs.

3. Hold the laces close to the ends with the index finger and thumb and loop together to tie a single knot.

4. Pull the laces tight.

5. With the two loose ends, make two loops, one in each hand.

6. Hold the base of the loop between the thumb and index finger of each hand.

7. Cross one loop over and under the other and tie as a single knot.

8. Pull both loops tightly.

9. Tie the loops again if a double knot is needed.

BACKWARD CHAINING

In backward chaining, the instructor alone carries out the entire procedure of a task except the last step, which the child completes; the child is prompted to complete more and more of the task, progressing backward until the entire task is mastered, while the adult's participation gradually lessens. This method allows the child to experience the success of completing a task at every attempt. It is useful for tasks such as dressing. For example, if a child is learning to put his or her pants on, the instructor may initially put them on for the child, except for pulling the pants up over the hips. The child does this step. Once mastered, the child then pulls them from the knees up. Next, the child pulls them from the ankles and then learns to put each foot in the pants legs one at a time. After mastering each step and adding to what he or she already knows, the child is then expected to locate the tag in the back of the pants and put them on independently.

MODELING

Modeling a behavior, in which the adult performs a technique and encourages the child to imitate it, is most effective for very young children with some degree of vision. It is useful for teaching skills such as how to hold a spoon.

MOTORING

Motoring, a technique of physical prompting, such as using hand-under-hand teaching or physically helping a child progress through the full or partial motions of an activity, may help children who have very limited or no vision to learn specific techniques and movements involved in daily living tasks. Motoring is useful for teaching a child such techniques as holding a washcloth and locating the soap when bathing. The instructor places the child's hand over his or her own hand as a systematic search pattern is demonstrated in locating the soap. The child is able to physically feel the movements of the instructor as he or she learns the motor pattern needed for the skill.

DEMONSTRATION

Demonstration is similar to modeling except that it is used to teach an entire task rather than a single behavior. Demonstrating an activity is not always effective, as young children may lose interest in an activity in which they do not participate. It is helpful if the instructor focuses his or her attention more on the activity than on the child during demonstration, as this directs the child's attention to the activity. Demonstration is useful for teaching the child with low vision such tasks as stirring ingredients for a recipe.

USE OF ROUTINES

Routines are predictable chains of related events used to structure activities that teach a broad range of communication, cognition, motor, sensory, and social skills (Carriero & Townsend, 1987). Routines allow the child to know what to expect from certain people and in what order daily tasks occur, such as bathing, eating, dressing, and the like. Such consistency lends itself well to transdisciplinary teaming (see Chapter 11) and incorporation of activities into natural contexts at home and school. For example, the routine of bedtime for a preschooler can be broken down into the following steps: undressing, putting dirty clothes in the hamper, getting out pajamas, running the bath water, going to the bathroom, getting in the tub, washing the hair and body with shampoo and soap, rinsing soap off, drying off, brushing teeth, putting on pajamas, and getting into bed. Starting the routine with the cue of "It's bedtime—time to get undressed" and ending with the cue of "Night-night" as the child gets into bed helps mark the beginning and end of the routine.

REINFORCEMENT

Positive reinforcement is helpful in any activity; it can be used most effectively with other methods. Verbal praise, physical contact (such

as a hug or pat on the back), and providing tangible (such as a favorite treat) and intangible (such as a favorite activity) rewards all reinforce a skill for future repetition.

Daily Living Skills for Children with Multiple Disabilities

Children with multiple impairments may require additional assistance in learning and performing many activities of daily living. Patience is needed to give the child more time to complete an activity. More motoring and physical prompting may be needed to assist
the child with additional disabilities. Ultimately, questions regarding the child with multiple impairments' potential for independent
functioning may have to be addressed. Partial participation in activities of daily living may promote self-esteem and dignity for some
students if it is balanced with full participation in other activities.
It is important to avoid limiting expectations of ultimate self-suffi-
ciency at an early age because many children eventually master
some of the activities of daily living in spite of mental or physical
disabilities. See "Considerations in Teaching Daily Living and Recreation and Leisure Skills to Children with Multiple Disabilities" for
specific suggestions.

Activities of daily living, used throughout life, provide ample opportunities for young children who are visually impaired to feel self-
reliant and as though they are contributing members of their family, classroom, and community. Whatever daily living tasks children
can master at an early age put them that much farther ahead as they
make their way toward independence. Believing in the abilities of a
child who is visually impaired and encouraging him or her while
avoiding frustration help the child reach the goals of competence
and independence sooner.

PARTICIPATION IN ACTIVITIES FOR RECREATION AND LEISURE

Recreation is defined as a means of refreshment or diversion, and
leisure as a time free from work or duties. These are activities that are
fun for people and provide a balance to life. Often children who are
visually impaired do not experience the same opportunities for recreation and leisure that children with no vision loss have in the early
years. Sometimes, this lack of experience may be attributed to the
child and the impact of his or her vision loss, sometimes to the
child's family, and sometimes to others in the outside world. Young

CONSIDERATIONS IN TEACHING DAILY LIVING AND RECREATION AND LEISURE SKILLS TO CHILDREN WITH MULTIPLE DISABILITIES

The following suggestions may be helpful when teaching both daily living skills and recreational skills to children with multiple disabilities:

➜ Carefully assess the individual child's visual, language, cognitive, and motor abilities. Communicate with other professionals and family members who may have important information on the child's level of functioning and abilities (for example, the physical therapist, the speech therapist, the classroom teacher, and the optometrist).

➜ Closely observe the child in his or her natural environments to see how some of the needs are manifested.

➜ Make adaptations when necessary to allow for more independence or participation.

➜ Use materials that are used in the child's daily environment to increase familiarity and generalization.

➜ Teach skills in the natural environment whenever possible.

➜ Use natural cues in the environment as a signal for a routine (for example, turn on the bath water when it is bath time).

➜ Be careful not to use materials or do activities that may overstimulate a child, especially if the child has processing or sensory integration problems.

➜ If the child has a motor impairment, make sure the child is comfortably positioned and supported before he or she attempts to learn a skill.

➜ Allow additional time for learning most skills, and show patience as the child attempts a new task.

Rona L. Pogrund

children who are visually impaired have a right to be exposed to a variety of recreational activities to see if there are things that they enjoy beyond the routine activities to which they are accustomed. Besides just being enjoyable or relaxing, recreational and leisure activities can provide an avenue for the development of motor skills, social skills, language skills, and fitness (Sanford & Burnett, 1996).

There are a variety of reasons why so many young children who are visually impaired do not participate in typical recreational activities. Many young sighted children may request to do certain activities because they see friends or neighbors doing them or see something on television or at movies that piques their interest. There is a natural inclination for most young children to want to copy what they see others doing if it looks like fun. For example, young children want to learn to ride tricycles and then bicycles because they see siblings or neighbors' children riding them and they want to join in. These models serve as a motivation to try to learn new skills that can provide many years of pleasurable leisure time. The child who is visually impaired is limited in observing many recreational activities and may often just be unaware of what choices are available. There may also be a fear of trying new things, even when an activity is suggested. The child may feel insecure in his or her motor abilities because of too much passivity or may be afraid of injury when trying something new.

Although most families do not intentionally exclude or discourage their child from recreational activities, families may unknowingly contribute to their child's limited recreational activities because of their own preconceived notions of what a person with a visual impairment can or cannot do. Parents may not even realize all of the possible recreational and leisure activities in which people who are blind or visually impaired participate. They may bowl, play golf, swim, snow ski, water ski, wrestle, play beeper baseball, ride bikes, and play musical instruments. Sometimes families are very protective of their children who are visually impaired. They may still be coping with acceptance of their child's vision loss and may feel very responsible for his or her safety. Protecting a child from injury and frightening experiences is one of a parent's primary tasks, but being overly protective by discouraging a child who is visually impaired from trying new activities may not be in the child's best interest.

Even if a child who is visually impaired and his or her parents are open to new recreational experiences, they may find roadblocks from others outside the family. Preschool classmates and teachers may exclude the child from many activities because they do not understand vision loss. Some community recreational programs may discourage participation of a visually impaired child, expressing liability concerns. For older children, team sports may be discouraged by coaches who have no knowledge of adaptations that can be made to include a child with a disability. The result of all these barriers to participation may be that the young child who is visually impaired spends a great deal of free time alone in passive situations, leading to increased social isolation and lack of confidence to try new activities.

It is important to think very broadly when identifying possible recreational and leisure time activities to try with a young child who is visually impaired, so as not to limit options. Thinking creatively in terms of how a child can participate in a given activity, even if not fully, and how age-appropriate and safe adaptations can be made opens many doors of recreation and leisure. (See McGregor & Farrenkopf, 2000, for more ideas on recreation and leisure for children who are visually impaired).

The following guiding principles may be useful in identifying appropriate recreational activities for young children who are visually impaired:

- Family interests and priorities should always be considered.

- The ability level of the child (both cognitive and motor areas) should be assessed.

- The interests of the child can guide the activity choices.

- The activities that sighted peers of the same age do can serve as a benchmark in selecting activities.

- The activities available in the community and geographic area often determine recreational activities from which to choose.

Many children with low vision can participate fully in a variety of activities with few adaptations once they have experience in them and their confidence builds. Sidebar 7.1 identifies some possible recreational activities in which young children who are visually impaired may participate. "Making Adaptations for Recreational or Leisure Activities" provides some general guidelines for ways of adapting recreational activities for participation by young children who are visually impaired. It also lists some examples of adaptations for different activities. The more creative and innovative one is, the more adaptations to allow participation that can be tried.

It is the role of the vision professional to help the family with ideas for appropriate recreational activities, to help the child learn skills to increase participation, to suggest adaptations when needed, and to encourage the development of fun and appropriate recreational and leisure activities based on each individual child's interests and abilities and family preferences. It is most beneficial when family members are aware of the need to expose the child who is vi-

SIDEBAR 7.1 **RECREATIONAL ACTIVITIES FOR YOUNG CHILDREN WHO ARE VISUALLY IMPAIRED**

The following list of possible recreational activities and adaptations that may be appropriate for a young child who is visually impaired can be used as a springboard for ideas.

GROUP ACTIVITIES/LESSONS

→ Play groups with other visually impaired and/or sighted children

→ Gymnastics classes

→ Swimming lessons

→ Community music classes

→ Story time at local library

→ Parachute games

→ Relay games

→ Martial arts (judo is especially appropriate for persons with visual impairments)

OUTDOOR ACTIVITIES

→ Water sports—swimming, boating, tubing with an adult, fishing

→ Playing in the sand and water

→ Sledding with an adult or older child

→ Jumping rope

INDOOR ACTIVITIES

→ Pretend play (for example, playing house, doctor, school)

→ Dancing

→ Arts and crafts

→ Hobbies and colletions (for examples, coins, Beanie Babies)

→ Board games (with partners, if needed)

→ Playing with cars and trucks

→ Building toys (for example, blocks, Duplos)

→ Computer games with friends

FAMILY ACTIVITIES

→ Hiking and camping with the family

- → Movies
- → Gardening
- → Concerts
- → Spectator sports with the family
- → Bumper bowling
- → Snow skiing with the family (with specialized instruction)
- → Children's museums (especially those that encourage touch and interaction)
- → Looking at holiday lights with the family (playing holiday music can enhance the activity)
- → Going to local parks or playgrounds.

Rona L. Pogrund

sually impaired to as many age-appropriate recreational and leisure activities as possible. These activities should fit the lifestyle, culture, and interests of other family members as well, since many recreational activities are done with family. The child can develop confidence in an activity with repeated practice. It is appropriate to expose a child to a variety of recreational activities, but it is best to prioritize activities that could easily fit into the family routine. For example, it would make sense to prioritize teaching a child a lot about fishing if the family enjoys fishing regularly.

It is also important for both families and professionals to remember that if a child appears resistant and upset when trying a new activity for the first time, it may be necessary to repeat the experience several times in a consistent manner until the child begins to feel some control over the situation. New skills can be improved by breaking them down into smaller tasks and can be paired with a successful activity while learning. It may take a number of tries before a child who is visually impaired can build confidence in his or her abilities and begin enjoying an activity more. It may soon become comfortable enough to be an activity of choice. If, after giving enough adjustment time to a particular activity, it does not seem enjoyable, then it is probably time to move on and try something else. It is important to keep in mind that the reason many young children who are visually impaired spend much of their free time alone (Schneckloth, 1989) listening to tapes or CDs, spinning, and rocking may be that they are not aware of all the vast possibilities of other ways to spend their leisure time.

Teachers of students who are visually impaired, orientation and

MAKING ADAPTATIONS FOR RECREATIONAL OR LEISURE ACTIVITIES

The following suggestions may be useful when deciding on adaptations for participation of a child with a visual impairment in recreational and leisure activities.

Principles for Making Adaptations

→ Initially, analyze an activity to see if a child with a visual impairment can participate fully without adaptations. Start with a "How can it be done?" attitude.

→ If there appears to be no way that the child can participate, then try to think of an adaptation that allows for full participation.

→ See if the child can partially participate with no adaptations or with adaptations, if necessary.

→ Decide whether the child needs a visual, tactile, or auditory adaptation or a combination to be able to participate.

→ Sometimes the equipment being used by sighted children or the rules of the activity can be slightly modified.

→ Sometimes specialized equipment needs to be obtained.

→ Some modifications require only allowing more time or being paired with a sighted partner.

→ Sometimes specialized instruction and practice are all that is needed for participation.

→ The guiding principle for adaptations is to make the least modifications necessary for the greatest amount of participation in any given activity.

Examples of Adaptations

→ Play commercially made games with tactile adaptations (see Resources section for catalogs with adapted products).

→ Put a big, bright colored stripe around a ball so child sees it "flicker" when moving.

→ Use sound localization cues for targets (for example, beepers on basketball goals and T-ball bases).

→ Use a beeper ball for T-ball participation.

→ Use beeper boxes for relay races.

→ Use large balls, bats, and other equipment to make them easier to see and use.

→ Have a family member sit by the child during a movie and give descriptions or use descriptive video, where available.

→ Take a portable radio and headphones to sporting events or when watching games on television to get more verbal descriptions of the game.

→ Encourage the chlid to play games with a partner.

→ Let the child turn rope for jump roping if he or she does not want to jump.

→ Use bumpers and a rail for bowling.

→ Use hand holding in circle games to allow for equal participation.

→ Use adult assistance in learning new movements for hand and body gestures in songs, gymnastics, dance, and playground equipment.

→ Use materials that are tactilely different for arts and crafts projects.

→ Allow more time on many activities, especially when the child is learning something new.

Rona L. Pogrund

mobility specialists, and early childhood specialists can help families develop intervention strategies to address these key areas. Such intervention plans should reflect the family's priorities and be easily implemented within the daily routine. A functional approach, in which skills are introduced and taught within the natural context of occurrence, may be incorporated into the instructional plan.

Children who are visually impaired who participate in activities of daily living and who experience a variety of recreational opportunities will be better prepared for future inclusion and independence. The value of providing specialized instruction and developing competency and confidence in these areas cannot be overestimated.

BEHAVIORAL FOCUS

Developing Positive Behavioral Supports

CONTRIBUTOR

Kay M. Pruett

B ehavioral supports are a set of methods and thought patterns that help parents and professionals guide children in establishing positive behaviors that facilitate development and learning. Children who are visually impaired, like all children, may display behaviors that frustrate and confound the adults who work or live with them. Children with severely delayed communication skills may experience even more behavioral challenges. Unacceptable behaviors may disrupt family life, interfere with the child's learning, violate appropriate social and classroom expectations, or interfere with other children's learning. Such behaviors can be modified through the use of positive behavioral supports.

The Individuals with Disabilities Education Act (IDEA) requires that the child's IFSP or IEP team address behavior that interferes with the learning of the child or others—for example, hand flapping, eye poking, or noisy outbursts—and determine appropriate positive behavioral interventions and strategies. IDEA requires functional behavioral assessment, which addresses the purposes of a child's behaviors, but does not specify how it must be conducted. (Functional behavioral assessment is discussed in more detail later in this chapter in the section on "Examining Social and Physical Environments.")

Most of the methods in this chapter have been developed and used with people whose behavior is significantly different from typical expectations for a given age group. Often, these individuals have been

The author wishes to thank Jeri Cleveland, Peg Brisco, and Lauren Newton in the Texas School for the Blind and Visually Impaired Special Programs Department for their assistance with this chapter.

FOCUS POINTS ON BEHAVIORAL SUPPORTS

The following key ideas are addressed in this chapter.

➜ Behavioral supports are a set of methods and thought patterns that help families and professionals guide children in establishing positive behaviors that facilitate development and learning.

➜ Young children with visual impairments should be expected to learn appropriate behaviors that will facilitate their development into capable, competent, and caring adults.

➜ Behaviors communicate the needs of the child.

➜ Maintaining a positive focus is at the core of a successful positive behavioral support program.

➜ Clear definitions of current behaviors and the needs those behaviors represent are an important foundation to the selection of appropriate strategies to support behavioral change. The behaviors must be observable and measurable.

➜ It is important to prioritize behavioral goals so efforts of families and professionals can focus on an achievable plan for behavioral change in the child.

➜ The goal of a functional behavior assessment is to understand the meaning of behaviors so that changes in the social and physical environments that support the child can be made.

➜ Strategies for behavioral change include instructional strategies, scheduling strategies, adaptations of physical environments, social strategies, and reinforcement strategies.

children and adults with severe cognitive delays. These methods are necessary and effective to support improved behavior of such students. However, they are equally effective in supporting behavioral change in learners with less severe behavioral challenges, including children with visual impairments who have no additional disabilities.

A chapter focused on behavior is most likely to attract readers seeking to change a child's frustrating behavior, and these methods are appropriate for such situations. However, they are also effective for supporting the behavioral changes that occur with development and learning. Teachers and parents who apply these procedures are able to help children to learn and develop by making positive changes in their behavior.

The strategies addressed in this chapter are based on several assumptions, which are listed in Sidebar 8.1. The specific strategies that will be developed in this chapter are listed in "Components of Positive Behavioral Support Systems."

Young children with visual impairments can and should be expected to learn appropriate behaviors. Wolffe (1999) stressed the importance of having expectations that children with visual impairments can and will "grow up to establish families of their own, live interdependently in their communities, and work to support themselves and their families" (p. 18). Keeping in mind the long-term goal of the child developing into a capable, competent, and caring adult helps professionals and parents teach young children appropriate behaviors.

Seeking to understand the communication and meaning of frustrating behaviors is at the heart of creating satisfying solutions to the conflicts these behaviors create. Mesaros (1995) claimed that behaviors are a child's way of "speaking" about his or her needs. Donnellan, Mirenda, Mesaros, and Fassbender (1984) also emphasize the communicative function of challenging behaviors. Researchers (for

COMPONENTS OF POSITIVE BEHAVIORAL SUPPORT SYSTEMS

Positive behavioral support systems for young children with visual impairment generally include the following components:

→ Valuing the child by attempting to understand the communicated meanings of the child's behaviors.

→ Clear communication of carefully selected expectations, including information about the actions of others that is only available visually.

→ Instruction in appropriate communication behaviors that have the same purpose as the challenging behaviors and guidance in where to use these alternative behaviors.

→ Nonaversive, concrete instruction in appropriate skills and concepts.

→ Naturally occurring, positive ways for children to acquire needed stimulation, escape, attention, tangibles, and other needs.

→ Modification of the physical or social environments to eliminate the opportunity to engage in problem behaviors (for example, helping siblings place important possessions out of reach). This strategy must be supplemented with other strategies to provide the child other options for meeting the need communicated by the problem behaviors.

→ Predictability, choice, and opportunities for independent success.

→ Reinforcement of positive behaviors with preferred reinforcers.

Kay M. Pruett

example, Brown, et al., 2000; Carr & Durand, 1985) have had success in reducing challenging behaviors by teaching students to use communication to express the same needs that the challenging behaviors had communicated.

This chapter will present only positive behavioral support strategies. The importance of choosing a positive focus for helping children learn desired behavior cannot be overemphasized. O'Neill, Horner, Albin, Storey, and Sprague (1990) stressed the importance of the dignity of the person by acknowledging "that a person's behavior is reasonable from that person's perspective" (p. 4). McGee and Menolascino (1991) emphasized the importance of valuing the people we work with and building relationships with them in which we are also willing to be changed. Teachers and parents who pay attention to capabilities, strengths, and positive behaviors of a child contribute to a positive social context where behavioral change can be initiated and nurtured.

Many teachers and parents seek a behavior management solution to a child's frustrating actions. Two types of behaviors tend to frustrate adults working with children. One is dealing with undesired behaviors, such as when a child with visual impairment repeatedly crinkles up a sibling's papers. The other is the challenge of dealing with absent desired behaviors, such as when a child with visual impairment does not eat lumpy foods. These challenging situations indicate a mismatch between the needs and abilities of the child and the requirements of the environment or a mismatch between the needs and abilities of the child and the needs of other people.

Behaviors communicate the needs of the child. This chapter covers a variety of techniques to help change children's behavior and improve the match between the child and the child's physical and social environments. It presents strategies to support and encourage positive behavioral changes in young children who are visually impaired with or without other impairments. Ways to define, prioritize, and promote positive behavior in young children who are blind or visually impaired will also be addressed. The sequence and components of this process are important because identical or similar behaviors may have different functions in different children or even at different times in the same child. It is therefore not possible to give particular strategies for any specific behavior without proceeding through this process, at least mentally.

DEFINING AND PRIORITIZING POSITIVE BEHAVIOR

Maintaining a Positive Focus

Behavioral support strategies are most effective if used in a stimulating positive environment that values the child. Sometimes young children with visual impairments, like other young children, engage in behaviors that other people do not perceive as positive. They make noises, rock in place, throw things, make messes with their food, fail to do tasks parents and teachers want them to do, and engage in other behaviors that frustrate adults. At these times, it is helpful for the adults to gain or maintain perspective, focus on their own feelings, and seek the meaning of the behavior. This background provides a good foundation for participation in an effective behavioral program.

Maintaining a positive focus is a challenging but powerful factor in the pursuit of positive behavioral change. The accompanying box, "Maintaining a Positive Focus," provides strategies for keeping a positive attitude.

Understanding the Behavior

Behavior does not occur in isolation. Considering their own feelings and responses gives teachers and parents background perspective and some initial data that is helpful in discovering the meaning of the child's behaviors. Separating out one's own needs, feelings, expectations, values, and issues reinforces and helps clarify what is going on with the child. Team members will be more prepared to implement a behavior intervention program after analyzing their own feelings, positions, and perspectives. They may write down their feelings or talk with someone safe, trusted, and positive who would not be in violation of the child's confidentiality rights. People working with children who display frustrating behaviors especially need to consider their own feelings. Questions to consider include:

- What do I think that the child is expressing to me through the behavior?

- What do I want to express to the child?

- How do I feel about the child and the behaviors?

- What are my rewards?

- How is this affecting me?

- What about this behavior troubles me?

- What are my wants, needs, and expectations in this situation?

- What do I want from and for the child?

Understanding Mannerisms

Mannerisms are repetitive behaviors commonly seen in children who are blind or visually impaired. They include rocking, eye poking, finger flicking, and head movements. Like other behaviors, mannerisms express needs which are reasonable from the perspective of the child. Seeking to understand the purpose of the behavior works especially well with mannerisms. Mannerisms generally manifest themselves in the child's early years to meet a need for sensory

---

FOCUS ON EFFECTIVENESS

MAINTAINING A POSITIVE FOCUS

When pursuing positive behavioral change, it is important to keep in mind the following strategies:

→ Teachers and caregivers need to focus on the positive with one another and with the child.

→ The child is more than the behavior and needs to continue to be valued.

→ Behavior indicates needs of the child that are reasonable from the child's perspective.

→ Shifting the focus of attention from the frustrating behavior to the child's abilities is sometimes enough to bring improvement in behavior.

→ Perspective may be gained by listing positive behaviors, capabilities, and characteristics opposite the frustrating ones.

Kay M. Pruett

stimulation and often continue as a habitual comfort. Sometimes they are then used as an escape from uncomfortable situations.

While mannerisms may be reasonable behavior from the child's perspective, there are important reasons to consider helping the child change these behaviors. Eye poking creates visual stimulation but can also create structural damage over time. Mannerisms can be uncomfortable for people to watch and, therefore, can affect perceptions of the child's social competence. These behaviors may not be consistent with the image of competent, capable adulthood. They can also take the place of more useful activities and in this way restrict the child's learning.

Waving the fingers in front of the eyes, sometimes called finger flicking, creates visual stimulation for children with low vision. Rocking and head movements create vestibular stimulation through movement of the fluid in the semicircular canals. The need for this increased sensory stimulation is directly related to the visual impairment, which reduces visual stimulation available. Visual impairment may also contribute to reduced activity levels that in turn cause reduced vestibular stimulation.

Understanding that these activities communicate a reasonable need for sensory stimulation can pave the way for providing such stimulation in more socially acceptable settings or activities. For example, the child's need for vestibular stimulation may be satisfied by swinging in a swing or running. More ways to give positive behavioral support to the child with needs for increased stimulation are presented in the strategies section of this chapter.

In contrast to children who use mannerisms to increase stimulation, other children use these habitual activities to block out or escape circumstances that they find to be aversive. Focusing their attention on the activity of the mannerism may protect these children from experiencing situations that they find frightening, confusing, frustrating, or uncomfortable. In this case, understanding that these activities communicate the need for reasonable coping mechanisms may pave the way for a better match between the children and the environment. Sometimes, changing the situation is appropriate either on a short- or long-term basis. Ideal long-term solutions include helping children to learn other ways to communicate their distress and helping them to learn other coping mechanisms for dealing with uncomfortable situations that cannot reasonably be changed. Ways to help the child who is expressing the need to avoid or escape a situation are also included in the strategies section of this chapter.

Defining Behaviors

Clear definitions of current behaviors and the needs those behaviors represent are an important foundation to selection of appropriate strategies to support behavioral change. At the heart of an effective behavioral support program is the practice of defining behaviors. A specific definition and description of each behavior of concern is essential for a clear plan to change behavior. It is more helpful to know that a child does not respond to another child's greeting, for example, than to know that the child behaves rudely. Likewise, it is more useful to know that a child strikes his or her head with an open palm than that the child has self-injurious behavior. It is more helpful to know that a child scoops soft foods with a spoon and stabs and lifts chunky foods with a fork than that he or she eats nicely. With a precise definition, the behavior can be more easily monitored, discussed, measured, and changed. The more precisely defined the behavior, the more possible it will be to change it.

Many young children with visual impairments, with or without additional impairments, withdraw their hands from tactile contact. Children with this and similar behaviors have often been given the label of "tactilely defensive." Also, the label of "tactilely selective" has come into use. (Additional information on tactile defensiveness and tactile avoidance can be found in Chapter 9.) In a positive behavioral support program, such labels are unnecessary and may be counterproductive by giving adults expectations that these withdrawing behaviors are, and always will be, present in the child. Nielsen (1990) suggests that hand withdrawal behavior is a reaction to the practice of adults taking over control of the child's hands and restricting the child's ability to explore. Withdrawal of the hands may also indicate children's surprise when they have been unaware of the approaching contact. In a positive behavioral support program, the behavior will be described in observable and measurable terms and the contexts of the behavior will be assessed to determine the function of the behavior. Strategies to increase active interaction with the environment are addressed later in this chapter, in the section on typical needs of young children with visual impairments.

Behavioral support programs need an observable and measurable definition for each behavior that is targeted for change. In this way, negative value judgments and labeling of characteristics are reduced. Clearly defined behaviors are more easily changed and less limiting than negative labeling and perceptions. Finally, communication and understanding among families and professionals are increased by a common observable and measurable definition.

Thought processes and understandings cannot be directly observed, but their presence is often evident in observable behavior. For example, knowing the way to the bathroom is not directly observable, whereas walking to the bathroom can be directly observed. In a behavioral focus, the cognitive processes are inferred by the behavior. Therefore, behavioral support programs focus on observable behaviors.

These observable behaviors must be clearly described and measurable. O'Neill and colleagues (1990) have suggested describing five aspects of each behavior of concern (see Sidebar 8.2). Measurement is necessary to document the behavior and to be able to recognize whether efforts to change it are effective or not. "Measuring Behaviors" in this chapter presents some different ways to measure behaviors. With clear definitions of behaviors, the educational team is ready to prioritize behaviors and analyze the contexts of the behaviors in preparation for helping the child change the desired or undesired behavior.

Setting Behavioral Goals

By prioritizing and selecting behavioral goals, the team of parents and teachers focuses their efforts on a manageable set of behaviors, thus creating an achievable plan for behavior change. If there are ten behaviors to change, it will be most helpful to begin with the most important one or two. For example, biting other children would be a higher priority for intervention than whining in the grocery store. High priority behaviors for intervention are safety issues, behaviors that hamper the child's own learning, behaviors that are highly disruptive of the learning of others, behaviors that communicate intensely felt unmet needs, and behaviors that fit the developmental level of the child.

Wise selection of behavioral goals helps the child move positively toward the long-term goal of competent adulthood. Stating behavioral goals in terms of desired behaviors helps maintain a positive focus. Examples of positive goals include:

- When requested to do so, Susie will sit still in her carseat to be buckled in.

- Ben will increase the period of time he remains in the learning area during instruction.

- Amy will lift food in a spoon from the bowl to her mouth.

Goals to increase desired behaviors that are incompatible with the undesirable behavior can reduce the undesired behaviors in a positive way. A child with hand flapping, finger-flicking, or eye-poking behavior would probably be best served by a goal and supports to increase a behavior that uses the hands in another way. Increasing two-handed exploration of objects would address this need. Behaviors selected for intervention should be consistent with long-term high expectations and goals. They should also be reasonable expectations considering current capabilities and developmental levels of the child. For example, it is unreasonable to expect a child who does not yet use his or her hands for tactile exploration to discriminate among braille letters. Goals must be observable and measurable to have clear knowledge of when they have been accomplished.

Safety issues are highest priority. They cannot be ignored. Behavior that is life- or health-threatening should be considered first. Children manifesting serious life- or health-threatening behaviors need the expertise of a behavior specialist on their educational team. Behavior that injures or is likely to injure the child or others must be reduced and then eliminated. Harmful behaviors such as head banging, hitting, eye poking, biting, and running into traffic will need to be eliminated. Safety practices, such as getting into and using a car safety seat, may need to be developed. The contexts and communi-

MEASURING BEHAVIORS

There are many ways to measure behaviors. Examples of these include:

➜ Counts made from permanent work such as classroom papers. For example, the teacher may count the number of correct braille letters produced by the child.

➜ Event recording in which an observer makes a tally using pen and paper or a variety of counting devices. For example, each time a child verbalizes the need for help or puts a spoon with food on it into the mouth may be tallied.

➜ The duration of a behavior or the duration without a behavior can be documented. For example, the length of time a child spent lying on the floor crying may be recorded, or the length of time the child spent engaged in an activity without crying may be recorded.

➜ Frequency of a behavior over a particular duration of time can be recorded in a variety of ways. For example, the number of letters a child identifies correctly in a minute or the number of tactile contacts with objects made in a minute by a child with multiple impairments may be recorded.

➜ Measurements may be taken continuously or during selected intervals of time. For example, behaviors that occur at a very high frequency may be counted for just three minutes of each activity period. Infrequent behaviors may be recorded each time they happen throughout the day. Behaviors relevant to only one activity may be recorded just during the time of that activity.

Kay M. Pruett

cated meanings of these behaviors will assist the team in selecting appropriate intervention strategies.

Behaviors that interfere with the child's or other children's learning must be addressed to meet IDEA requirements. Changing behaviors that affect learning opportunities of the child or others can have a double impact. The positive effects of the targeted behavior change are multiplied by the increased availability of the child to the learning situation. These behavioral goals may include such things as increasing interactions with materials and people while reducing mannerisms. Another example is increasing appropriate verbal requests for help or attention while reducing disruptive attention seeking behaviors. Behaviors that keep parents or teachers from including children in community outings also need to be addressed.

Strongly felt needs of the child, professionals, and family should be addressed in an effective plan. Needs expressed by the child's behaviors need to be included. For example, a child who is expressing a need for more vestibular stimulation through frequent rocking needs an increase in behaviors that provide socially acceptable vestibular stimulation. Teachers and classmates need a certain amount of order in the classroom that may be in conflict with a child's need to move independently and explore the environment. In this case, creating a defined space full of interesting materials and equipment in which the child may move and explore independently, while limiting exploration in other areas of the classroom, may effectively address this conflict of needs.

A child with intense needs for instruction and assistance in eating may be part of a family that has a cultural value for a peaceful family dinner hour. Like the previous classroom example, separation of the needs may lead to a satisfactory solution to this conflict. Eating skills may be addressed at other times and feeding the child may even occur before or after the family meal. The child may be given quiet toys or other assistance to be included as a less disruptive part of the family gathering time. Other families may be very comfortable with lots of noise and messes while eating dinner. Each family and each child have their own unique needs.

Understanding the developmental level and needs of the child is critical to selection of appropriate behavioral goals. Behaviors appropriate to a child's level of development can be changed much more easily than behaviors that are significantly beyond developmental levels of the child. IDEA requires developmental assessment of infants, toddlers, and preschoolers receiving services. Information from such assessments is essential in selection of appropriate behavioral goals for children of all ages. For example, a child with developmental skills consistently in the 2- to 3-year-range is unlikely to learn to read fluently and independently in the current year. Toilet training is unlikely to be effective with a 5-year-old whose skills are all clustered around the 12-month level. Parents or some of the professionals on the child's early educational team may feel strongly about a goal that is significantly beyond the child's current developmental level. In this case, behavioral goals may be selected which address developmentally appropriate portions of these tasks. Reading readiness goals such as exploring books, listening to stories, and playing rhyming games may be appropriate for a child with development in the 2- to 3-year-range. Goals such as walking to the bathroom, cooperating with hand washing after a diaper change, or assisting in pulling up pants may be appropriate for the child with overall development in the 12-month range. (See Chapter 7 for more information about age-appropriate behavior.)

Another developmental issue in prioritizing behaviors for intervention is the developmental need for a given behavior. Some behaviors are developmentally appropriate and necessary for learning. Exploring food tactilely and eating with the fingers are necessary steps in learning to eat. Throwing and dropping objects are part of the cognitive development of understanding the properties of objects. Saying no is part of developing an independent sense of self. Walking or running around handling objects is part of developing motor skills, mobility skills, spatial understanding, and understanding of objects. These types of behaviors are more adequately addressed by educating the adults involved, changing expectations, and adapting physical environments and schedules than by a program to eliminate the behaviors. For example, placing the child with emerging eating skills on easily cleaned surfaces makes life easier for caregivers while allowing the practice opportunities needed to develop better eating skills.

Finally, positive behavioral goals need to be selected with long-term life goals in mind. The earlier example of increasing exploration while decreasing hand flapping is a developmentally appropriate goal that has lifelong implications. Increasing manual exploration is usually a positive choice for children with visual impairments, who as a group tend to need encouragement to be active in their learning. This exploration teaches a skill that opens all kinds of doors to learning opportunities and activities. Active exploration is also more likely to provide some stimulation, which is often the need that is expressed in eye poking, hand flapping, and finger flicking.

In summary, several factors need consideration in prioritizing behavioral goals. Issues of safety are critical. Addressing behaviors that affect learning of the child or other children is required by IDEA and improves behavior while increasing learning opportunities. The needs expressed by the child's behavior and the needs of others in the home or school environment must be addressed in selecting behavioral goals. The child's levels of development are integral to understanding the needs of the child and creating successful plans for behavioral change. A positive vision for the child's future in the long term leads to meaningful goals.

EXAMINING THE SOCIAL AND PHYSICAL ENVIRONMENTS RELATED TO BEHAVIOR

Behaviors do not occur in isolation. They happen within social and physical contexts. Variations in these environments lead to variations in behavior, creating a behavioral dialogue between the child and the social and physical environment. Behaviors are reinforced in various ways within these contexts. Functional behavioral assessment is the study of behaviors within these environments. The goal of a functional behavioral assessment is to understand the meaning of behaviors and to make changes in the social and physical environments that support the child to make positive behavioral changes.

Functional behavioral assessment may be as informal as saying, "I think the child does the behavior because____." However, for complex, continuing problem behaviors, more extensive functional behavioral assessment is necessary. Such assessment includes data collection and specific functional assessment procedures such as those specified by Quinn, Gable, Rutherford, Nelson, & Howell (1998) or O'Neill and colleagues (1990). Both suggested multifaceted processes that include:

- indirect assessment, such as interviews of those who know the child best,

- direct assessment, through observations of the child within the contexts where behavioral change is sought,

- analysis of the assessment data, and

- hypothesis testing through systematic manipulation of variables to be able to predict occurrence of the behaviors.

As stated previously, it is important to remember that behaviors communicate a child's needs. Examining the social and physical environments of behaviors of concern helps to clarify the communicative dialogue and to understand what the child is expressing by these behaviors. As in other assessment situations, the assessment team must consider the effects of the child's visual impairment on interactions in both social and physical aspects of the environmental context. These effects must be considered in all assessments of the child's environments.

Visual impairment affects a child's interactions with people and the environment. Without intervention, children with visual impairments have significantly less interaction with social and physical environments than children with normal vision. Visual impairment affects eye contact between child and caregiver. It reduces or eliminates the social smile feedback (see Chapter 6). Visual impairment reduces or eliminates visual incentive to reach out and interact with objects. It severely restricts opportunities to learn from imitation of others (see Chapter 4). How the child with a visual impairment perceives the environment is a critical factor in understanding the behavioral dialogue and developing strategies to support positive behavior. For example, a child with visual impairment who sits without interacting or exploring in a preschool classroom full of toys, materials, and children may not be able to see the toys or how the other children play with the toys. Therefore, this child may not recognize the option to participate in the play and exploration.

The goal of examining the environmental contexts of a child's behaviors is to understand what the child is communicating behaviorally. This section will address three levels of environmental contexts. It will begin most broadly, considering quality of life issues. Next, the situations in which selected behaviors occur or do not occur are addressed. Also at the intermediate level of analysis, discrepancy analysis can identify and clarify differences between expected or desired behaviors and what the child currently does. Finally, the narrow focus of events immediately surrounding the behavior is addressed in analysis of antecedents and consequences of the selected behaviors.

Quality-of-Life and Lifestyle Contexts

The broad view looks at the multidimensional character of the child's natural contexts. These environmental contexts include quality-of-life and lifestyle issues. The child's entire daily and weekly schedule needs to be considered. "Assessing Quality-of-Life and Lifestyle Contexts" contains specific ideas on assessing quality-of-life and lifestyle issues.

Situational Context

Within the broad quality-of-life context, the specific environments of high-priority behaviors are examined. In each situation related to a behavior of concern, the specific context is addressed. "Assessing Specific Behavioral Contexts" lists who, what, when, where, and how questions to ask in the environment or context of a specific behavior. Analyzing the answers to these questions for each situation and each behavior may clarify factors related to the behaviors of concern. For example, do the child's behaviors happen or not happen with particular people, during particular activities, at particular times, in particular locations, or during particular internal biological or emotional states?

Discrepancy Analysis

Also at the intermediate level of analysis, discrepancy analysis, described in more detail in Chen & Dote-Kwan, (1999) and Lueck (1998), is especially useful for behaviors that need to increase. The

ASSESSING QUALITY-OF-LIFE AND LIFESTYLE CONTEXTS

To assess the child's environment broadly in terms of his or her quality of life and lifestyle, the child's daily and weekly schedules need to be examined. Specific aspects to focus on include:

→ *Variety of activities:* In what activities does the child participate? What does the child perceive? What does the child do in each activity?

→ *Variety of environments:* What places does the child go? How do the places vary from one another in such characteristics as size of space, lighting, temperature, and acoustics?

→ *Variety and stability of social environments:* With whom does the child interact? What are the age, gender, culture, and style of interaction of each person? How stable are the relationships?

→ *Attention to physical needs:* How are the child's individual physical needs such as rest, sleep, food, water, cleanliness, and medications met?

→ *Relative independence:* To what extent does the child have success without assistance?

→ *Predictability:* To what extent does the child know what will happen from regularity of schedules or from cues and prompts in the environment?

→ *Choices:* What choices does the child make? How often does the child choose? How does the child communicate those choices?

→ *Deference to the child's preferences:* To what extent are the child's preferences honored? In what circumstances?

→ *Active engagement with objects:* What is the amount or ratio of time the child is actively engaged with objects? What are the objects?

→ *Active involvement with people:* What is the amount or ratio of time the child is actively engaged with people?

Kay M. Pruett

task is broken into its component parts, with expectations listed for each part. A plus sign is placed beside each component of the desired behavior that the child does. A minus sign is placed beside components for which there is a discrepancy between expectations and performance. From this discrepancy analysis, an instructional plan may be created to teach the missing skills. If the skills are not appropriate instructional goals, adaptations may be used for successful completion of the discrepant parts of the task.

ASSESSING SPECIFIC BEHAVIORAL CONTEXTS

When assessing the situation surrounding specific behaviors, asking the questions who, what, when, where, and how can help clarify the behavioral context.

➜ *Who* is present? (Considers the social situation in which the behaviors of concern happen or do not happen.) For example, the number, genders, ages, and familiarity of the people, proximity of the people to the child, and the nature of the interactions.

➜ *What* is the activity? (Considers the action context.) For example, expectations for the child, child's actions, and materials.

➜ *When* does it happen? (Considers the scheduling context.) For example, how often this situation happens, the time of day, the day of the week, and preceding events.

➜ *Where* does it happen? (Considers the physical location.) For example, room characteristics, furniture, lighting, and noise level.

➜ *How* is the child? (Considers variables within the child.) For example, recovering from an illness, excited about a coming event, stayed up late, and exposure to allergens.

Kay M. Pruett

Antecedents and Reinforcers

Finally, the focus of the behavioral analysis is narrowed to the situations immediately preceding and following the behaviors of concern. Within an understanding of the broader context, these factors are examined to understand the communicative function of the behaviors. This analysis is sometimes referred to as ABC analysis, referring to *a*ntecedents, *b*ehavior, and *c*onsequences (Taylor-Peters, 1992). Antecedents are the factors present in the situation before a behavior happens. They will be addressed after the discussion of consequences. Consequences immediately follow the behavior. Consequences that increase a behavior are reinforcers. They are what the child escapes or receives from a given behavior. For example, a consequence when a child yells may be removal from a difficult lesson. When a child asks for and receives a snack, the asking behavior may be reinforced by receiving the snack.

REINFORCERS

Reinforcers fall into two main categories. Behavior is reinforced by getting something desired (*positive reinforcement*) or avoiding something unwanted (*negative reinforcement*). Positive reinforcement increases behavior because something is given (for example, the infant increases eating behaviors when soft music is played). Attention, sensory stimulation, tangible items such as food or objects, and activities can be positive reinforcers. Negative reinforcement increases behavior because something negative is removed (for example, the infant increases eating behavior when loud music is turned off). Escape from difficult tasks, feared situations, or uncomfortable sensations can be negative reinforcers. Negative reinforcement is not the same as punishment. Punishment decreases or eliminates a behavior by following the behavior with an undesired consequence (for example, the child who is throwing food decreases the behavior in subsequent feedings because the parent turned off the child's favorite music when the child threw food) (Taylor-Peters, 1992). Punishment is not used in positive behavioral support plans.

Negative reinforcement, or avoidance of something perceived as undesirable, supports an increase in behavior. Avoidance of a variety of things may increase (reinforce) behaviors. Behaviors can be reinforced by avoidance of overly stressful stimulation. Sometimes avoidance of challenging learning situations reinforces undesirable behavior. Carr (1994) suggested that behavior can also be reinforced by avoiding uncomfortable social contacts.

Paclawskyj and Vollmer (1995) studied preferred positive reinforcers of school-age boys with visual and other impairments. They found that the stimulation of being presented any reinforcer was preferred more often than was the case in previous studies of sighted children. In a forced choice situation, the boys as a group chose the reinforcers in this order of preference: music, vibration, clapping/praise, candy, cracker, juice, and a string ball. This finding may demonstrate a need to provide more reinforcers in general for these children.

As discussed in the section on keeping perspective, behaviors of those working with children are also reinforced during their interactions. Teachers and parents are positively reinforced for using effective teaching strategies by getting the responses they want from the children. Sometimes, however, an undesirable behavior loop gets established through negative reinforcement of an adult working with the child. This pattern typically happens when the adult tries to reduce the child's undesirable behavior by introducing an unpleasant consequence. For example, an adult may scold the child. For the moment, the child's behavior stops and the adult is reinforced by escape from experiencing the child's undesirable behavior. The next time the behavior appears, the adult again scolds and again the behavior stops. However, over time the occurrence of both the child's undesirable behavior and the adult's scolding increase. The adult's scolding behavior is being rewarded by the immediate escape from the child's behavior. The child's behavior is being reinforced by receiving the adult's attention. This is "positive" reinforcement because the child is getting something desired, even though the tone of the attention becomes far from positive in such a loop. Positive behavior support programs attempt to change behaviors by providing desired reinforcers that are acceptable to the child, the professional, and the parent.

Identifying reinforcers clarifies the communicative function of behaviors. Donnellan and colleagues (1984) suggested meanings of behaviors that are maintained by particular kinds of reinforcers. Table 8.1 gives examples of behaviors maintained by different kinds of reinforcers.

Understanding what the behaviors are communicating leads to selection of appropriate interventions. Smith and Levack (1996) recommended that the intentionality of communication also be considered. A child who intentionally communicates needs through behaviors is a good candidate for instruction in appropriate communication behaviors with the same meanings as the undesirable behaviors. When the behavior communicates needs without evidence of the child's intent to do so, modifications in the social and physical environment may be more helpful than attempting to teach direct communication skills at this time.

ANTECEDENTS

Antecedents are the situations that precede behaviors. They are the specific events that trigger the occurrence of the behavior. What prompts the child's behavior? The general situation has already been analyzed. At this level, the events immediately preceding the behavior are considered. For example,

- *What is the sensory input:* noises, lighting, smells, things in contact with the child, child's movement, and other environmental input? (For example, the sensory overload or blocking effect of loud noise may be the antecedent to the behavior of dropping immobile to the sidewalk.)

- *How is the child positioned?* (For example, being placed on the stomach may be the antecedent to crying behaviors.)

- *What are the materials?* (For example, experiencing an unpleasant texture in food might be the antecedent to gagging or spitting behaviors.)

- *What is the focus of the child and other people in the situation?* (For example, an adult talking on the phone may be the antecedent to attention seeking behaviors.)

- *What prompts have been given?* (For example, the prompt "time for bed" may be the antecedent to whining behavior or teethbrushing behavior.)

Knowing the antecedents or prompts to a particular behavior is important because changing the antecedents can lead directly to a change in behaviors. One may be able to reduce antecedents that trigger problem behaviors. Most importantly, changing the an-

TABLE 8.1 **COMMUNICATIVE FUNCTIONS OF BEHAVIORS MAINTAINED BY VARIOUS REINFORCERS**

BEHAVIOR THAT IS REINFORCED BY:	SUGGESTS COMMUNICATION OF:	EXAMPLES:
Avoidance	"I don't want to do this any more." "Stop." "No!" "I don't understand; I want out."	Pulling hands away or spitting out lumpy food.
Blocking out excess sensory input	"I'm anxious, tense, excited, nervous, overwhelmed." "Help me."	Placing hands over ears and humming
Attention	"Pay attention to me." "Hello!" "Look at me, I'm silly," "Play with me." "Look at me," "Help me."	Yelling
Receiving food, object, or activity reinforcers	"I want _____."	Whining for cookies
Stimulation of the senses	"I'm not getting the input I want." "I'm bored."	Rocking

Source: Based on material from A. M. Donnellan, P. L. Mirenda, R. A. Mesaros, & Fassbender, L. L. Fassbender. "Analyzing the communicative functions of aberrant behaviors," *Journal of the Association for the Severely Handicapped, 9,* (1984), pp. 201–212.

tecedents is often a key factor in increasing infrequent and absent behaviors. Most instructional techniques and prompts are antecedent events.

STRATEGIES FOR PROMOTING POSITIVE BEHAVIORS

Once one or a few behaviors have been selected as priorities for helping the child change, and the functional assessment of behavior has been done to suggest what purpose or communication the targeted behavior serves, the team is ready to apply strategies for behavioral change. The following types of strategies will be addressed:

- Instructional strategies usually involve changing the level of information provided by the caregiver to a young child.

- Scheduling strategies involve changing activities or the times and order in which they happen.

- Adaptations of physical environments to include specialized equipment and how space, equipment, materials, and supplies are arranged.

- Social strategies are changes made with regard to who interacts with the child and how they interact.

- Reinforcement strategies include being aware of what rewards the child's behavior and the adult's behavior and making changes in the consequences that follow a behavior.

The application of these strategies differs depending on the purpose or communicated meaning of the behavior being addressed. Therefore, strategies are for five groups of children:

1. Strategies often needed by children with visual impairments.

2. Strategies for children with needs for increased sensory input.

3. Strategies for children with needs for escape and avoidance.

4. Strategies for children with needs for attention.

5. Strategies for children with difficulty expressing needs for tangible objects or activities.

Typical Needs of Children with Visual Impairments

INSTRUCTIONAL STRATEGIES

As noted earlier, children who are blind or visually impaired need to be given expectations of capable functioning in adulthood. They need to be taught skills and concepts that children with vision pick up through watching. Specifically, they need specialized instruction in the expanded core curricular areas of compensatory communication modes, orientation and mobility, social interaction skills, visual efficiency, independent living, recreation and leisure, career education, and technology (Hatlen, 1996). Lueck (1998) has provided a systematic process for identifying concepts needing to be taught for specific tasks a child is learning. Examining necessary skills and concepts from a discrepancy analysis helps instructional teams select appropriate instructional objectives in concepts and skills.

SCHEDULING STRATEGIES

Young visually impaired children need schedules that include a developmentally appropriate variety of activities and environments that cover the expanded core curricular areas. The child's time needs to be broken into many small chunks of varied and meaningful activities. Children with visual impairments do not get the rich information from looking around that a sighted child receives. Therefore, the child with visual impairment needs more frequent changes in position and stimulation (for example, rotating toys and alternating interaction with a person and interaction with toys). A large proportion of the child's time needs to be spent in environments where the child has a significant degree of developmentally appropriate autonomy, independent success, and choice making, as described in the next section.

Predictability in their environment and activities is important to children who are visually impaired. Predictability can be achieved through indications of change in activity that the child is able to perceive (such as small rituals that signal diapering and bathing) and some regularity in the child's schedule. Touch cues, object cues, calendar boxes, calendars, and consistent auditory cues (for example, using the same few words or same song before an activity with a child who hears) are positive strategies for providing predictability.

Predictability can be increased by giving consistent auditory and tactile cues before changes in activity or position (for example, one might signal time to be lifted up by telling the child each time and then touching the sides of the torso under the child's arms). For children with low vision, visual cues within their visual and developmental capabilities would also be used. An adult holding up the child's shoes might indicate "time to put on your shoes and go outside." Olfactory cues may be appropriate for some activities, especially those that have a naturally occurring odor such as the smell of lunch or the smell of clean diapers and wipes.

The schedule for infants who are visually impaired needs to include a significant amount of time spent in positions where the infant's actions would have a predictable effect on the environment. (See the next section on "Adaptations of Physical Environments" for suggestions.) The infant's schedule also needs to include frequent, extended carrying in physical contact with an adult from which the child would gain vestibular stimulation, body image feedback, and a feel and expectation of movement patterns (for example, carried in a front pack, sling, or backpack).

ADAPTATIONS OF PHYSICAL ENVIRONMENTS

A stimulating and interactive environment that the young child with a visual impairment can successfully relate to is essential to the child's development of a full compliment of desired behaviors. As noted in the previous section, the physical environments of these children need consistency and predictability. In addition, objects to explore and specialized equipment for unique needs must be easily accessed by the child. Having objects in consistent places (for example, a favorite crib toy in the same corner) facilitates the learning of object constancy and independent mobility. Specialized equipment also helps infants with visual impairments to develop manual motor skills, cognitive concepts, and understanding of spatial relationships. The toys and materials listed in "Specialized Equipment that Provides Consistency of Placement and Opportunity for Exploration" give opportunities for child-directed active exploration.

As the child begins moving independently, consistent placement of furniture, toys, clothes, and household items helps the child learn spatial concepts and contributes to independence and autonomy. Specialized equipment related to visual impairment (for example, braillewriters to write with, magnifiers and closed-circuit television systems [CCTVs] to look at objects with) need to be introduced and accessible in consistent places during the preschool years.

Some physical adjustments enhance the social interactions of young children with visual impairments. Skellenger, Hill, & Hill (1992) suggested enhancing the social environment of a child with visual impairment by placing desirable materials such as toys that are attractive to other children at a table where the child sits as a way to enhance the child's social environment. This practice invites the other children into accessible proximity to participate in social interactions.

SOCIAL STRATEGIES

Infants who are visually impaired need the close proximity of a caregiver who will respond to cries for food, changing, and attention. The child needs frequent tactile, auditory, and close visual contact. This closeness to a responsive person teaches the child to expect that communication will receive a response, which encourages the development of more intentional communication behaviors and social skills.

Children with visual impairments are limited in what can be learned from simple visual observation of the surroundings. Unlike children with normal vision, they receive little incidental learning from observation. Therefore, it is crucial that intentional

SPECIALIZED EQUIPMENT THAT PROVIDES CONSISTENCY OF PLACEMENT AND OPPORTUNITY FOR EXPLORATION

Young children who are visually impared need to spend time in environments where they are able to explore independently, make choices, and experience the effects of their actions on their surroundings. For them to be successful, objects in the environment need to be accessible and in consistent places. The following equipment is suggested for providing consistency of placement and motivation for exploration:

➜ *"Little Room"* (Nielsen, 1992)—a large, three-walled, box-like apparatus with objects hanging by elastic from a Plexiglas ceiling. Objects are placed to meet the child's individual needs. They are positioned where the child will perceive them and where something will happen when the child makes movements that are appropriate to individual development. The child lying in the Little Room can interact with the consistently placed objects by moving different parts of the body. Use of the Little Room promotes increased interaction, motor skills, spatial orientation, autonomy, cognitive development, and often speech and language.

➜ *Scratch boards*—a variety of textures attached to a board that is placed beneath the child's hands. Boards may be made with a child's preferred textures. These boards encourage independent exploration and use of fingers to scratch, rub, and explore the textures.

➜ *Stroller bars*—bars of toys that attach to strollers or seats of young children. These toys have a consistency of location and provide interesting noises, sights, and tactile experiences.

➜ *Infant discovery gyms*—bars with toys hanging down that are placed over a baby lying on his or her back. The baby can kick and bat at the toys.

➜ *Position boards* (Nielsen, 1992)—custom-made boards that are typically attached to wheelchairs or tables. Interesting objects are attached to the board by elastic. The child can handle the objects, let them go, and locate them again and again.

➜ *Echo bucket* (Johnson, Griffin-Shirley, & Koenig, 2000)—A bucket with objects hanging from its edges is suspended upside down over the child. It echoes back to the child the auditory effects of actions the child performs with the objects.

Kay M. Pruett

opportunities be provided for learning what others around them are doing. Adults and other children can be taught through instruction and modeling to unobtrusively provide information about what is happening that is otherwise only available visually. An adult sitting with the children may state this information without interrupting the activity. For example, "Sarah is poking holes in her Playdough with her finger. I am handing Steven a fork. Steven is tapping the fork on his Playdough and on the table," or "I have my cup of pudding. I'm putting my spoon in the cup. Now I'm putting the spoon in my mouth. Mmm. I kept all the pudding in my mouth and swallowed it. Now, I will get another bite." Both adults and children can learn these methods of enhancing the social environment for young children who are visually impaired. While this method can be quite effective in providing information to children with visual impairments so they can model their behavior after the behaviors of others, it should not be used all the time. Children also need a considerable amount of time for processing and exploring without ongoing verbal commentary.

Mutual tactile attention (also described as "mutual touch,") (Miles, 1999) is a child-directed method for sharing activities and experiences. As the child touches something, the adult's hands join the child's under the little fingers to share in the exploration. This technique is similar to mutual visual attention (for example, pointing and looking), a facilitating factor of early communication for most children. This shared experience also provides opportunities for communication that are directly and immediately related to the child's experiences.

REINFORCEMENT STRATEGIES

Keeping a positive behavioral focus includes being aware of reinforcers of both the child's and adult's behaviors. If frustrating behaviors begin, assessing the communicative function of the behavior and making adjustments quickly creates positive behavioral support. For example, if a parent determines that crying in the grocery store signals a need to avoid or escape confusing noises, the child may be more secure carried in a front pack rather than sitting in the basket. Being aware of the child's preferred reinforcers and how they are paired with desired behaviors in the natural environment also helps create and maintain positive behavioral support. For example, active playground play includes vestibular stimulation.

Need for Increased Sensory Input

As noted earlier, children who engage in mannerisms are often expressing a need for sensory input. The need for more stimulation, a common need among young children with visual impairments, may also be indicated by other behaviors communicating boredom. Caretakers and professionals should, however, be cautious not to just present a lot of sensory input randomly. Sensory opportunities need to be very meaningful for the individual child. The strategies described in this section for promoting positive behavior would enhance the lives and education of many children with visual impairments whether or not they display mannerisms.

INSTRUCTIONAL STRATEGIES

Children who display mannerisms may need instruction in skills used in other activities that provide needed stimulation or they may need instruction in communication skills to express their needs. Children displaying vestibular mannerisms such as rocking and head movement may need instruction in and opportunities for gross motor movements such as running and jumping. Children displaying visual mannerisms such as finger flicking may benefit from a program to promote increased use of vision. Once they have learned other activities that provide the stimulation they seek, children can be taught to request these activities through words, phrases, object cues, or gestures. Most of these children will also benefit from instruction in social skills (see Chapter 6).

Supporting the development of positive age-appropriate activities—such as using a slide independently—provides stimulation and reduces the need for mannerisms.

SCHEDULING STRATEGIES

Enriching the sensory environment of these children throughout their day can be implemented through scheduling changes. Children with visual impairments need a variety of stimulating activities in a variety of environments (for example, running in the gym, running in the park, clapping games, exploring books, and swinging). Activities matched to the sensory need should be included throughout the day. For example, children with needs for vestibular stimulation require periodic activities such as swinging, rocking, spinning, running, and jumping. Children with visual needs may benefit from several daily opportunities to interact with materials that promote the use of vision, such as light boxes, flashlights, and bright shiny objects.

In creating a schedule for these children, opportunities for a variety of sensory input should be included. Easily accessible opportunities for active involvement need to be present throughout the day. Preferred modalities of stimulation and opportunities for the child's choice-making need to be provided. For example, a child could choose between playing with objects on the light box or playing with a mirror. Opportunities for independent success in a variety of interactions and activities are crucial.

ADAPTATIONS OF PHYSICAL ENVIRONMENTS

Environmental adaptations include rocking chairs, rocking horses, swings, small trampolines, resonance boards, Little Rooms, and equipment and materials that promote the use of vision. Adapting the environment to have independently accessible materials always easily available to the child is essential. For the child who is not yet mobile, this adaptation may mean using a Little Room or position boards with objects attached (see "Specialized Equipment that Provides Consistency of Placement and Opportunity for Exploration" earlier in this chapter for descriptions). Sitting the child in the middle of a resonance board (Nielsen, 1992) causes round items that are dropped to return to the child as they roll downhill to the middle of the board. As the child develops sitting skills, easily accessed, preferred objects can be placed on a table or tray in front of the child or in the child's lap on the floor. Even when the child is independently mobile, materials still need to be consistently located and easily accessed.

SOCIAL STRATEGIES

Social interaction is an important form of stimulation. It is a basic human need, and it often becomes a powerful reinforcer. Since children with visual impairments often miss visual cues, they need specific instruction in social skills (see Chapter 6). Increasing social interaction may also increase and enhance other forms of stimulation such as visual, sensory–motor, auditory, tactile, and kinesthetic stimulation. Opportunities for active play with peers and social interactions may create a useful level of stimulation while the child develops social skills.

REINFORCEMENT STRATEGIES

Children who display mannerisms often need more stimulation. Socially appropriate forms of the stimulation the child wants and needs are powerful reinforcers for other desired behaviors. For example, a child who uses two hands for playing with Playdough (and thus refrains from hand flapping) may be reinforced by play with a shiny pinwheel, which provides socially appropriate visual stimulation.

Need for Avoidance or Escape

INSTRUCTIONAL STRATEGIES

Many children with needs to escape can be taught more desirable escape-requesting behaviors. Children who have some intentional communication may be taught to communicate their desire to avoid a situation or to request adaptations that help them cope with the situation. At the first sign of agitation in a situation that is associated with undesirable behavior, the child can be prompted to request escape through gestures, signs, words, or phrases. Following this communication, the child would be given a brief break from the difficult situation. For example, a child may be taught to say or sign "need break." Following approximations of this communication, the child is given a brief break.

Children may also be taught to use and request adaptations that help them cope with situations they find uncomfortable. For example, the child needing escape from auditory sensory overload may be taught to use headphones alone or with a system playing soothing music. Initially, such a system may be used all the time in noisy situations. Later it may be used for intermittent breaks from the noise. A child who is bothered by bright lights may be trained to shield the eyes, wear sunglasses, or move away from bright areas of the classroom. A child who feels crowded may be taught to ask for help, ask for more space, move away, or self-distract in a favorite appropriate activity.

If avoidance behaviors are interfering with teaching situations, adapting the situation is part of positive behavioral support. The teacher needs to consider whether instruction is appropriately tailored to the individual child. Skill instruction needs to be focused on skills that the child has the prerequisites and developmental level to learn. For example, to succeed at braille reading and writing, a child must be able to use his or her fingers separately, track efficiently, demonstrate understanding of basic spatial concepts, and gather and process tactile information. Young children with visual impairments need to be instructed using concrete experiences from which they can learn the concepts that are not available visually. Such experiences may include touching vegetables in the grocery store and other real objects beyond auditory descriptions or pictures. Children may feel more success in their instructional experiences if skills are broken into small steps, or if prompts are given so that the child can experience success while learning. However, for some children instruction may be aversive because it is boring. These children may need more challenge in their instruction.

SCHEDULING STRATEGIES

Changes in the child's schedule and physical environment can create a smoother fit with the child's learning characteristics and needs. Positive behavior patterns are supported when the child has fewer aversive experiences. Eliminating unnecessary aversive activities is occasionally possible (for example, turning off the vacuum if the child is bothered by the noise). Rescheduling some to a better time for the child may be possible. Regularly scheduling favorite activities as part of the aversive activity or immediately following the activity may help the child cope. For example, a child who dislikes bathing may tolerate baths better at a different time of the day, with a snack to eat in the bath, or if regularly followed by snuggle time in the rocking chair or other preferred activity.

ADAPTATIONS OF PHYSICAL ENVIRONMENTS

Physical arrangements may be changed to create different types and levels of stimulation. For example, an infant who cries when the TV news is turned on may need to be settled with someone or with soothing music in another room before the TV is turned on. The TV volume may also need to be turned down. When things that are aversive to the child are necessary, the overall situation can be made less aversive by the addition of positive elements or activities to the situation, thus buffering the effects of the unpleasant aspects of the situation. For example, taking a strongly flavored medicine may be both aversive and necessary. Buffering it with a small spoonful of chocolate syrup before and afterward may make the overall situation less aversive and make it possible for the child to take the medicine in a more positive way. The child who dislikes bathing may tolerate it better with music playing in the background or favorite toys in the water.

Materials may be changed or adapted to provide more interest or a different level of instruction to buffer the aversiveness of an instructional task. For example, difficult academic tasks may be less aversive using high interest materials. High contrast, visually pleasing materials, or use of visually interesting computer programs may make instructional tasks more positive for young children with low vision.

SOCIAL STRATEGIES

Providing a "safety signal" that indicates a no-demand situation (Carr & Durand, 1985) or imminent escape from the demand situation (O'Neill & Reichle, 1993) may help a child refrain from undesirable escape-motivated behaviors. For example, if items are placed within the child's visual field so the child can see when there is just one more item to complete before a natural escape, the child may more easily refrain from the behaviors that create escape. A safety signal indicating a no-demand situation might be when the materials from the demanding task are removed from the work table. Structuring social situations with attention to space and predictability issues may help some children have more success and less need for escape from social situations.

REINFORCEMENT STRATEGIES

For the child with avoidance needs, brief breaks from an unpleasant situation can be an effective reinforcement for appropriate requesting behaviors and increased coping behaviors. In instructional settings, successful completion of work may be followed by intervals without demands. Positively communicated requests for escape in appropriate situations need to be reinforced with opportunity for positive escape.

Providing short-term escape and avoidance that the child needs to maintain positive behaviors helps the child be more receptive to the learning situations in the long run. Initially, providing positive means of escape slightly more often than what the child has obtained through undesirable behaviors helps the child choose the positive behaviors.

Teachers or parents may be reluctant to reduce instruction or interaction time by providing escape breaks. However, it is important to remember that the child needs the breaks and has already been getting them through undesirable behaviors. By providing what the child needs in positive ways, both teacher and child will be more attentive to the learning situation for the long term.

Carr and Durand (1985) have suggested extinguishing the undesirable escape-motivated behavior by continuing instructional demands after such behavior. For example, when the child does something undesirable to avoid doing what has been asked, the teacher or parent asks again and continues to expect the child to do it. Continuing the instructional demands after escape-motivated behaviors stops the reinforcement of these behaviors. The needed escape is provided at other times when the undesirable behavior is not occurring.

Need for Attention

It is critical to remember not to discuss or focus on undesirable behaviors that are reinforced by attention, in the child's presence. Any behavior that increases after getting attention is most likely reinforced by attention. This relationship is true even if there are other reasons for the behavior. An example is a 5-year-old who regularly wets her bed about once a week. Her parents put her to bed each night in disposable training pants and say nothing about it when she is wet in the morning. At her annual well checkup, the parent, doctor, and child discuss the possibility of a medical cause for bedwetting and possible treatments. That night and every night for a week the child wets the bed. The parents continue to deal with it as before, giving their attention to other things. Bedwetting returns to the lower frequency of about once a week.

In the child whose behaviors are reinforced by attention, any behavior can be reinforced in this way. It is important for everyone who works with such children to understand this pattern and give lots of attention only to behaviors they wish to see increased. Discussion heard by the attention-seeking child needs to focus on whatever behaviors teachers and parents want to see more frequently. Undesirable behaviors must be discussed only when the child is not present and could not hear the discussion.

INSTRUCTIONAL STRATEGIES

The child whose behavior communicates a need for attention may benefit from instruction in communication and social skills. Specifically, ways of greeting, seeking assistance, showing work, asking for feedback, nonverbal social behaviors, and reciprocal interactions may be taught. (See Chapter 6 for strategies to promote social skills.)

SCHEDULING STRATEGIES

Children whose behaviors are reinforced by attention need a schedule that includes more opportunities for positive attention built into it. Adding interactive activities with people who give attention for positive behaviors may provide some of the needed attention in positive ways. Such activities include taking walks with someone, cooking with an adult, playing games, one-on-one reading time, going to social groups and activities with ample child-focused social interactions, telling jokes, imaginative play, playing musical instruments, and putting on plays. Having regular, predictable times of undivided attention is another positive support for the child with attention needs. Until the child learns more appropriate behavior for seeking attention, it may be helpful or necessary to temporarily reduce the child's time with people who cannot break out of the loop of giving attention for undesirable behaviors and who are unable to learn to give positive attention for positive behaviors.

ADAPTATIONS OF PHYSICAL ENVIRONMENTS

The environment may be structured in a way to encourage interactions that give attention for desired behaviors and discourage interactions that get attention for undesired behaviors. For example, toys that the child usually uses appropriately can be made available, while objects that the child uses inappropriately for attention are stored elsewhere. Toys and materials that invite positive interaction and attention may include a piece of cloth for playing peek-a-boo, dress-up clothes, and games that involve taking turns.

SOCIAL STRATEGIES

Adapting the social environment is at the core of a positive support plan for children with strong attention needs. Recognizing and giving attention for positive behaviors reinforces more desirable behaviors in the social environment. Helping others in the environment learn to provide ample positive attention to this child separate from the undesired behaviors is critical. Both children and other adults can be helped to change their response to the attention needs of these children through modeling and instruction. Understanding the reinforcing nature of negative attention for negative behavior helps others to change the social environment of the child. Bringing in another adult or older child to play, eat, or read with the child can provide some extra needed attention. Creating more opportunities to play with peers may enrich the environment for the preschool child with visual impairment.

REINFORCEMENT STRATEGIES

Professionals and families need to be consistent in providing immediate responses to the child's communicative attempts to gain attention. For example, when a child asks to be talked to and he or she is ignored, a tantrum may result. Attention should also be given consistently and frequently during times of acceptable behavior throughout the day. Attention reinforcement is especially important when the child manages in situations of low attention for increasing lengths of time. For example, when the teacher or parent is called away from an activity and the child manages without exhibiting past undesirable behaviors, the teacher or parent needs to provide attention, perhaps through a positive comment that describes the positive behavior.

With adequate skills and many opportunities to gain attention for positive behaviors, occurrences of the undesirable behaviors should not be followed by attention reinforcement. Ignoring these behaviors eliminates the reinforcement that has been maintaining them. However, parents and teachers need to be aware that part of the extinction cycle when reinforcement is withdrawn is an initial increase in the behavior before the behavior decreases. People in the child's environment need to be prepared for this increase. If the behavior is such that it cannot be ignored, it is preferable to make the minimal response to stop the behavior than to allow the behavior to increase and to then give the attention reinforcement to higher levels of an undesirable behavior.

Need or Desire for Tangible Objects or Activities

INSTRUCTIONAL STRATEGIES

All people have needs for tangible objects (for example, food, water, clothing, and so forth). This section includes some strategies that may help both children and their caregivers meet their needs. When children's behaviors express a need in ways that are of no concern to others, the team should consider whether simply providing for the need could be appropriate. This response is particularly effective if one can provide for the need before the child displays the undesirable behavior.

For the infant or older child with development typical of an infant, behaviors unintentionally expressing tangible needs can be taken as clear communication. For example, the child who cries when wet or hungry needs a prompt response to meet the need. This response teaches the child that others are listening. A child who expects a response to communication becomes prepared to learn intentional communication in the future. The child whose behavior intentionally expresses needs for tangibles such as material objects, activities, and things to eat or drink may be taught requesting communication skills or socially appropriate requesting. Use of object cues, gestures, signs, words, phrases, or augmentative communication devices may be taught and reinforced by access to the desired things at appropriate times. Movement skills necessary for independent access to the needed objects may also be taught.

For the preschooler or toddler who is visually impaired, teaching turn-taking skills may be appropriate. For the child with language skills, description of turn-taking behaviors of others will provide visual information unavailable to the child. Following this awareness building, the child may be prompted to allow an adult or another child to play with a toy for a brief time with the assurance that it will be returned soon.

For the child who is younger or has developmental delays, Nielsen (1990) has described a way of inviting exchanges. She begins by playing next to the child, using similar materials in similar ways to the child's typical play. Often this play invites the child to participate in basic turn-taking dialogue. The child may reach out and take the adult's materials, touch the adult, or begin to play in a turn-taking rhythm with the adult.

SCHEDULING STRATEGIES

Adjusting the schedule to include a variety of activities with access to the desired objects or activities reduces the need to use undesirable behaviors for this purpose. For example, a child who drops to the floor at the end of an occasionally occurring walk to keep the walk from ending may need more opportunities to take walks. Following the walks with another highly desired activity that is predictably available in the classroom may help prevent the child's undesired behavior as well.

Increasing the predictability of access to food, objects, and activities may help the child wait for those times of access. For example, for the child just described, taking walks at the same time every day may reduce his or her need to protest at the end of a walk.

ADAPTATIONS OF PHYSICAL ENVIRONMENTS

The environment may be enriched by making the desired objects and activities available more often and in a wider variety of settings and activities. Mace and Roberts (1993) suggested that perceivable evidence of the future availability of the object or activity may support positive behaviors. For example, seeing or hearing the snack cups set on the counter may help the hungry child wait for the snack. However, for very young children it may intensify their need to eat. In such situations, withdrawal of the object or its signal may be associated with undesirable behaviors. Increasing the children's control over when they get these things may also reduce undesired behaviors.

SOCIAL STRATEGIES

The social environment may be enriched by providing social situations in which the tangible objects and activities are available. For example, children may participate in snacks or meals with a variety of people. Children may participate in favorite activities or play with favorite toys in a playgroup.

REINFORCEMENT STRATEGIES

The reinforcement of access to food, drink, objects, or activities needs to be withheld immediately following inappropriate behaviors. However, parents and teachers need to be prepared for the initial increase in inappropriate behaviors that precedes the reduction of the behaviors. Reinforcement needs to immediately follow appropriately communicated requests, especially during instruction of these requesting behaviors. However, children can learn appropriate settings for requesting these items. Therefore, these reinforcers would not be provided in settings where they are not appropriate or where requesting behaviors are not appropriate, such as some community or library sponsored story times or worship services. Food, drink, objects, or activity reinforcers may also be effective with these children for increasing other desired behaviors.

DEVELOPING A CONSISTENT APPROACH TO SUPPORTING POSITIVE BEHAVIORS

Teamwork is the key to understanding the meanings of children's behaviors and developing consistent support for positive behaviors. When behaviors are serious or implementation of strategies used in this chapter are not effective, a behavioral specialist will need to be part of the team working with the child. Improvements in the behavioral dialogue that come from positive support strategies can be extended to all of the people working with the child. Including all team members spreads the consistency of positive behavioral support throughout the child's life. Communication between team members facilitates the process. Selecting positive supports with ongoing, naturally occurring reinforcers present in the activities helps maintain positive support over time with less effort from those working with the child. For example, setting the table is reinforced by eating, and playground activity is reinforced by vestibular stimulation.

Eating a meal in a restaurant includes the natural reinforcement of food. Performing in recitals or plays includes naturally occurring attention. In these activities, no one has to specifically remember to provide the reinforcers. Generalization strategies teach children to discriminate between situations with differing expectations (DePaepe, Reichle, & O'Neill, 1993). Maintaining a vision of positive long-term expectations guides the team in planning and executing successful programs of behavioral support. Team planning creates behavioral support plans that can be carried out by each team member, providing consistency for the child in different settings.

There are various ways to work and communicate in a team. (See Chapter 11 for more ideas on teaming strategies.) For infants and toddlers, IDEA requires that one service coordinator be the main contact with the family. Additionally, assessment of behavior and behavioral support plans requires the viewpoints of a transdisciplinary team. For example, one member may have expertise in recognizing the child's communication signals, while another understands the stages of motor development. A teacher of students who are visually impaired is a necessary team member who brings an understanding of the effects of the visual impairment.

Valuing and respecting the child is at the core of consistent behavioral support. Teams who understand and respond to the child's needs and the child's part in the dialogue draw the child into life-enhancing, interdependent relationships. Interdependent dialogue with the child drives behavioral support programs.

Several things are communicated within an effective behavioral support team. Effective team members know and can communicate their own feelings and reinforcers. Each team member needs to understand and state the communicative message of children's behaviors. Shared expectations for the child depict a vision of the desired future.

As noted in the previous section, children can learn to discriminate between situations in which to use and not use certain communication behaviors when the behaviors are reinforced in certain situations and not in others (DePaepe, et al., 1993; O'Neill & Reichle, 1993). It helps if the child can predict that needed reinforcers will be available soon after the period of unavailability. For example, a child with visual and multiple impairments asks for a flashlight while walking outdoors on an O&M lesson. The teacher states that the flashlight is at school. The teacher also provides a rich variety of social reinforcers by carrying on a conversation and singing with the student at his or her request until they return to school, where the child is given the flashlight.

Working together, the team is able to maintain a focus that includes a long-term positive vision of the child's future. Understanding and respecting what a child says through behaviors lays a foundation for interdependent behavioral dialogue. Positive behavioral support programs give children the ability to access naturally occurring reinforcers, function successfully in natural environments, and learn skills for life.

MOTOR FOCUS

Promoting Movement Experiences and
Motor Development

CONTRIBUTORS

Chris A. Strickling

Rona L. Pogrund

Exploring the environment through movement in order to interact
with objects and people is essential to the optimal development of
every child (Bunker, 1991). However, many children with low vision
or blindness face predictable developmental risks that often include
delays in motor development and postural differences (Adelson &
Fraiberg, 1977). In the most general sense, children with significantly decreased visual functioning have a qualitatively different
level of access to the physical world than their sighted peers do. Vision helps children "gain access to the environment by providing
motivation to move toward people and objects of interest in it and
indirectly by promoting their overall development" (Shon, 1999,
p. 161). Children who grow up without the help of useful visual information are at risk for delayed gross motor development (Kastein,
Spaulding, & Scharf, 1980), postural differences (Barraga, 1976), and
diminished or altered self-image (Sonsken, Levitt, & Kitsinger, 1984).
Though some children develop motor and perceptual skills without
specific intervention, despite their visual impairment, many others
need help learning basic motor skills, object concepts, and social expectations in order to participate in daily activities with their peers.

For the purpose of this discussion, motor development includes
both gross motor skills involving large muscle movement and balance and fine motor skills involving the use of smaller muscles, as
well as sensory integration (organizing sensations from the body and
the environment in order to use the body effectively). Promoting

Parts of this chapter are adapted from the section on "Gross Motor Development," by Jessica S. Lampert, pp. 88–94 in the 1992 edition of this book.

motor development in young children with visual impairments leads to a higher probability of success in developing mobility skills, social skills, recreational skills, and daily living skills as the child grows and develops. Improved health and fitness in the future are additional benefits from early motor development experiences. These early movement experiences facilitate the development of muscle tone, balance, strength, coordination, posture, and stamina (Cratty, 1971). All these motor functions lead to control of the child's body for safer, more efficient, and more graceful movement.

In this chapter, typical motor development of young sighted children is contrasted with that of peers of the same age who have visual impairment. Children who grow up without the benefit of vision usually progress through the same stages of motor development as those with vision, but they acquire some skills later, and the quality of their movement is frequently compromised. Knowing what to expect in terms of motor development for both groups can help families and professionals formulate realistic expectations and know when to intervene. Motor differences that are commonly seen in children with visual impairments will also be covered. An overview of sensory integration and the impact of visual impairment on it is provided. A section about motor development issues unique to young children with multiple disabilities is also included. Assessment strategies and intervention strategies for promoting motor development are offered as well.

EXPECTED MOTOR DEVELOPMENT OF YOUNG SIGHTED CHILDREN

In the first few weeks of life, a baby's motor system works to make the adjustment between the prenatal world and a new life with the family. During this time, the child learns to move out of total body flexion (the prenatal folding of the body) into extension patterns (stretching the spine, head, arms, and legs out into space). Primitive reflexes help the child develop these extension movements, which will be important in all later motor functions. Movement varies widely from child to child, depending on factors such as muscle tone, general health, environment, nutrition, and the amount and type of stimulation offered by the environment. Table 9.1 offers an overview of motor skills acquired between birth and 36 months of age, with an emphasis on specific gross motor milestones that many parents and caregivers anticipate. In the next section of this chapter, skills and activities of children with low vision or blindness in corresponding age categories are presented to highlight both the differences and similarities in development between the two groups. The charts are intended as guidelines only, since all children develop at their own individual rate. However, if one is working with a child who has not developed the skills noted for any specific age category, it is important to confer with a teacher, pediatrician, therapist, or orientation and mobility (O&M) specialist for further information on developmental skill acquisition.

It is especially important to understand skills and activities of typical motor development that are heavily influenced by vision as a way to understand some of the motor problems experienced by children with visual impairments. Several motor milestones mentioned in Table 9.1 are discussed in the following sections to help the reader better understand their importance.

Prone-on-Elbows Position

Between 2 and 3 months of age, children begin to raise and stabilize their heads in an erect position while lying on their stomachs, using weight bearing through the elbows to prop themselves up. The back and neck muscles contract into an extension pattern; the arms move in toward the body (adduction); and the elbows move under the shoulders to provide support. This position allows the child to see people and objects nearby. It also allows free movement of the head in all directions.

Accomplishing this movement is an important moment in development because prior to this milestone, most head movement is associated with larger, whole-body movements. This new "dissociated" movement is the beginning of head control. The head can move by itself and the rest of the body remains still, largely because the rest of the body is serving as a support base. This ability to isolate head movements is absolutely essential to later development of coordination. (For example, if the child's whole body turned to the left each time the head turns left, it would be difficult to organize purposeful movement.) Visual stimuli usually prompt the child to raise and turn the head from this position. During this period of time, children begin to gaze at nearby people and objects and attend to the actions of others (Levack, 1994).

A recent position on infant positioning and Sudden Infant Death Syndrome (SIDS) from the American Academy of Pediatrics' (AAP) (1992 and revised in 1997) recommends that infants not be placed in the prone position for sleeping; the supine (on back) position is preferred as it has the lowest risk for SIDS. (A side position also carries a lower risk than a prone position, but the infant's dependent arm should be brought forward to reduce the chance of the baby rolling into a prone position.) This position is somewhat controversial in that, while it has confirmed health benefits for the infant, it may not be in the best interest of motor development for some children because they cannot begin to raise their heads and push up with their arms while on their backs. The AAP task force did, however, encourage "tummy time" while the infant is awake and observed, for developmental reasons. Because of this recommendation for "back sleeping," many infants, both with and without vision, are spending less and less time on their stomachs. Infants who do not get enough "tummy time" may be at risk for additional motor delays. It is even

TABLE 9.1 **SEQUENCE OF GROSS MOTOR SKILLS ACQUISITION FOR SIGHTED CHILDREN**

USUAL AGE FOR SKILL	GROSS MOTOR SKILL OR ACTIVITY OBSERVED
Birth to 4 weeks	Initial physiological flexion, asymmetrical posturing (due to primitive reflex involvement); visual response to faces, light, some shapes
1–2 months	Movements into extension through spine, arms and legs move out into space, begins to lift head against gravity while prone (prone-on-elbows position); visual interest in objects and actions of people in the environment
3–5 months	More symmetry in movement, visual development assists with dissociation of head movement from upper body movement; visually directed reaching, first with two hands, then one hand; head control improves; independent rolling
6–8 months	Sits independently after being propped, using one or both hands for support; grasps, releases and transfers toys and other small objects; begins moving in and out of sitting position; primitive reflexes are integrated; creeping and crawling emerge as a way to access people or objects (purposeful movement through space)
9–11 months	Pulls to stand with minimal assistance, manages all transitional movements independently (such as sit-to-stand and stand-to-floor); goal-directed movement through space continues; stands alone momentarily, begins walking
12–14 months	Walks with one hand held or begins walking independently; chooses between walking and crawling depending on the task; moves onto and off of low furniture
15–18 months	Walks well independently on level surfaces; begins to negotiate inclines and declines, needs help with steps
21–24 months	Manages stairs with minimal assistance and a handrail; running begins; accesses rocking toys, uses push and pull toys; spinal posture is usually established by this time
36 months	Runs, kicks, balances briefly on one foot, jumps in place, alternates feet when climbing stairs

Sources: Adapted in part from N. Bayley, *Bayley Scales of Infant Development—Motor Scale Kit* (2nd ed.) (San Antonio, TX: Psychological Corporation, 2001); Furuno et. al., *Hawaii Early Learning Profile (HELP): Activity Guide. Enrichment Project for Handicapped Infants* (Palo Alto, CA: VORT Corp., 1979); and E. Adelson & S. Fraiberg, "Gross Motor Development," in S. Fraiberg, Ed., *Insights from the Blind: Comparative Studies of Blind and Sighted Infants* (New York: Basic Books, 1977).

more important than ever that infants spend significant time in their waking hours in the prone position.

Visually Directed Reaching

The earliest "reaching" behavior is actually more of an activation response; the child sees an object or person and arms and legs begin to move in response to that stimulus. Between 3 and 5 months of age, children begin to refine these movements and use their two arms to reach for objects that they see. Reaching is primarily a response to a *visual* stimulus at this stage. No additional cognitive concept is needed. By 4 to 5 months of age, motor coordination and visual tracking are well enough established that most sighted children begin to reach with only one hand, which will usually become their dominant hand (Levack, 1994).

Sitting

Most infants can sit with the head steady and the trunk erect by 6 months of age, as long as they have good support through the hips. At first they have trouble keeping their balance. By 9 months, most infants can sit with good postural control, without support. Sitting requires balance and protective responses in forward, backward, and side-to-side directions (Bobath & Bobath, 1964). Sitting is a motivating position because it brings the child into visual contact with objects and people not visible from the floor. In sitting, the child assumes and maintains vertical alignment of the spine and becomes familiar with visual verticality. Sitting is also important because it frees the arms and hands for further use and exploration, and it increases head control, balance, and strength for future motor skills. Most infants can also go from sitting to prone position and back by 9 months.

Purposeful Movement Through Space

Between the ages of 6 and 8 months, children begin to move toward and away from objects or people independently. In order to do that, they must be motivated to move through space on their own, and they need enough coordination and strength to successfully go from one place to another. Three major sensory systems work together to help children understand spatial relations and develop body awareness and balance:

- *Proprioception:* awareness of body position in space, derived from sensory apparati called proprioceptors embedded primarily in joints, muscles, and tendons that are activated by

bearing and shifting weight through the joints. Proprioception can be conscious, as in our awareness of our position
sense during voluntary activities such as sports, or uncon-
scious (based on reflex responses, which inform our muscle
action) (Laskowski, Newcomer-Aney, & Smith, 1997). Proprioception helps a child know how to move by supplying sensory information about the position of the limbs in space and
influencing judgment on how fast and how far to move in
order to reach a target.

- *Vision:* the ability to receive and interpret information through
  the eye.

- *Vestibular function:* the ability to detect and interpret acceler-
  ation and deceleration of the body (especially related to
  movement of the head) and the pull of gravity, derived from
  receptors in the inner ear. Spatial orientation, balance and
  equilibrium depend on proper vestibular function. Vestibular input to the nervous system stabilizes the eyes in space
  during head movements, which "reduces the movement of
  a fixed object on the retina" (Brugge, 1996). Vestibular function interacts with visual and proprioceptive information
  to allow a child to move with efficiency and coordination
  (Kasai, 1991).

When the child moves toward a toy, for instance, vision serves
as the motivator. Because the movement requires the child to
bear and/or shift weight, the child also receives proprioceptive
feedback, which helps with coordination. Information from the
vestibular system helps clarify whether the object is moving, or
the child is moving, so that appropriate motor responses can be
elicited. If one of these sensory systems is deficient, the others
are often compromised. This interaction means that visual impairment cannot be considered simply as a loss of one sensory
system, since along with it comes disruption of vestibular and
proprioceptive processing.

Creeping and Crawling

Researchers and theorists have not yet agreed about what produces
crawling. Early research from Gesell (1946) and McGraw (1943) assumed that crawling was an effect of the maturing central nervous
system, a "neural maturationist" theory (Maida & McCune, 1996).
More contemporary research emphasized the cognitive bases for
crawling and theorized crawling as an internally driven motor con-

sequence of cognitive interfaces with the environment (Piaget, 1952; Bruner, 1973). Recent work on crawling supports McGraw's original description of the sequence of motor skills used in crawling, but assumes neither that crawling is merely maturational nor that it is solely cognitively based (Maida & McCune, 1996). Instead, crawling as a movement outcome that demonstrates the synthesis of many systems working together cannot be separated from "the motives that inspired it, the information that guided it, and the body parts that produced it" (Maida & McCune, 1996, p. 120). Maida and McCune (1996) report that their exploratory study of crawling in both children with or without vision determined that the ability "to reach for an object and to move to or from the sitting position appear to be the two most critical precursors to the actual execution of crawling" (p. 130). Vision plays a role in these prerequisite skills. Transitioning into and out of sitting is often learned incidentally, by watching and imitating. Reaching for interesting objects or people is prompted by first visually locating them. Together, they provide the developmental background for crawling.

The age at which a child crawls varies widely depending on physical and environmental factors. Some infants will "creep" on their stomachs for several months, using their arms to pull forward in a "commando" position, before they begin using a hands-and-knees crawling pattern with the tummy off the floor. Some infants crawl as early as 6 months, others wait several more months to start. Some babies never crawl at all; they pull to stand, walk for a period of time holding onto furniture or other support, and then begin walking independently. Crawling is a complicated motor task that requires stability at the shoulder and the hip, enough spinal extension and abdominal strength to keep the tummy off the floor, and excellent head control. Weight-bearing through extended wrists and through knees and hips provides proprioceptive input into the joints that contributes to shoulder and hip stability, and moving into and out of all-fours requires rotational movement through the trunk, which helps develop the strength and coordination for later walking.

Standing

Children do a kind of early "standing" beginning somewhere around the fourth month, which consists of straightening their legs and taking some weight on them when placed in a standing position with their feet on a support surface. By 6 months, many children can stand briefly when placed into a standing position, with minimal support. This kind of "standing" is not functional, because they cannot move into or out of it independently, but it does provide some experience in weight bearing and briefly changes the baby's spatial orientation. The head is brought into alignment so that the child can maintain a meaningful visual connection with the world. By approximately 9 months, most children can pull to stand and then maintain that position for at least a few moments. They can stand for much longer periods if they can hang onto a chair or other furniture for support. The primary incentive is often visual. The child begins to look at things that are out of reach, then pulls to stand in order to obtain or view them (Bly, 1980). Coming to stand in free space, with no support, and being able to sit back down again unassisted is the ultimate goal.

Walking

Walking usually begins with cruising, taking steps (often sideways) while holding onto furniture or a wall. Most walking is motivated by the desire to reach a destination; children want what they can see. Children use two hands for cruising at first, and then one as balance improves. Walking with the support of a parent's hand or holding onto a weighted push toy precedes independent walking. Most infants take their first solo steps between 13 and 15 months, but walking can begin anywhere from 9 to 18 months, depending on factors such as muscle tone, motivation, coordination, and environmental stimulation.

Developing a "Map" of the Environment

Vision motivates independent movement through space and helps the child understand distances, planes of movement, spatial arrangements, and even social contexts. Vision tells the sighted child how the environment is set up, which makes it easy to negotiate the space and understand activities taking place. The brain "maps" the space, using vision, and the child has an almost automatic sense of where he or she is in that space. Once a child understands how a particular physical environment is structured, it is possible to move through that space confidently. This ability to comprehend the dimensions and other particulars of space and to negotiate that space is called "spatial organization." The three most critical components of spatial organization are:

- *motor exploration*—the ability to move around in space and test out the boundaries,

- *tactile development*—the ability to use tactile information to interpret and reinforce other available sensory information, and

- *spatial representation*—using tactile, proprioceptive and auditory input to understand the spatial relations between objects in the environment (Wheeler, Floyd, & Griffin, 1997).

Incidental Learning

Many later motor skills are learned incidentally, by watching and imitating peers. Gross motor skills for accessing playground equipment or climbing onto and off of furniture, for instance, are often learned incidentally by watching. Fine motor skills, such as how to hold a spoon or a pair of scissors, may also be learned in this way. (For more information on incidental learning, see D'Arcangel, 2000.)

IMPACT OF VISUAL IMPAIRMENT ON MOTOR DEVELOPMENT

Some children who have visual impairments seem to develop motor skills as effortlessly as their sighted peers. For others, motor development is more of a challenge. Differences in postural tone, early movement experiences, motivation, and perception often alter the rate and sequence of motor skill development. Table 9.2 presents the ages at which base motor skills are typically developed by children with low vision and blindness. This outline can be compared with the typical development of sighted children as presented in Table 9.1. As noted earlier, these are rough guidelines, and all children develop at their own rate. In the sections that follow, some of the developmental issues outlined in Table 9.2 are addressed as a means of highlighting some of the important differences in motor development between sighted children and their peers with visual impairment.

Postural Tone

In addition to motor delays associated with lack of visual motivation for movement and inadequate cognitive mapping of the environment, children with visual impairments sometimes experience motor difficulties based on decreased postural tone.

Low postural tone is evidenced by "floppy" muscles, or instability at the major joints (hips, shoulders, and spine) that sometimes takes the form of a slouched posture or excessive movement through the upper body when walking. Low postural tone has been linked to reduced physical activity in blind infants, based on the idea that low tone makes it more difficult to move against gravity (Maida & McCune, 1996). As children grow older, diminished postural tone also influences their movement, especially gait and transitional

TABLE 9.2 **SEQUENCE OF GROSS SKILL ACQUISITION FOR CHILDREN WITH VISUAL IMPAIRMENT**

USUAL AGE FOR SKILL	GROSS MOTOR SKILL OR ACTIVITY OBSERVED
Birth to 4 weeks	Initial physiological flexion (a bending movement), asymmetrical posturing (due to primitive reflex involvement); touch, movement, and sound are the primary stimuli
1–2 months	Movements into extension through spine (arms and legs move out into space), prone-on-elbows positioning remains difficult; interested in play on the body, attends to rhythms and physical handling
3–5 months	More symmetry in movement, tendency to avoid prone positioning; head control emerges in supported sitting, likes supine (on back) position; hands remain lightly fisted
6–8 months	Sits independently after being propped, using one or both hands for support; will briefly hold objects placed into the hand, sometimes mouthing them, sometimes simply releasing them; will move from sitting to supine position and pivot in a circle; limited crawling in pursuit of objects or people
9–11 months	Pulls to stand with minimal assistance; may be up on toes for several months; manages all transitional movements independently (such as sit-to-stand and stand-to-floor); may begin goal-directed movement through space, if encouraged
12–14 months	Walks indoors with one hand held, sometimes with two; crawling continues, though some completely skip crawling as a means of locomotion; may cruise on furniture
15–18 months	Walks independently on level surfaces; begins to negotiate indoor inclines and declines with physical assistance from an adult; may move down declines using a crouched position and searching with hands; limited exploration of outdoor or unfamiliar environments
21–24 months	Manages stairs with moderate assistance and a handrail and/or adult assistance; walks independently in familiar surroundings; begins learning simple routes for daily activities and how to use landmarks in ambulation
36 months	Travels indoors independently in familiar settings; dynamic balance developing; age-appropriate motor skills like running, jumping, and kicking balls usually are not yet established

Sources: Adapted in part from N. Bayley, *Bayley Scales of Infant Development—Motor Scale Kit* (2nd ed.) (San Antonio, TX: Psychological Corporation, 2001); Furuno et. al., *Hawaii Early Learning Profile (HELP): Activity Guide. Enrichment Project for Handicapped Infants* (Palo Alto, CA: VORT Corp., 1979); and E. Adelson & S. Fraiberg, "Gross Motor Development," in S. Fraiberg, Ed., *Insights from the Blind: Comparative Studies of Blind and Sighted Infants* (New York: Basic Books, 1977).

movement. Postural tone can often be improved through early intervention and experience, and children can be taught ways to adapt their activities to minimize the effects of low postural tone. (See the section on "Strategies for Promoting Motor Development" later in this chapter for specific activities to help postural tone.)

Prone Positioning

As indicated earlier, spending time in prone position helps develop upper body strength and encourages important head and neck movements. Children who have limited visual function may avoid prone positioning for play because, from this position, it is more difficult to interact with others or to play on the body (play with fingers, toes, clothing, and so on). Most play that occurs in prone positioning involves nearby objects (reach is limited in prone) and is motivated by a desire to watch a person or an event. Children who are visually impaired will not have this visual motivation. Since object concepts often develop later in children with visual impairments, they are not as motivated to assume and maintain this position in order to play with or watch the actions of objects. Low postural tone makes it feel like work to hold the head up against gravity, which also makes prone positioning less desirable. "Prone-on-elbows" position may develop much later for children who are visually impaired, emerging around 6 to 8 months. This compromises the integrity of the shoulder girdle, as well as the head and neck muscles, which will have an important impact on body posture and fine motor development (Adelson & Fraiberg, 1977). The shoulder girdle consists of the clavicle (collarbone), scapula (shoulder blade), and the top end of the humerus bones (upper arm bones) and their connecting joints; its function is to provide an attachment point for the numerous muscles that allow the shoulder and elbow joints to move. Spending time in the prone position, even if there is protest, is very important for the infant with visual impairment in order to promote proper motor development.

Purposeful Movement Through Space

Lacking visual motivation to explore the environment, these children sometimes prefer play on their own bodies over pursuing play with nearby objects. This behavior limits purposeful movement through the environment. Vision works with proprioception and vestibular feedback to help organize the movements of sighted children, and vision deficit contributes to diminished proprioceptive awareness and vestibular processing, which also impacts purposeful movement

A mother's voice and smile can provide an infant with the necessary motivation to lift his head while in the prone position.

through space. If a child is having difficulty with awareness of body position in space and cannot efficiently respond to gravity or other forces acting on the body, then moving through the environment in a goal-directed way may present too great a challenge in the absence of specific encouragement to do so. The lack of purposeful movement through the environment puts the child with visual impairment at risk for delayed development of spatial relationships and other concepts. Infants need to be allowed free access to their environments, so time in the stroller, baby carrier, walker, saucer, or playpen should be limited in order to encourage movement.

Sitting

Children with visual impairments generally reach "stable" motor milestones, such as sitting alone or standing with the support of an adult's hand, or even standing alone, at about the same time as their sighted peers. Sighted children tend to reach the "sits alone momentarily" milestone at around 5 months of age, and children with visual impairments reach it near the end of the sixth month, a discrepancy of just over one month (Shon, 1999; Bayley, 2001; Adelson & Fraiberg, 1977). The "mobile" milestones, such as "getting into and out of sitting" (2.7 months discrepancy) and "walks alone across the room" (7.15 months discrepancy) are harder for children with visual impairments to achieve. However, some infants with visual impairments may need considerable practice sitting with the support of a pillow, bolster, or an adult's body before they are ready to sit alone. If a child has additional motor impairments and does not have enough control of the trunk muscles to sit independently, some type of adaptive positioning or equipment may be needed so that the child gains experience in the sitting position with hands free to engage in functional activities. Some children try to get a wider base of support when sitting to increase their stability. They may use the "W sit" position, bending the knees and externally rotating the leg from the hip so that the feet rest near the buttocks. This position allows children with low muscle tone to feel stable, since it effectively widens the base of weight bearing support, but it puts considerable pressure on the head of the femur (the long bone of the leg) and may contribute to hip displacement. "Tailor sitting" (legs crossed in front) or side sitting (both legs bent at the knee, both feet pointed the same direction) are preferred postures, as long as there is sufficient range of motion in the hamstrings to allow the spine to stay aligned.

Many children with visual impairments will learn how to get into and out of a sitting position at roughly the same age as their sighted peers (8 to 11 months), but they will continue to move into and out of sitting, staying in the same area of the room, for many months after their peers have learned to crawl toward an interesting object or activity (up to 18 months).

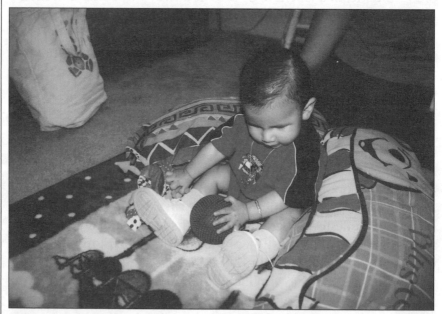

Pillows provide added support to a 6-month-old as he tries to master sitting.

Creeping and Crawling

Adelson and Fraiberg (1974) noted in their study of infants with visual impairments that crawling begins only after the child has begun to reach out toward sound sources, which occurs later in children with visual impairments than it does for sighted children. As previously discussed, crawling results from a dynamic interaction of the child with the environment, and it depends on the child's ability to get into and out of sitting, which is a "mobile" milestone that is sometimes difficult for children with visual impairments to achieve. Because visual motivation is lacking and motor skill development is often delayed, crawling can be significantly delayed in these children (Ferrell, 1998). It is not uncommon for infants with low vision or blindness to advance to walking and standing without going through the crawling stage of motor development. In some of these children, low muscle tone and decreased ability to stabilize the neck and shoulder girdle may make crawling too difficult to be efficient. Other children may give up crawling quickly, preferring to walk or scoot upright on their bottoms, to minimize unexpected collisions with objects in the environment. Often they will scoot or "pivot" in a circle while seated on their bottoms, using their legs as "feelers" to clear the space of any threatening object. For children who persist in scooting on their bottoms instead of crawling, caregivers may have to offer more support and encouragement (for example, guiding the child into all fours position and moving alongside).

Standing

Children with visual impairments will usually pull up to standing from 9 to 11 months, like their sighted peers, but may wait as late as 13 months to achieve this motor skill. It is not uncommon during this early phase of motor development for both sighted children and children with visual impairments to stand with their heels off the floor, on their toes. This position increases sensory feedback (by putting the calf muscles on stretch and setting off proprioceptors) and redistributes more weight onto the forefoot. Most children will use this posture only for a few weeks and can easily come down onto their heels. If the child is up on the toes for more than three to four weeks after weight bearing is established, and especially if it is difficult to move the child's foot into a flexed position, conferring with a pediatrician or therapist about possible ways to help that child come down into a more functional weight-bearing stance is recommended. Any furniture that a child uses for pulling to stand should be stable and "baby proofed" (corners or edges padded).

Walking

Walking without support is another motor milestone that is often delayed in young children with visual impairments (Ferrell, 1998). Many children, regardless of their visual ability, initially walk by keeping their feet wide apart and holding their hands and arms up high (a *high guard* posture). These behaviors decrease over time as confidence and balance increase. Some children with visual impairments may eventually lower their hands to their sides but continue using the broader base of support as they walk. Continued use of such a wide base of support can impact the foot, causing breakdown in the midfoot because of the way the weight is distributed when walking in this pattern. There is a tendency to shift weight to the inside of the foot, causing pronation of the foot.) Activities to improve

A "high guard" posture initially helps the child maintain balance when learning to walk.

balance (using a trampoline, rocking board, or seesaws) can be useful, but may not significantly impact a child's gait pattern, since this widened base may be employed because of weak hip flexor muscles, pelvic instability, and/or low postural tone. Conferring with a physical or occupational therapist is recommended if a child uses an unusually wide base of support.

Children who are learning to walk will have more confidence if they know how to protect themselves when they fall. Using a large inflated ball, with the child leaning tummy down over the ball, helps develop falling protection as the child learns to reach out and "catch" him- or herself when the ball is rolled forward. Any activities that encourage the infant to shift weight from side to side will help with transitions from sitting to standing to walking. Using weighted push toys encourages walking while providing some protection from obstacles in the environment (See Chapter 10 for more suggestions on the use of toys, adaptive devices, and canes as the child with visual impairment learns to walk).

Mapping the Environment

Children who are able to use vision to understand their environment can experience a physical space in an integrated, holistic way. Long before they understand dimension, the composition of objects, or the social contexts of physical spaces, sighted children can discriminate between a bathroom and a living room just by looking at them. Visual cues, along with some lived experience, are all they need to determine where they are and what is expected. A child with vision can have a visual map of where items are stored or the arrangement of a room in an instant. For the child who is blind or visually impaired, though, these aspects of the environment have to be learned sequentially through part-to-whole learning (as opposed to holistically, in a "right brain," nonlinear fashion), and in early development, they have to be learned through systematic tactile exploration that is reinforced with language. This challenge for mapping the environment can also contribute to the hesitancy to move through the environment. It is not motivating to move into unknown space for many children with visual impairments.

Incidental Learning

Without vision, learning motor skills through imitation is extremely difficult. Children who rely on verbal and physical cues to acquire motor behaviors, however, typically learn them at a slower rate and often have to overcome fear in order to even try new motor tasks.

This hesitancy is evident in children who have physical motor problems like cerebral palsy or muscular dystrophy, as well as with children whose vision is limited. Fear needs to be acknowledged, and the activity should be adapted to ensure the comfort of each child when trying novel motor tasks.

Skill versus Quality of Movement

In addition to these differences in *motor skill* development, children with visual impairments sometimes exhibit different ways of moving or a different quality of movement. Some of these differences are indicated in Table 9.3. Recognizing them can help teachers, parents, and therapists structure meaningful interventions, as discussed later in this chapter.

DOES DIFFERENCE MEAN DIFFICULTY?

Several of the motor differences that were noted in the preceding section can have significant impact on later development of motor skills. As discussed in the following sections, if these developmental differences are noticed in a child who is visually impaired, it is important to follow up with a more in-depth examination of that child's movement.

Low Muscle Tone in the Trunk

Though muscle tone is sometimes difficult for the nonprofessional to assess, it has some common manifestations in children with low vision or blindness. Low tone contributes to difficulty maintaining an erect posture, causes "loose" movement patterns because the hips and shoulders are overly mobile, and can cause clumsiness and slouching through the upper back. If a child shows these motor differences, it would be prudent to ask for an evaluation by a physical or occupational therapist.

Static and Dynamic Balance Diminished

Children develop two kinds of balance in the early years. *Static* balance refers to the ability to assume and maintain still positions, like sitting or standing. *Dynamic* balance is the ability to keep the body upright and organized while moving. Many children with blindness or low vision have difficulty with both static and dynamic balance when they first begin to walk. This balance problem causes frequent falls or reluctance to let go of supporting surfaces, but usually resolves as the child gains more experience with movement. If balance

TABLE 9.3 **MOTOR DIFFERENCES IN CHILDREN WITH VISUAL IMPAIRMENT**

Postural characteristics (trunk and pelvis)	Low tone through trunk and pelvis, weak abdominal muscles Static and dynamic balance reactions diminished
Head and neck	Head often deviated to one side (visual or auditory accommodation) Head "stacked" (face up, resting on upper spine) or dropped forward In early development, head is often used as a support point Head sways or moves nonpurposefully, especially when child is bored
Shoulders, arms, hands	Unstable shoulder girdles with poor proximal control ("floppy") "Winging" at scapulae (shoulder blades protruding) Weakness of arm muscles and intrinsic hand muscles Forearm supination and pronation diminished Poorly developed arches of the hand (due to decreased arm weight-bearing and lack of visual motivation for manual object manipulation)
Legs and feet	Legs externally rotated from hip, "toe out" Hypermobile knees and hips Toe-walking (secondary to tight muscles and/or poor sensation) Wide support base at feet (to get more sensory feedback and to add stability) Shoulders often elevate to get more stability in the trunk Excessive movement through the trunk while walking Persistence in high guard posture (hands up, like a toddler) Pronation (rolling foot inward) at midfoot

Note: Table 9.3 was developed from unpublished material presented by Mary Beth Langley (1998) (author of *Visual Impairment and Students with Severe Neurodevelopmental Disorders: Facilitating Visual Potential*. Gibsonia, PA: Distance Learning Center) at the Texas School for the Blind and Visually Impaired, and from personal experience of the author.

problems persist after the child has been walking for six to eight months, evaluation by an occupational or physical therapist is recommended.

Deviated Head Position

Children will usually assume the head position that allows them to use whatever vision they have in the most efficient way. When considering whether or not to correct a child's head position (as in the case of treating a child with scoliosis), it is important to consider that head position may be related to visual function, and accommodation should be made accordingly. Children should be taught the social implications of a deviated head position, and then be taught ways to choose to correct the head position selectively when desired (for example, reorienting the head to be in alignment with a speech partner's head when having a conversation, as a way of showing interest in the conversation).

Nonpurposeful Head Movements

Children with blindness or very low vision have no way of knowing that people hold their heads in specific ways during conversations or that these head positions have social meanings. They sometimes engage in nonpurposeful head movements, such as rocking or swaying, or they will keep the head down instead of orienting toward a speaker. Typically, the rocking or swaying of the head diminishes when a child is fully engaged in an activity, and simple verbal or nonverbal cues help the child learn what is acceptable in interaction. If a child shows constant head movement or seems unable to control the movement, a sensory integration evaluation may be indicated. Sensory integration therapy can be useful in teaching a child to identify stillness as opposed to movement and can provide an organized and appropriate source of the kind of sensory information that the child may be seeking. (See the section "Sensory Integration" later in this chapter for information on sensory integration therapy.)

Fisted Hands

Without a visual stimulus, a child may have less motivation to extend the hand and reach for an object. In addition, decreased prone positioning results in limited upper body weight bearing and contributes to continued fisting of the hands. Weight-bearing motor experiences along with the use of objects of varied weight, texture, and shape can help decrease the fisting and encourage tactile exploration that is so essential to the child with visual impairment.

Limited Wrist Rotation

Among sighted children, wrist rotation is primarily a visually motivated and reinforced activity. Early wrist rotation is an economy of
movement for the visual learner and serves as a method of obtaining different visual perspectives on an object without having to actually change the grip on the object. Wrist rotation is important as
the child gets older because of all its functional uses (for example,
opening doorknobs, opening containers, and turning on the faucet).

Unstable Shoulder Girdle Muscles

Low postural tone and diminished early prone positioning often contribute to poorly developed shoulder muscles because weight bearing
and weight shifting, in addition to basic neurological status, give
muscles their tone. In order for the arm and hand to be mobile and
move with coordination, the shoulder has to provide stability (mobility proceeds from stability). Unstable shoulder muscles cause what
looks like weakness in the arms as well as a noticeable hypermobility
of the shoulder blade. Instability at the shoulder impacts all fine motor skills and should be addressed in children up to 6 to 8 years of age.
After that age, treatment is less effective and postural tone is set.

"Toe-Out" Pattern

Many children who use wide-based gaits walk with their toes pointing out instead of straight ahead of them. This gait usually originates
as instability at the hip, so that the leg itself rotates laterally and the
foot follows. Toe-out gaits are compensatory, which means that the
child is using the toe-out pattern in order to compensate for some
weakness or lack of sensation that is hindering the development of
a more functional gait. If addressed early, sometimes the causative
factor can be eliminated. Toe-out contributes to the collapse of the
midfoot if it continues over a period of years, so it is best to intervene early. As noted earlier, many children use the toe-out pattern
when they first learn to walk, but if it persists past the first year of
ambulation, it should be addressed.

Pronation at the Midfoot

Often as a result of using a toe-out gait pattern, the arch collapses,
and the child begins to walk with the inside border of the foot in
contact with the floor surface and the outside border of the foot
slightly raised. If this position persists, it can cause later hip and back
problems and foot pain. There is no period in which walking in

pronation is acceptable or beneficial to the child, and it should be addressed as early as possible.

Walking on Toes

Many children walk on their toes when they are just beginning to walk. Up on the toes, the leg muscles provide more sensory feedback than when the heel is down, so children with sensory feedback problems will often opt for toe-walking. Long-term, it has detrimental effects on the calf muscles and the bony alignment of the foot, so it should be interrupted as early as possible. If a child stays up on the toes and cannot come down into heel contact with the floor, an orthopedic evaluation is needed. If the child can still come down on the heel, but does not unless instructed or assisted, referral to a pediatric physical therapist is in order.

It is important for families and teachers of children with visual impairments to be aware of any motor differences and to observe the child carefully so that motor problems can be identified early and appropriate interventions implemented. Many different approaches have been used by professionals to enhance motor skills in children with low vision and blindness; among them, sensory integration therapy has often been successful.

SENSORY INTEGRATION

The term "sensory integration," as defined by Ayres (1989), refers to:

> the neurological process that organizes sensation from one's own body and from the environment and makes it possible to use the body effectively within the environment. The spatial and temporal aspects of inputs from different sensory modalities are interpreted, associated, and unified. [p. 11]

Ayres' theoretical work helped bring into circulation the idea that the brain can modulate its own activity, and sensory integration treatment strategies evolved from that assumption. (For a discussion of sensory modulation, see Wilbarger & Stackhouse, 1998.) Sensory integration is the process through which sensory information is received through the body's sense organs (such as eyes, ears, nose, skin, joints, and tongue), relayed through the central nervous system, then "integrated" into action, perception, or other experience.

Ayres identified a pattern of behaviors labeled *sensory integration dysfunction,* or SID, which includes difficulty processing auditory and tactile information (tactile and auditory "defensiveness") and a tendency to be either over- or understimulated by the sensory experiences of daily life (Sherman, 2000). Clinical signs of sensory integrative dysfunction include:

- dyspraxia (trouble with motor planning),

- clumsiness,

- inability to filter out background stimuli from primary stimuli, and

- resistance to tastes and smells.

Whether sensory integration dysfunction is distinct from other disorders that produce similar behaviors, such as attention deficit hyperactivity disorder (ADHD) (a disruptive behavior disorder in which an individual displays abnormal levels of inattention, hyperactivity, or their combination) remains to be established. Research indicates possible links between ADHD and visual system disturbances (see Lerner, 1995).

Sensory Integration Therapy

Sensory integration therapy acknowledges that motor and cognitive development depend on the adequate function of the basic sensory systems (tactile, vestibular, visual, auditory, olfactory, gustatory, and kinesthetic) and sufficient stimulation to assist the central nervous system in meaningfully "knitting together" or "integrating" information received from those systems. A sensory integration approach to intervention begins with an evaluation of how the sensory systems are currently influencing development (Ayres, 1989), and the treatment provides sensory (or sensorimotor) activities that address the body's needs. The success of sensory integration treatment depends on the accuracy of the evaluation and the formulation of an effective treatment strategy that addresses the identified deficit areas. The treatment strategy works from the idea that sensory input can be provided systematically, and that when such input is provided, the central nervous system is forced to process it. For example, if a child has difficulty processing proprioceptive information from the body (evidenced by an inability to assume and hold stable positions, coordinate movements, or sustain resistance against movements), sensory integration therapy would focus on providing organized proprioceptive input through jumping, bouncing, deep pressures applied passively, and resistive activities. Providing targeted sensory input prompts the central nervous system to process that input. Sensory integration theory suggests that the more processing the central nervous system has to do, the more efficient it becomes, which yields more efficient motor output (and indirectly assists cognitive development).

Sensory integration, as a therapeutic approach, is widely practiced with children who have neurological disorders, as well as with children who are blind or visually impaired. Those who support SID as a diagnosis and sensory integration therapy as an intervention with blind children emphasize the connections between the tactile, vestibular, and proprioceptive systems in helping a child understand and master the environment. These three systems, along with vision, help the child develop the body awareness that provides the foundation for functional movement. This emphasis seems especially important for children with visual impairments because, as discussed above, vision impacts the interpretation and processing of proprioceptive and vestibular sensation, and deficits in these two areas are common in this population. Sensory integration therapy specifically addresses the tactile system, primarily in terms of helping children who have trouble correctly interpreting touch, by providing touch input combined with deep pressure (proprioceptive input) or bombarding the nervous system with organized tactile input (providing systematic sensory input like brushing or icing of the skin). Since tactile discrimination and the ability to interpret tactile information accurately is so important to independent functioning for children who are blind or visually impaired, emphasizing tactile system function is a valuable way to help children reach their maximum potential.

Impact of Visual Impairment on Sensory Integration

Because visual information informs and helps interpret so much of one's other sensory experiences, vision loss could be said to produce a degree of sensory integrative dysfunction. Without vision, the proprioceptive feedback generated by receptors in the body would be more difficult to interpret. For example, when sighted children hold out a hand, they can see it, and the feeling of holding their hand out is reinforced by visual information. Without vision, a child has to depend on proprioception for the "meaning" of that movement, and proprioceptive feedback is not as easy to interpret as visual information. Without vision, kinesthesia (body awareness produced by movement) also has less meaning. The connections between vision and vestibular input are clear. Visual information helps the vestibular apparatus prepare us to process gravitational forces on the body and interpret movement around us. Vision integrates our proprioceptive, tactile, kinesthetic, and vestibular experiences. Without it, sensory integration is compromised.

Visual impairment often results in tactile defensiveness, a major issue in sensory integration, which is exhibited as an unwillingness to make tactile contact with novel objects and a tendency not to explore tactilely. This behavior may not be "true" tactile defensiveness, which is based in central nervous system dysfunction, but could be a more emotionally or experientially based tactile avoidance. A therapist with sensory integration certification can help determine the cause by using subtests of the Sensory Integration and Praxis Test (SIPT) (Ayres, 1989). No matter what its origins, tactile defensiveness (or tactile avoidance) has major ramifications for learning. For children with visual impairments, whose learning depends on tactile exploration, systematic searching, and exploring the physical qualities of objects in order to learn about function, shape, weight, composition, and texture, tactile avoidance can have serious ramifications. (For more information on tactile defensiveness, see Chapter 8.)

Children with visual impairments frequently exhibit the kind of dyspraxia (difficulty with motor planning) seen in children with SID. Vision loss makes motor skills harder to develop, as already discussed, but if there is also a motor planning problem due to broader sensory integrative deficits, nonpurposeful, idiosyncratic movement patterns can develop. Children with SID also show hypersensitivity to auditory and tactile stimuli and resist noisy or crowded environments. The child with a visual impairment may already have this kind of avoidance of crowded, close situations. This hypersensitivity to auditory and visual stimuli can lead to hyperkinesis (excessive movement, difficulty getting and staying still), which is disruptive to all forms of instruction. SID is also accompanied by a tendency toward decreased spatial awareness with resultant lack of organizational skills. These children are unable to organize their classroom or personal materials, tending to either handle the materials excessively or avoid contact with them. All of these sensory integration problems have the potential for long-term implications that affect movement patterns and future learning opportunities. With appropriate early intervention, however, many of these sensory problems can be significantly decreased or eliminated.

MOTOR DEVELOPMENT ISSUES FOR CHILDREN WITH MULTIPLE DISABILITIES

For children who have more than one disability, visual impairment may be just one part of a larger developmental picture. For them, motor development is especially challenging. Often, motor difficulties make it hard for adults to determine which cognitive abilities are intact, since motor skill influences communication, whether spoken, signed, or gestural.

During early infancy and throughout their lives, children with multiple disabilities often experience less movement than their age peers. Many children with multiple disabilities cannot move from tummy to back or reposition their heads to get a better visual orientation. Children with severe spasticity, for instance, cannot even effectively change their position in space by themselves. Body awareness and spatial orientation fail to develop fully because these children primarily experience movement in a passive way, when they are held or moved by someone else. This passivity reduces the amount and restricts the type of proprioceptive and vestibular stimulation the child receives and makes it difficult to interpret these sensations. Because they cannot move out into the environment and get sensory stimulation from that movement in what is considered an "appropriate" way, these children will sometimes develop "self-stimulatory" movements. Most adults and children without disabilities have a certain repertoire of acceptable, nonpurposeful movements (such as flicking a pen while talking on the phone or tapping a foot when standing in line), but most are able to move in a myriad of other ways, too, so that these movements do not interfere with motor skill development. For children with multiple disabilities, these self-stimulatory movements are often the only ones that can be reliably reproduced. Repeated enough, without interruption or redirection, these movements sometimes become mannerisms, behaviors so engrained that they are hard to extinguish (see Chapter 8).

Joint Action Routines

Many children who have severe multiple disabilities are unable to develop expressive communication through speech or other communicative form because they lack the voluntary motor control to communicate in the usual ways. Fortunately, the body usually communicates in many ways, and often the nonverbal information the body provides is more accurate than what is said. For children with multiple disabilities, even this nonverbal communication is often disrupted. Because their motor control is diminished, it is even hard to "read" what their bodies are saying without careful observation. For these children, establishing *joint action routines* can sometimes be the key to communication. Joint action routines are "ritualized interaction patterns" that provide repetition of predictable events and specific kinds of stimulation or prompts in order to build anticipation as a foundation for communication (Hagood, 1997). As the child learns the routine and learns what to expect, he or she begins to anticipate the next step in the routine. In moments of anticipation, the child can use any available movement, or even changes in breathing or gaze, as a signal. Routines allow communication between people who have only the language of the body at their disposal.

A joint action routine is a ritualized interaction pattern with the following features (Hagood, 1997):

- joint focus and interaction among all participants

- unified by a specific theme or goal

- logical sequencing, including a clear beginning point

- a specific role for each participant, with specific response expectancies

- structured turn-taking

- planned repetition

- exchangeable roles

- a plan for controlled variation

Hagood's (1997) book offers an exhaustive discussion of joint action routines, including how to structure, implement, change, and evaluate their impact.

Joint action routines based on motor activities can be particularly valuable for children with multiple disabilities. They provide some much needed movement, reduce the physical distances between child and adult, and offer a vehicle for eliciting communication using whatever means is available to the child. The following is an example of using a joint action routine with a young girl who has multiple disabilities:

Janelle is a 4-year old girl who shows choreoathetosis—a type of cerebral palsy resulting in involuntary random movements, especially in the face, arms, and trunk. She has very low vision and no expressive communication. It is not clear whether she has receptive language because she has no way to communicate anticipation or to let caregivers know what she understands. She does not use her hands for any functional activities but is able to flex and extend her arms purposefully when her head, trunk, and pelvis are supported properly. She has a rudimentary hand-opening response when attempting to recontact an object that interests her.

It was decided to use activity routines to teach Janelle how to interact with objects. Children with visual impairments must learn about their environment through language and auditory information, and through touch and movement. Touch and movement are difficult for Janelle, because of her motor impairments, and it is unclear how well she processes language. Because of these barriers, it is of paramount importance that Janelle be given structured opportunities to learn about objects by assisted tactile contact and exploration of objects.

The first objective with Janelle was to encourage her to purposefully contact objects. One way to get her to contact objects was to set up situations in which contacting an object produces a desired effect. For example, as she was lying on her left side with her right hand free to move, a brightly colored vibrating ball was presented within her reach. It was moved slowly, since she appears to see things that are moving better than things that are fixed. Her hand was brought out to touch it, and at the moment that she touched it, it would be switched on. She responded by smiling and laughing and thus communicating that she liked that activity. This cycle was repeated several times (10 or more), trying to show her that touching the object would make it "go" (vibrate). After the first several tries, Janelle touched the object independently and then continued to respond in this way for several more turns. She was able to touch activate the ball when it was held in three different positions, visually relocating it each time it was moved. She had not previously been observed to visually track an object or to reach to touch an object.

The kind of structured interaction with an object used with Janelle has two aims:

1. to teach that *objects can represent activities*

2. to teach her to *isolate a specific voluntary movement* to access something

There was interest in these two teaching aims because mastery of these ideas or concepts would help prepare Janelle for making meaningful activity choices (for example, by touching an object that represents an activity, she could choose between a lotion rub or a mat activity) and prepare her to be more active in controlling her environment by enabling her to access a switch (which might control a toy, a radio, a fan, or a television). The set of actions carried out with Janelle make up a joint action routine, because they comprise a structured, predictable sequence of events that takes place with a partner and are repeated in order to teach a skill or concept.

Other Routines

There are some children with multiple disabilities who cannot even change the planes of their movement—that is, they cannot move up, down, or sideways; move into headfirst position; or maintain erect postures. For these children, incorporating motor-based routines that put the child into different planes of movement, as in rolling up and down a wedge cushion, rolling forward and backward over a bolster, or swinging from a swing, will often produce increased alertness, spontaneous movements, and supporting reactions. Occupational and physical therapists can help develop strategies for incorporating this kind of stimulation for children with severe disabilities and clarify what the precautions are for children with seizure disorders, shunts, and other medical issues. Once the child can tolerate positioning and movement in many planes of motion, purposeful movement can be more effectively encouraged through these types of routines.

STRATEGIES FOR ASSESSING MOTOR DEVELOPMENT

Meaningful assessment of motor development is at best a difficult task because children vary so widely in the rate at which they learn and develop. Formal testing that compares sighted, typically developing children and children with visual impairments, blindness, or multiple disabilities offers caregivers guidelines for developmental expectations and predictable sequences but is not always a good predictor of what a specific child may accomplish. Professionals and family members who are concerned with inadequate assessment strategies are beginning to formulate new evaluation tools that incorporate observations by family members and friends in order to provide a more complete picture of the child's overall competencies. Formal assessment data is still necessary in many instances, however, to establish the need for services, the eligibility to receive services, or to assess progress. The following are possible resources for assessing motor development in children who are visually impaired:

- *Oregon Project for Visually Impaired and Blind Preschool Children* (Brown, Simmons, Methuin, Anderson, Boigon-Davis, 1991): The Oregon Project is a nonstandardized, criteria-based assessment, for use with children from birth to 6 years of age. Items assess motor (gross and fine) skills, self-help, language, cognition and socialization.

- *Callier-Azusa Scale* (1978): The Callier-Azusa Scale was designed specifically for students with deaf-blindness and can be used with most students with severe disabilities. Subscales relating to visual, auditory, and tactile development make it useful for a wide variety of children. The "G" scale, intended for use by teachers and/or family members, assesses motor development. The "H" scale is designed for use by those with professional training related to the disability. This assessment is not standardized.

- *LINKing Assessment and Early Intervention* (Bagnato, Neisworth, & Munson, 1997): This publication provides an informative review of many assessments now available.

Much of the assessment of motor skills done by occupational and physical therapists, however, is based on clinical observation and physical interaction with the child instead of on normative standards. The accompanying box, "Assessing Motor Development," lists some of the physical motor skills and quality-of-movement indicators that help therapists determine when children need help with motor skill development. Families and other professionals are often aware of these issues and are encouraged to use their observational skills in natural environments with functional tasks to help determine the need for assistance or intervention.

STRATEGIES FOR PROMOTING MOTOR DEVELOPMENT

Once specific motor problems have been identified in the young child with visual impairment, there are a variety of strategies which teachers and families can use to promote motor development. It may be as simple as changing the placement of a material presented, creating activities which encourage movement, positioning oneself differently in relation to the child, or adapting standard techniques to match the motor development level of a particular child. Some general strategies for promoting motor development are offered below, followed by more specific suggestions.

Stimulation versus Engagement

For decades, intervention with young children has focused on improving skill levels in order to maximize independent function. Putting the emphasis on gaining skills has lead to an emphasis on *stimulation*. Stimulation is a tool, a way to provide experience and sensory material, but stimulation, as an approach, falls short. In order to enhance development on any level, whether cognitive, social or motor, the primary goal should be *engagement*. Skills should be

ASSESSING MOTOR DEVELOPMENT

The following factors are important to include when assessing motor development:

➜ *Stability of trunk, pelvis, and shoulder girdle:* This stability impacts coordination of movement; clinical test involves manual muscle evaluation, resistive activities, and observation to determine whether the child can stabilize one body part so others can move freely and functionally.

➜ *Muscle tone and strength:* Accuracy of testing for muscle tone depends on the evaluator's level of experience, since it is largely a subjective test with young children. Strength can be empirically measured with testing equipment. Low tone is often implicated in low strength. As a first effort to think about tone, the clinician might ask: Does the child's body feel like mine (normal tone), like a rag doll (hypotonic), or stiff, like a plastic doll (hypertonic)? Is the child able to lift and carry items, to bend and pick up items from the floor?

➜ *Joint range of motion:* Every joint of the body has a potential full range of motion, which is the amount of movement allowed by the structure of the joint. The thumb has a specific range of motion, as do the shoulder, the hip, and every other joint. Many factors can impede that full range, such as spasticity, bone changes, posture, affect, and muscle atrophy, and so on. If passive or active range of motion is limited, further evaluation and intervention is imperative. If a child cannot fully move the arm from the shoulder, or if it is difficult for a child to bend at the knee or come down to weight bearing through both heels, a range of motion evaluation should be completed.

➜ *Static versus dynamic standing balance:* The ability to balance, holding body parts upright, influences motor coordination planning and safety. Balance develops from head to toe.

   Static balance: Children who are visually impaired should be able to stand on one foot for at least 5–10 seconds by the age of 6 (norms are established for sighted children).

   Dynamic balance: Dynamic balance is evaluated as a reflection of functional ability. Can the child move over obstacles, shift weight, and recover balance independently?

➜ *Reflex integration:* A careful observation of the quality of movements, with emphasis on determining whether primitive reflexes interfere with voluntary movement, will help establish the need for therapeutic intervention. Two major reflexes to consider are the asymmetrical tonic neck reflex (ATNR) and symmetrical tonic neck reflex (STNR). Both of these reflexes produce movement through the arms as a result of head movement. In the ATNR, when the head moves to one side, the arm on the "face" side extends (straightens) and the arm on the "skull"

(continued)

side reflexes (bends). If the ATNR persists, it will be difficult for the child to develop functional voluntary hand movement. The STNR is often called the "puppy position" reflex, because when the head is raised, the arms extend. If the child is prone, whenever the head is raised, the arms extend and the hips flex, which precludes most purposeful movement like crawling or creeping. Persistence of reflex activity past late infancy is usually an indicator of some type of neurological impairment, and this impairment should be identified and addressed.

➜ *Bilateral coordination:* This term refers to the ability to use the two sides of the body together cooperatively, as in midline play (playing with objects by manipulating them with both hands at the body's midline), jumping jacks, clapping, skipping, or holding a container with one hand and opening the lid with the other. By crossing the midline of the body, the child is able to integrate the left and right sides of the body and thereby increases overall functioning. Can the child hold a bottle with two hands, clap, and so on?

➜ *Motor planning:* Presented with a new task, can the child create a "motor plan" to deal with the situation? For example, can the child climb down from a platform, get up onto an unfamiliar swing, negotiate a ramped incline, or pick up a novel object independently? Additionally, can the child learn and generalize a motor skill after it is demonstrated, such as opening a container or stepping over an obstacle?

➜ *Transitional movements:* All children need to be able to move from one position to another on their own. Transitional movement is extremely important, because without smooth transitions, mobility and safety are greatly reduced. Does the child move from sitting to standing independently, or does he or she pull up on furniture (or an adult's body)?

If problems are observed in any of these motor areas, or if there is a question of quality of movement in these areas, it is important that referrals be made to an occupational or physical therapist for further assessment.

Chris A. Strickling

taught to children so that they will be able to meaningfully participate in their world. For children without visual or other physical impairments, stimulation leads easily to engagement. By providing a stimulating environment that is rich in interaction and complex tasks, caregivers offer the child not only an opportunity to learn the tasks at hand, but ways to apply this knowledge in many situations, and use that knowledge in other contexts. Mastery of each new task or skill brings with it a whole milieu of possible social connections, connections maintained from a base of shared interest.

For children with visual impairments or multiple disabilities, a stimulating environment may not foster any skill development be-

Active engagement in climbing activities helps a child with visual impairment master many motor tasks.

cause the requisite exploration does not take place and the applications are not clear. For these children, "stimulation" needs to be subordinated to engagement. Children who are blind, especially those with other disabilities, learn to play alone and sometimes isolate themselves, preferring to engage in highly ritualized, repetitive patterns of movement or action on objects instead of engaging with others. At that point, stimulation in itself has little value.

Ricky is a 3-year-old blind boy who prefers to play by himself, using a few highly ritualized, repetitive movements and actions on objects in his environment. He is happy with that kind of play, but his parents are concerned that he does not interact with them or with age peers. His occupational therapist is concerned because instead of learning new manipulation schemes for objects, he repeats the ones he already knows. He uses every toy that he handles to produce a sound. Once he has made that sound, he drops the object. The therapist offers him stimulation in the form of new motor experiences and new toys, but he refuses. The therapist's goal is to expand Ricky's skills. But Ricky's goal is different. He just wants to explore the way things sound. To him, play is meaningful and fun.

In order to see eventual progress on skills, the adults who care for Ricky need to reduce their focus on teaching him higher level skills and focus on *interactions* that let Ricky know that adults can bring something interesting into play, not just impose their agendas. He has to be prepared to be instructed, or taught, by learning that there is reward in interaction.

Initially, the therapist introduced a battery-operated toy that vibrated. Ricky needed to signal his therapist to restart the toy at intervals, because it was turned off every minute or so. Because he was motivated by the vibration and the sound of the toy, he was willing to stay in tactile contact with the therapist's hand, which was something he had always avoided, and to signal her to restart the vibrator. The therapist showed him how to restart it, by placing her hand underneath his (hand under hand) when she pushed the button to start the toy. Ricky was learning to use the therapist as an assistant, learning a way to engage her to get something he wanted, and also learning that she had something to offer him that was at least as interesting as his solitary play.

In essence, engagement allows the child to pick the "topic" of the play and teaches him or her that there is reward in interaction. Once the child understands the value of interaction, the avenue is open for teaching.

Using Sensory Integration

As discussed earlier, sensory integration therapy is widely used for children with visual impairments. Because sensory integration involves age-appropriate sensorimotor activities, teachers and families can use these ideas in many contexts. If one child in a class or group needs sensory integration therapy, peers, and siblings can join in the fun, too. Occupational therapists and physical therapists who have been trained in sensory integration can help families set up appropriate motor activities at home. Following are a few suggestions for incorporating sensorimotor activity into classroom and home settings:

- Use an obstacle course to teach directional concepts like "up" or "over" while teaching transitional movement and providing movement on different planes.

- Incorporate a slow, repetitive movement activity, such as swinging in a suspended hammock, or swing, as an option for a child who shows a tendency toward excitability.

- For children who are afraid to move out in space, provide a peer as a buddy and use an exciting vestibular stimulus, such as a scooter board, or a rocker board, or use a small rebounder trampoline for proprioceptive input as a preparation for walking.

Replace Incidental Learning with Systematic Introduction

Since children with visual impairments cannot learn by watching, they have to be introduced to most new fine and gross motor tasks. As much as possible, new motor activities need to be introduced in supportive, no-demand contexts in which peer or adult interaction is available. It is important to help the child solve problems about each transitional movement so that exploration is safe. Likewise, it is important to encourage children with visual impairments to move through their physical environments as independently as possible. Lifting and carrying a child with a visual impairment to another area of a room, for example, deprives the child of the chance to develop a map of the environment and may be confusing. Some examples of occasions when systematic instruction may be needed include when the child is:

- crawling or climbing onto and off of a sofa, bench, or chair;
- climbing on and off gym equipment and riding toys;
- going up and down the stairs using a handrail; and
- skipping, hopping, jumping, and running.

Structuring Peer Interactions to Promote Exploration of the Environment

Typically, motor skills are considered to be highly individual. In fact, they are. But what motivates many of our motor activities is the desire to be in contact with others. Planning for peer interaction during a motor game or even during walking, may help motivate the action, especially for children whose movement is slow to develop or who may be hesitant to explore the physical environment. Examples include:

- using a buddy system in preschool games (for example, Red Rover, duck-duck goose),
- running with a partner to experience freedom of movement, and
- pairing up to use playground equipment (for example, see-saw and slide).

Early Orientation and Mobility

O&M instruction can be crucial to the child's motor development, especially for children with very low vision and blindness. Modifying the environment so that objects can be located and relocated easily and creating safe boundaries are essential for easy early mobility. Early O&M instruction provides many benefits to motor development, including:

- understanding of body concepts and how to move body parts in a functional manner;

- learning how to systematically explore the environment for safe, efficient movement; and

- use of appropriate mobility devices, increasing exploration and confidence of movement as well as improving muscle tone, balance, and coordination.

Additional suggestions to facilitate motor development in young children with visual impairment are offered in the accompanying box "Promoting Motor Development." Also see Chapter 10 for more extensive information on O&M instruction for young children.

In organizing activities and lessons, it sometimes helps to define spatial boundaries, with a blanket or carpet square for instance. In addition, although it is sometimes easy to focus on learning a skill, in general the skill should not be removed from its functional realm. The child's developmental status should also always be kept in mind. For example, it makes sense that a child should be able to stabilize his or her shoulder and trunk before using forearm protective techniques, to avoid promoting atypical movement patterns.

Using a Team Approach with Child-Centered Goals

The goal of any motor program is to maximize a child's ability to interact safely, efficiently, and gracefully with the environment. Families, therapists, O&M specialists, teachers, and others can work together to promote typical movement experiences for the child with visual impairment. However, different professionals and family members are likely to have their own, sometimes conflicting, ideas of what constitutes "progress." It is important that all team members coordinate their efforts to focus on the child's goals, not the individual goals of each team member. (See the section on teaming in Chapter 11 for more information on using a team approach.)

Instead of working separately on occupational therapy, physical therapy, or O&M goals, the child will be better served if team members confer with each other and with the child and his or her family and develop child-centered goals. Once the goals are established, each member of the team can devise a strategy for helping the child

PROMOTING MOTOR DEVELOPMENT

The following strategies are useful in promoting the motor development of young children who are visually impaired. It should be noted that in cases in which children are receiving physical or occupational therapy, or in which there is any motor development concern, a physical therapist or occupational therapist should be consulted regarding the appropriateness of any of these for intervention purposes. Every student has unique needs, and general suggestions such as these listed cannot take the place of a planned individualized program.

→ Provide the infant with a variety of movement and positional experiences. Short, comfortable experiences may be more easily tolerated at first than 10–15 minute sessions. Tolerance can gradually be extended from a few seconds to greater periods of time.

→ To break up body play, give compression (applying pressure to a joint) to the arm or hand of the child, and then put a substitute object in the hand (such as a piece of PVC pipe corked with a weight inside so the child gets some proprioceptive feedback). Joint compression is done by putting two joints in alignment, stablizing both manually, then applying sustained pressure for up to 30–45 seconds.

→ Use the adult's hand or body for the child to push against when trying to teach a skill such as squaring off to a child who is disorganized. Giving resistance helps stabilize any body part before using it for an O&M skill.

→ To encourage midline orientation of the hands and visual attention, use a patterned cover on an infant's bottle. High-contrast patterns are best. Encourage the infant to hold the bottle during feeding.

→ Add different textures to infant and toddler objects and toys as there are too many plastic and soft objects commercially available and children with visual impairments have trouble differentiating them.

→ To orient the child to forward space and movement, it is helpful to work in front of the child rather than always from behind.

→ To promote body awareness, concept development, and visual skills while the child is on his or her tummy, place toys in front to either side. Encourage the child to shift his or her weight onto one arm and reach for the toy with the other.

→ Use big balls, bolsters, and rolled pillows to help with rolling forward to facilitate shoulder girdle and arm development.

→ With the child sitting on the floor or straddling a small bolster (with supervision only), place a set of items (such as blocks) on one side and empty containers on the other. Have the child take one item at a time and place it in an empty container. This activity addresses the goals of concept development (such

(continued)

as empty/full, in/out, in front, beside, behind, turn, and up/down). Other areas addressed are visual skills, body awareness, and systematic search. Consider placement of containers to work on specific skills and concepts.

➜ Teach functional activities, like opening doors and jars or turning on faucets, which promote motor skills such as wrist rotation.

➜ To promote body awareness, concept development, independent movement, and route travel, use a scooterboard in a variety of ways. Have the child push or pull him- or herself across the room, follow a visual or tactile path, or hold a hula hoop while the specialist holds the other side, with the child indicating the speed and directions. Have the child go through an obstacle course.

➜ Scooterboards can be used with various positions (sitting, using legs to propel; sitting cross-legged and propelling with hands or being pulled, lying on back). Never use a scooterboard without providing much (preferably hands-on) supervision, and always check with an occupational or physical therapist before initiating scooterboard activities.

➜ Encourage the child to cruise for short distances holding on to a variety of surfaces at varying heights. For incentive and to add purpose to the activity, place a favorite toy or food a short distance from the child and have him or her cruise to locate it.

➜ Place a tactile marker or a favorite motivating toy or other object at the child's place at a table and have the child cruise (eventually trail) to locate it. O&M areas addressed include independent movement, beginning use of basic skills, and beginning use of landmarks. The marker may be visual for the child who has vision.

➜ To promote body awareness, social skills, and concept development, play robot or ballerina by balancing a beanbag or book on the child's head. Have the child try to keep the chin level as he or she sits or walks while balancing the book or beanbag. Be aware of atypical posturing, and discontinue this activity if any is noted until checking with a physical therapist or occupational therapist for ideas.

Adapted from J. S. Lampert, "Gross Motor Development," in R. L. Pogrund, D. L. Fazzi, & J. S. Lampert (Eds). Early focus: Working with Young Blind and Visually Impaired Children and Their Families (New York: AFB Press, 1992), *pp. 38–94.*

advance toward those goals. Instead of prioritizing the goals of each kind of service (in which the occupational therapist, physical therapist, and other providers would each develop separate goals and then devise activities to help the child reach those goals), teams can work toward identifying what the child most needs to learn and making those skills the "goals" (in this model, the occupational therapist, physical therapist and other providers then decide how they will help the child achieve the identified goals). This shift in thinking reduces the number of goals each child is expected to achieve, focuses the energy and creativity of all involved in a way that benefits the child, and ensures maximum success in the child's motor development.

10 MOBILITY FOCUS

Developing Early Skills for Orientation and Mobility

CONTRIBUTORS

Tanni L. Anthony Working Definitions and Program Components, O&M Considerations for Infants and Toddlers, Body Concepts and Spatial Relationships (in O&M Considerations for Preschoolers), O&M Assessment

Hannah Bleier Echolocation (in O&M Considerations for Preschoolers)

Diane L. Fazzi O&M Considerations for Preschoolers, Basic Skills, Mobility Devices, Environmental Considerations

Daniel Kish Echolocation (in O&M Considerations for Preschoolers)

Rona L. Pogrund O&M Considerations for Preschoolers, Basic Skills, Mobility Devices

The area of orientation and mobility (O&M), with its emphasis on movement, actually encompasses all developmental areas. For the young child who lacks visual input, movement through the environment may not occur naturally. Sight is a motivator for movement, and through movement young children learn about the world. Through the process of purposeful movement, young children with visual impairments are able to interact with the environment and develop conceptual understanding that leads to growth in all other areas of development.

The process of teaching "travel skills" to people who are blind or visually impaired is called *orientation and mobility* or in its abbreviated form, O&M. As a profession, O&M was founded as a rehabilitation process for the war-blinded veterans of World War II. Over the past 50 years, the profession has revised its teaching strategies to better focus on the needs of children. A particular emphasis has been placed on the early O&M skills of infants, toddlers, and preschoolers with visual impairments, especially within the last two decades.

With the inclusion of children, from birth to 5 years of age, the field of O&M continues to refine both instructional philosophy and

FOCUS POINTS ON ORIENTATION AND MOBILITY

The following key ideas are addressed in this chapter.

➜ Orientation and mobility (O&M), with its emphasis on movement, actually encompasses all developmental areas.

➜ O&M specialists must work closely with families, teachers, and other professionals in order to develop and provide high quality O&M programs for young children who are blind or visually impaired.

➜ Sensory skills and concept development are important components of O&M programs for young children.

➜ Encouraging purposeful and self-initiated movement in children who are visually impaired should begin early and continue as children move through and explore increasingly complex environments.

➜ It is through movement that young children learn about the world, develop muscle tone and coordination, and become actively engaged with other people and their surroundings.

➜ The basic skills of using a human guide, protective techniques, and trailing can be valuable skills for young children who are blind or visually impaired when taught in conjunction with the use of an appropriate mobility device.

➜ Motivating instruction in the use of appropriately selected low vision and mobility devices can facilitate independent travel for many children who are blind or visually impaired.

actual teaching techniques. A developmental approach has helped to shape the actual definitions and program components of O&M for infants, toddlers, and preschoolers.

WORKING DEFINITIONS AND PROGRAM COMPONENTS

As traditionally defined, "Orientation is the process of using the remaining senses to establish one's position and relationship to all other significant objects in one's environment," (p. 3) and "Mobility is the capacity, the readiness, and the facility to move" (p. 115) (Hill & Ponder, 1976). These definitions are both simplified and expanded when the focus is on early childhood. *Orientation* involves knowing oneself as a separate being, where one is in space, where one wants to move out into space, and how to get to that place. To determine this information, the child must be able to use available sensory information and have a basic understanding of his or her location in space and the environmental settings in which he or she will move. With very young children, orientation can be directly tied to the cognitive mastery of concepts of body image, spatial constructs, causality, means and ends, and object permanence. In addition, orientation involves the refinement of each individual child's sensory skills as a means of acquiring information about him- or herself, other people, and the environment.

Mobility refers to the physical process of moving through space in a safe and efficient manner. For the very young child, mobility refers to general gross motor development, including the normal integration of reflexes, acquisition of motor milestones, refinement of quality-of-movement skills, and purposeful, self-initiated movement.

Expanded service components of O&M programs for very young children ensure that programming embraces a developmental approach. New components reflect a bottom-up style of program, reinforcing the understanding that all O&M skills are founded in the early years of life within the home environment of the child. As the child experiences typical outings in the home community, O&M concepts and skills can be reinforced in these environments. Hill, Rosen, Correa, and Langley (1984) noted the following facets of an O&M program: sensory skill development, concept development, motor development, environmental and community awareness, formal orientation skills, and formal mobility skills. Environmental and community awareness and formal orientation skills were new components of the traditional O&M model. The Preschool O&M Project by Hill, Smith, Dodson-Burk, and Rosen (1987) added fine and gross motor skills. Anthony (1993) noted the need for two additional areas of specific O&M program focus: purposeful and self-initiated movement. "Developing an Appropriate O&M Program for Young Children" in this chapter provides some tips for developing an O&M program for young children who are blind or visually impaired.

O&M CONSIDERATIONS FOR INFANTS AND TODDLERS

Philosophical Approach to O&M and Early Intervention

The O&M specialist must work closely with the family and local service providers to accomplish the joint goals of the early intervention program. Both team- and family-centered approaches are critical to the success of the program.

DEVELOPING AN APPROPRIATE O&M PROGRAM FOR YOUNG CHILDREN

The following general suggestions may be helpful in developing an O&M program that is appropriate for young children who are visually impaired:

➜ Read all relevant medical and background information available. Clinical and functional assessments of vision (where appropriate), health condition diagnoses, and developmental assessments will each be important in planning O&M assessments and ultimately designing individualized O&M programs.

➜ Meet with the family and listen closely to their descriptions of the young child's strengths, family concerns, and cultural background. Ask questions as appropriate to determine their priorities for and comfort level with services. Take time to make sure that they understand the scope of O&M services that can be provided to young children who are blind or visually impaired, including those children who have multiple disabilities.

➜ Observe the child in a full range of natural environments (home, yard, neighborhood, or preschool) as appropriate to determine his or her individual strengths (such as motor coordination or level of curiosity for exploration) and needs (such as balance or expectations for independent movement from others) in the area of orientation and mobility.

➜ Conduct the O&M assessments, either individually or as part of a team assessment process, as approved by the family. Determine the child's physical readiness for independent or semi-independent movement (such as motor milestones achieved and overall quality of movements), the child's cognitive understanding of his or her surroundings (such as attainment of object permanence, understanding of body concepts, and awareness of spatial layout of rooms in the house), and motivation for movement and exploration (such as child's interest in exploring new and familiar environments or expectations for getting places independently from family members and other teachers).

➜ Consult with other team members (such as family members, occupational or physical therapists, eye care professionals, the teacher of students who are visually impaired, and the preschool teacher) when additional disabilities are present that impact the child's physical ability to move independently, for example.

➜ Develop an individualized O&M program for the child and family in collaboration with all team members, so that the program can be integrated throughout the child's day during natural times and family and school routines, as appropriate.

➜ Provide follow-up with families and other professionals to make sure that the O&M program is being implemented appropriately and anticipated progress is being made. Follow-up meetings are important to address any areas of confusion that may arise and also to maintain team vigilance for follow-through on O&M approaches.

Diane L. Fazzi

In a team approach, the goals of the family and each professional discipline can be embedded into the developmental activities of the child's day. For example, the activity of dressing can address a number of skills. One such skill is advanced object permanence as the toddler remembers that his or her pajamas are located in the bottom drawer of his or her bedroom bureau, and another orientation skill is reinforced as the toddler finds the dresser in the bedroom. Upper extremity strength and coordination are needed to help open the drawer. Finally, there is evidence of self-help mastery as the toddler assists his or her mother with putting on pajamas. In this manner, a number of early skills are addressed without arbitrary tasks that do not lead to the completion of a daily routine of the child.

A family-centered approach is one that includes active respect for family values, culture, socioeconomic diversity, and child raising philosophy (NEC*TAS, 1991). Such an approach will give definition and direction to the programmatic activities. Parents are considered key team members with full decision-making power of what the goals of the program will be and how they can best be reached. It is the responsibility of the professionals to provide the family with ample information so that they can make well-informed decisions about their child. The O&M specialist's program goals for the young child can be easily embedded into the overall program of the child. To be effective, the O&M specialist must have a solid understanding of early childhood development, as well as knowledge of the implications of blindness and low vision upon early development. Global program emphases will have four main focus areas (Anthony, 1993):

First, *continually to expand the child's understanding of his or her own body, daily settings and location within each environment;*

Second, *to encourage, then refine the child's means of movement;*

Third, *to reinforce his or her purpose to move within his or her environment so that he or she is motivated to explore and is capable of accomplishing a goal which requires movement as the means to achieve that goal; and*

Fourth, *to assist the family and service providers in analyzing the daily environments of the child for safety factors and for possible modification that will maximize self-initiated and goal-oriented movement. Attention to the child's first learning environments such as the crib or first floor play space promotes the understanding of spatial relations and purposeful movement exploration.*

For the purpose of this section of the chapter, the areas of sensory, cognitive, and gross motor development will be explored as to their role in the evolution of O&M skill development during the first two years of life. In addition to these areas of human growth, the developmental domains of fine motor, communication, self-help, and social skill acquisition will be briefly addressed for their role in orientation and mobility skill acquisition. Further information about these domains can be found in Chapters 4, 6, 7, and 9.

Sensory Development

Exposure to sensory stimuli is important to the development of the infant's ability to take in information about the world around him or her. Caregivers and early intervention personnel must be sensitive to the developing infant's ability to organize sensory information. All team members should work together to provide the child with meaningful sensory input that is graded to the child's individual needs and tolerance level. Too often young children are bombarded with sensory information in a naïve attempt to provide "all possible information". Greeley (1997) recommended that only one sensory–modality stimulus be offered at a time, as multiple types of input may be too overwhelming and complex for a child with additional disabilities to understand and process. Too much sensory information can be as fruitless as too little information. Children with fragile central nervous systems and/or cortical visual impairment overload with too much information or may not engage with too little.

Determining what types and possible combinations of sensory input to offer the developing infant may well be one of the first tasks of the teacher of students who are visually impaired and/or the O&M specialist. Over time, the goal is to fine-tune the child's ability to respond and utilize sensory information (Anthony, 1993).

Knowing the status of the child's sensory skills will provide information about the influences of noise and lighting, potential need for prescriptive optical devices, and the suitable teaching style. Rather than completing only a functional vision assessment on the child, a complete sensory profile should be developed. This profile can yield information on what types of sensory information alert, calm, and overload the young learner. It is also a more appropriate assessment for a child who is blind and who would not benefit from the traditional functional vision assessment. Knowing this information will assist the team in identifying possible motivators for exploration and movement (Anthony, 1998). For example, a sensory profile assessment might indicate a preference for objects of a certain color or for a sequence of sensory stimuli before a child will engage in visual activities. The latter has been found to be especially important for children who have combined vision and hearing losses (Greeley & Anthony, 1995). Some children may need to listen, then touch, and then look at an object.

Sensory profile assessment information will also help the O&M specialist identify how sensory stimuli can be used by the young child for decoding important environmental information (Anthony, 1993). The team should then work together to identify how the infant's sensory skills can be used for orientation purposes within the daily routines. One family decided to use visual, olfactory, and tactile landmarks in different rooms of their home. The crib mobile had an attached fabric bag of a soft potpourri fragrance that filled the room with a specific aroma. The bathtub had a black and white contact paper "picture" adhered to one side. This turned out to be a great landmark for the child; he would immediately turn to the picture and touch it upon entering the tub. For more details on how to develop a sensory profile see "Completing a Sensory Profile."

All sensory systems are involved in the learning process. The four senses of hearing, vision, touch, and smell are important for purposes of the awareness of the surrounding environment. Each sense will be briefly reviewed from a perspective of early orientation and mobility skill development.

THE SENSE OF HEARING

Too often, the sense of hearing is taken for granted with the young child with visual impairment. When vision is impaired, the role of hearing plays an especially vital role in the child's learning, communication, and movement development.

The sense of hearing can offer critical information about one's environment. It is vital that the child who has a diagnosed visual loss also be examined for any hearing concerns. Even temporary hearing loss as a result of an ear infection can negatively impact a child's communication development and balance. A more serious hearing loss has great implications on both communication and the ability to use auditory information for orientation purposes. Early identification can lead to appropriate assistive listening devices, as well as specialized programming that addresses the impact of hearing loss upon development. The child who has a combined vision and hearing loss (deaf blindness) will need specialized programming that accounts for this unique situation.

The ability to determine the direction and identify the source of a sound is a highly usable orientation skill. The sound of a familiar voice can signal that sister is home from school, water running means someone is getting the bath ready in the bathroom down the

COMPLETING A SENSORY PROFILE

A sensory profile assessment of a young child who is blind or visually impaired can yield important information that will help professionals and parents be sensitive to the child's needs and preferences and work more effectively with the child. It involves the following steps:

1. Gather medical information about the child's vision condition, hearing status, diagnosis of other conditions, and listing of any medications the child is taking.

   a. Hearing. Is hearing within normal limits? Does the child need or have any type of assistive listening devices? Is there a history of ear infections? Is the child on any medications that might influence hearing abilities?

   b. Vision. Is the vision loss due to ocular visual impairment or cortical visual impairment or both? Is vision better in one eye than the other? Is there field loss in either eye? Is the child on any medications that might influence visual abilities?

   c. Physical/Medical. Is there a diagnosis of additional disabilities or health concerns such as cerebral palsy, seizure disorders, or medical fragility? Is the child on any medications that influence balance or alertness? Does the child require any special equipment for positioning?

2. Observe the child in several environments and notice what types and/or combinations of sensory stimuli elicit certain responses from the child:

   a. What calms the child (e.g., rocking, mother's voice, quiet)?

   b. What alerts the child (e.g., music, bright colors, familiar objects)?

   c. What cues the child to look at an object (e.g., movement, color, familiarity, contrast, sound, wait time)?

   d. What cues the child to touch an object (e.g., visual cues such as movement, color, contrast; sound cues; touch cue to wrist or top of hand)?

3. Observe the child's sensory preferences:

   a. Hearing: soft sounds versus loud sounds; sounds presented within a certain hearing range from the child, need for a quiet environment.

   b. Vision: certain colors and/or levels of contrast, certain lighting conditions, specific focal ranges, quiet faces versus talking faces, specific areas to avoid in the visual field, familiar objects versus novel objects, movement cues of a visual target, sound cues with a visual target.

   c. Touch: soft versus firm touch; preferences for places on body to be touched versus places to initially avoid such as the face or hands, touch announced by a visual cue, touch announced by a sound cue.

   d. Kinesthetic: movement when supported (e.g., holding baby close to body while moving versus holding baby out in space while moving), slow movement versus fast movement.

Compiled by Tanni L. Anthony

hall, and the ringing of the doorbell announces someone at the front door. To reinforce the young child's curiosity and understanding of the sounds in his or her world, it is helpful to note his or her response to the sound and, as appropriate, investigate the source of the noise. Label new sounds so that the child can learn that each sound has a name. More importantly, allow the child to experience firsthand the source of the sound, such as traveling to the laundry room and touching the vibrating washing machine, and then later, when the sound stops, taking the wet clothes out to put into the dryer. As the child becomes mobile, encourage him or her to travel to the sound or voice to see where, what, or who it is.

It is important to understand the developmental sequence of auditory localization, as these skills will tutor the child in reaching and/or moving out in space that cannot be visually observed. The typical infant learns to localize sound in the following sequence (Kukla & Thomas, 1978):

1. sounds presented directly at ear level;

2. sounds presented at ear level and downward;

3. sounds presented at ear level and upward;

4. sounds presented directly upward, and

5. sounds presented in front of his or her body and at almost any other angle by about 21–24 months.

Too often, an infant without vision is enticed to reach out to a sounding object that is placed directly in midline. Detecting a sound source directly in front of one's body is a skill that develops last in the sequence of auditory localization. If the child has low vision and can see the sounding item, he or she has an additional cue to reach toward the object. Without sight, the child is faced with an auditory skill that is credited as a 21–24-month skill (Kukla & Thomas, 1978). This fact means that an 8-month old child who is blind may be asked to do a much higher-level skill if she or he is expected to reach for a sounding object in front of her or him. The skill of reaching to an unseen sound source is complicated further by the child's understanding of object permanence, as will be reviewed in the upcoming cognition section of this chapter.

THE SENSE OF VISION

Visual–motor skills such as fixation, tracking, and shift of gaze develop typically within the first six months of life (Bayley, 1993). Eye contact is usually well established within the first two to three months of life (Parks, Furuno, O'Reilly, et al., 1994). By six months of life, the infant should demonstrate coordinated eye movements during tracking (following a moving object) and shift of gaze (fixation on one object, then another) tasks. When a baby has a visual impairment, there may be delays in developing visual milestones and, depending on the amount of vision loss, certain visual milestones may not be feasible. If there are additional disabilities, such as cerebral palsy, eye movement abilities may be affected.

It will be important for the team members to work together to address the visual abilities of the child. Care should be taken to determine what types of visual stimuli are appropriate for the developing infant and how to determine appropriate visual development objectives for the child. Information should be shared with the family about the importance of grading visual information along with other sensory stimuli. If a child is expected to visually attend to a presented face, toy, or other object, it will be important to ensure that he or she is in a balanced, supported position. In such a position, the child can direct his or her energy into looking and not dividing his or her concentration in both looking and maintaining balance. Later, as the child is upright and moving, the O&M specialist can address how the child can use vision as a means of finding specific environmental clues, such as visual landmarks or changes in contrast indicating steps.

The following suggestions can be used to encourage *visual fixation* with a very young child:

Encouraging Visual Fixation

→ Select objects that have the appropriate sensory characteristics related to the visual abilities of the child. For example, a child with light perception may be responsive to shiny objects such as silver pie tins that are hung overhead as a play mobile. As the air current catches the tins, they will move and sparkle in the sunlight. A child with gross form perception may be responsive to brightly colored objects that are placed on a high contrast solid background. A yellow and red striped ball on a white floor mat may entice a child's visual attention.

→ Care should be taken to give the child time to visually respond to a face and/or an object.

→ As a child visually notices objects in his or her environment, these items will serve as a lure for movement: a reach, a roll, or a crawl.

→ As the child is able to fixate on objects, attention can be given to increasing the visual complexity of a visual task by decreasing the size of objects being viewed, decreasing the contrast surrounding the object, and increasing the distance of the object from the child. Of course, all of these suggestions must be geared to the physiological capabilities of the child.

Once a child can direct his or her gaze to an object for a sustained period of time (sustained visual attention or fixation), the next visual skill will be *tracking* the object. Tracking involves maintaining focus on an object that is moving. The object or face of interest can be slowly moved from midline to either side of the face, then back to midline. Visual tracking typically proceeds from nose to forehead, nose to either side (not crossing midline), side to side (crossing midline), full vertical (lower chest to above forehead), and then in circular motions. In the best of circumstances, tracking is completed with both eyes moving together. Depending on the child's visual status in either eye, this movement may or may not be possible.

The following suggestions can be used to encourage tracking in very young children:

Encouraging Tracking

→ Tracking activities can be deliberately set up with the child, and they can occur spontaneously in the environment as a person or household pet moves by the child.

→ If tracking tasks are deliberately set up with the child, care should be taken to select an object that is of interest to the child (a spoon with food or a favorite toy) and to grade the movement of the object so that it does not move too quickly.

→ Games can be set up where the child follows the object to a location where there is a surprise waiting for him or her, such as a hand that opens up with a small toy.

Atkinson (2000) describes the sequence of the development of *shift of gaze* skills in the developing infant. Shift of gaze describes the ability to shift one's visual attention from one item to another. Shift of gaze, which is typically evident in the first months of life, is accomplished first with items that are located in the same depth range or distance away from the child's eyes. By 6 months, the infant can shift his or her visual attention from one object in one depth plane (such as near range) to another in a different depth plane (such as far range). At the end of the first year, the child can follow an adult's point to a visual reference of another object and, as such, shows the skill of a shift of gaze from another person's hand to an object in distant space.

The following suggestions can be used to encourage shift of gaze in very young children:

Encouraging Shift of Gaze

→ When working with a child to shift his or her visual gaze, begin with similar objects that are held the same distance from the child's face.

→ It may be necessary to give a little wiggle of one object to elicit the child's attention to that object. Once attention has been gained, the second object can be jiggled to divert attention to it. This method can be used in a meaningful context of showing two choices of items: first one toy, then another toy or a piece of food.

→ Just as in tracking and fixation tasks, there will be natural opportunities for shift of gaze to develop and be refined. For example, the infant may be looking at a toy in his or her hand when Mom appears and he or she shifts gaze from the toy to her face.

Visual information about the environment can assist the child with low vision in determining where he or she is in space and where he or she may want to travel (Anthony, 1993). Light, color, and form perception all can give varying levels of orientation information. The ability to detect the source of a light, for example, may confirm the lit kitchen at the end of the hallway or the patio window on a sunny day. Sensitivity to high contrast may be used to discern a dark door from light-colored walls. Color vision may be used to note a particular landmark, such as a red couch in the living room or a certain house on the neighborhood block.

Analysis of the child's everyday environment is important to determine what aspects of the environment assist or hinder the child's visual abilities to develop orientation skills. Attention to lighting, use of high-contrast colors, reduced visual clutter, and distinctive visual landmarks are all ways to visually enhance the home and caregiving environments (Anthony, 1993). These effects can be accomplished by looking at the room from the child's perspective, if possible by using a low vision simulator. There are both commercial and homemade vision simulators. One way to simulate acuity loss is to place several sheets of plastic sandwich bags over one another until a certain degree of visual acuity loss is achieved when looking through them. The collected plastic bags can then be placed in front of one's eyes while looking at the home or classroom environment. Be sure to look at the room at different times of the day, as the lighting will change depending on the use of lamps, overhead lights, and incoming sun.

The goal is to make simple and realistic adaptations rather than major home or classroom alterations. For example, a high-contrast rug in front of the staircase may be used to signal the presence of stairs, or glare may be reduced on a sunny day by adjusting the window blinds. These adaptations contribute both to the physical safety and visual comfort of a child.

The best solution, however, is sometimes to let the child figure out the best way to maneuver in the environment just the way that it is, as in the following example:

In one home, a family realized that the child was confused by the color change from the living room carpet to the kitchen tiles. The child, a relatively new walker, would consistently stop, feel the floor, and then crawl over the surface change before then getting back up to his feet to continue walking. This child had poor depth perception and had had an experience of falling on a step recently. The family decided that the child had made the appropriate adaptation and that they did not need to do anything to alter their home environment. Within a couple of weeks of tactilely "checking it out," the child began to walk confidently from one room to the other without stopping to feel the surface change.

As with hearing, vision can serve as a powerful motivator to travel. For example, a toddler might learn to bring toys to a front window where he or she could check out their reflective or translucent color qualities in the sunlight. This interest may have been discovered when the child found interest in a stained glass ornament on the front window. Parents might choose to purposefully put the toy box near the window to expand the travel of the child; encouraging him or her to crawl first to the toy box, then to the front window with his or her acquired treasure.

SENSE OF TOUCH

The role of touch cannot be underestimated in an infant's understanding of his or her world. It is vital that young children have multiple opportunities to use their hands in a positive way to gain information about the world. Some children use their mouths and even parts of their faces for tactile exploration. For example, a toddler with a significant visual impairment might bring objects directly to his or her cheeks, touching them gently against his or her face as a way of learning more about the item. Mouthing typically fades as a means of exploration once children learn to use their hands for this purpose.

Miles (1998) recommends that objects be presented to the child's hands as a means of inviting tactile exploration. Hand-over-hand guidance may cause the child to pull back from the object to be explored. Tactile information will assist the young traveler in identifying objects encountered along his or her way and recognizing familiar landmarks such as the cement patio in the backyard or the wooden fence in the front yard.

SENSE OF SMELL

The sense of smell may play an occasional role in a child's orientation in the environment. The smell of dinner cooking in his or her home may confirm the location of the kitchen, just as the smell of lilacs might signal the flowering tree in front of the house. In the community, certain smells may assist the child in identifying the gas station, bakery, fast food restaurants, and other indoor and outdoor aromatic environments.

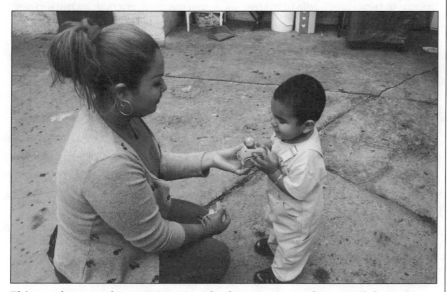

This mother gently presents a toy for her son to explore tactilely.

Some smells will be overpowering to the young child, and care should be taken not to subject the child to overly potent smells that may trigger a neurological response. Olfactory information should be presented within its normal context and not as a form of deliberate stimulation with young children, especially with those who have additional disabilities (Farber, 1982).

Cognitive Development

From the moment of birth, the infant begins to learn about the world. The next 24 months mark a time period unparalleled in one's lifetime for learning mastery of new ideas and capabilities. The first two years of life literally transform the reflexive-bound, fully dependent infant to an independently ambulating, communicating toddler with seemingly a mind of his or her own. The transition from a bundle of joy to a bundle of self-propelled energy unfolds with a combination of basic maturation and environmental opportunity. No matter the innate potential of each individual child, the first 2 years of life are of major importance for establishing the early foundation of learning. The presence of a disability may have a variety of influences on the developing child. For the child with blindness or visual impairment, the first 2 years provide both opportunity and challenge for developmental growth. Additional disabilities to the visual impairment will further compound the child's developmental path.

The first 2 years of life are the "sensorimotor period" (Piaget, 1952a). During this time frame, the young child's learning is guided by an interwoven relationship of sensory and motor experiences. Movement for the sake of movement is demonstrated, as is movement for the sake of exploring the environment. Both are important for mastery of motor skills and ongoing learning.

It is important to recognize the tug-pull relationship of a child's ongoing understanding of the world because of his or her ability to move within it and, in the process, becoming more mobile because of an expanded understanding of the world. This premise undergirds many of the early O&M activities of the young traveler. Leong (1996) credits this concept to Galloway (1981) by describing the following process:

> As children who are blind begin to master the environment and adequately move within it, they often grow cognitively and physically, their motivation to move and explore further increases; their greater motivation, in turn, ensures the continued expansion of their learning, control, and independence. (p. 145)

Three components of cognitive development, in particular, have great influence on the child's acquisition of early travel skills: the developing understanding of: object-permanence, means-end relationships, and the early constructs of spatial relations. Each concept area is developmentally intertwined to the other. (See Sidebar 10.1 for a list of concepts that may be learned during the first 2 years of life.)

SIDEBAR 10.1 CONCEPTS LEARNED IN THE EARLY YEARS:
BIRTH TO 24 MONTHS

The following list provides a general overview of key items that may be tied to early O&M concept development. It is not intended to be exhaustive of all of the concepts that are learned during the first two years of life.

The items were drawn from the following early childhood assessment tools: *Carolina Curriculum for Infants and Toddlers* (Johnson-Martin, Jens, Attermeier, & Hacker, 1991) and the *Hawaii Early Learning Profile (HELP: Birth to Three)* (Parks, et al., 1994). Neither of these tools have normative data for children with visual impairments. For that reason, age ranges have not been noted, and, in some cases, the items are not appropriate for a child who is totally blind.

OBJECT PERMANENCE

→ Shows interest in people and toys.
→ Reacts to disappearance of object.
→ Finds partially covered object.
→ Looks for family members and pets when named.
→ Plays peek-a-boo.
→ Finds totally hidden object.
→ Unwraps a toy.
→ Remembers location of toys that are put down for a few minutes.
→ Remembers familiar place where objects are kept.
→ Reaches for an object out of sight after it no longer makes noise.
→ Brings objects from another room upon request.
→ Reaches in correct direction of object that has made noise in several places.
→ Remembers where objects belong and puts them away upon request.

CAUSE AND EFFECT / MEANS END

→ Watches hands.
→ Uses hands and mouth for sensory exploration of objects.
→ Shakes rattle or bangs toys placed in hand.

(continued)

→ Slides toy on surface.

→ Overcomes obstacle to retrieve an object.

→ Guides action on manual toy (pushes buttons, pulls lever, and so on).

→ Drops objects systematically.

→ Understands that different toys are activated by different actions.

→ Retrieves object using another item.

→ Solves simple problems with tools.

→ Demonstrates common use of objects.

IMITATION

→ Enjoys repeating newly learned activity.

→ Imitates new gesture.

→ Engages in simple imitative play.

→ Imitates adult behavior using props.

→ Provides "help" in simple household chores—imitates adults.

BODY IMAGE

→ Moves hand to mouth.

→ Watches hands.

→ Brings hands together at midline.

→ Plays with own hands, feet, fingers, and toes.

→ Touches spot on body where a toy or object is touching.

→ Brings feet to mouth.

→ Transfers objects from hand to hand.

→ Identifies self in mirror.

→ Names one, then three, and then six body parts.

SPATIAL RELATIONSHIPS

→ Inspects surroundings.

→ Visually searches for sound.

→ Shifts visual attention or body orientation from one object to another.

→ Watches hands.

→ Plays with own hands, feet, fingers, and toes.

→ Turns to direction where name is called.

→ Brings feet to mouth.

→ Glances at one toy, then another when a toy is placed in each hand.

→ Reaches for nearby object in view.

REACHES FOR AN OBJECT OUT OF REACH, BUT STILL IN SIGHT

→ Drops objects systematically.

→ Searches for objects moved out of visual field.

→ Takes stacking ring apart.

→ Stacks rings on pole (though not in correct order).

→ Nests two, then three cans.

→ Places pegs in pegboard holes.

→ Places round piece, then square piece, and then triangle piece in form board.

→ Points to distant outdoor objects.

→ Explores cabinets and drawers.

SELF-INITIATION

→ Enjoys repeating a newly learned game.

→ Waits for an adult to take his or her turn in a turn-taking game.

→ Continues a familiar game by initiating movements involved in game.

→ Repeats action that elicits laughter from others.

→ Moves away from a caregiver who is in the same room.

→ Makes simple choices about books, food, and so on.

→ Gets own toys to play with from familiar place.

→ Uses adults to solve problems.

→ Approaches peer or adult to initiate play.

→ Solves simple problems without adult assistance.

→ Explores new environment.

Compiled by Tanni L. Anthony

The child who has a visual impairment must learn these early concepts firsthand, through actual functional experience with the involved objects. Concepts should be taught first in a natural context, and then reinforced in many different environments and with a variety of objects. Learning occurs best when the child is a participant and in a manner that initially involves the child's body. (See "Reinforcing Concept Development" for more specific suggestions.)

REINFORCING CONCEPT DEVELOPMENT

The following suggestions provide strategies for assisting young children who are blind or visually impaired in developing understanding of early concepts:

→ Introduce the concept in a natural context, such as introducing the concepts of wet and dry while taking a bath and drying with a towel, or, similarly, while washing dishes or watering plants.

→ Reinforce concepts across different environments and situations using a variety of objects. For example, opportunities for reinforcing the spatial concept of "in front of you" can be generated with different objects during play in the yard (such as "the ball is in front of you" while helping the child extend arms forward to locate the ball), at the dinner table (such as "your glass of water is in front of you"), and while shopping at the market (such as "there are two shopping carts in front of us in the line").

→ In general, start to teach concepts by involving the child's own body or body movements. For example, learning the concepts of "on" and "off" can begin with taking diapers or clothes on and off the child and later be reinforced by taking a doll's clothes on and off or turning a radio on or off.

→ Support generalization of concepts through comparative learning such as by looking at high-contrast pictures of different sizes of dogs and comparing those to pictures of different sizes of cats, for example. Such an activity can be followed by a visit to a neighborhood pet shop or kennel to see or touch the real thing.

→ Help develop complete concepts by involving young children who are blind or visually impaired in full activities. For example, having the young child help to take the bread out of the bag, put it in the toaster, and spread the butter on the warm toast will help the young child to understand that bread does not magically appear toasted and buttered.

→ Encourage young children to retrieve and return favorite toys from storage areas. By doing so, children learn the spatial layout of their homes and the permanence of objects.

Diane L. Fazzi

For example, the child can learn the concept of "in" as he or she crawls or is placed into specified space such as a laundry basket filled with toys. This concept can be reinforced further by putting a hand into a pocket, objects into a container, the toothbrush into the cup after brushing, and the dirty clothes into the hamper.

Comparative learning is important and care should be taken not to assume that a concept would be generalized without giving the child multiple experiences. The small metal spoon that is used for eating may not be generalized for the large plastic spoon that Mother uses to stir the evening meal. The world is filled with items that are in the same category, but are different in design. Caregivers and the early intervention team can spend time with the child just looking and touching objects that expand the child's repertoire of information, such as, cups, shoes, and writing tools.

Too often, children with visual impairments may develop fragmented concepts because of lack of opportunities to experience the full sequence of an activity. Objects appear out of nowhere as opposed to involving the child in their retrieval. From a mobility perspective, it is important to embed "getting the objects" and "putting away the objects" as a part of the routine of playing with or using the objects. This process provides a perfect opportunity to teach the child about the contents of his or her environment, as well as age appropriate responsibilities of helping out around the house.

CONCEPTS OF OBJECT PERMANENCE

Object permanence in layperson's terms simply means "out of sight, *not* out of mind." For approximately the first 9 months, the infant does not have the memory capacity to search for an item completely removed from view, or in the case of a child with visual impairment, out of touch. This realization has profound implications from an O&M perspective.

During this time period, the sighted infant demonstrates steady progress in the area of memory and search skills. At approximately 4 to 6 months of age, an infant will find an object that is touching his or her body (Johnson-Martin, Jens, & Attermeier, 1986). The sighted infant will briefly search for a newly dropped object and deliberately uncover a partially hidden object at 6 months of age (Johnson-Martin, et. al, 1986). By 9 months, the infant learns that an object continues to exist even if it is covered from view. A favorite interaction game at this age is the classic peek-a-boo.

Fraiberg (1968) noted that sound is not a substitute for sight; between 6 and 7 months of age, hearing and holding are two separate events for the infant who is blind. As this age, the infant does not realize that the object that was just moments ago sounding outside of his or her hands is the same one now placed in his or her hands. Fraiberg's research revealed that the first beginnings of search behavior occurred between 7 and 9 months of age.

The child who is visually impaired may have a unique timetable as he or she develops a conceptual understanding of object permanence. Individual level of functional vision will play an ongoing role in the child's ability to discern a world outside of immediate touch.

The presence of vision, however obscure, will assist in the cognitive confirmation of the presence of a near-range object.

For all children with a significant visual impairment, it may be important to mediate an understanding of object permanence by paying close attention to the infant's signals (if not an actual reach) that he or she is interested in the sounding object or a silent object or person newly removed from touch. For example, does the child cease movement or babbling when an object is sounded nearby, or are there new hand movements that may signal the child's interest in the object? These cues should be reinforced as signals that the infant wants to continue to interact with the object or nearby person: "You hear the toy bell. I will touch it to your hand so you can feel it."

The child who is blind may need tactile cueing to initiate a reach of a desired object. The object can be touched to the child's hand and then slightly distanced from the hand in an attempt to draw the hand to the object. As the child becomes more proficient with his or her understanding of a world beyond touch (expansion of object permanence), these touch cues will become less necessary.

In addition, a reactive spatial environment is important. Too often, the object is dropped or lost in space before the infant has a chance for a second handling experience. As the object distances from the child, the opportunity for immediate second-time feedback is lost, and the child moves on to another object. It may be helpful to design a play space where objects have consistent locations for repeated interactions. This design can be accomplished by attaching objects to a play board so that they cannot fall or roll away from the child. Nielsen (1992) created the notion of a "Little Room," a self-contained play space for a single child in which objects are attached to the ceiling. The idea is to provide a play setting where reaching skills can be practiced over and over. As the child reaches out in space, he or she is learning about the world beyond his or her body and, with repetition, remembering the exact location of favorite playthings. This reaching begins the first process of spatial mapping away from the body.

As object permanence is mastered, the ante can be upped so that the child is gradually applying more memory skills to the location of objects within his or her environment. The consistent location of the toy box, the kitchen cupboard where "his" or "her" cooking pans and utensils are located, and the net of bath toys right by the tub can all serve to assist the child's more advanced object permanence skills. The toddler can help retrieve a new diaper, put dirty clothes in the hamper, or fetch the evening storybook from the bedroom bookshelf. All of these routines involve memory of where objects are located and invite meaningful mobility routes where the child understands how to navigate to a specific location in the house from different starting points.

CONCEPTS OF MEANS-END RELATIONSHIPS

The ability to solve problems with an end result in mind is called means-end behavior. This ability indicates that a child is able to understand what means (actions) will result in a certain end (result). Over the course of the first two years, the child learns to think of a simple goal and then uses the motor skills within his or her repertoire to achieve that end result.

The young infant, however, does not initially realize that his or her body movements produce a certain sensory result. Early body movements are not associated with reactions such as the visual sway of a swatted mobile or the chime bells of the kicked Happy Apple toy. During these early days, the infant is practicing newly acquired volitional movement as motor reflexes are fully integrated. Movement occurs for the sake of movement alone. With repetition, however, the infant begins to discover that his or her body movements can make something happen. One of the first indications of intention occurs with deliberate hand watching behavior. During this phase of very early development, the infant will look at his or her hands with newfound interest. Hand watching behavior usually occurs around the first three months of life and begins when the baby visually notices his or her hands as they move toward and away from his or her face. With the discovery of hands as a working part of the body, an infant of 4 months learns to reach for nearby objects. As such, the infant first learns that his or her hands are personal tools to bring items to the mouth or manipulate an end result of a toy (such as shaking and banging).

In these early days of learning, it may be helpful to heighten the reactivity of the environment. A resonance board may be used to give children feedback of their body movements. This board, designed by Nielsen (1992), is a thin strip of wood that is attached to a quarter-inch, 4' × 4' sheet of birch plywood. The idea is that it provides vibratory feedback to the child's movements as he or she lays and moves upon the board. Each movement, however intentional or nonintentional, will result in a vibration that the child can feel. A wooden or tile floor may provide the same type of feedback when the infant moves his or her body across the surface of the floor.

Other means end behaviors include early use of objects as tools. The child learns to pull a string to obtain the attached toy, to scoop food with a spoon, and to use an object to acquire a toy just out of reach. Clarke (1988) noted that tool use has great implications for a child's ability to successfully utilize a mobility device or long cane during the toddler and preschool years of development. As children use toys or other objects such as kitchen utensils to probe alongside their body, they are learning to use a tool to check out the space beyond their reach (the ultimate purpose of a cane).

As the child expands his or her understanding of the space beyond the body and has the physical readiness to move out into space, the reach is extended from an isolated arm movement to a full body movement. This skill is the beginning passage into purposeful movement; the child can begin to use self-propelled ambulation (the means) for an end result. His or her worldly travels have begun, from a mobility perspective, whether in the form of a roll from back to front or a long stretched reach while in a prone position that results in forward movement toward the object or person of interest. Tool use is expanded as the child learns to move forward while holding onto a wheel or push toy or to walk across the room or outside using an adapted mobility device or a long cane.

CONCEPTS OF SPATIAL RELATIONSHIPS

An understanding of spatial relationships includes early concepts of position, location, direction, and distance from one's own body (Morgan, 1992). Spatial constructs have three primary categories:

- spatial awareness of one's body,
- awareness of both near and distance space as it relates to one's body, and
- awareness of the space dimensions between objects.

All three of these areas have developmental beginnings in infancy. A full sequence of body image and spatial relations (Anthony, 1992) will be reviewed in the "O&M Considerations for Preschoolers" section later in this chapter.

The infant learns about his or her body as he or she learns to move each body part and as people touch and move him or her. With maturation, the infant will master voluntary movements such as hand watching, midline hand play (interacting with an object held at the middle of the body), and bringing feet to mouth. These movements give him or her information about the dimensions and parts of his or her body. This process can be referred to as *body mapping.* As the infant reaches for his or her foot, he or she is participating in the discovery and confirmation of where his or her feet are located on his or her body. As the child learns to cross midline, she or he has expanded his or her knowledge of the sides of his or her body and the direction and extent of where one arm can reach into space. These body movements will later assist with the ability to use adaptive mobility devices that require specific arm posturing.

Baby massage provides a wonderful avenue of proprioceptive input to the infant about the spatial dimensions of his or her body. For example, as the arm is rubbed from shoulder to fingertips, the infant receives information about the length of his or her full arm. As the baby develops, touching interaction games, such as saying "I'm going to get your . . . !" and then naming and touching various body parts, as well as placing the child in a variety of body positions, are also natural teaching strategies for reinforcing the infant's sense of body. For example, the young infant will see and feel different things when he or she is on his or her tummy, back, side, and in a reclining position. Different positions will give surface pressure input into different body parts. For example, when the infant is on his or her tummy, he or she will feel surface input throughout the length of the front of his or her body. As he or she pulls away from the floor surface, the infant will feel muscles activate throughout the tummy, upper chest, and shoulder/neck area.

Bathing and dressing routines will further shape a child's understanding of body parts. Dressing and undressing actions give meaning to prospective body parts. "Put your arm through the sleeve" involves more purpose than a request of "Show me your arm." Fun body play activities, such as trying on different hats or shoes, can enhance the child's understanding of what and where different body parts are on his or her body and other's bodies.

Coinciding with spatial mapping of his or her body, the infant will begin to explore the immediate parameters of the surrounding world. Toys located on the body and next to the body will be the first ones explored. As the infant has repeated reinforcement for random movements out into space, he or she will begin to actively search for what is out there. Organized play areas with defined spatial boundaries and content will soon invite his or her visual and tactile search for people and toys.

With the advent of an understanding of object permanence and motor readiness, the infant will learn to search for objects and people at farther distances. With newfound ambulation of crawling and ultimately walking, he or she will begin to explore larger spaces and learn about the parameters of new rooms and their contents. Team members can help to teach orientation by actively calling the child's attention to specific landmarks such as, "You are at the refrigerator; can you come to me at the table?"

Gross Motor Development

Gross motor development encompasses both static body postures, such as sitting and standing, and all movement skills, such as reaching out to touch a desired object or using an adaptive mobility device or a long cane for the purpose of independent travel. Gross motor skills dictate the way in which a child moves through his or her environment. This section reviews early challenges to motor development and ultimately O&M skill attainment due to blindness or low vision.

DEVELOPMENTAL PATTERNS ASSOCIATED WITH GROSS MOTOR MILESTONE ACQUISITION

Gross motor skill development is tied directly to the integration of motor reflexes, acquisition of equilibrium/righting (balance) and protective reactions, and postural tone. (A detailed review of motor development can be found in Chapter 9.) For the purposes of early O&M programming, it will be especially important to understand influences such as low postural tone on the development of motor skills. Teamwork with a motor therapist will be helpful, especially if the child has additional physical challenges such as cerebral palsy.

The child's ability to move and explore his or her environment will be directly tied to postural readiness to move in space. Postural tone refers to the amount of tension in the body when it is at rest or moving. If a child has low postural tone (hypotonia), she or he may be less able to move with speed and agility than a child with normal postural tone. If a child has high postural tone (hypertonia), she or he will also experience difficulty in moving fluidly and purposefully. A certain amount of tension in the muscles of the body is required to provide readiness for the body to move and act against gravity (Campbell, 1982). Postural tone must be high enough to support the body (stability), but low enough to allow the body to move (mobility). Postural tone is the foundational base for all types of motor tasks, such as sustaining an independent sitting position, as well as moving activities such as rolling, crawling, and walking.

The rate of gross motor milestone development is influenced by a visual impairment. While the integration of reflexes such as the asymmetrical tonic neck reflex (ATNR) happens at the same time in children with visual impairments as with children without visual impairment, there is evidence of delay in movement skills such as rolling, crawling, and walking. This delay may be due in part to the possible presence of low postural tone, the interdependent relationship of movement, and understanding object permanence and/or auditory localization skills. All of the factors can influence the child's ability to move against gravity and out into space.

Infants with visual impairments often have low postural tone (Jan, Robinson, Scott, & Kinnis, 1975). Brown and Bour (1986) report the theory that the reason many babies who are visually impaired have low postural tone is because of a lack of experience in the prone (tummy) position, which is an important position to strengthen the infant's upper body. (See Chapter 9 for more information on prone positioning.)

Brown and Bour also report that another theory is that due to the lack of vision, the ability to utilize optical righting (righting head in alignment with the visual horizon) is impaired. Without optical righting, there is reduced motivation to move and turn the head. This pattern dominos into a reduction of practice of head control that influences the muscles that control development throughout the neck and overall trunk.

Although the reason for the presence of hypotonia has not been fully researched, the end result appears to be a delayed readiness for some infants due to reduced postural stability. The infant who is blind or visually impaired may have difficulty moving against gravity. For example, when a baby is on the tummy, he or she may have trouble lifting his or her head up due to a combination of low postural tone and lack of visual reward for lifting the head. This age is an important time for intervention—it is never too early to address motor skill development. Programming may begin by gently putting

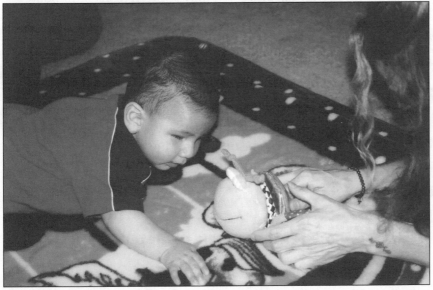

The O&M specialist presents a brightly colored toy to encourage this 6-month-old to lift his head while in the prone position.

one's hands underneath the infant's prone chest, so that the arms come forward and he or she can begin to feel his or her body's weight on the arms. This input will send proprioceptive input up through elbows and into the shoulder and neck. As the infant strengthens these muscles, it will give him or her increased head control in the prone position. In time, the increased motor strength in the upper extremity will assist the child in using an adaptive mobility device. In motor skill acquisition, all roads lead back to early foundation skills.

In addition to delayed movement milestones, low postural tone is felt to have a negative impact on the child's *quality of movement* according to Brown and Bour (1986). Quality of movement refers to the level of refinement of a particular gross motor skill. Low postural tone often will compromise the refinement integrity of motor skills involving balance and strength. Balance reactions, trunk rotation, and actual motor milestones may be influenced. For example, a child may be able to sit independently, but the actual sitting posture may be compromised. A rounded back with the legs situated far apart may be the only way the child can achieve independent sitting. Due to low trunk tone, the child may need to establish a wide base of support to maintain an upright sitting posture. Compensatory patterns that emerge in sitting are likely to show up in the child's gait, as they are symptomatic of the same problem—low postural tone of the trunk. Compensatory patterns may become habitual. If repeatedly used over time, the child is at risk for physiological change in his or her muscles; some may lengthen and some may shorten to accommodate the compensatory posture. If left untreated, it is possible that an orthopedic deformity such as scoliosis may develop (Campbell, 1983).

It may be wise to consult with a physical and/or an occupational therapist to ensure that the child's motor skills are developing in a manner that reflects good quality of movement. A motor therapist should definitely be consulted if there are any concerns about the child's motor development and/or if there is a diagnosis such as cerebral palsy. Information can be offered to the team about the need for any specialized equipment to improve motor functioning, how best to position the child, and any special activities to strengthen the child's trunk muscles.

Other Developmental Domains Related to O&M

FINE MOTOR SKILLS

The fine motor skills of associated upper body strength and grasp patterns factor into the orientation and mobility skill acquisition equation. The child's ability to perform and sustain a grasp and to ultimately manipulate a mobility device and/or a long cane are directly tied to upper extremity strength and prehension (hand use) skills. Other fine motor–related O&M skills include identifying tactile landmarks, trailing, using body protection techniques, and using organized search patterns. All of these skills involve at least one of the following types of fine motor skills: grasp, directed reach, wrist rotation, arm extension/flexion (straightening/bending), and pushing an object in a forward motion. It is important to note that low postural tone will influence upper body strength.

COMMUNICATION SKILLS

Both receptive (listening) and expressive (talking) communication skills will influence the child's understanding of verbal instruction and ability to request assistance and acquire important travel information. An example of the latter would be a child requesting where a favorite toy is located, which will ultimately initiate his or her travel search for the item. By 9–14 months, the child is capable of responding to simple requests; by 15–18 months, the child can bring an object from another room upon request; and by 21–24 months, the child can remember where objects are located and return them upon request (Parks et al., 1994). Care should be taken not to bombard the young child with too much verbal description. The focus should be upon the task at hand and giving salient information to help the child learn about the objects in his or her world and how to navigate new places using familiar language. For example, if a familiar landmark can be referenced, it will help in navigational directions. "You are at the table. Your cup is on the table."

SELF-HELP SKILLS

The activities of daily living reinforce the child's purpose for independent route travel. Feeding, bathing, dressing and undressing, and toileting schedules typically occur at routine times and locations throughout a young child's day. Self-help independence includes the ability to move to the location where the activity occurs. Rather than carrying the child to the bathroom for bath time, the child can be encouraged to seek the sound of running water. The first time, the child might be placed right next to the tub; then, as time goes on, the child can be encouraged to move toward the tub from a greater distance, such as from his or her bedroom just down the hall from the bathroom. Parents and early interventionists can reinforce route travel to these locations within the child's home setting.

SOCIALIZATION SKILLS

Socialization skills involve both the child's ability to bond with care-givers and the ongoing ability to socialize with peers. The first is para-mount to the infant as it indicates that he or she is emotionally con-nected to his or her caregivers. The bonding process in the early months is tied to consistency of care and accurate reading of the in-fant's signals. It is important that service providers assist the family, as needed, in these behaviors.

Emotional security is paramount to early mobility, as the infant needs to feel safe before venturing outward. This concept is evident with young toddlers who stay in touch with their caregivers in new environments.

For example, one child with low vision was observed to venture to greater and greater distances from his mother during a parent meeting. First, the child inched a foot away and then scrambled back to his mother. As the evening progressed, he distanced himself over 15 feet from her—shifting from physical contact to an "auditory check-in" as he became more confident to be away from her.

The implications of social interaction cannot be stressed enough for their role in defining purpose to the child's travel and for the re-inforcement of peer-supported travel independence. For example, a plastic swimming pool in the backyard may be a highly motivating route for the young toddler who knows his or her brother also likes to play in the pool.

PURPOSEFUL AND SELF-INITIATED MOVEMENT

Not only should the quality and skill level of the child's movement be encouraged and reinforced, but its purpose and self-initiation also should (Anthony, 1993). Purposeful movement involves having an end goal to the movement; whether it is to investigate a sound, re-trieve an object, or find someone in another room. Self-initiated movement infers that the child is moving on his or her own volition.

Families and service providers can encourage purposeful and self-initiated movement with very young children. An infant can be en-ticed to reach for his or her bottle with a visual or touch cue or to touch his or her father's face when he leans forward, talks to, and nuzzles his child's face. All team members should be taught how to present objects to the child in a way that invites the child to touch, grasp, and ultimately reach for the person or object. For example, rather than placing all objects directly into a child's hands, the child can be asked to find the object mentioned: "I have your ball. Can you find it in my hands?" A slight touch cue to the child's hands or wrists might be used to announce the presence of the object, but the actual pursuit of the object (even if it is less than half an inch away) should come at the initiative of the child.

This early reaching behavior can be transferred to movement as the child learns how to roll, scoot, crawl, and/or walk. Once the child has a means of reliable ambulation, the motivating item can be placed at farther and farther distances. "Come to Mommy" can be a fun interaction game that involves very purposeful (and rewarding) ambulation. The Oregon Skills Inventory (Brown et al., 1991) notes that by 16 months, many young children can locate a familiar object kept nearby in a familiar place. By 2 years, the child is beginning to locate a familiar object placed in another room. Also at this age, the child is learning to actively avoid hazards such as stairs (Brown et. al, 1991).

Purposeful and self-initiated movement also signals the child's confidence of moving without assistance. The more opportunities for practice of his or her motor capabilities and subsequent reinforcement of the objects that he or she discovers along the way, the more the infant will want to explore. Independent exploration and route travel will provide the child with improved orientation to a setting.

There is much to learn about child development in the first two years of life, practically as much as the young infant has to learn during this fast-paced skill acquisition period of life! Knowledge of early childhood development is as important as how to adjust this information base to meet the unique needs of every child with a vision loss. For the child who has a visual impairment, it will be important that both a team and a family-centered approach are utilized. The direction of an O&M specialist who has a background in early childhood development is important to this process.

The optimal learning environment for the child is his or her home and the familiar environments of his or her family's activities. The seeds of travel independence come from opportunities of movement exploration in these early years. Infants should be provided with environments that reinforce the wonder as well as the pleasure of their movement explorations into both familiar and new settings.

O&M CONSIDERATIONS FOR PRESCHOOLERS

While this discussion of O&M considerations for young children who are visually impaired has been divided into two distinct sections for organizational purposes—one for infants and toddlers and one for preschoolers—the skills that young children use for independent movement develop along a continuum. Each of the skills and strategies discussed in the previous section form a foundation upon which to expand the approaches used to facilitate independent and purposeful movement in young children who are blind or visually impaired, including children who have additional disabilities.

For many preschool children who are visually impaired, ages 3–5, the use of sensory skills and understanding of concepts will be applied to movement and travel through increasingly complex environments. Instruction in formal mobility skills (such as human-guide or long-cane instruction), which may begin earlier, will likely assume a greater emphasis during this preschool period, including the development of basic skills and the use of low vision and/or mobility devices in home, school, and community environments. The following list provides only a sampling of some of the important O&M achievements that may occur during this period:

- use of echoes to locate and avoid large obstacles in the path,
- use of a hand-held magnifier to examine leaves that fell from a tree onto the sidewalk or a monocular to locate branches on a tall tree,
- use of systematic tactile exploration to identify a familiar landmark along a route,
- use of the understanding of two sides of the body to demonstrate good body position for upper body and forearm protective technique, or
- use of the long cane as a probe to explore school and community environments.

Children who have additional disabilities may experience similar accomplishments and may need some adaptations in technique or devices (such as modified grip on the long cane) or supplemental instructional approaches (such as the use of reverse chaining in which the child is assisted through each portion of the task except the last, which he or she completes independently, thereby experiencing the successful completion of the task). For a detailed review of reverse chaining and other instructional strategies for teaching O&M to children who have multiple disabilities, see Fazzi (1998).

Sensory Development

O&M specialists will continue to work with preschool age children to assist them in organizing, interpreting, and using sensory information to move about the environment. The four senses of hearing, vision, touch, and smell will be discussed in relation to how they can be used to foster the development of O&M skills.

HEARING

It is important to realize that to a young child who is blind, hearing is at least as important as vision is to a sighted child. An infant who is blind with normal hearing will immediately begin using hearing as a primary means for gathering information about the environment.

Some children who are blind also have hearing loss. Some causes of blindness, such as genetic factors, meningitis, and prematurity, can also cause deafness. Children who are also prone to respiratory illnesses, such as infants born prematurely, are prone to middle ear infections (otitis media). Chronic otitis media can cause temporary hearing loss or irreversible hearing loss in extreme cases. It is important for all children to receive hearing tests—especially infants who are blind. Some children with hearing loss can be helped with hearing aids. This option should be explored immediately to expand on the young child's learning potential as early as possible. Of course young children who are deaf-blind can still receive information about their environment and can still learn. However, they require different intervention strategies than young children who are blind with normal hearing. (See Huebner, Prickett, Rafalowski-Welch, & Joffee, 1995 for information on intervention strategies for children who are deaf-blind.)

For children who are blind, hearing becomes the dominant sense for guiding movement, perceiving space, and recognizing events. Hearing, being the predominant distance sense, becomes responsible for conveying most spatial information about the world and enabling dynamic interaction between the blind child and the world. It takes the place of vision in this respect and can do so to a highly advanced level. Hearing in children who are blind should be deliberately cultivated for this critical use.

There are several ways to help young children who are blind use hearing to facilitate movement:

Using Hearing to Facilitate Movement

→ *Establish fixed sound references to help young children who are blind learn to maintain their orientation in their environments.* A clock on the wall, a fish tank, a refrigerator, wind chimes outside, a softly playing radio—all can provide points of reference that blind children can use to develop orientation skills. Such sonic cues can be used in any environment—home, classroom, or playground. Only one or two references are usually needed for any given space. These cues should be pointed out to blind children until they start using them automatically to help determine where they are and where they want to go.

→ *Associate common sounds to desired objects or events.* For example, if a particular bell is permanently attached to a child's spoon, he or she may quickly learn to identify the sound with the spoon and may become animated upon hearing it. By placing the spoon or other desired objects, also tagged with sounds, just out of reach, the child can be encouraged to move toward it to retrieve it.

→ *Encourage young children who are blind to interact with balls or other highly mobile objects when there are sounds attached.* Balls with bells are common. An inexpensive and easy way to make an item noisy is to tie it securely in a plastic grocery bag (for use under total adult supervision only). It causes the item to make a delightful racket with every little movement, so the child can interact with it easily.

→ *Encourage young children to discover the sources of interesting sounds.* A very common question among young blind children is, "What's that noise?" This is similar to the equally common question, "What's that?" from sighted children. These expressions of curiosity are wonderful opportunities to encourage blind children to move toward what they hear, if possible, and explore it for themselves. Instead of just telling the child the answer, adults can ask the child questions in return, such as, "What do you think it is?" "Do you think it's big or small?" or "What does it sound like?" to help the child understand and learn more.

When using sounds, it is important not to flood the environment with sounds or make sounds too loud. Very quiet sounds can go a long way for children who are blind. They learn to register soft sounds that sighted children would likely dismiss or ignore. Avoiding unnecessary or loud sounds will help blind children gain information and keep them from becoming distracted or overwhelmed. As young children who are blind continue to develop an awareness and interest in sounds and sound sources, they may be ready to use echoes to navigate as they move about with greater purpose.

Overview of Echolocation. Echolocation is an important skill that individuals who are blind may use to help maintain orientation and assist with safe travel in the environment. The term *echolocation* refers to the ability to hear and interpret sound waves. People usually think of echoes as resulting from specific events, like firing a gun in the mountains or calling out in caves. In fact, all waves of sound can create echoes. The auditory system processes echoes as they travel from their source, bounce off surfaces, and enter the ears. Children who are blind can get a great deal of information about the environment by interpreting the sound waves that return to them from objects and surfaces around them. Using echoes, a blind child can perceive information from distances far beyond the reach of the longest cane. Echoes give information about where objects are (locations); their size and general shapes (dimensions); and how hard, soft, solid, or sparse they are (densities). Using his or her hearing, a blind child can learn to detect buildings, play equipment, room size, walls, doorways, poles, stairs, or parked cars.

Making a Clear Sound Signal. Children who are blind need to make clear sound signals so that the information that comes back to them in the form of sound waves will be clear and easy to interpret. A handclap is one example of a clear sound signal. It is short, clear, and sharp. Another good way a child can make a sound signal is to use a hand-held clicker. Plastic clickers, usually toy noisemakers in the shape of crickets or frogs, are available commercially. The clicker should be large and simple enough for the child to hold onto and press. Continuous clicking should be avoided; the child needs to leave space between clicks to hear the sound waves coming back. Cane tip tapping (as in two-point touch cane technique) and even footsteps have been used as echo signals. Though ground level objects may be detected well with such signals, the displacement from the ears causes the returning echoes to be depleted of detailed information under most circumstances. Tongue clicks are the most effective way for children to make clear sound signals, because the sound returns right back to the child's head, close to his or her ears. (Echoes made with the hands return to the level of the child's hands and are more difficult to hear.) Clicks made with the tongue can be varied easily in volume and direction to match the requirements of the environment. Soft clicks are usually best for indoors, while much louder clicks may be necessary while walking in crowds or noise.

Also, louder clicks may be needed to detect objects that are further away. Any tongue click that a child can make will work. One good example of a tongue click is the sound grown-ups make when they are saying, "tsk, tsk, tsk" to a child who is being naughty. Another is the one a rider might use to get a horse to go faster.

As young children gain confidence in using echolocation for independent or semi-independent travel, it is practical to discuss the type and volume of signal most appropriate to use in different social situations. For example, it would be more socially appropriate to use a soft tongue click than a loud handclap in a library where people are expected to be quiet. Similarly, a child may need to refrain from using clicks while sitting on the carpet and paying attention during story time. There may not be full acceptance of the young child using echolocation in some social situations because some people may be unaware of the purpose of the clicking sound or are uncomfortable with the difference it creates. Therefore the child's use of this skill should be discussed openly with people in the child's life.

Teaching Echolocation. Many children who are blind will be intrinsically motivated to use echoes to help navigate as they move about; some children will develop echolocation skills without any instruction or support from others. Echolocation skills can be introduced or enhanced as a part of the formal O&M program.

The following factors are important to consider before helping a preschool-age child use echolocation:

Factors Affecting Echolocation

→ *Child's quality of hearing.* Broadly speaking, the better a child's hearing, the better the child's potential to use echoes as a tool to help him or her travel. However, many useful echo cues may still be available to children with a hearing loss. Though these cues may be more difficult to learn, they may still be effective. It is important to have detailed information about what sounds a child is able or unable to hear.

→ *Child's ability to concentrate.* Since echo information is relatively subtle, it requires some continued concentration to be used effectively for navigation. Many preschoolers who are blind are very interested in echoes, and young children tend to concentrate most on what interests them. However, some blind preschoolers may be uninterested in echoes. One can attempt to elicit interest by incorporating very basic echo tasks in fun activities. Functional echo skills can thus be brought along at the child's pace.

→ *Background noise.* Background noise can mask echoes. Because echoes are so quiet, noise absorbs them. Echo signals carry well in quiet places. Echolocation exercises should begin in a quiet environment.

→ *Surface reflectivity.* When helping a preschool child detect objects using echoes, make sure that the objects the child is trying to detect will reflect as clear a signal as possible. Large, hard, solid surfaces, like walls or buildings, are easiest to detect and can be detected at the greatest distances. Objects near the head are typically easier to detect than those below the waist or knees are. Small or sparse objects are more difficult to detect. It is easier to detect an object that stands alone than an object standing among other objects.

The following are some strategies for helping preschool-age children develop echolocation:

Teaching Echolocation

→ *Noticing strong echo signals.* When preschoolers are moving around the house or other environment, help them notice the presence of strong echoes. For example, many children who are blind love to play sound games in highly reverberant environments such as restrooms, breezeways, or stairwells. Children can be encouraged to sing; repeat words; or clap in a bathroom, garage, or other large, uncarpeted place that does not have a lot of furniture or other objects that absorb sound. If children make noises in places with strong echoes, they can notice that their voices sound different in these places than in other places. An adult can clap with a child in a room where strong echoes are present (like a tiled bathroom) and then move with the child into a less reverberent environment (like a carpeted hallway), and clap again, encouraging the child to compare and contrast the two sounds. Corners in a room also usually emit stronger echoes than other areas of the room.

→ *Observation.* It is important to know what echolocation skills the child is already using. Staying behind the child, but close enough to prevent injury, the instructor can observe existing echolocation skills. For example, instead of requiring children to trail along a hallway, they can be allowed to walk along the hallway without any instruction or interference. With this approach, O&M specialists can determine if children are able to control their movements between two walls and if they are able to perceive when a wall or door is in front of them. When children are walking in a play area, O&M specialists can note if they stop independently before bumping into pieces of play equipment and determine whether or not their movements are directed. Young children who are able to do these things may be demonstrating some basic echolocation skills. Encourage them to do so. Some children demonstrate good skills at an early age with no instruction, but good instruction always helps improve skills.

→ *Locating large objects.* A building is a simple object to echolocate because it is large, solid, and freestanding. As children get closer to buildings, O&M specialists can ask them to notice what is happening to the echo. The click will sound louder as they approach the building. Echolocating and recognizing large objects allows children to find them at will, avoid them, or use them as landmarks. Young children may know where an object is but will not necessarily turn their bodies to move in the correct direction. They may need reminders to turn their bodies so that the object is in front of them. Eventually, turning so that they are facing an object becomes habitual. As children's skills improve, the distance to objects can be increased. As skills further improve, smaller objects can be located, such as trees, basketball hoops, and poles. Children can also begin to locate spaces between buildings or open doors in hallways, based on the change in echo signal that these openings produce.

Developing a heightened awareness of sound and knowing basic echolocation skills can help young children who are blind to move about the environment with greater ease and safety. It is incumbent upon O&M specialists to assist young children who are blind to develop and utilize hearing as an effective tool for independent orientation and movement.

THE SENSE OF VISION

Differences in color, contrast, and illumination will continue to be important sensory cues for preschool children who have low vision.

(See Chapter 3 for a review of promoting the use of functional vision in young children who are visually impaired.) The O&M specialist, together with teachers and families, may find ways to enhance the visual environments in which the child lives, learns, and plays. Such modifications should be similar for children who have additional disabilities. For example, increasing natural lighting in a living room by keeping the curtains open could make it easier for a three year-old to locate toys of choice independently as he or she plays with siblings or friends. By incorporating preferred colors (possibly red or yellow for a young child who is cortically visually impaired), increasing contrast, and tailoring illumination to the needs of the individual child, the O&M specialist can make it easier for the young visually impaired child to use his or her vision to more fully participate in many aspects of daily life.

Visual skills. While O&M specialists may work to support the infant's or toddler's efficient use of vision for spotting and identifying objects in the environment, shifting gaze from one object or person to another, and completing tasks that require eye–hand coordination, some preschool-age children may be able to begin to more fully develop or refine the use of three key advanced visual skills that can be used to travel safely and efficiently:

- *tracing:* visually following a stationary line such as a painted line on the playground,

- *scanning:* visually searching in a systematic pattern such as looking high, middle, and low to find obstacles on a pathway, or

- *tracking:* visually following a moving target such as a friend sliding down a slide.

O&M specialists can help children learn these visual skills by designing highly motivating games and activities that incorporate tracing, scanning, or tracking. Functional activities can also be used to develop visual skills so children with low vision can practice them regularly. The following are some approaches that can be used to develop these skills:

Developing Visual Skills

→ *Tracing.* A five-year-old can be asked to trace (visually follow the line created by environmental features) a variety of fences, building lines, or hedges in order to locate treasure hunt clues. Similarly, young children can be encouraged to visually trace along a garden hose in order to locate the nozzle and then be helped to water the lawn in a systematic scanning-pattern fashion, making sure that all of the grass and plants are watered.

→ *Scanning.* O&M specialists can encourage young children who have low vision to practice use of visual skills while they are participating in class field trips, such as scanning at the zoo to count the number of gorillas in an exhibit. For a functional activity, scanning can easily be incorporated into clean-up time so that children are encouraged to scan the floor and playroom for toys that need to be put away.

→ *Tracking.* For example, a very soft and colorful ball can be suspended from a tether, and children can push and swing the ball and visually follow its movements. Various games can be developed once the child has confidence in tracking the moving ball. Similarly, brightly colored balloons can be tracked while the child tries to keep them up in the air with a hairdryer (set on cool) or by batting them with his or her hands. Visual tracking also serves functional purposes, such as tracking the movement of people in a line at a grocery store in order to keep one's place in line and to know when it is your turn to place items on the counter.

When working outdoors with children who have low vision, O&M specialists need to make sure that their students are wearing appropriate glare protection (such as hats or visors with a minimum 3-inch brim and good quality sunglasses or filters). By doing so, O&M specialists are ensuring that their young students are able to use their vision to the maximum potential and that they are as comfortable as possible in outdoor lighting.

Each of these visual skills will support later independent travel that is both safe and efficient. The O&M specialist will have a wealth of activities to pick from that will be fun and functional for young children to try.

Use of Optical Devices. Young children who have low vision and can benefit from magnification can be taught to use a variety of optical devices. An optometrist specializing in vision rehabilitation will likely prescribe devices as appropriate, but it may be up to the O&M

specialist to find some creative ways to help preschool children develop the necessary skills for their proper use.

Hand-held magnifiers can be used on O&M discovery lessons as children are encouraged to closely examine objects of interest such as plants, tree bark, large insects, fences, and mailboxes. For children with multiple disabilities who lack the ability to grasp a hand-held magnifier, alternative magnifiers, such as those that can be worn around the neck with a chain and propped against the chest, can be used. Closed-circuit televisions can be used back in the classroom as the preschool child returns from O&M lessons with snippets, such as leaves and flower petals, from the day's travels to examine them in closer detail. In training preschool-age children who have low vision to use monoculars, O&M specialists can start with toilet paper rolls to practice spotting objects in the environment. Students may enjoy decorating their own toilet paper roll. Games of "I Spy" can take place in the classroom, playground, or community to encourage looking and eye–hand coordination. Some preschoolers may like pretending to be a pirate and enjoy wearing a costume while searching for treasures in the backyard (Duncan, personal communication, 1997). With practice, young children may be able to make the transition to low-powered monoculars, which may be easiest for initial training due to larger fields and more stable images. Many monoculars come with rubber-coated housings so breakage concerns are minimized. By wearing the neck strap children are less likely to drop the expensive device. For more ideas on teaching optical device use to children see D'Andrea & Farrenkopf (2000).

As with all visual skills, O&M specialists can start with lessons that are simple and add complexity as the child gains confidence and skill with the optical device. There is no reason to wait until a child reaches elementary school to start appropriate optical device training. Preschool children who have low vision will enjoy looking at interesting objects, and their curiosity and motivation for exploration will be piqued.

SENSE OF TOUCH

Preschool-age students who are blind or visually impaired will continue to benefit from tactile exploration of their environment. Of course tactile exploration will support the development of object concepts, especially for children who have dual sensory impairments. Preschool-age children may be expected to become more systematic in their exploration, such as exploring an object starting from the top and working downwards or exploring with the right hand while holding an object in the left hand and then switching. To model this skill, O&M specialists, teachers, and family members can use a hand-under-hand approach in which the child places his or her hands on top of the adult's hands as the object is explored initially. Systematic exploration helps the young child to develop a more complete picture of the objects being examined. By doing so, young children will be better equipped to identify the unique characteristics of landmarks found along travel routes and to distinguish between them as they travel. For example, a unique door handle can be a landmark to a specific room, if the child is able to distinguish the unique shape and texture. Systematic search patterns, such as moving the palm of the hand or cupped fingertips in concentric circles or from left to right and back (similar to reading a page of braille), will also be helpful when young children are trying to locate dropped objects, such as a spoon on the floor or a matchbox car on the carpet.

Young children will also receive tactile information through their feet as they walk along a variety of textured surfaces (such as asphalt, grass, wood chips, cement, carpet, and linoleum). They can be encouraged to think about these surfaces and identify when changes occur. Children who use long canes will also receive tactile feedback through their canes. For more detail on canes and preschoolers, see the section "Use of Canes with Preschoolers" later in this chapter.

SENSE OF SMELL

Olfactory cues may become increasingly useful as the preschool child who is visually impaired travels with increased independence in home, school, and community environments. The fresh smell of powder may be used to help locate Mom and Dad's bathroom. The smell of tacos may help the preschool child anticipate lunch and assist him or her in locating the lunch area. Fragrant roses may be a cue that the child is nearing the neighbor's house. Young children may enjoy outings to the grocery store to investigate various smells and can learn to match the name, feel, and smell of certain fruits and vegetables. Similarly, trips to garden centers or parks can be useful in exploring the smell and textures of certain plants. Each experience adds to the child's understanding of the environment and, one hopes, to his or her interest in exploring and learning more.

Concept Development for O&M

A very important component of a quality O&M program for young children who are blind or visually impaired is concept development. Cognitive development, including the understanding of object permanence, means-end relationships, and early spatial relationships, are discussed earlier in the section "Cognitive Development." O&M specialists share the responsibility for concept development with other teachers and family members, but have the unique teaching opportunity as specialists who work in the community to expose young children to a variety of concepts that will be relevant to independent orientation and mobility (especially preschool-age children who may begin to have more formal travel experiences in the neighborhood). Since body concepts, spatial relationships, and environmental awareness are key to developing O&M skills, they are addressed below, but for more details on concept development, see Chapter 4 and Fazzi & Petersmeyer (2001).

BODY CONCEPTS AND SPATIAL RELATIONSHIPS

Body awareness has long been recognized as the foundation of O&M concept development (Hill, 1986). Concepts of spatial relationships are tightly interwoven with the development of body concepts. The two cannot be fully separated, as they are interdependent upon one another. As an infant learns about the spatial dimensions of his or her body, he or she is learning about his or her body image. As the infant learns about space away from his or her body, he or she will use the body as the reference point to judge the spatial distance. A comparison of the two sequences is provided here, along with suggestions for activities that may be useful in developing such concepts.

In general, body mapping is the earliest form of body image and understanding of space. Body "mapping" refers to an internal awareness and understanding of one's body space including the following concepts:

- where one's body begins and ends in space;

- the physical dimensions of one's body;

- where pressure is felt on the body from a supporting surface such as a floor, bed, or chair; and

- which body parts are moving or still at any given period.

A proposed sequence of the development of body image that includes the aforementioned components and encourages programming from infancy through preschool follows. The six levels should not be viewed in isolation but as a general guideline of what typically occurs from step to step. Children may cross over to a new area before fully developing skills in another area.

Development of Body Image

1. *Awareness of touch; movement by the whole body.* The infant begins to understand the layout of his or her body during the first months of being touched, carried, and positioned. Proprioceptive (sensitivity to the position of the joints, which gives postural information), kinesthetic (awareness of body movement or motion), and tactile (awareness of touching or being touched) inputs are primary modes of assisting the infant with building body awareness. As the child is placed in various positions on the tummy, back, side, or in a reclining posture, he or she feels the input into different parts of the body. The input from the surface where the body is resting serves as a physical reminder of where the child's body is in space and serves further as a working surface to move against gravity. The latter is important as it allows the child an opportunity to develop muscle strength and control over his or her body. For example, when the child is on his or her tummy, he or she will build neck and upper extremity muscles every time the child works to lift the head off the floor.

   Infant massage and bathing are excellent ways for a young infant to learn about the dimensions of his or her body. As the infant feels another person rubbing or washing the full length of his or her back, front, legs, and arms, he or she experiences tactile feedback of the dimensions of the body. A firm touch is preferable to a light touch, as the latter may feel tickly instead of relaxing.

2. *Awareness of body parts through movement.* Activities such as hand watching, clasping hands at midline, and moving feet to mouth are examples of this level of awareness of the body. The child begins to understand how his or her body is connected from top to bottom by moving his or her own body parts. As the process unfolds, the child begins to "map" proximal (parts of the body near the trunk) space and begins to learn about the immediate space around the body.

3. *Identification of body parts.* Body part identification is typically assessed through the cueing of a series of rote responses, such as "Where's your _____?" Children learn the identification of parts of the body best when the body parts are involved in motivating activities. Play involving the fingers or parts of the body is ideal for the preschool child; coactive bathing, in

which the parent uses hand-under-hand movement with the child to explore body parts while bathing, may be a more basic activity for a toddler or infant. While naming body parts and playing tickle games may be motivating and stimulating for both family members and the visually impaired child, many body identification activities can be incorporated into functional routines for the preschool-aged child. "Put your arm through the sleeve" involves more purpose than a request like "Show me your arm." "Blow your nose with the tissue" is more relevant than simply telling a child, "Touch your nose." More elaborate play activities that incorporate body part identification and movement may promote socialization, self-confidence, and increased dramatic play.

4. *Identification of body planes.* Body plane identification includes the understanding of one's body from the perspectives of top to bottom, side to side, and front to back. Internally, it may not include the child's labeling of the body planes. Activities that involve body planes are ideal for reinforcing the understanding of this concept. Putting on hats, shoes, and mittens or having a back rub are examples of such activities.

5. *Understanding of the relationship of body parts and body planes to movement* (laterality and later directionality). At this level of understanding the child comprehends the planes of his or her body: left to right, front to back, and top to bottom. The child now understands bilaterality, colaterality (relating to pairs of limbs), and differentiation of the halves of the body. Many mobility skills can be taught at this stage. The child may be developmentally ready to utilize a posture from a protective technique in an appropriate situation. The child may be more able to respond consistently to a landmark or travel cue by relating the positions of such landmarks and cues to the position of his or her body. Language is especially important at this stage. Concrete terms should be used when asking the child to move his or her body in a certain way. An understanding of the relationship of self to object and of spatial relationships grows out of this phase of skill development. For example:

The mother of one 5-year-old child who was blind brought her daughter to a community exercise program for young children. All went well once the instructor was asked to use concrete language when giving directions to the children in her class. Instead of just say-

ing, "point your 'birdies' to the sky" without any further explanation, the instructor began to give one direction at time, pausing before moving on to the next direction until she could see that the child was following along (with the physical assistance of her mother). The new directions were much more concrete: "Pretend your toes are birdies; when you are sitting on your bottom with your legs straight out in front of you, keep your heels on the floor and point your toes or little birdies up in the air." With time and some physical guidance, the child soon knew all of the nuances of the body positioning language and could comply with the exercise routines.

Had this child not had the benefit of first knowing all of her body parts and then language specific to moving the body parts, the exercise class would have been an even more overwhelming experience.

6. *Identification of self in relationship to objects and space.* At this stage, young children develop a greater cause-and-effect understanding. They may begin to move to familiar objects in the environment. Routes can be utilized to travel to desired locations, persons, or objects. The child with a severe visual impairment may initially need some degree of prompting or physical assistance in completing these types of tasks.

The following is a brief listing of the proposed sequence in which a child develops basic spatial-relationship concepts:

Development of Spatial-Relationship Concepts

1. *Mapping of the immediate body* (comparable with the first level of the development of body image). Mapping refers to the child's developing understanding of the spatial dimensions of his or her body. At this stage, the infant is not aware of the names of the body parts that are being touched or moved but knows only that there is a tactile sensation or motion of the body.

2. *Mapping of proximal space* (comparable to the second level of the development of body image). The child begins to search for items at near range, first those touching the body and then those within reach of the body. The use of a defined space is especially important at this early level because it as-

sists the child in setting internal parameters concerning where he or she is within a particular environment. Objects should initially be connected to a stable site, such as to the child, the crib, or a table or tray where the child is situated. Later, the objects can be placed randomly around the child for discovery and interaction.

3. *Mapping of distant space.* At this level of understanding, the child understands sound cues within the environment, is able to recognize landmarks within the environment, and moves with goal-oriented intention (for example, rolling toward a parent's voice). The child should have the experience of moving to a sound cue. If a child hears the dishwasher from across the room and shows an interest in the sound, it would be beneficial to take him or her to the source of the sound. The child can then experience the dishwasher as the sound's source and the spatial aspects of the machine's location within the room.

4. *Mapping of near-range object-to-object relationships.* The child begins to use objects together, understanding such concepts as playing with toys with lids, organization of food in bowls or on a plate, use of tools to obtain objects, and the meaning of more complex search patterns.

5. *Mapping of body-to-objects relationships.* The child expands his or her understanding of space and learns prepositional concepts, body and movement games, negotiation of barriers, use of push toys or a cane, more complex search patterns, travel on routes to put away or retrieve familiar items, and trailing skills.

6. *Mapping of size and shape relationships.* In this phase, the child learns to use functional objects in varying sizes and shaped container toys. The understanding of seriation also occurs. Body games that require the child to be "small," "tall," "wide," and so on facilitate an understanding of size relationships.

7. *Mapping of part-to-whole relationships.* Use of puzzles, use of a part of an item or room, and recognition of landmarks through partial touch are skills demonstrated at this level.

As with the phases of the development of body concepts, the seven phases of the understanding of spatial relationships should not be viewed as strictly sequential. Once the child progresses beyond the second phase, there is no linear model. Some components of various phases may be learned simultaneously.

ENVIRONMENTAL AWARENESS

Through encouraged exploration and interaction with the environment in both structured and unstructured formats, young children with visual impairments develop an awareness of their environment. This awareness is the first step in creating motivation for the young child who is blind or visually impaired to move. Learning environmental concepts assists the child in making sense of the world, which in turn facilitates the development of orientation skills as the child develops. It is the role of families and professionals to provide experiences in the home, school, and community that will expand this awareness.

Home. Young children spend the majority of their time at home, their most natural environment. Therefore the home environment is the logical place in which to provide the child with a good initial opportunity for learning many environmental concepts. Families may have opportunities within the daily routine to teach concepts related to body image, as well as positional and functional concepts, which are the "foundations of environmental awareness" (Hill et al., 1989, p. 52). For example, the young blind child in the scooting stage quickly learns to avoid the family pet's dish when he or she learns that the dish is located next to the refrigerator, that the dish holds the pet's food, and that the rule is to keep hands off. Knowing this series of conceptual relationships builds images in the young child's mind, which assist in the development of understanding the connection between the child and elements of the environment.

Making sure the child has opportunities to explore various parts of the house in a systematic manner helps the child piece together the environment in a meaningful way. As the child begins moving by crawling or cruising, providing verbal descriptions of the household environment is beneficial. It is useful to talk in terms of relationships, such as, "You're touching the couch, which is next to the kitchen door." Environmental awareness starts the process of *landmarking,* in which the child designates certain objects as landmarks; landmarking is a very important orientation skill for the child who is blind. Making sure the child is familiar with more than one or two rooms of the house means that the whole concept of "house" is eventually understood. Noting tactile differences (such carpeted, tiled, and wooden floors) and auditory cues (such as toilets flushing, garbage disposals grinding, radios playing, and wind chimes ringing) heightens the child's environmental awareness through the senses, which also serves as a foundation for future orientation skills.

School. The preschool environment, another natural environment, can also be a rich learning experience for the young child who is blind. It is important that the child's awareness of school not be limited to the routes from the bus or car to the entrance to the classroom and to the bathroom and play area and back. Does the child know that there are many rooms off the hallway on both sides? Does the child know that there are stairs leading to a second floor at the end of the hallway? Does the child know that there is a kitchen with appliances and counters and shelves, where lunch is prepared, and that meals do not magically appear on a tray from nowhere? Has the child had the opportunity to explore the entire play area in a systematic manner, or does he or she only know about a favorite swing? Are the relationships between each part of the school and the functions of each understood?

The child with a visual impairment deserves to know about the total school environment so that his or her conceptual knowledge increases and "gestalts" of the world are built. Learning certain travel routes to follow by rote sometimes has its functional purpose and may be necessary, but the blind child's world must be expanded with the help of trained professionals if generalized travel is to be a future goal. For some children with severe cognitive delays or for children with spatial orientation problems, rote route travel may be the primary travel method in learning needed functional routes. The child with multiple disabilities, however, also deserves the opportunity to explore his environment in a more generalized sense, even if the child is unable to transfer orientation strategies and concepts to larger environments. For specific strategies see "Encouraging Children with Multiple Disabilities to Explore" on the next page.

Community. Children who are sighted learn about their community outside the home and school by going to the bank, the store, the post office, the fast-food restaurant, and so on with their parents from an early age and observing the environments around them. They see the colors and shapes, the uniforms the workers wear, the buildings inside and out, and all the many features and activities that teach them about each community environment they visit. They also learn a tremendous amount about the outside world from the visual media. Television and movies open up many unknown worlds to the preschooler who is sighted.

ENCOURAGING CHILDREN WITH MULTIPLE DISABILITIES TO EXPLORE

The following strategies can be used to encourage young children who are visually impaired and have additional disabilities to explore their enviroment:

➜ Attach toys with suction cups to tables, highchair trays, or certain flooring surfaces so that children can explore and manipulate them independently without losing track of their location.

➜ Place child-safe toys in an easily accessible place for children who may not be ambulatory so that they can retrieve them independently or semi-independently. For example, plastic bins in contrasting colors can be used on the floor to store toys.

➜ Create pleasurable experiences for children to explore objects of various textures (such as wooden spoons, metal whisks, or dry and wet sponges). Such experiences are generally more positive for children when they are given opportunities to anticipate the new experience and are not forced to touch things that may be new or different. Children may also feel more secure to explore new things while being held by their caregiver or while lying on a familiar cozy blanket.

➜ Describe key landmarks or features along a route to children while giving them time to explore, repeating the same descriptions each day as the route is walked or traveled. For example, along the walk to the preschool-age child's bus stop, a mailbox, oak tree, and wooden fence are encountered. While describing these three landmarks, encourage the child to explore (such as through hand-under-hand modeling) or look at (possibly by physically assisting the child to direct his or her gaze or by emphasizing the color of the object) each feature. With time and repetition, children may be able to anticipate the sequence or order of the landmarks and communicate this through language, the use of basic signs, or with a communication board.

➜ Collect or help children collect interesting objects (such as fallen leaves, twigs, and rocks) encountered along a familiar or new route. Talk about where the object came from and why it is there. Children who use wheelchairs can keep a piece of cardboard with them, on a tray, or in a sack, to attach items found to the cardboard with two-sided tape. Items found can be compared and later placed in a memory book or special container for later exploration.

➜ Assist children in participating in daily living activities to the extent possible (such as placing toothpaste on a toothbrush using a pump dispenser, using margarine or very soft butter to spread on toast together, or selecting a shirt to wear from two choices given).

Diane L. Fazzi

Children who are blind do not have these vast opportunities to take in the world visually and expand their conceptual understandings. They are only aware of the places and activities in the community to which someone has exposed them and carefully explained what is happening. Tactile, auditory, olfactory, and visual (if available) exploration accompanied by meaningful verbal descriptions provide the only way the child with a visual impairment can make sense of the world around him or her. Otherwise, the child has only bits and pieces of a very fragmented world, which leave often confusing and inaccurate images of the environment.

Outings into the community should be an important component of the young visually impaired child's O&M program. Families and professionals can create opportunities for the child to experience pet stores, grocery stores, airports, restaurants, gas stations, post offices, taxis, office buildings with elevators and escalators, bus rides, and bowling alleys. Each new experience in the community at an early age adds another piece to the conceptual puzzle. It is not unusual to find an older congenitally blind child, ready to learn street-crossing skills, whose understanding of "intersection" is inadequate. Understanding may be limited to the tactile and proprioceptive feedback received underfoot while walking with a guide down a flat, smooth surface, stepping down a drop-off, walking over a rougher surface, and stepping up again. He or she may also have been aware of a variety of confusing surrounding sounds. He or she may not, however, have been aware of the parkway to the side, the driveways passed, the houses on the other side, the way the curb runs, the gutter, or the wheelchair ramp at the corner. He or she also may not have any idea how the two streets cross to form an intersection and may not know about the other two corners, the systematic way the traffic flows, or the traffic light overhead. How can this child be expected to cross the street safely and remain oriented, given such large conceptual gaps?

Families and professionals have an important responsibility in teaching young children who are blind about their community and the world at large. Verbal descriptions alone are not enough, or the *verbal unreality of the blind* described by Cutsforth (1951) may occur, in which the blind child grows up with intricate verbal descriptions of the world but with no true understanding of the environment and little ability to interact functionally with it. For the child with multiple disabilities or the very young child with little or no receptive language, nonverbal methods of communicating about the environment must be employed. Co-active exploring, movements, and manipulation of objects, such as touching the various textures on a new quilt together, walking with Daddy on top of his toes, or uncovering a toy that is hidden by a cloth diaper with assistance are valuable experiences. When these activities are paired with labels and verbal descriptions for young children who are blind and visually impaired, they provide a necessary bridge for this communication gap. Early, meaningful instruction in environmental awareness is the only way to create future success in this area.

Awareness of all these environmental concepts can begin at a very early age, as families and professionals expose the child to the outside world and take the time to explain this complex environment carefully. It is not possible to teach everything about the environment to the preschool-aged child who is visually impaired, but whatever he or she learns about early on will provide that much more of a head start when the child competes in a sighted world and applies O&M skills in the future.

BASIC SKILLS

Instruction in basic skills is typically an integral part of most O&M programs for young children who are visually impaired. Basic skills include, but are not limited to, human guide technique, protective techniques, and trailing. The instructional techniques, usage, and potential benefits of these basic skills may differ from the techniques and benefits commonly associated with older children and adult populations. For specific strategies for teaching basic skills to young children see the box, "Teaching Basic Skills to Young Children in O&M."

FOCUS ON EFFECTIVENESS

TEACHING BASIC SKILLS TO YOUNG CHILDREN IN O&M

The following strategies may be helpful in teaching basic skills in O&M to young children who are blind or visually impaired:

➜ Collaborate with other specialists (such as an occupational or physical therapist) to develop an age-appropriate arm strengthening program to support the young child's physical ability to use protective techniques and trailing.

➜ Play games like Pin the Tail on the Donkey with other children while encouraging the use of good protective techniques for locating the wall, poster, or other motivating target.

➜ Allow young children who enjoy dress-up activities to wear "magic gloves" to practice upper and lower protective techniques.

➜ Use a feather duster to practice trailing walls, fences, railings, or play equipment in order to develop an understanding of maintaining contact with a surface and to develop skills in walking parallel to each (Fazzi & Petersmeyer, 2001).

➜ Attach interesting items (such as a balloon, brailled message, or sticker) with tape along a familiar trailing surface for the young child to locate to increase motivation for maintaining contact while trailing.

➜ Combine instruction in the use of protective techniques or trailing with instruction in the use of an appropriate mobility device to increase safety along routes traveled.

➜ Play games like red light, green light while practicing trailing along a wall, or practice the use of protective techniques in open areas to increase the fun and motivation in lessons (Fazzi & Petersmeyer, 2001).

➜ Use music (tape recorded or sung) to motivate children to practice basic skills. For example, the O&M specialist could turn on the tape recorder when the child is demonstrating a given technique properly as a form of positive reinforcement (Fazzi & Petersmeyer, 2001).

➜ Switch roles—have young children be "teacher" and instruct O&M specialists or other children in how to travel properly with a guide.

➜ Create a human guide obstacle course, using cardboard boxes, orange cones, and other items found in the area to practice the many facets of traveling with a guide (such as narrow passageway or switching sides). An imaginary tale can be added and told while negotiating the course. Other children who are learning how to be a guide can also participate and earn points for correct techniques and not touching obstacles along the way.

➜ Give in-services and provide follow-up for families, teachers, assistants, other professionals, and children, as appropriate, to make sure that everyone is using the same techniques consistently.

➜ Adapt techniques, as appropriate, to meet the individual needs of children. For example, a very small child may need to grasp the guide's fingers when traveling or a child who has additional physical disabilities may not be able to cup his or her fingers and may need to assume a different position for trailing a wall with his or her hands.

Diane L. Fazzi

Human (Sighted) Guide Technique

As young children with visual impairments start to walk, they can begin to benefit from the use of the human guide technique. Either a person with sight or a person with a visual impairment can serve as a guide, as appropriate. In using this technique, the person who is blind holds on to the guide's arm and walks a half step behind and

Young children may need to use an adapted grasp, such as holding the guide's wrist, when walking with a human guide.

to the side of the guide, following the guide's body movements. Rather than always holding the young blind child's hand and pulling him or her through unknown space, adults can use a modified grasp with the child, in which the child holds the guide's index finger or hand in such a way as to obtain a sense of control while walking. As the child grows older, the grasp may move closer to the guide's elbow (from the finger to the hand to the wrist to the forearm). The technique is a safer, more efficient way to lead a child who is blind than walking side by side and holding the child's hand. For example, a young child using a modified guide technique is more likely to avoid people and obstacles because the child can interpret the body movements of the guide.

Instruction in guide techniques should not be limited to the young child and the immediate family. Instruction can be extended to other adults, such as the preschool teacher, child-care worker, teaching assistant, other specialists, and extended family and friends who may come in contact with the child. In addition, peers and playmates can be instructed in the proper use of the technique. Eventually, the child who is visually impaired will be required to take a more active role in instructing those around him or her in the proper techniques. This training should begin as early as possible to avoid the passivity often demonstrated by many young blind children who are frequently pulled about by their well-meaning peers.

Protective Techniques

When young children who are blind move through their home, school, and play environments independently, there may be unexpected obstacles. Protective techniques are one defense against bodily contact with some of these hazards. Children between the ages of 1 and 5, depending on motor development, level of physical coordination, and attention span, may begin to learn to use protective techniques appropriately when walking about. When executed properly, the upper forearm protective technique, in which the arm is bent at the elbow and the forearm is placed across the body at shoulder height parallel to the floor with the palm outward, will guard young children from head- and chest-level obstacles. There may be instances in which an O&M specialist may prefer that the child's forearm be placed at a diagonal upward position in front of the face. For example, in familiar areas where children know to expect a head-level cabinet, the diagonal position can provide greater protection.

Similarly, the lower body protective technique, in which the arm is extended downward and diagonally across the body at the hip area with the palm toward the body, guards against contacting obstacles at waist-to-upper-leg level. When used with consistency, however, these techniques may become physically tiring for the young child. Selective use of protective techniques in unfamiliar areas, in familiar

This preschool-age child is working to refine the upper forearm protective technique.

areas where certain obstacles are known to exist, or when other persons give verbal warnings of potential hazards, is more appropriate and realistic than continual nondiscriminatory usage.

Protective techniques are limited in the amount of protection they provide, particularly in unfamiliar areas. Even in cases of perfect execution of these techniques, individuals may bump into obstacles with the knees, shins, ankles, and toes. It takes a refined traveler to be able to adjust forearm protection for obstacles of differing height. The less sophisticated traveler, who is unable to distinguish the height of head-level obstacles, is at risk for upper-head-level injuries. Because of the high level of muscle tone and motor coordination required for proper use of protective techniques, young children commonly exhibit inexact technique and are prone to unexpected collisions. Collisions may discourage the young blind child from using the techniques daily.

Although protective techniques are valuable skills to be used in selected travel situations, the reality is that in isolation these skills have significant limitations. If a young blind child's only sources of protection for independent movement are forearm and lower-body protective techniques, the risks of movement may ultimately outweigh the motivation to explore the environment. These skills are most beneficial when taught and used in conjunction with the long cane, a more reliable, independent protective device, which is discussed in the next section, "Mobility Devices."

Trailing

The basic skill of trailing, in which the traveler extends the arm at a 45-degree angle in front and to the side of the body to follow a surface with the hand, has multiple functions. It can be used as a method of alignment, as an approach for gathering information, as a method for locating landmarks and destinations, and as a form of protection during movement. As with protective techniques, the usefulness of trailing may be limited and may depend on the accuracy and consistency of the arm position and the concentration of the traveler. Modifications in trailing for young blind children involve varying arm and hand positions, depending on the particulars of the environment and the child's motor capabilities.

Cruising—holding on to a surface for support while side-stepping—is commonly used by young toddlers for balance and support prior to walking independently. Cruising is a preliminary form of trailing that should be encouraged. Typically, children will progress from holding on to a table or couch edge with two hands to holding a furniture edge with just one hand to trailing the edge of a surface.

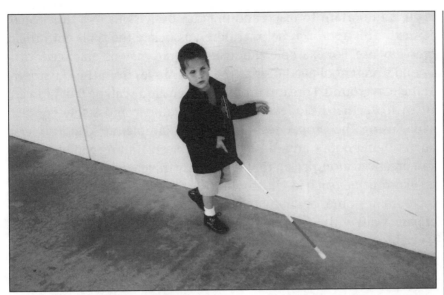

Trailing techniques are safer when used in conjunction with the long cane.

Cruising is important because it facilitates movement, exploration, and independence for young children.

For young blind children who are able to walk independently, trailing a surface edge or wall may provide a general sense of security as they move through the environment. Trailing technique can be enhanced when taught and used in conjunction with the long cane. The cane not only provides extra needed lower-body protection for the young traveler, but it also allows the trailing hand more freedom of movement for exploration of the trailed surface.

Teaching Skills in a Functional Context

Traditionally, a large amount of time has been devoted to teaching basic skills to young children who are visually impaired, and yet they rarely fully incorporate these skills into their daily routines. Basic skills too often become associated only with O&M lessons. Young children need to understand the purpose behind the use of such techniques. When blind children internalize the cause-and-effect relationship between the use of techniques and safe and efficient movement, they are more likely to be motivated to use their skills. For children with poor muscle tone or with physical impairments, protective techniques and trailing may be very difficult to master because they require shoulder-girdle strength and arm and wrist rotation. For children with additional physical disabilities, consultation with a physical therapist should occur prior to instruction in these more challenging motor skills.

It is important to teach and practice basic skills in a functional context. This approach helps children associate the skills with their everyday use. For example, guide techniques may be practiced with a child's preschool-aged peer as the class moves from the classroom to the playground. Forearm protective technique can be taught in an area with actual head-level objects the child could safely contact while using the proper technique (for example, air conditioners, open cabinet doors, and dining room tables). Trailing can be taught and practiced along a wall that is typically traveled during the child's regular routine (such as classroom to bathroom, kitchen to the family room at home, or cubby to the classroom door). Associating use of basic skills with their functional purposes helps children, families, specialists, and teachers to understand, accept, reinforce, and utilize these techniques in an appropriate context.

MOBILITY DEVICES

No one disagrees about the importance of movement for young children with visual impairments. It is through movement that young children learn about the world, develop muscle tone and coordination, and become actively engaged with other people and their surroundings. There may be a range of viewpoints, however, regarding the most appropriate devices, techniques, and teaching strategies to best promote this movement. A mobility device for a person who is blind or visually impaired is a device that is used to serve as a probe or bumper in the environment. Adapted devices may also provide additional support for balance. Mobility devices for young children may fall into several broad categories, including infant appliances (such as walkers), toys, adaptive devices, and long canes.

These devices may have selective use with individual children at various developmental stages, with individual children who have various motor capabilities, children who have additional disabilities, and individual children as they interact in various social situations. In the long-term perspective, most children who are blind and many who have low vision will ultimately utilize the long cane for independent travel. With this goal in mind, and with those goals of promoting movement, exploration, autonomy, socialization, and improved gait and posture, decisions regarding the appropriateness of specific mobility devices should be incorporated into the O&M program. A certified O&M specialist (COMS) should make the determination of the most appropriate mobility device, with input from family members, other specialists and teachers. Fazzi (1995, 1998) has suggested the following considerations when selecting, adapting, or designing a mobility device:

- ability of the child to hold the device in some manner,
- ability of the child to maintain static and dynamic balance,
- ability of the child to maintain attention or focus on mobility tasks,
- ability of the child to move or push a device with one or two hands,
- the child's motivation to move in various environments,
- the child's level of visual functioning,
- the child's need for hand trailing or other contact with the environment,
- the age-appropriateness of the device(s),
- the environments in which the device(s) will be used, and
- child and family preferences.

An occupational therapist or physical therapist should also be consulted when there is any question about the device's impact on a child's balance, posture, gait, or motor development.

Infant Appliances

Early childhood specialists, special educators, physical therapists, parents, physicians, and manufacturers disagree over the possible pros and cons of such infant appliances as jumpers and infant walkers. Although these appliances may provide some early movement experiences for young children, they should be used only with extreme caution. Jumpers are appliances that are mounted in a doorframe and have a canvas seat attached to coiled springs. Infants can bounce in the seat by pushing off from the floor. Even when used with constant supervision, baby jumpers have been associated with sprained ankles, leg injuries, and detached retinas.

Walkers typically consist of a wheeled base with a rigid frame that holds a fabric seat with leg openings. Some are equipped with bouncing mechanisms, mounted plastic toys, and play trays. Nonambulatory children can propel the walkers rapidly by pushing on the floor with their feet. The National Association of Children's Hospitals and Related Institutions (NACHRI) and the American Academy of Pediatrics (AAP) (1995) state that baby walker accidents have sent 25,000 young children to hospital emergency rooms every year. Rolling down stairs was the most common cause of injuries cited. NACHRI and AAP recommend that baby walkers be replaced with saucers (like walkers without wheels), playtables, infant swings, or highchairs.

Infant walkers may act as a buffer between the child and the environment during the early movement stages. However, their use requires constant supervision by a responsible adult. Blind children in walkers may easily topple down drop-offs or stairs. Infant walkers may move very quickly along noncarpeted surfaces, causing collisions and spills, especially in movement over changing surfaces. The use of infant walkers may inhibit development of normal motor patterns and balance and may decrease opportunities for creeping and crawling (Clarke, 1988; American Academy of Pediatrics, 1995). Given the special motor development needs of young children with visual or multiple impairments, it is essential for educators and families to consult with physical therapists regarding the appropriateness of any infant appliance.

Toys

As the young child with a visual impairment begins to stand, take first steps, cruise, and move through the environment, a variety of toys or objects may be used for support or may provide some degree of protection. Some toys and objects may be used in conjunction with an adult to provide initial movement experiences. These experiences, which still depend on the presence or assistance of another person, may serve as transitions from use of a guide to independent movement as distances are extended between the guide and the child (Clarke, 1988). Examples include hula hoops, rubber rings, broom handles, or any object that is held by a person as the blind child also holds it for support while walking.

When the child is ready to move more independently, toys such as beach balls, hula hoops, toy shopping carts, push toys with wheels, and toys that are ridden may be used for support or as bumpers for protection from collision with obstacles in the environment. Children may use some of these items to navigate in appropriate play situations.

Although some of these toys and objects may have a certain value for children in need of support for balance and for certain social situations, they also have inherent limitations. Some toys may not withstand the weight of a child in need of support, so care must be taken to ensure safety through adaptations (weighting toy shopping carts with sandbags or pushing them in reverse, for instance). Some of the items are bulky and provide more protection from the environment than is necessary (for example, pushing a large hula hoop may limit the areas accessible to the young child and may limit hands-on contact with the surroundings).

Using many of these toys may seem natural in a play setting for a young blind child, but the same toys may appear out of place in other settings. For example, a hula hoop used by a preschool child who is blind may be accepted on the playground but may be totally unacceptable in the lunchroom. A toy shopping cart may be used appropriately on a route to collect milk from the kitchen at school but may be less appropriate to take routinely to the bathroom. A beach ball may serve a useful purpose in the home as the young child pushes it to avoid collisions with furniture but would not be appropriate to use in a store or in the general community. If toys are used in a safe, functional, and socially appropriate manner, they may be useful for some children who are visually impaired in the early stages of walking. Using toys that are not safe, functional, or socially appropriate may serve to inhibit movement, decrease generalization of travel skills, and increase social isolation.

Adaptive Mobility Devices

Mobility devices may be designed or adapted by O&M specialists or may be commercially available. Witte (1993) found a variety of adapted mobility devices being developed, field-tested, and utilized in residential schools across the United States. O&M specialists are designing alternatives and adapting more traditional devices for young children who are blind and who have low vision, as well as for children who have multiple disabilities. LaPrelle (1996) provides step-by-step instructions for constructing mobility devices for young children from polyvinyl chloride (PVC) pipe. In addition, the book provides specialists with some general guidelines for their use with preschool age children who are visually impaired. Appendix E of *TAPS* (Pogrund et. al, 1993) also has an extensive resource for O&M practitioners who wish to construct their own adaptive mobility device. Adaptive devices may include:

- long canes with dual handles (one for the child and one for the instructor to coactively move),

- long canes with dual grips (for the child to use with both hands in order to maintain a centered position with greater ease),

- long canes with alternative grip materials (to make grasping the cane and/or positioning the finger easier),

- long canes with wheels, casters, or gliders (to facilitate easier side-to-side movement),

- PVC devices with curved tips, tubed rollers, or four legs and wheels (to provide the young child with a wider base of protection or support for balance), and

- PVC arc definers (used by the O&M specialist while walking backwards to give the child a guideline for proper arc width).

Wheeled devices may reduce the amount of tactile feedback from the environment received by the child. Note that devices with wheels should be used with caution as they may limit reaction time for drop-offs and cause children to step down abruptly or fall. Figure 10.1 shows two examples of adapted mobility devices that can be used with young children.

Many of these adaptations have been designed to meet the individual needs of children who are visually impaired and who have additional physical disabilities and/or attention span deficits, and who are initially unable to successfully utilize the traditional long cane. Clarke, Sainto, and Ward (1994) found that adaptive mobility devices are most commonly used when there is a need for additional support for balance or more consistent protection from environmental obstacles.

O&M specialists may find it beneficial to use a variety of devices to supplement specific O&M activities or to use one device as a transition to another (Fazzi, 1998). In many cases, adapted mobility devices can be used as transitions to the long cane by shaping the skills necessary to use the cane. For young children who are visually impaired, including those who have additional disabilities, who will eventually be able to use the long cane, it is beneficial to do so at an early age, as this is the mobility device the child will likely use in the long term. The long cane is also the device most likely to be accepted and understood in the larger community, as some of the adaptive devices may be confused with devices used by persons with orthopedic disabilities.

Pogrund et al. (1993, p. 268) developed the following questions that can help the educational team make an appropriate adaptive mobility device decision.

- Does the device motivate the student?

- Does the student have a severe physical or cognitive disability that interferes with the student's ability to protect himself or herself with a cane?

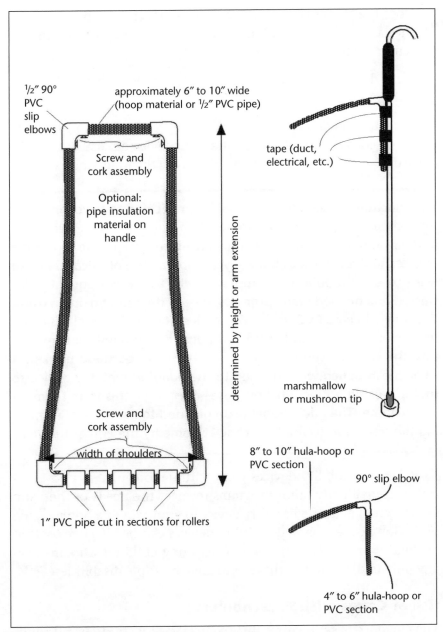

Figure 10.1. Examples of Adapted Mobility Devices

A variety of adapted mobility devices such as the hoopcane (left) and the L-bar cane (right), can be constructed from a few basic materials.

Reprinted with permission from R. Pogrund, G. Healy, K. Jones, et al. *Teaching Age: Appropriate Skills: An Orientation & Mobility Curriculum for Students with Visual Impairments,* 2nd ed., Appendix E, pp. 276, 285 (Austin: Texas School for the Blind and Visually Impaired, 1995).

- Does the student have deficits in proprioception and kinesthesia that interfere with the student's ability to protect himself or herself with a cane?

- Is the device socially appropriate for the student's age and environment?

An educational team can use the questions in conjunction with the factors to consider in selecting a mobility device discussed earlier to make decisions about mobility devices, as in the following example:

The educational team for 4-year-old Ben decided to have him use a four-wheeled PVC device at home when going for walks with Dad in their neighborhood, while introducing the use of the long cane at preschool. Even though the 4-year-old had the physical ability to learn to use the long cane appropriately, Ben was frequently distracted and needed many prompts to keep the cane tip out in front. The four-wheeled PVC device was easiest for family members to supervise at this time, and using it at home encouraged the family to take the child on motivating trips to the neighborhood market. A small mesh pouch was attached to the adapted mobility device so that it took on a functional purpose—carrying items from the market to home. The educational team planned to have Ben start making the transition to the long cane at home by the end of the year.

Adaptive mobility devices will continue to evolve as O&M specialists individually tailor programs to meet the needs of their students. Whether as the mobility device of choice or as a bridge to use of the long cane, adapted mobility devices can be effective tools in facilitating purposeful movement in young children who are visually impaired, including those who have multiple disabilities.

Use of Canes with Preschoolers

The sequence of skills currently used in O&M for children and adults was originally developed for adults. In accordance with this sequence, mastery of so-called *pre-cane* skills, such as guide techniques, protective and information-gathering techniques, and understanding of a variety of spatial and environmental concepts, were required prior to the introduction of cane skills. Because of the prevalence of this philosophy, the introduction of cane skills was commonly delayed until a child was at least 8, 9, or 10 years of age and after the basic skills had been refined. A term preferable to pre-cane skills is *basic skills*—those skills basic to all travel, which are not necessarily

The use of the long cane is routinely taught by O&M specialists to preschool-age children.

a prerequisite to use of a cane. During the late 1980s, there was a shift in thinking and practice regarding the introduction of long canes to children as young as age 2. In current practice, long canes are routinely introduced by O&M specialists to toddlers and preschoolers.

ARGUMENTS FOR AND AGAINST EARLY CANE USE

Several reasons traditionally have been used to support the delay of introducing cane skills. These reasons and responses to them are presented in Sidebar 10.2. Moreover, late introduction of the cane may have long-range social, physical, and cognitive implications. These include:

- development of inappropriate gait patterns (shuffling, taking small steps, slapping the feet) and postural positions (head down, stiffened movements) in response to moving in an uncertain environment and fearing a loss of balance.

- development of fear of movement, with resulting passivity; protective techniques do not offer enough warning or protection against low obstacles and changes in terrain.

- lack of exploration of the environment, leading to development of inaccurate and incomplete environmental concepts.

- development of lack of confidence in the ability to control oneself and the environment; lack of autonomy leading to "learned helplessness."

- possible difficulty with the family, the child, peers, and others accepting the cane when it is finally introduced.

There are several potential advantages to introducing the long cane early. These include:

- increased freedom of movement,

- increased ability to explore the environment, resulting in increased knowledge of the environment,

- development of a more secure, natural gait and a more appropriate and relaxed posture,

- increased stimulation of the vestibular system, resulting in a decreased need for self-stimulation,

- increased self-confidence and autonomy as the child appears more competent to others, and

- early acceptance of the long cane by the child, family, peers, and others.

The long cane may also be helpful for some children with low vision. If the decreased vision interferes with movement and travel, the cane may be used for lower-body protection, as well as to help identify the child as a visually impaired person. Walking with a cane enables the child to use existing vision to gather relevant information from the environment rather than having to keep the eyes on the ground constantly in fear of obstacles, drop-offs, and terrain changes.

TEACHING USE OF THE LONG CANE

The development of cane skills in young children is relatively slow compared with development of the same skills in adults. Instruction involves shaping the skill and giving the child enough time to acquire it. It is also important to make learning to use a cane a fun and positive experience for the young child. General suggestions for introducing and teaching the use of the long cane to young children are provided in "Instructional Approaches and Adaptations for Teaching the Use of the Long Cane to Young Children."

Mastery of many of the concepts, cognitive abilities, and motor skills previously considered necessary before introduction of the long cane are, in reality, not prerequisites. For the visually impaired child who has no other physical impairments, two motor abilities are key to success with the long cane: the ability to hold the cane in some fashion, and the ability to walk independently with adequate balance so as not to need to use high- or medium-guard positions (in which the arms are bent upward at 90-degree or 60-degree angles, respectively, for balance) or help from a person or balance device. If a young visually impaired child has additional physical impairments

INSTRUCTIONAL APPROACHES AND ADAPTATIONS FOR TEACHING THE USE OF THE LONG CANE TO YOUNG CHILDREN

O&M specialists may incorporate the following suggestions within instructional approaches and adaptations used when teaching the use of the long cane to young children.

INSTRUCTIONAL APPROACHES

→ Finding ways to use the cane as a "tool" before using it for walking may reinforce its purpose as a probe (for example, sitting on the floor and reaching objects or reaching for objects high up can increase understanding of the length of the cane).

→ When selecting the proper cane, each child should be considered individually. The child's weight, strength, coordination, skill level, and ability to respond to tactile feedback determine which cane is most appropriate. For example, the lighter NFB (National Federation of the Blind) fiberglass cane may be more suitable for some children than the heavier aluminum-shafted cane.

→ Initially, trailing the baseboard where the wall meets the floor with the tip of the cane can assist the young child in kinesthetically learning the diagonal position.

→ Use of the cane as a bumper and probe should be taught because the very young child will use the cane primarily for these purposes.

→ Alternative techniques may be taught initially according to the child's needs and motor abilities. These include modified diagonal technique with the cane arm relaxed at the child's side, modified diagonal technique used while trailing, constant-contact technique, and two-point-touch technique.

→ Safety rules should be taught, emphasizing that the tip of the cane initially stays on the ground at all times and that the cane stays in front at all times when the child is walking.

→ Cane skills can be integrated into basic skill instruction and development of concepts, language skills, and body awareness, rather than treating them as an isolated instructional activity. For example, trailing the wall to locate a landmark can be taught in conjunction with diagonal cane technique; squaring off (putting one's back and heels against a flat surface to gain alignment) can be practiced while using the long cane in crossing a hallway; cane usage can facilitate the acquisition of environmental concepts through increased movement and exploration; and spatial concepts such as "down," "center," "back and forth," "across," "forward," and "front" are reflected in long cane instruction.

→ Methods of holding the cane while using a guide should be taught, as this will be a frequently used skill for the young child as he or she goes to and from lessons and travels with friends, parents, and teachers.

➜ Names of the parts of the cane should be taught in order to establish a common terminology, if the child has sufficient language and cognitive ability.

➜ Cane use should be incorporated into daily activities as soon as possible in order to provide many natural opportunities for practice.

➜ Family members, other children, and related professionals should receive in-service training before the young visually impaired child uses the cane in the given setting. It is important to create an environment of acceptance for the use of canes by family members. They should be exposed to examples of older children and adults using canes regularly as role models (such as with speakers at parent programs, posters of a cane user prominently displayed, or observation of an older child at an O&M lesson with a cane).

➜ The young child should have an assigned place to store the cane when it is not in use. Folding canes are usually best kept with the child's personal belongings, in order to foster a child's sense of autonomy and responsibility.

➜ Allowing the child to hold or periodically check his or her cane arm with his or her free arm may initially help the child maintain the cane arm in proper position.

➜ Correct terminology is important, but it is also helpful to pair the new term with something that makes sense to the child (for example, pairing *arc* with *sweep it back and forth*).

ADAPTATIONS

➜ Marshmallow, mushroom, and teardrop tips for canes are useful because they tend to glide over uneven surfaces more easily than do other tips; they are slightly heavier than other tips, and they provide additional cues for keeping the cane tip down.

➜ Hip holsters that can be attached to the child's belt or pants loop can serve as a convenient storage place for a folding cane not in use. (Cane holders are available from HandiWorks—see the Resources section.)

➜ Marking the cane's grip with a paper clip and masking tape or with a piece of felt, or using a specially designed grip with a finger ridge for young children helps the child know where to grasp the cane.

➜ Unique key chains can be attached to the elastic strap so that children may identify their canes from one another.

➜ For the child in a wheelchair, using a short-shafted cane with a small tip and grip allows the child without vision to trail the wall without bumping his or her wheelchair into it (Fazzi & Petersmeyer, 2001).

Rona L. Pogrund

that preclude holding the cane or using it while maintaining an acceptable gait pattern, it is recommended that the O&M specialist consult with a physical therapist.

Expressive language abilities are not a necessity in receiving instruction in cane travel. Modeling, nonverbal communication, physical prompting, and receptive touching (for example, interpreting a touch on the shoulder as a message to stop) are effective instructional tools for use with children who have limited receptive-language abilities.

Only a limited awareness of objects in the immediate environment is necessary for cane instruction. An understanding of object permanence, cause-and-effect relationships, and the function of the cane as a bumper can actually be facilitated through cane instruction and movement activities. Similarly, spatial concepts and environmental awareness can be promoted. For example, a child who is visually impaired does not need to be able to identify or locate specific body parts in order to use a long cane; the child only needs to be able to utilize functionally some of those body parts in order to be successful (Pogrund & Rosen, 1989).

When working with young children, it is important not to try to work on everything at once. Learning to use the long cane or any mobility device should be a motivating experience for the child. With the continued development of O&M programs for infants and preschoolers, new information and ongoing research will be needed.

O&M ASSESSMENT

Identification of the need for an early intervention O&M program begins with an assessment of the child and family. An O&M assessment can occur for the first time anytime during the child's first two years of life. Many of the early concepts and motor skills associated with O&M can be supported by a teacher certified in the area of visual impairment and supporting professionals such as a physical therapist. There is, however, benefit in gaining the perspective of an O&M specialist who has early childhood training during these early years. An O&M specialist will provide a unique contribution to the early intervention team and work with the team to ensure that the child is developing into a competent and confident early traveler. For more detailed information about planning for and conducting O&M assessments, see Fazzi & Petersmeyer (2001).

Assessment information is gathered by interviewing the parents and directly observing and interacting with the child. An assessment and subsequent report should include:

- background information,

- clinical impressions,

- a summary, and

- recommendations.

The section on background information should include specific, pertinent information such as the child's currently diagnosed eye condition, medications, additional disabilities, and involvement in other educational and therapeutic programs. The clinical impression section should consist of the names and brief backgrounds of the assessment techniques or instruments utilized, child-specific behavioral notes (for example, how the child was feeling or acting during the assessment process), and an environmental analysis of the assessment site. The summary of assessment results, including the child's functional vision should be clearly written and understandable to families and involved professionals. The final section should list any recommendations for further testing, as well as specific programming suggestions.

A general developmental assessment yields considerable information pertinent to an early intervention O&M program. Not all this information must be assessed directly by the O&M specialist, but it can be obtained from other professionals in an interdisciplinary or transdisciplinary style (see Chapter 11).

An O&M assessment can occur as a separate assessment or within a team model of assessment. For example, if a transdisciplinary model of assessment is used, where all of the team members evaluate the child at the same time, the O&M specialist can be present at the assessment to evaluate the specific concepts and motor skills associated with early O&M programming. The beauty of a team assessment is that all team members, including the parents, are there together to talk about the prioritized needs of the child. If a motor development need, for example, has been identified, the entire team can work together to build a program to support motor development based on the knowledge of how motor skills may be tied to a cognitive understanding of space, a sense of security, and a purpose to move.

In addition to overall developmental information, the O&M specialist should be concerned with the child's level of functional vision and auditory, tactile, and specific mobility skills. Finally, the specialist should consider the natural environmental opportunities presented to the child within the conditions of the assessment and their possible influence on the child's observed performance.

The frequency of an O&M assessment can follow two courses. First, it can mirror the assessment frequency of other developmental domains. Infants and toddlers with Individualized Family Service Plans are evaluated every six months, while preschool children with school district Individualized Education Programs are evaluated on an annual basis. In these scenarios, there is a mandated frequency of assessment. If O&M programming is an inherent part of the child's programming in the early years, the child's concepts and skills associated with O&M should be evaluated on a routine basis. A second course of action would be to base the assessment frequency on the needs of the infant and toddler. If the programmatic needs have not changed significantly over the six-month period, it may not be necessary to have a full reassessment.

In addition to assessment or information gathering relating to the child's specific mobility skills, information should be collected on his or her general developmental functioning. The following list indicates the areas of developmental functioning to be addressed and their implications for O&M skills:

Assessing Developmental Functioning

→ *Sensory skills.* Knowing the status of the child's functional vision, hearing, and tactile development will provide information about the influences of lighting and noise, potential need for prescriptive devices, and the kind of teaching style that is suitable.

→ *Cognition.* It is important to understand how a child processes information about the world and his or her level of problem-solving competence. Body image and time, space, and object-interaction concepts are included in this area. Orientation concepts are grounded in these early cognitive areas.

→ *Fine motor development.* Prehension (grasping) patterns and general upper-extremity strength are building blocks for protective responses and techniques, trailing, and cane use.

→ *Gross motor development.* In addition to such developmental milestones as rolling and crawling, the child's *quality of movement* (strength, balance and coordination) should be analyzed. This variable is important for the child's balance capabilities and quality of gait.

→ *Receptive language and communication.* Understanding the child's level of language provides a guideline for how instruction should be presented to the child.

→ *Self-help*. Activities of daily living may incorporate the use of *functional routes* (routes necessary for active participation in daily routines) for the child to practice. One such route might be the route to the highchair for mealtime.

→ *Social-emotional development*. Social situations may be motivating for travel. It is important to know if a child is responsive to praise or is reinforced by peer interaction in order to carry out route planning and determine style of instruction.

All children who are visually impaired should be assessed by a qualified O&M specialist to identify possible needs and periodically reassessed to determine whether their needs have changed and if O&M services are needed. Not all children with visual impairments will need O&M services at all times. Young children who are able to engage successfully in the same activities as their peers and whose present O&M needs are met may not need specific O&M training until a later date. Other children who may have a similar diagnosis or visual condition may not be able to keep up with peers, move with safety or confidence, or maintain orientation in the home or school environment. These children may benefit from O&M services. The young child's expected activities at home, at school (if applicable), and in relevant community settings can be addressed as prioritized by the family.

ENVIRONMENTAL CONSIDERATIONS

In determining environmental considerations for young children who are visually impaired, the O&M specialist must make suggestions that will enhance the accessibility of natural environments, improve the motivation for efficiency of early movement, and ensure the safety and security that are essential to confident movement. The O&M specialist may be asked to make such suggestions in the home, in the yard, at school, or on the playground. Environmental considerations are important for visually impaired infants, toddlers, and preschoolers, as they may serve to inhibit or to enhance independent movement.

Considerations for Infants

Sleeping, feeding, and bathing areas for infants who are visually impaired may be adapted to provide a stimulating environment for waking hours in which the infant is receptive to interactions. An interesting and accessible environment can promote initial explor-atory behaviors that provide the foundations for early movement. Visual, auditory, and tactile development represent a few of the com-ponents from which the motivation to move stems.

The essential considerations for such adaptations should be the safety of the visually impaired infant and the general interest level of the environment to an infant with a vision loss. Safety issues are similar to those for sighted infants:

- Pillows, blankets, and stuffed animals should not be given to small infants, who may smother themselves as they try to ex-plore the objects or wriggle in their cribs.

- Objects given to infants should be large enough so that they cannot be swallowed as the child mouths them.

- Larger toys and objects should not have smaller, removable parts that may find their way into babies' mouths.

- Infants who are visually impaired should not be left unat-tended in infant walkers or swings.

- Safety straps should be used on the changing table and high-chair to avoid dangerous falls, even if the infant is there only a few minutes.

- Cords from window shades and blinds should not be left dangling where children can reach them as they can strangle themselves with the cords.

Taking the time to move about the house on hands and knees pro-vides caretakers with the opportunity to look at possible hazards from their child's vantage point and can be helpful in eliminating potential danger spots. For more detailed information on infant safety, there are many manuals and resources available from health centers, infant safety classes, libraries, and bookstores.

Suggestions for increasing the interest level of the visually im-paired infant's environment with the intention of prompting reach-ing and exploratory behaviors to promote movement may include:

Enhancing the Environment for Infants

→ Natural lighting can be maximized during waking hours for infants who are visually impaired (for example, by opening drapes and curtains or placing the crib or infant seat in a well-lit area). Optimal lighting may help the child with low vision to see contrasts, shapes, shadows, objects, and faces more clearly.

→ High-contrast (black and white) mobiles (with short strings for safety) can be placed within grasp of the infant who is visually impaired to promote reaching, a sense of causality, and awareness of the outside environment.

→ Securely mounted shiny objects, Christmas lights (kept out of reach), and mirrors can be used to form mobiles or mounted against contrasting backgrounds (for example, by the changing table) to provide structured visual activities that promote reaching, head movements, visual tracking, and exploration.

→ High contrast among bathtub, soap, and bathtime toys may promote vision use by infants during bathing.

→ During daytime feedings, optimum natural lighting can be used to facilitate increased infant–caregiver attachment. Under optimum lighting conditions, infants who are visually impaired may be better able to see the silhouette, shape, or details of the caregiver's face.

→ Musical items may be used as mobiles for infants who are blind. It is important to remember that while eye–hand coordination typically develops in the sighted infant at approximately 4–6 months, ear–hand coordination does not typically appear until approximately the 10–12 month developmental period. Although auditory stimulation is of great importance to the blind or visually impaired infant, adult expectations of the child reaching towards the sound source must realistically consider this time differential.

→ Adaptations can be made in the home that may heighten the infant's awareness of the environment. For example, a soft-sounding wind chime hung in a doorway may alert the blind infant to people's entrance into a room. This type of warning may also give the infant a greater sense of control and security. In addition, it may lead to attending behaviors such as head turning, reaching, and babbling sounds that strengthen the child's interaction with the environment. These kinds of skills and involvement with the environment are some of the important precursors to purposeful movement.

Considerations for Toddlers

Environmental considerations for toddlers who are visually impaired may be slightly more complex than those for infants. Not only must the child's surroundings provide security, motivation for movement, and opportunities for exploration, but arrangements must also take into account the toddler's need for support during cruising and other attempts at first steps and walking.

SAFETY

Adults should be concerned about objects with which the toddler may unknowingly or unsuspectingly come into contact while crawling or cruising.

- Corner protectors are commercially available for tables, shelves, and countertops to protect children from injuries caused by falling onto or running into sharp furniture edges.

- Objects at head level are of particular concern for young children with visual impairments and their families.

- Care should be taken to ensure that tablecloths are not hanging over the table edges where the child can pull on them and spill hot food or knock over candles.

- Electrical socket plug covers are available, as are electric-cord shorteners, which keep cords out of children's reach and limit entanglement and tripping.

MOTIVATION

Many sighted toddlers begin their first movements in response to a desire to reach an interesting object or person. That same motivation needs to be present for toddlers who are visually impaired. As visually impaired toddlers learn cause-and-effect concepts, they will receive enjoyment from reaching favorite toys or objects and being able to manipulate them. As they expand in their social interactions, toddlers who are visually impaired will be reinforced to move through meaningful contact with significant people in their lives.

Some of these motivating factors, which seem to occur as a matter of course, need to be well thought out for the toddler who is visually impaired. Discovering likes and dislikes, such as types of textures, types of sounds, or fun activities, and incorporating that information into programming may foster positive early movement experiences for the visually impaired toddler. Those early experiences help to expand the young child's environment and broaden the physical and social interactions contained within the child's experiences.

SUPPORT

Toddlers often use furniture to gain support for upright movement. Sighted toddlers have the advantage of being able to plan visually a trail of support for getting where they want to go. The visually impaired toddler cruising along the edge of a couch may be at a loss as to where to go next. Furniture may be arranged to provide support for the toddler who is visually impaired in a logical sequence that allows for movement to meaningful locations, such as the child's toy box. Once the furniture is arranged to meet some of the toddler's needs, as well as the needs of the family, it should be left in place as much as possible. This physical stability allows the child to begin using basic mental mapping and orientation skills. Initially, stability is important to the formation of foundations in orientation processing and application. In later childhood, however, it will be important for visually impaired students to have opportunities to experience and adapt to changes in the physical environment. If changes in furniture are necessary, it is important to reorient the young child by giving verbal descriptions and physically guiding the child to the new furniture placements to ensure that he or she understands the changed spatial relationships.

Considerations for Preschoolers

Preschool children with visual impairments who are fully ambulatory require a whole new set of considerations. The environment should be secured for the young, inexperienced traveler, but it can also become a tool for use in the development of initial travel orientation skills.

SAFETY

In response to similar concerns expressed regarding safety for the toddler, the home and school environment for the preschool child who is visually impaired should be examined for head-level obstacles; knee- and shin-level obstacles; cords, wires, and throw rugs that may cause tripping or slippage; and stairs and other drop-offs that may catch the young child off guard.

- Commercially available corner and edge protectors can significantly diminish the danger of bumping into obstacles.

- Rubber housings for loose cords and wires can prevent the curious youngster from being entangled.

- Various types of plastic and rubber mats are available for placement under throw rugs. These mats significantly reduce slippage and turned-up corners on area rugs.

- Secure safety gates can be used to block off stairways in the home to allow the child with a visual impairment to move more freely during playtime.

For the preschool child who has low vision, the use of color and contrast may be used to increase safety in the home or at school:

- A dark area rug on top of a light-colored carpet (or vice versa) can alert the child who has low vision to the location of a coffee table or other piece of furniture.

- A dark-colored cloth or drape can help the young child with low vision detect a glass tabletop or other piece of furniture with glass, which would otherwise be difficult to see.

- Contrasting placemats and dishes can reduce the number of accidental spills and breakage.

- Planned color choices for cupboards and furniture or brightly colored decorations can reduce collisions for children who are visually impaired in their preschool classroom.

TRAVEL AND ORIENTATION

As the visually impaired child's ability to move increases, the child's environment expands and its personal relevance increases. Families play an instrumental role in encouraging their young children to move about and explore the growing world around them. (See "Strategies for Families to *Support* Movement and Exploration" for specific suggestions on this topic.) Certain considerations can help to create home and school environments that are both accessible and meaningful to the young child with a visual impairment.

For example, fenced-in yards provide ample opportunities for safe and independent movement. If outdoor toys are routinely stored in an accessible area, the environment then possesses a natural motivation for the young child to move, when it is the child's responsibility to retrieve and return his or her toys.

In addition, walkways and surface changes (such as grass to gravel, cement to dirt, hedges to open areas, and carpet to linoleum) can provide both indoor and outdoor landmarks and easily followed routes to favorite areas in the home, yard, or school. These types of ready-made or adapted environmental characteristics can assist the

STRATEGIES FOR FAMILIES TO *SUPPORT* MOVEMENT AND EXPLORATION

The following suggestions can be offered to families. When put into practice they spell *support* for a young child to move about and explore the home environment.

→ Support children's orientation by keeping the placement of objects in the home (such as furniture, storage for toys, and laundry baskets) fairly consistent and by using clear spatial terms to describe locations (for example, "Your tricycle is next to the trash can").

→ Understand the importance of encouraging children to move about independently or semi-independently to retrieve toys, books, clothing, or even a snack, and allow children to do so even if it takes extra time.

→ Provide a safe home environment for children, whether they are sighted or visually impaired, to independently explore (for example, using electrical outlet covers, keeping mini-blind cords out of reach, or placing all the "breakables" in a different room so that children can play in a given room more freely).

→ Positively accept the use of low vision and mobility devices in the home, school, and community. Children can be very sensitive and determine when a family member has a negative attitude about the long cane, for example.

→ Optimize lighting and the use of color and contrast in the home to facilitate ease of movement and exploration for young children who have low vision, (for example, opening drapes to light a family room so that children can more easily locate toys independently).

→ Require children who are visually impaired to assist in completing household and family chores alongside siblings or parents (such as helping to put away the groceries or take the clothes out of the drier) to promote participation in family activities and hands-on experiences with functional concepts (such as location and storage of different food items—cold foods in the refrigerator and canned foods in the cupboard).

→ Take time to encourage children to look at, listen to, and explore new objects or actively participate in events so that they can expand conceptual understanding of their surroundings. For example, encouraging children who are blind to tactilely explore the mail slot in the door and listen to the sounds that different size letters and cards make when they fall on the wood floor can help them to better understand the daily event when the letter carrier delivers mail.

Diane L. Fazzi

child who is visually impaired in orientation processing and decrease the child's dependence on adults for movement.

Environmental considerations for young children who are visually impaired and for families who want to be actively involved in promoting their child's desires and abilities in regard to movement should not be overlooked. Although some considerations may require more effort, time, and expense than classroom teachers or families are able to expend, most adaptations will require minimal investment of time and money. The O&M specialist should plan to devote ample time to observing the child indoors and outdoors and in both the home and school. Careful observations of movement and interaction patterns should determine which environmental considerations are priorities to be addressed. Ongoing observations will help update modifications to keep in step with the changing needs of the visually impaired child as he or she matures and develops.

CONCLUSION

As the population served by O&M specialists changes to include more infants, toddlers, and preschoolers, the role of the specialist changes as well. The specialist's major responsibility continues to be the encouragement of optimal independence and the provision of motivation for young children who are blind or visually impaired to travel within a variety of environments. A responsibility of the field as a whole is to develop further and refine appropriate methodologies to achieve these goals. This effort will require more than a shift from the formal O&M techniques and applications to a developmentally appropriate approach. The latter will demand further research and collaboration within an early childhood spectrum of education for children with vision loss.

TEAM FOCUS

Current Trends, Service Delivery, and Advocacy

CONTRIBUTORS

Vivian I. Correa Current Trends in Service Provision

Diane L. Fazzi Service Delivery

Rona L. Pogrund Team Models, Advocacy

Although early intervention services have been available for many years, new knowledge about the importance of the early years of a child's life (Carnegie Corporation of New York, 1994; Nash, 1997) and the role of the family (Hanson & Lynch, 1995) has resulted in a significant expansion of these services, culminating in legislative support. The 1986 amendments (P.L. 99–457) to the Education for All Handicapped Children Act (P.L. 94–142), while addressing a variety of educational services, had two major areas of impact for young children with disabilities and their families. It extended special education services to include all children with disabilities from 3 through 21 years of age, and it provided strong incentives for states to offer services to eligible children from birth. The 1997 amendments (P.L. 105–17) to P.L. 99–457 (by then called the Individuals with Disabilities Education Act, or IDEA) further strengthened and clarified early intervention services for children with disabilities. They included multidisciplinary assessment for eligible children from birth to age 3 and the development of an Individualized Family Service Plan (IFSP), a written guideline of the goals, objectives, and specific services to be provided to eligible children and their families.

This emphasis on early education is not new. Original drafts of P.L. 94–142 contained provisions for early education. During the financial and political "refinements" of the subsequent drafts of this law, however, the age for eligibility was changed to 6 years, in part because of a pervasive belief that mandated services would violate the family's right to full responsibility for the development of their young child. Thus, P.L. 94–142 only supported competitive distribution of discretionary funds for a limited number of demonstration projects

FOCUS POINTS ON TEAMING

The following key ideas are addressed in this chapter.

➔ Increases in the number of young children with disabilities are a reflection of improved outreach services through child find efforts at the state and local level.

➔ Professionals in the field of visual impairment need to stay informed about the current trends and laws in early intervention in order to adequately serve the population of children who are visually impaired.

➔ Effective teaming among the various professionals working with a young child with a visual impairment is essential in planning and implementing a good early educational program.

➔ The use of a transdisciplinary team model results in a less fragmented program for each individual child and family.

➔ Young children who are visually impaired can be served in a variety of program options, including home-based, center-based, or combination programs.

➔ Teachers of students who are visually impaired and O&M specialists play an esssential role in the early intervention and early education of young children who are visually impaired, and collaboration between these two professionals minimizes overlap of services and maximizes team effectiveness.

➔ Families and professionals working together as a team create the strongest force when advocating for improved programs and services for young children who are blind or visually impaired.

serving young children, the Handicapped Children's Early Education Program (HCEEP). The 1986 amendments redesigned the criteria for distribution of discretionary funds and made them available, on a noncompetitive basis, to all states and territories that chose to comply with the criteria, including: criteria that reflect the importance of the family in the young child's development; interagency coordination with parent representation; the family's right to refuse services and protection of their rights of due process, and the IFSP. Passage of this law was the most significant indication of changing current trends in early education. The law has had a major influence on every aspect of services. The 1997 amendments strengthened the law regarding services to children who are visually impaired by noting the need for specialized services by experts in visual impairment.

This chapter will provide an overview of the current trends and laws in early intervention and their implications for children who are visually impaired. There is an extensive section on teaming models, including the transdisciplinary team approach. Program options for young children who are visually impaired are described with a focus on the need to identify the most appropriate placement for each child. A description of the professionals who work with these young children and their roles is also addressed, along with the issue of class and caseload size. The chapter concludes with a section on advocacy for young children who are visually impaired with specific suggestions for effective advocacy efforts.

CURRENT TRENDS IN SERVICE PROVISION

Professionals in the field of visual impairment are increasingly being asked to collaborate with early interventionists, preschool educators, and related service professionals in meeting the needs of young children with visual impairments. Critical to the success of early education programs for this population is the required collaboration between families and professionals in service delivery. The early intervention system (that is, educational services for children with disabilities birth through age 5) is complex and requires professionals to work together to meet the needs of families and children. Some of the issues facing early intervention professionals include: child find services, contemporary practices in early intervention, and personnel preparation.

Child Find Services

The numbers of young children with disabilities receiving services under the sections of IDEA known as Part C (which covers children from birth through age 2) and Part B (ages 3 through 5) continue to increase. The increase reflects improved outreach services through "child find" efforts at the state and local level. Furthermore, child find requirements have been extended to children with disabilities in private and parochial schools. Services for children three years old and up are provided by each state's department of education. However, programs for children under age 3 are provided by different agencies in different states. Sometimes the department of education will handle all of these programs; in other states it may be the health department or another agency. Much variability exists in the degree and quality of services provided across states.

What are known as child find programs are the earliest forms of screening and assessment for identifying children who have disabilities or who are at risk for disabilities, and they are maintained by IDEA. Child find services are directed by each state's lead agency for identifying and diagnosing unserved children with disabilities. While child find looks for all unserved children, it makes a special effort to identify children from birth to six years old. The child find system includes public awareness activities that provide parents, professionals, and the community at large with information on the importance of identifying children with or at risk for developmental delays and disabilities, and procedures for screening, referral, assessment, and early intervention services.

Although the number of children receiving services has increased, not all of the children needing early intervention services are being reached. Child find services may not be reaching families who do not use public health services or well-baby clinics, do not speak English, have just arrived in the United States, or who do not suspect a delay or problem with a child. Diligence with outreach must be taken to make families aware of the free diagnostic and early intervention services available in their communities.

For families of children with visual impairments, finding out about early intervention services is often dependent on health professionals' knowledge of the child find system. In particular, health care professionals and eye care specialists (for example, ophthalmologists, pediatric neurologists, neonatal intensive care nurses, and physicians) will be the first to diagnose a visual impairment in newborns and toddlers. These health care professionals need to provide families with information on early intervention services so that families and children receive services as soon as possible. Hatton (2001), however, noted that there is often a time lag between when a visual impairment is diagnosed and when a referral is made to specialized services. Established-risk children, those with a known diagnosable condition (for example, retinopathy of prematurity or congenital cataracts), are most likely to be identified by the medical community. Those at-risk children, the ones with any number of biological or environmental factors that contribute to developmental delays (approximately 75% of children seen in special education), are often not identified by the medical community. Medical professionals may miss some children with low vision, cortical visual impairment, and other neurological impairments.

Ongoing efforts must be made by professionals in the field of visual impairment to educate medical professionals, public health personnel, child-care providers, and generic early interventionists about the importance of early referral to vision specialists knowledgeable in the impact of vision loss on development (Hatton, 2001). A young child with visual impairment has little reason to explore interesting objects in the environment and, thus, may miss opportunities to have experiences and to learn. This lack of exploration may continue until learning becomes motivating or until intervention begins. Furthermore, because the child cannot see parents or peers, he or she may be unable to imitate social behavior or understand nonverbal cues (National Information Center for Children and Youth with Disabilities, 2001). Without early intervention services, children with visual impairments can have difficulties in learning and developing independence.

Contemporary Practices in Early Intervention

Various trends are evident in programs serving young children with disabilities. Most of the intervention services provided for these young children are also recommended practices when serving young children with visual impairments. Sidebar 11.1 highlights some of the contemporary practices in the early intervention system and how they relate to serving young children with visual impairments.

Although empirical evidence of the effectiveness of early intervention models on young children with visual disabilities is scarce, discussions of recommended early intervention practices have been documented (see Davidson & Harrison, 1997 for a review). Several contemporary guidelines emerge from the literature on early intervention for young children with visual impairments. The focus of early intervention for improving development in young children who are visually impaired should include:

- motivation or interest in the external environment;

- body concepts or increased awareness of the hands and feet for independent exploration;

- opportunity for increased physical play at home;

- object permanence for people, objects with sound, and silent objects;

- sound localization;

- sensitivity to the fear of objects thrust within the infant's space without verbal warning or introduction (Sonksen, Levitt, and Kitsinger, 1984); and

- support of positive caregiver–child interactions (Dote-Kwan, 1995).

SIDEBAR 11.1 **CONTEMPORARY PRACTICES IN EARLY INTERVENTION AND IMPLICATIONS FOR CHILDREN WITH VISUAL IMPAIRMENTS**

EARLY INTERVENTION PRACTICES

IMPLICATIONS FOR CHILDREN WITH VISUAL IMPAIRMENTS

Individualized Family Service Plan

Unlike the IEP, the Individualized Family Service Plan IFSP focuses on the family and requires a family-directed assessment of resources, priorities, and concerns of the family.

Family concerns related to O&M, educational intervention, and medical and social services should be addressed in the IFSP. Family intervention should focus on specific skills in how to interact with their infants with visual impairments.

The IFSP addresses issues of teaching children with disabilities in their natural environments with young children without disabilities, utilizing service coordination, and building a transition plan to pre-school services under Part B of the Individuals with Disabilities Education Act (IDEA) serving ages 3–21.

The settings for serving young children with visual impairments can vary in the home, family day care, child-care center, special visual impairment program, or special early intervention center. It is hoped that, to the extent appropriate, children with visual impairments will be placed with nondisabled peers of the same age. Transition of services at age 3 can also vary by setting, including residential programs, special education schools, or more inclusive programs in regular public or private schools.

The IFSP must be reviewed every six months.

It is important to monitor the development of young children with visual impairments in the areas of mobility, sensorimotor development, language, and social communication by conducting developmental assessments frequently, documenting gains on charts and graphs, interviewing parents, and videotaping parent–child and parent–teacher interactions.

Interagency Coordinating Councils (ICCs)

States are required to create ICCs and interagency agreements with all agencies (education, health, and social services) serving children birth to age 3 under Part C of IDEA, in an effort to decrease fragmented services to children and families.

In the area of visual impairment, interagency coordination must occur with agencies serving visually impaired populations, such as the state and local educational services for children who are visually impaired, private agencies, rehabilitation services, Division of Blind Services, and Lion's Clubs.

Family-Centered Services

Early intervention programs recognize that the family is the constant in the child's life and respect the equality of the family–professional partnership.

Vision specialists must connect closely with families, providing them with specific information resources for parenting their child with a visual impairment. Families should be equal partners in their child's education and should provide the early intervention team with information on the needs, concerns, and priorities for their child.

Ecological System of Intervention

Early intervention programs adopt a view of children as part of a larger social scheme embedded within the family, school, neighborhood, and community.

Vision specialists must be sensitive to the various environments young children with visual impairments navigate and help families understand how to make various environmental accommodations for their children's needs.

Early interventionists recognize the social, cultural, and economic factors that impact the family and understand how to work with all families, including families who are "at-risk" due to poverty, violent and abusive environments, homelessness, substance abuse, or family members with HIV/AIDS.

Vision specialists should understand the risks of visual impairments with certain conditions (such as poor prenatal care, prematurity, "shaken baby syndrome," or HIV/AIDS).

(continued)

Culturally Reciprocal Early Education

Early intervention programs reflect recommended practices in multicultural education and meet the needs of children who are from non–English-language backgrounds (Derman-Sparks, 1989; Gollnick & Chinn, 2002; Greey, 1994).

Many of the recommended practices for working with bilingual young children can be used when serving young children with visual impairments who come from non–English-speaking backgrounds. However, issues related to braille use in languages other than English will need to be addressed.

Early intervention personnel are aware of their own cultural beliefs and practices and evaluate the extent to which they retain biases.

Vision specialists should approach the diversity of the children they serve as an opportunity to learn and grow professionally. The first step in becoming a culturally responsive educator is to understand your own culture, values, and beliefs. Biases related to children outside of the fringes of blindness should be examined (such as severe multiple disabilities).

Early intervention personnel understand the family's beliefs and values related to the education of their children and engage in respectful problem solving approaches that acknowledge the cultural and ethnic beliefs of the family. (Kalyanpur & Harry, 1999).

Blindness and visual impairments may carry unique ideologies in different cultural groups. Vision specialists must understand those ideologies as well as the parenting practices of culturally and linguistically diverse families.

Assessment and Evaluation

Naturalistic observation approaches to assessing young children often include a transdisciplinary model of evaluation where one member of the team serves as a play facilitator for the child while other team members observe the child's development

Children with visual impairments will need special accommodations for assessment and evaluation. Vision specialists must collaborate with the assessment team in making accommodations and assist in making careful interpretations of

(Linder, 1993; McGonigel, Woodruff, & Roszmann-Millican, 1994).

the assessment results. Knowledge of the unique development of children with visual impairments is critical. Assessment in uses of technological devices for children with visual impairments will need to be added to the evaluation as well as in other areas of the core curriculum unique to children who are visually impaired (such as functional vision, listening skills, and O&M).

Curriculum and Strategies

Multiple approaches to teaching young children with disabilities include developmentally appropriate practices, behavioral intervention strategies, and activity-based instruction.

Curricula together with intervention strategies specifically designed for young children with visual impairments should be considered. Palazisi (1986) & Joffee (1988) provide a framework for intervention with young children with visual impairments. Skill development in sensory awareness, olfactory identification, tactile discrimination, kinesthetic awareness, and vestibular awareness should be emphasized in the multiple approaches to intervention.

Vivian I. Correa

In partnership with families and health care professionals, the vision specialist can play a critical role in the success of early intervention programs for young children who are visually impaired. Early intervention is most critical for children with visual impairments within the first 12 months of life, when they need to be exploring the world around them, beginning to crawl and walk, and developing early language skills. Educational vision specialists must understand the impact of vision on early cognitive, motor, social, and language development and possess the skills necessary to intervene and stimulate development with very young children.

Personnel Preparation

High-quality teachers and specialists are the key to providing effective intervention services to young children with disabilities and their families. Regrettably, as noted in Chapter 1, there is a critical shortage of qualified professionals to serve this population. A current trend in the preparation of early interventionists is to blend personnel preparation programs across different disciplines such as early childhood, early childhood special education, speech and communication disorders, and school psychology. Preparing professionals in the field of visual impairment should also include the integration of content related to early intervention.

According to the National Association for the Education of Young Children (NAEYC) (1996), personnel preparation content should include the following components:

- the uniqueness of early childhood as a developmental phase,

- the significant role of families in early education and intervention,

- the role of developmentally and individually appropriate practices,

- the preference for service delivery in inclusive settings,

- the importance of culturally competent professional behavior, and

- the importance of collaborative interpersonal and interprofessional actions.

As stated earlier, professionals in the field of visual impairment are fully prepared to understand the powerful effects of vision loss on development at an early age. Educational vision specialists are essential members of the early intervention team. They provide excellent linkages with health professionals and early interventionists and assist in better understanding the child's visual and developmental needs. Professionals in the field of visual impairment should stay informed of the current trends and practices in early intervention and continually examine the effectiveness of those practices for children who are visually impaired.

The Law and Children Who Are Visually Impaired

The 1997 amendments to IDEA made significant improvements in services for young children who are visually impaired, as noted in Chapter 1. Previously, visual impairment and specialized services for these children were not even mentioned in P.L. 99–457, the 1986 amendments now referred to as Part C of IDEA. The 1997 amendments added vision services to Part C of the law as one of the possible early intervention services to be offered. These services are specifically defined in the accompanying regulations. In addition, orientation and mobility (O&M) specialists are included in the list of qualified personnel who would be providing early intervention services. Even though these specialized services and personnel are mentioned in the law, it is important that families and professionals ensure that needs related to visual impairment are not overlooked or inappropriately met, particularly for the child who does not have an apparent eye anomaly or who is not exhibiting significant developmental delay. The primary focus of Part C is still on established conditions and developmental delay, and, in some states, on at-risk indicators.

A potential concern of the 1997 amendments to IDEA is that the law does not require that children be labeled or categorized in order to be eligible for early childhood services. The label of developmental delay can be used for children age 3 through 9. The practice of noncategorization can cause problems for the population with visual impairment because:

1. access to specialized materials is based on identification and labeling,

2. successful lobbying for a share of limited resources depends on an accurate reporting of the numbers of children identified with visual impairment, not just developmental delays, and

3. lack of accurate reporting makes it difficult for school systems to plan for the specialized resources and personnel required by children with vision loss.

The 1997 amendments to IDEA do, however, now give the state and local education agency the authority to change a child's label of "developmental delays" to "categorical" labels such as blindness when the child turns 3 years of age. This option may assist states and local education agencies in addressing some of the above-mentioned problems, if they choose to use it.

Special educators must become involved in the planning process at the state and local, as well as the programmatic, levels to ensure that young children who are visually impaired and their families have the specialized resources and intervention they require. Mobilizing and working with parents, including the involvement of organizations such as local affiliates of the National Association for

Parents of Children with Visual Impairments (NAPVI) (see the Resources section), in this advocacy effort is one critical strategy. Educating others who serve young children with special needs about visual impairment and vision resources is also important to the effort to ensure that appropriate services are provided. (See the section "Advocacy for Young Children Who Are Visually Impaired" later in this chapter.) Only through a true team effort will high-quality service delivery models be established for young children who are visually impaired and their families.

SERVICE DELIVERY

Included among the possible options in service delivery models for young children who are visually impaired and their families are the multidisciplinary, interdisciplinary, and transdisciplinary team approaches for serving individuals with special needs. Program options may also vary and may include center-based programming, home-based programming, and combination programs for young children and families. The most appropriate placements for young children who are visually impaired emphasize the meeting of all educational needs—those typical of other children of similar age and those particular to children with visual impairments. Class size, student–staff ratios, and professional preparation and competencies are all important considerations in making proper placement determinations. Open discussion and clear understanding of the professional roles of the teacher of students who are visually impaired, the O&M specialist, and related staff and specialists help to ensure the appropriateness of services rendered to young children who are visually impaired and their families.

Team Models

No matter what service delivery model is used for young children, a team is always involved. Effective team functioning is critical to planning and providing a good educational program for the child. The use of a team in education has been advocated by those who are interested in the whole child and those who feel that knowledge of the various aspects of the child must be integrated in order to help the child reach maximum potential. No one person can have all the necessary skills to meet all the child's needs.

Depending on the child's needs, the team of professionals working with a child with visual or multiple impairments may include, but not be limited to, any of the following:

- Parent or primary caregiver
- Other significant family members
- Special education teacher
- Administrator
- Psychologist
- Teacher of students who are visually impaired
- O&M specialist
- Early childhood intervention (ECI) teacher
- Physical therapist
- Occupational therapist
- Speech and language therapist
- Audiologist
- Ophthalmologist
- Optometrist
- Adaptive physical education teacher
- Nurse
- Behavior specialist
- Health care aide
- Social worker
- Parent advocate
- Instructional assistant
- General education teacher

Whenever teams work with a child, they may need to be alert to barriers that interfere with effective team functioning. Lack of communication can be the biggest barrier to effective functioning. This lack of communication often occurs during assessment, writing objectives, and IFSP or IEP meetings, as well as during implementation of the program. Members of the team may fail to communicate with each other on a regular basis, and specialists in one field may not have a clear appreciation of the skills another discipline wants to teach. Each discipline has its own jargon, and team members may not understand each other's terms. In addition, families and professionals may meet very few times during the school year, so interaction between them may be superficial.

Lack of coordination and collaboration is another barrier to effective functioning. Assessments, planning, and program implementation are three areas in which this can be seen. Assessments are frequently not coordinated among team members; therefore, they may duplicate one another. Objectives may be written with no consideration of the priorities of other team members, and each team member may implement only his or her own program. For example, an O&M specialist may plan to work on cane skills on a functional route to the lunch area without consulting with the teacher of students who are visually impaired. The teacher's primary focus might be on toileting, but the young child is not familiar with the route to the bathroom.

In addition, when team members have differing perceptions of a student's needs, the members may begin to feel that their professional judgment is being questioned. It is not uncommon for professionals to disagree about putting the emphasis on a child's needs for academics rather than social skills. When these differences are not dealt with professionally, discrepancies may lead to animosity among team members.

Follow-through is important to the workings of the team and the child's program. When team members do not follow through in providing services they have agreed to provide, trust is undermined. For example, teachers who agree to reinforce basic mobility skills in the classroom but do not follow through interfere with the student's progress and frustrate O&M specialists. Such behavior severely ham-

---

FOCUS ON EFFECTIVENESS

IMPROVING TEAM COMMUNICATION, COLLABORATION, AND COORDINATION

The following suggestions may help members of educational teams improve their working relationships with each other and negotiate obstacles to the smooth functioning of the team:

➜ Respect the specialized expertise of other professional team members, and listen to family members who are a significant part of any educational team. All team members have a contribution to make that will benefit the child.

➜ Make every effort to communicate and collaborate with other team members on an ongoing basis (via phone, e-mail, written correspondence, or in person) regarding all assessment and intervention planning and implementation.

➜ Have good listening skills when communicating with other team members.

➜ Use tact and diplomacy when negotiating with other team members.

➜ Follow through on what you agree to do (for example, provide a service, make a call, find a resource, or obtain materials). Dependability leads to credibility and respect by other team members.

➜ Disregard personality differences in other team members. Remain professional at all times in your interactions.

➜ Be confident in your own expertise and knowledge so that you are able to share what you know with others without fear of giving up control.

➜ Stay focused on the needs of the child and the family at all times.

Rona L. Pogrund

pers team functioning. Personality differences and other personal issues and dislikes, when allowed to dominate, can interfere with communication and team functioning. It is important to try to work past personal differences.

Finally, the issue of territoriality can be troublesome to teams. The feeling of needing to protect one's own area of expertise interferes with the team's efforts. This feeling often comes from insecurities about one's own professional abilities or distrust of another person's abilities. For example, an occupational therapist or physical therapist who does not trust the abilities of an instructional assistant may not spend the necessary time training the assistant in positioning strategies. Range-of-motion activities may not be shared for fear that other teachers or assistants may overstep professional bounds. When one has confidence in one's expertise and trust in others, sharing and communication take place. See "Improving Team Communication, Collaboration, and Coordination" for suggestions on addressing some of the barriers just mentioned and ways to improve team communication and collaboration.

The three primary models used for educational teams are multidisciplinary, interdisciplinary, and transdisciplinary (Erin, 1990; McCollum & Hughes, 1988). It is common to hear these terms being used interchangeably and inaccurately, yet there are distinct differences in the three approaches, as described in the following sections. Regardless of the term used to describe the educational team, however, the purpose of the team is always the same: to provide the best overall educational programming for a particular child.

MULTIDISCIPLINARY TEAM

The *multidisciplinary* team is a traditional practice based on a medical model. The child is seen by a variety of specialists at different times, in sessions usually carried out away from the classroom or home. Professionals involved seldom communicate, collaborate, or make common agreements with each other about service delivery. The preschool teacher or parents have little input regarding decisions about the child. Usually, the teacher or parent is a recipient of recommendations from different specialists that are most frequently provided in writing and that may conflict among the various team members. This model often results in a very fragmented program.

INTERDISCIPLINARY TEAM

The *interdisciplinary* model reduces fragmentation in programming. As a group, team members focus on one child's functioning, share assessment findings, and develop objectives together. The parent's and teacher's roles in this model are minimal, however. Team recommendations are often more ideal than practical because they are based on isolated views of the child and because each specialist has assessed the child separately in his or her area of expertise.

TRANSDISCIPLINARY TEAM

In the *transdisciplinary* model, one or a few people are responsible for direct contact with the child. Usually the teacher or the caregiver is the primary service provider. The composition of the team depends on the child's needs. Collaborative assessments, such as an arena-type assessment, where team members meet together to observe a child as one team member, such as the parent, interacts with the child, forms an excellent foundation to a successful transdisciplinary model (Smith, 1998). *Role release,* in which fixed roles are diminished, allows training and a particular specialty function to be carried out by more than one person. The specialist releases his or her role to the primary service provider. (For example, the physical therapist may teach the parent how to do range of motion exercises at home on a daily basis for the child with physical disabilities.) Direct care is handled by the persons closest to the child and those who work with the child most regularly, and team members offer consultative backup. The transdisciplinary approach has been defined as a deliberate pooling and exchange of information, knowledge, and skills, involving the crossing and recrossing of traditional boundaries by various team members (Hutchinson, 1974; Gallivan-Fenton, 1994; Holzhauser-Peters & Husemann, 1988; Woodruff & McGonigel, 1988; Smith, 1998).

For a transdisciplinary team to work, three elements must be present: (1) a joint team effort, in which a team performs aspects of the program together; (2) a staff development approach, in which team members train one another; and (3) role release, in which various professionals teach one another to implement training procedures and skills that by tradition have been considered the sole responsibility of one individual.

Role release does not imply that the professional abdicates professional responsibility. Professional accountability is not relinquished. Team members remain accountable for what they teach and how well the skills are learned. Role release involves sharing of knowledge and skills on three levels (Lyon & Lyon, 1980):

- *General information,* in which knowledge of basic skills and practices is communicated (for example, the O&M specialist teaches related staff to utilize adapted human guide techniques with young children who are blind).

- *Informational skills,* in which others are taught to make specific judgments or decisions about something that has been taught so that a skill may be reinforced (for example, the occupational therapist shares information on a child's self-feeding ability so that the classroom teacher may reinforce skills and hold consistent expectations of independence).

- *Performance competence,* in which others are trained to perform specific actions (for example, the physical therapist trains a classroom assistant in proper positioning and lifting procedures to use with a child who is physically and visually impaired so that lifting and positioning can be done in the classroom without the therapist present).

Considerations for using role release include the student's needs, the expertise available on a team, logistical constraints, and legal ramifications (for example, certain medical procedures should only be performed by the appropriate specialist).

The transdisciplinary model is based on the belief that therapies should be incorporated continuously and naturally into the child's daily activities at school or at home (Smith, 1998). Skills taught in short episodes twice a week may not be easily integrated into the child's repertoire. For example, if O&M skills are only practiced when the O&M specialist comes to the preschool, the child who is visually impaired will most likely not incorporate the skills into his or her everyday activities in a meaningful way. If the classroom teacher and assistant are shown the appropriate skills and have the child utilize them, then the daily reinforcement will help the child functionally interpret the skills.

In this scenario, the program facilitator plays a key role in the transdisciplinary model. The facilitator may be any member of the educational team. This person has the responsibility of coordinating and integrating the delivery of the various services provided. The educational facilitator gathers information from a variety of resources and disciplines and incorporates it so that effective intervention is carried out.

A good team facilitator must have the following characteristics:

- sound working knowledge of all the disciplines,

- knowledge of the psychology of coordination and group dynamics,

- possession of ample time and energy to complete necessary duties,

- willingness to serve as a team member,

- knowledge of how to bring families effectively into the team, and

- good group communication skills such as listening, negotiating, and exercising tact.

The transdisciplinary model initially seems more difficult to sustain than other models because it may be new and because participation in it seems to take more time. One of the biggest problems transdisciplinary teams face is finding the time to meet. Structuring these ongoing meeting times with other team members is essential. Looking for alternative communication methods such as ongoing e-mail, phone calls, and faxes of written documents helps as well when face-to-face meetings are not possible. Use of videotaping in the demonstration of specific strategies and skill instruction may also be a useful tool for sharing information when direct observation is not possible. Specific consultations where the specialist assesses, recommends, demonstrates in a natural context, and evaluates the results is a better model than a more general-type consultation. (Smith, 1998) Once communciation systems and implementation procedures are developed, the transdisciplinary model actually allows more students to be reached and is less time-consuming than traditional models. A well-run team makes significant contributions to the child's growth.

Program Options

Program options may vary for infants, toddlers, and preschoolers who are visually impaired and their families according to individual needs, service availability, and funding constraints. Familiarity with programming possibilities can assist professionals and families in locating, selecting, or providing appropriate services.

CENTER-BASED SERVICES

Center-based programs are available nationwide for young children with special needs. They are typically housed at public schools, private agencies, or in hospital settings. Not all center-based programs are alike, nor are they intended to be similar service delivery models. Some center-based programs are privately funded, while others must meet public agency guidelines. Programs may be generic in nature, working with young children who have a variety of special needs. Such agencies may or may not employ or contract for the services of professionals who have specialized training in the area of visual impairment. For example, a generic early childhood special education program may hire a physical therapist on a contractual basis to work with young children with motor difficulties or a teacher of students who are visually impaired to work with a young child with a visual impairment who may be enrolled in the program.

Disability-specific center-based programs provide another option for young children with special needs and their families. Such programs are designed to meet the needs of children with specific, primary disabilities—for example, children who have orthopedic disabilities, hearing impairments, or visual impairments. Specialized programs should be staffed by professionals with specialized training or experience that qualifies them to work with the specific population.

Inclusion with nondisabled peers may be incorporated to varying degrees in center-based programs. Integration may occur at a school site or facility where other children are participating in early childhood programs. Children with disabilities may be placed with nondisabled peers in Head Start or other preschool programs for all or part of the day. Some programs use an arrangement of reverse integration to bring nondisabled children into classrooms with children who have disabilities. This model provides social interactions with peers combined with the advantages of having a full-time teacher with specialized knowledge and experience in serving children with visual impairments. Reverse-integration programs frequently report having waiting lists for nondisabled children who want to participate, possibly due to small class sizes or quality programming. Center-based programs may create additional opportunities for inclusion within the community, such as picnics at a local community park where other young children may be at play during the day.

Family involvement is another element of center-based programming for young children with disabilities that may vary greatly. Some programs may mandate parental involvement as a requisite for a child's enrollment (often called preschool cooperatives or co-ops), while other programs do not mandate such a component. Family participation may include assistance with school fundraisers, chaperoning field trips, attending informal parent groups, making materials for class projects, or working with individual or small groups of children.

Center-based programs for young children with disabilities vary greatly in structure and scope. Young visually impaired children and their families may or may not find a variety of center-based options, depending on the availability of programs in their area. Specialized center-based programs for young children with low-incidence disabilities are more likely to exist in highly populated areas where a concentration of children of a similar age with similar disabilities exists.

HOME-BASED SERVICES

Home-based programs are another service delivery model for young children with special needs and their families. Home-based programming may incorporate direct service, consultation, or a combination of the two in the family's natural environment. Services may be provided by any number of professionals, including a nurse, social worker, occupational therapist, physical therapist, teacher of students who are visually impaired, O&M specialist, or early childhood interventionist. Frequency of home visitations varies from monthly to weekly and may vary from program to program. Home-based services may be provided by a school district, other local education agency, or private agency, and are typically provided to families with children who are under the age of 3. They may also be provided to older children who attend partial day preschool programs. Service programs vary across states, regions, and local areas but are ultimately determined through the IFSP or IEP process.

COMBINATION PROGRAMS

Other programs operate combination center-based and home-outreach service delivery in order to meet more diverse needs of the child and family. For example, parents may attend support group meetings at the center and receive direct service for their child at home. Some parents of infants who are visually impaired attend "mommy and me" or "daddy and me" classes at a center and then receive home-monitoring support. In these combined models, some children and families may receive one or both forms of service, based on family and child need or program organization.

While home-based services are incorporated into the natural environment for young children and their families, some families may express preferences for either home-based or center-based services. Sidebar 11.2 compares some of the factors that differentiate home-based and center-based services. Both types of programs have their distinct advantages in serving young children with visual impairments and their families. The availability of both provides families with an important choice so that they can utilize the services that best meet their needs, priorities, lifestyles, and preferences. Families are well equipped to make the choices that will be best for the development of their child and support for their family unit.

SIDEBAR 11.2 **COMPARISON OF HOME-BASED AND CENTER-BASED EARLY INTERVENTION SERVICES**

HOME-BASED SERVICES

➜ Services provided in the home are in a natural and familiar setting for the child and family.

➜ Children and families do not have to travel to another location for services.

➜ Intervention practices can be modeled with actual materials found in the home during natural routines (for example, moving a brightly colored spoon back and forth to encourage visual attention for eating applesauce during snack time).

➜ Specialists can more easily observe family dynamics (such as child rearing practices and expectations for siblings in the home who do not have disabilities) and help assist with intervention planning that will incorporate family values.

➜ Specialists can conduct assessments of the physical environment of the home and make appropriate suggestions for any necessary adaptations that would increase the young child's ability to participate more fully in family activities (for example, using a light meter to measure the lighting in various rooms in the house and recommending a higher watt light bulb or more open curtains to increase contrast for the child during play with toys).

➜ Appropriate family members can be directly involved in all aspects of the intervention program (for example, an occupational therapist working in the home can model a physical strategy to assist the young child with grasping an adapted drinking cup, and the family can then try the approach and get immediate feedback from the occupational therapist).

CENTER-BASED SERVICES

➜ Children receive more intensive (daily rather than weekly) services from specialists who are knowledgeable about the unique needs of infants, toddlers, and preschoolers with visual impairments.

➜ Children may have increased opportunities to learn from and interact with other children, including verbal interactions, sharing toys, and singing together during circle time.

➜ There are frequent opportunities for specialists serving young children to meet, discuss, and coordinate services for children and families at the center.

➜ There is decreased isolation and more opportunities for families of visually impaired children to interact with one another and benefit from formal and informal parent support networks.

➜ The center serves as a consistent resource to families and easy referrals to other services as needed.

Diane L. Fazzi

Most Appropriate Placement

Selecting the appropriate program model for the infant, toddler, or preschooler who is visually impaired can be challenging, to say the least. If a wide array of options is available, families must explore their own concerns, priorities, and resources in making appropriate determinations. Efficacy studies as to the effectiveness of different early childhood intervention models have been limited in scope, especially in the area of visual impairment in infancy and early childhood. There are few definitive studies that might suggest which program models promote optimum child development, caretaker–infant attachment, and family support and involvement.

The most appropriate placement (MAP) for young children who are visually impaired considers both the developmental needs that the young child shares with nondisabled peers and the child's disability-specific needs (Curry & Hatlen, 1988). The MAP is the optimum choice for an individual child at any given time and may change periodically. For example, a young child who is developing braille readiness skills may need the intensity of specialized instruction in a preschool class designed for children who are visually impaired. That same child may be included in a general-education academic program later in life, once adequate braille skills are developed.

Proponents who believe that inclusion is the most desirable option for all children insist that integration with nondisabled peers is the main intent of the least restrictive environment clause of IDEA. The least restrictive environment for children who are visually impaired is that placement deemed best to meet all the child's educational needs (Hatlen, 1990). Integration with sighted peers is one among many considerations when determining an appropriate placement for a young child with a visual impairment. Hatlen maintains that the most accurate interpretation of least restrictive environment is "the educational placement which least restricts the child's opportunity to learn" (p. 2). For many children with visual impairments, early years spent in a specialized setting promote the learning of disability-specific core curriculum skills that will facilitate successful integration in later school years and in adult life in society (Corn, Hatlen, Huebner, Ryan, & Siller, 1995). IEP and IFSP decision-making teams must make careful determinations based on individualized, comprehensive, unbiased assessments. A child's placement should reflect those assessed needs and the family's priorities and realistic concerns.

Specially Trained Professionals

Infants, toddlers, and preschoolers who are visually impaired have many unique needs that are directly related to their disability. Incidental learning, which is primarily a function of vision in early childhood, is severely limited for the young child who is blind. For this reason, visually impaired infants, toddlers, and preschoolers require the specialized services of teachers of students who are visually impaired and O&M specialists, who have specialized training that enables them to readily adapt curricula, utilize effective methodologies, modify the environment, and address the special needs of the population (Hatlen & Curry, 1987). Without specialized training in the area of visual impairment, generic special educators and early childhood specialists, who in all likelihood may have strong backgrounds and contributions to make in the area of general development, may not have the knowledge base or experience necessary to provide appropriate programming for young children with visual impairments.

When investigating possible program options for young children who are visually impaired, the extent and quality of specially trained professional involvement should be thoroughly researched, including the availability, training, and backgrounds of relevant specialists and their experience with young children with visual impairments. This involvement is a key element in meeting the unique needs of children with this low-incidence disability and their families.

Class and Caseload Size

Class size and student-to-staff ratios are both important factors to consider in evaluating a center-based program's appropriateness for young children who are visually impaired. Young children who are totally blind require much one-on-one attention from staff. Many learning activities may initially be done "hand-under-hand" to assist children with tactile exploration, to model a new skill for children, or to support children's participation in a certain activity. Young blind children may miss some of the subtleties of activities that occur in close proximity, and, without careful attention and planning, obtain limited benefit from those activities that occur beyond their reach. Auditory cues received by these young children relate less useful information in comparison to the visual input received by children of similar ages with other disabilities. Ferrell (1996) notes: "According to some researchers, vision is usually involved in 90% of the learning that takes place in early development" (p. 89). Young students with low vision also require more individualized attention to help them attend to and interpret relevant visual information that is sometimes limited, inconsistent, and confusing. In both cases, these children can benefit from the additional time, attention, and thoughtful use of descriptions and materials given by teachers and assistants in classrooms with small teacher–student ratios.

Smaller, more manageable class sizes are often more appropriate for children who are visually impaired. Based on state and national averages, class sizes for classes designed specifically for visually impaired infants or preschool-aged children with one teacher and one assistant should range from four to eight students. Kindergarten class sizes should range from six to ten students (Hazekamp & Huebner, 1989; CA Program Guidelines, 1997). It is also important to consider that additional assistance from aides, related service staff, volunteers, families, or older students may be particularly beneficial during feeding, toileting, dressing, and field trips to the community.

It is equally important to consider caseload size of staff when selecting home-based programming for infants or preschool-aged children who are visually impaired. Large caseload sizes may be associated with a low frequency of direct service by qualified professionals. Based on state and national averages, a caseload range of 13 to 17 students should be considered an appropriate guideline (Hazenkamp & Huebner, 1989; CA Program Guidelines, 1997). Professionals who serve children and families on a consultation basis may have slightly higher caseloads since they are not providing as much direct service. Geographic areas and driving distances served by itinerant or home-based professionals can greatly impact caseload sizes and their manageability.

In recommending or selecting a program for a young child who is visually impaired, it is important to consider the family's preferences. Families have different lifestyles; economic, physical, and emotional supports; and resources. They need to be comfortable with the philosophies and staffing of the child's program as well as with the more logistical aspects such as location, funding, scheduling, and family involvement. The family's comfort ensures a more positive parent–professional collaboration as well as a more positive outcome for the child.

Professional Roles

TEACHER OF STUDENTS WHO ARE VISUALLY IMPAIRED

In programs for young children who are visually impaired, the teacher of students who are visually impaired is a vital team member. This specialist is particularly qualified in the following areas:

- providing input to programming decisions,

- reviewing possible program options and placements,

- completing specialized assessments, including a functional vision assessment,

- serving as a case manager, service manager, or program facilitator,

- adapting assessment materials and procedures for other professionals,

- interpreting medical and functional eye reports for related professionals and families,

- adapting curricular materials,

- securing adaptive materials and equipment for educational purposes,

- incorporating functional use of vision within daily routines at school or at home,

- providing in-service training to preschool staff and students,

- delivering direct services to children who are visually impaired and their families in center-based or home-based programs, and

- providing consultation to families and related professionals on such matters as assessment, programming, placement, curricula, and direct service.

In providing direct service to young children who are visually impaired, teachers of students who are visually impaired may address areas of child development on which vision loss has an impact. For infants who are visually impaired, particular emphasis may be placed on visual, auditory, tactile, olfactory, and kinesthetic sensory development. The teacher of students who are visually impaired may also be involved in providing enriching activities and environments that promote language development, play skills, and movement. Additionally, he or she provides direct support to families in areas of concern related to general caretaking, including feeding, diapering, and bathing.

When working with toddlers and preschoolers who are visually impaired, this teacher's focus may be adjusted to include more structured aspects of development. Braille readiness is one of the structured educational components that is incorporated into the teacher's area of direct service. The preschool-aged blind child may be introduced to exercises that promote tactile sensitivity, page orientation, and tracking ability in regard to braille reading. Young children may also begin experiencing the use of braillewriters, learning correct finger placement, and developing necessary finger strength. The teacher of students who are visually impaired might help the preschooler with low vision learn to use a magnifier or closed-circuit television (CCTV) for looking at letters and pictures and to develop page-orientation and line-tracking abilities. Training in the use of optical and non-optical low vision devices is an important area to address at this young age.

Although auditory development is important, and concern related to it should begin with the visually impaired infant, teachers of students who are visually impaired place emphasis on more formalized listening skills during the preschool years. These listening skills will ultimately lay part of the foundation for preacademic and later academic learning for the child who is visually impaired, and they are also important in nonacademic, functional areas of the curriculum. Preacademic skills are also addressed by the teacher of students who are visually impaired. He or she secures adaptive materials (including braille books, large-print materials, books on tape, and so on) and equipment (such as braillewriters, CCTVs, and specialized computers) in order to maximize the participation of preschoolers who are visually impaired in classrooms with sighted peers.

Teachers of students who are visually impaired also address concept development, which needs to be developed in a formal manner with young children who are visually impaired. They are also concerned with daily living skills (for example, eating, dressing, personal hygiene, personal organization, and toileting), which may not be acquired automatically by the child through observation. Social and emotional needs are addressed as the teacher supports the child in family and peer interactions while attempting to build social and play skills that facilitate the development of self-esteem. When necessary, these teachers may assist preschool staff and families with developing positive behavioral supports that may be applicable to some young children who are visually impaired. For example, preschool staff may be confused about their role in dealing with the mannerisms or repetitive behaviors (such as eye poking or rocking) of some young blind children. The teacher of students who are visually impaired may have to suggest appropriate strategies (such as providing alternative activities to provide the child with stimulation) to reduce such behaviors.

Aspects of communication that may need remediation, including receptive and expressive language, are important parts of the teacher's role because this specialist is very sensitive to the amount of nonverbal communication that young children who are visually impaired may miss. These teachers also understand the need to provide instruction in nonverbal communication so that children who are visually impaired are able to make use of appropriate gestures and facial expressions that are integral components of communication. Career awareness is another mandated area the specialist should begin to address during the preschool period. Through stories, field trips, and structured role-play, young children who are visually impaired can become familiar with the vast array of jobs that people do and how they do them. As the child who is visually impaired grows older, the teacher of students who are visually impaired continues to work to promote optimum sensory development and purposeful functional usage of those sensory capabilities, including functional use of vision.

O&M SPECIALIST

The O&M specialist is another vital team member in programs for young children who are visually impaired. The O&M specialist is particularly qualified in the following areas:

- conducting home or school environmental assessments to suggest modifications to enhance motivation for movement or to provide additional safety during independent movement,

- completing specialized assessments, including functional vision assessments and assessments of independent and semi-independent movements and orientation,

- adapting assessment materials and procedures for other specialists, such as physical therapists, occupational therapists, and adaptive physical educators,

- interpreting medical and functional eye reports for related professionals and families,

- providing in-service training for preschool staff and students, including the proper use of human guide,

- securing adaptive materials and equipment related to O&M,

- providing direct services to children who are visually impaired and their families in center or home-based programs, and

- serving as a consultant to families and related professionals.

In providing direct service to young children who are visually impaired, the O&M specialist may address movement-related areas of development affected by vision loss. For infants who are visually impaired, particular emphasis may be placed on visual, auditory, tactile, olfactory, and kinesthetic development. The O&M specialist should be involved in designing safe immediate and surrounding environments that may motivate increased exploration and movement. O&M specialists may also assist families in developing caretaking practices that encourage young children who are visually impaired to become active participants in activities of daily living.

When working with toddlers and preschoolers who are visually impaired, the O&M specialist may focus on developing safe and efficient forms of independent and semi-independent movement for the child. Instruction in basic skills (such as human guide, trailing, and protective techniques) for the child who is blind, the family, and associated friends and peers may begin during this period. It is also the role of the O&M specialist to introduce appropriate mobility devices for use within the home, at school, in the community, and during O&M lessons. The long cane, the most prominent mobility device, may be specially ordered or individually modified in accordance with the size, weight, and strength of the individual preschool child who is blind.

The O&M specialist may also address areas of concept development that have a direct impact on the child's motivation and ability to move about the environment. These areas may include body concepts, spatial relations, and environmental awareness. The foundations of map reading, map use, and personal-space organization may begin as a part of the O&M specialist's direct instruction. The specialist may also be involved in training young children in the use of low vision devices, especially such distance devices as monoculars and telescopes. It is the O&M specialist's role to develop and encourage the use of any existing vision that might improve the young child's functioning. Similarly, it is important to assist children who are visually impaired in developing the use of available auditory information for safe movement in the environment. (See Chapter 10 for specific suggestions in visual and auditory training related to O&M.)

Overlap of Roles and Services

Many other professionals, including pediatric ophthalmologists, optometrists specializing in low vision, PTs, OTs, speech therapists, psychologists, adaptive physical educators, social workers, counselors, nurses, special educators, early childhood interventionists, and general education teachers may be involved with young children who are visually impaired and their families. The extent of that involvement is most likely to depend on the individual needs of the child and his or her family, the availability of services in the area, and the administrative structure and philosophies of the social or educational program that is providing services.

Many of the roles for teachers of students who are visually impaired, O&M specialists, and related professionals seem to overlap or at least to closely shadow one another. This overlap may be in evidence especially when these professional's are working with infants who are visually impaired and their families. At this early stage in the child's life, all the professionals involved want to optimize the child's general development, which will ultimately have an impact on their specialty area. Efficacy studies in early intervention indicate that direct service by various specialists in the first 12 months of a disabled child's life is less significant than all professionals working collaboratively in a transdisciplinary team model. The most significant factor in the child's development at this age is the caregiver's involvement. Those children whose caregivers are significantly involved do better than those whose caregivers are not. Professionals who facilitate this caregiver involvement, rather than providing direct service with the infant, make the most impact (Rosetti, 2001). Professionals are jointly interested in supporting families and serving as resources to families who may need information or relevant contacts. It should not be surprising that many of their goals and objectives reflect this intent.

Professionals may often overlap in their direct service roles; because assessment of young children who are visually impaired frequently is not a clearly defined area of responsibility, overlap in assessment services may frequently be seen. Although it is accepted that teachers of students who are visually impaired are responsible for assessing braille readiness skills, what about areas of concept development that may overlap with areas of concern for the O&M specialist? Which specialist should assess body concepts? It is clearly accepted that the O&M specialist is responsible for assessing independent travel skills, but what about visual efficiency? And which specialist should assess functional vision? It is not always clear who is most appropriate to administer a given assessment or which is the most efficient way to complete a comprehensive assessment of the young child who is visually impaired. Roles can most easily be clarified when specialists communicate prior to developing an assessment plan and work together to achieve the most complete and accurate information regarding the child and family.

Professionals in related fields, who may be most qualified to do assessments of speech and fine and gross motor development, may be less familiar with the impact of vision loss than the teacher of students who are visually impaired and the O&M specialist are. When appropriate, these specialists should provide assistance to other professionals who are asked to assess the young child who is visually impaired (such as, suggesting modifications for assessment items that require vision, helping to interpret responses of young children with multiple disabilities, and assisting in the administration of assessments to increase the quantity and quality of students' responses). Suggestions for best positioning or seating, for optimum lighting and glare reduction, and for adaptation of assessment materials and procedures may help to obtain a more accurate picture of the visually impaired child's developmental potential. Assessments conducted cooperatively among teachers of students who are visually impaired, O&M specialists, and other professionals may increase the efficiency and accuracy of the overall assessment of the child. The sharing of information at the assessment level improves the ability of families and professionals to interpret the assessment results. Increased understanding of results, in turn, better enables team members to make appropriate programming decisions for the child who is visually impaired and the family.

In regard to assessment as well as service delivery, the transdisciplinary approach inherently reduces the amount of overlap of professional roles. When considerations of what is most appropriate for young children and their families come into play, the transdisciplinary model limits the number of different professionals who work directly with the young child and his family. As noted earlier in this chapter, professionals from different disciplines provide information, training, and consultation to the family members or staff members working directly with the child. This same kind of role release occurs during the assessment process, as professionals give input and make observations during assessment, but the number of specialists who actually perform the hands-on assessment is limited. In addition, the transdisciplinary model may limit the number of specialists with whom families must deal directly in the home, at school, or at agencies. For example, the teacher of students who are visually impaired may assume the primary service delivery role for a specific child. The occupational therapist or physical therapist may share specific positioning techniques for the child with the teacher, while the O&M specialist may provide consultation on environmental considerations at home. The family would deal consistently with just one professional, but that one professional would have the benefit of shared expertise from two others. The transdisciplinary model appropriates professional resources in a way that reduces the redundancy of service delivery in early childhood and enhances the ability of professionals to provide quality service to children in their caseload.

For agencies and educational systems that do not employ the transdisciplinary model, effective organization and open communication among professionals can be helpful in minimizing role overlap. In general, one key to diminishing assessment and direct service overlap is organization. The following suggestions may be helpful in reducing unnecessary overlap:

- Professionals can review assessment tools to identify potential overlap.

- Professionals can preplan assessments to identify who will address which areas.

- Professionals can conduct assessments together and combine observations.

- Professionals can share assessment results with one another.

When professionals work together to preplan and organize assessments, redundancy can be reduced or eliminated. When programming decisions are collaboratively made by families and professionals working together as a team, unnecessary direct service overlap can be eliminated before it is begun. Proper organization of staff resources should not only maximize the quality of service but also minimize the confusion often experienced by young children who are visually impaired and their families.

In situations where professional responsibilities do overlap, cooperation and open communication are essential. Exploring service delivery options together may help professionals more clearly define their individual roles with the young child who is visually impaired. Through open discussions, they may find that not all teachers of students who are visually impaired or O&M specialists are alike.

Although university training programs are similar in regard to many standards and competency areas, training at different universities may emphasize work with populations of different ages (adults, school-age or preschool children, or infants). Course offerings, such as electives in child development, early childhood special education, and parent–professional collaboration may be dependent on the expertise and interest of the university teaching staff or faculty in associated departments. Open discussions can help professionals to become more familiar with coworkers' backgrounds and training.

When working collaboratively, it is also important for professionals to explore previous teaching experiences with one another. These positive or negative experiences may have a genuine impact on specialists' skills, enthusiasm, and interest level in working with young children and their families. Sharing prior experiences may help to highlight individual teaching strengths and areas for support that are important to service delivery. Although many specialists may be well-rounded in training and experience, it is not unusual to find people who have developed strong interests in working with specific populations, teaching specific skills, or assessing specific areas of development in young children who are visually impaired. These areas of interest often blossom into areas of professional expertise and, when shared with others, can be a tremendous benefit to team functioning.

Service delivery models for young children with visual impairments and their families may vary in philosophy, structure, professional training, and assessment and service delivery approaches. A wide array of program options enables families and professionals to explore various models in order to determine the program that will most closely meet the assessed needs of a particular child who is visually impaired.

ADVOCACY FOR YOUNG CHILDREN WHO ARE VISUALLY IMPAIRED

Like other children, young children who are visually impaired have difficulty advocating for themselves. Thus the role of advocate or active supporter falls mainly on others who believe in and are concerned with the development of the young child. Families and professionals in the field of visual impairment must be the key advocates for infants, toddlers, and preschoolers who are visually impaired. Families and professionals working together as a team create the strongest advocacy force. The need for advocacy often arises when things are not going well. Advocacy can be the force for change to improve services, communication, laws, policies, and rights. It is through advocacy in its many forms that positive changes occur that can significantly influence the lives of young children who are visually impaired.

Families are often thrown into advocacy without the tools to be successful. They are often expected and forced to become advocates for their child when it is recognized that the child has a visual impairment. The first time parents become advocates may be at the hospital or with medical personnel when they are told to make difficult decisions about their child's medical needs. These decisions may have to be made when they are emotionally distraught or in shock. They learn very quickly that, in most cases, they are the ones ultimately required to make critical decisions on behalf of their child. They may feel intimidated by medical personnel and other "experts" who advise them on the best path. Without effective tools of advocacy, they may allow others to make decisions that may not always be in their child's best interest.

As the young child who is visually impaired grows older, families may need to advocate for appropriate intervention services; related services such as physical therapy, occupational therapy, or O&M; program options; and equipment and materials. Advocacy may occur in relation to the IFSP or IEP process by professionals and administrators, when goals and objectives are prioritized. Changes may occur at the local level in all these areas through effective advocacy. Parents should be made aware of their rights to due process so that they can have access to proper channels if there are unresolvable disagreements. Maintaining a nonadversarial attitude throughout any due process procedures and keeping the focus on the needs of the child help ensure ongoing team relationships between families and professionals.

Some families discover that advocacy within a local program does not bring about change, and they find themselves forced to advocate on a broader basis. Often the roadblocks to obtaining the necessary services for their child are outside local schools or agencies. These roadblocks may occur at the state or federal policy or legislative level. Advocating for changes in policy or law at the state or federal level can be started by one parent who feels a particular law or policy is harmful to his or her child, but most changes in the law come about through active support or advocacy on the part of many concerned individuals. There is usually, therefore, an initiator who recognizes that power exists in numbers. Joining together with other families of children who are visually impaired and sometimes with families of children with other disabilities creates a stronger voice to be heard by policymakers. Family members who become vocal advocates have made many significant changes in the law, including the passage of the original Education for All Handicapped Children Act. Families who believe their young child who is visually impaired should be taught by someone knowledgeable about the impact of vision loss on learning, for example, may advocate for changes in state teacher certification laws that do not require disability-specific credentialing for teachers who work with children who are visually impaired.

Professionals in the field of visual impairment, especially those who work with families of young children who are visually impaired, must take on the role of advocate as one of their primary roles. Because of the low prevalence of children who are visually impaired, few voices are speaking out who are knowledgeable about this population's unique needs. Strong voices are needed in working with medical and social service personnel, at the local school and agency level, and at the state and federal policymaking levels. Because of their unique expertise, specialized vision professionals are often the most qualified to facilitate needed changes. Professionals in the field of visual impairment no longer have the luxury of remaining apolitical. If they do not become active, vocal advocates for the children and families they serve, others less knowledgeable will make significant decisions that directly, and often negatively, affect the lives of children who are visually impaired.

The most powerful advocacy teams are those made up of both families and professionals. A professional who is knowledgeable about the laws, the system, and appropriate educational services and strategies, paired with a family member who knows what is best for his or her child and who has the passion and commitment to communicate these beliefs, form a voice that cannot easily be ignored. It is important in many situations that this team work together. It is also equally important that professionals assist families in obtaining their own advocacy tools so that when the families move on to other settings and advocacy arenas as their child gets older, they feel capable and competent to advocate on their own if they do not have a professional teammate. Effective advocacy tools may be used throughout the years as a child develops. It is also important that families and professionals begin giving the young child who is visually impaired his or her own advocacy tools and strategies as soon as possible so that the goal of self-advocacy can be realized. Ultimately, the child will have to learn how to advocate for changes on his or her own behalf.

There are a variety of arenas and ways in which one can be an advocate for young children who are visually impaired. These include:

Becoming an Advocate

➜ supporting IFSP or IEP development and implementation,

➜ ensuring that families know their due process rights,

➜ ensuring the availability of appropriate specialized personnel at the local level,

→ ensuring that appropriate medical and social services are available to families,

→ assisting with the recruitment of trainees for personnel preparation programs in the areas of visual impairment and O&M, with a focus on early childhood so that specialized personnel will be available,

→ joining professional or parent organizations,

→ staying informed about current issues and trends within the field by reading organizational newsletters, serving on boards, serving on legislative committees, and going to conferences,

→ assisting advocacy groups and organizations financially or by volunteering to raise funds for them,

→ educating friends, family members, and co-workers about the needs of children who are visually impaired and current problems, as they are the constituents of the decision makers,

→ meeting with state and federal legislators or their staff assistants to educate them about the needs of children who are visually impaired and current problems (families and professionals need to remember that they know more about this area than any public official making decisions),

→ writing letters, making phone calls, and sending e-mails on relevant policies and bills at the state or federal level that may affect children who are visually impaired,

→ writing editorials for local newspapers informing the public about the needs of children who are visually impaired and current problems with service delivery, policies, and laws,

→ participating as a member of interagency coordinating councils developed at local and state levels as a result of IDEA (as noted in Chapter 1, these councils often do not have representation by individuals knowledgeable about the unique needs of infants, toddlers, and preschoolers with visual impairments),

→ joining or forming coalitions of consumers, parents, professionals, and agencies with common concerns about the rights and needs of young children who are visually impaired, and

→ providing testimony at public hearings, hearings before legislative committees, or other public forums on any issues affecting young children who are visually impaired.

"Guidelines and Tools for Effective Advocacy," provides suggestions for professionals and families about how to make these efforts as effective as possible.

GUIDELINES AND TOOLS FOR EFFECTIVE ADVOCACY

Basic guidelines and tools for effective advocacy include the following:

➔ Be assertive in communicating concerns (not passive or aggressive).

➔ Have a clear goal in mind when asking for change—what is it specifically that you want?

➔ Have a brief written statement of your concern, proposed change or solution, and rationale ready to give to any policymaker who may be unfamiliar with the issue.

➔ Go through proper channels first to see if a problem can be solved at a lower level instead of going straight to the top.

➔ Find out who is responsible for current policy so that time is not wasted with the wrong persons.

➔ Utilize personal contact with public officials, if appropriate, in order to get to see them.

➔ Use a public relations approach by inviting a public official to speak at a meeting or event and inviting the media for publicity.

➔ Use positive, polite communication skills when advocating—do not be intimidating, argumentative, or condescending.

➔ Advocate with no more than two or three people at a time, with at least one articulate spokesperson and the others for support.

➔ When writing letters or meeting with policymakers, always ask for a response to your request or their position on the issue.

➔ Be prepared by doing your homework before a meeting, but if you do not know something, admit it, and offer to find out and get back to those present later.

➔ Negotiate, negotiate, negotiate! Realistic compromise without giving up your cause or principles is the key to successful advocacy.

Rona L. Pogrund

It is important to realize that not all individuals have the same time or energy available for advocacy. Some families may choose not to participate in advocacy activities, either because their focus and energy are directed toward more basic human needs, or because they simply prefer not to become involved. This is their right. Families and professionals alike may vary in their abilities to contribute to important causes at different times in their lives. If all individuals concerned about young children who are visually impaired are willing to do what they can, from testifying at a hearing to folding fliers at home for a mailing, the process of advocacy will be vital and effective. Everyone doing something is what makes the difference in effecting positive changes.

Realizing that most advocacy efforts do not create immediate changes helps one focus more realistically on the process of advocacy. Advocacy begins with the planting of seeds that over time and with nourishment lead to desired results. In the legislative arena, for example, the process often begins with focusing on the language of legislative intent, followed by mandating a law, followed by a budget bill that provides the necessary funding to carry out the original intent. Patience and persistence are essential to successful advocacy.

Momentary crises are what often fuel the fires of advocacy. It is, however, important to look ahead and to be farsighted in determining when one should be proactive for the future. Families and professionals advocating for the needs of infants, toddlers, and preschoolers should also be ensuring that programs, services, and safeguards for rights will be in place as these children enter future educational and rehabilitative arenas. Considering the evolutionary process of system change, it is important that a long-term perspective be taken as one clears the pathway for the young children who are visually impaired of today and ensures that appropriate services will be available for the children of the future.

REFERENCES

Adelson, E., & Fraiberg, S. (1974). Gross motor development in infants blind from birth. *Child Development, 45,* 114–126.

Adelson, E., & Fraiberg, S. (1977). Gross motor development. In S. Fraiberg (Ed.), *Insights from the blind: Comparative studies of blind and sighted infants.* New York: Basic Books.

American Academy of Pediatrics (1995). Injuries associated with infant walkers. *Pediatrics, 95*(5), 778–780.

American Academy of Pediatrics Task Force on Infant Positioning and SIDS (1992). Positioning and SIDS. *Pediatrics, 89,* 1120–1126.

Anastasiow, N. (1986). Cultural differences in the development of meanings and use of language. In N. Anastasiow (Ed.), *Development and disability* (pp. 183–209). Baltimore: Paul H. Brookes.

Anderson, P., & Fenichel, E. (1989). *Serving culturally diverse families of infants and toddlers with disabilities.* Washington, D.C.: National Center for Clinical Infant Programs.

Anthony, T. (1992). Body image and spatial relationships. In R. L. Pogrund, D. L. Fazzi, & J. S. Lampert, (Eds.) *Early focus: Working with young blind and visually impaired children and their families, Movement Focus Chapter* (pp. 85–88). New York: AFB Press.

Anthony, T. (1993). Orientation and mobility skill development. In *First steps: A handbook for teaching young children who are visually impaired* (pp. 115–138). Los Angeles: Blind Childrens Center.

Anthony, T. (1998). Sensory learning: A framework of early O&M skill development. In E. Siffermann, M. Williams, & B. B. Blasch (Eds.) Conference proceedings: The ninth International Mobility Conference (pp. 279–280). Atlanta, GA: Rehabilitation Research and Development Center.

Ashcroft, S. C., Henderson, F., Sanford, L., & Koenig, A. J. (1991). *New programmed instruction in braille.* Nashville: SCALARS Publishing.

Ashcroft, S. C., Sanford, L., & Koenig, A. J. (2001). *New programmed instruction in braille* (3rd ed.). Nashville, TN: SCALARS Publishing.

Asher, S. R., Renshaw, P. D., & Hymel, S. (1982). Peer relations and the development of social skills. In S. G. Moore & C. R. Cooper (Eds.), *The young child: Reviews of research* (Vol. 3) (pp. 137–158). Washington, DC: National Association for the Education of Young Children.

Atkinson, J. (2000). *The developing visual brain.* New York: Oxford University Press.

Ayres, A. J. (1989). *Sensory integration and praxis tests.* Los Angeles: Western Psychological Services.

Bagnato, S. J., Neisworth, J. T., & Munson, S. M. (1997). *LINKing assessment and early intervention: An authentic curriculum-based approach.* Baltimore: Paul H. Brookes.

Barraga, N. (1976). *Visual handicaps and learning: A developmental approach.* Belmont, CA: Wadsworth.

Barraga, N. (1980). *Program to develop efficiency in visual functioning.* Louisville: American Printing House for the Blind.

Bayley, N. (1993). *Bayley scales of infant development II* (2nd ed.). San Antonio, TX: The Psychological Corporation.

Bayley, N. (2001). *Bayley scales of infant development (BSID-II): Motor Scale Kit* (2nd ed.). San Antonio, TX: Psychological Corporation.

Berenson, A., Wiemann, C. M., Rowe, T. F., & Rickert, V. I. (1997). Inadequate weight gain among pregnant adolescents: Risk factors and relationship to infant birth weight. *American Journal of Obstetrics and Gynecology, 176,* 1220–1227.

Blind Babies Foundation (1998). *Pediatric visual diagnosis fact sheets.* San Francisco, CA: Blind Babies Foundation.

Bly, L. (1980). *The components of normal movement during the first year of life.* Chapel Hill, NC: University of North Carolina.

Bobath, K., & Bobath, B. (1964). The facilitation of normal postural reactions and movements in the treatment of cerebral palsy. *Physiotherapy, 50,* 246–252.

Bolinger, R., & Bolinger, C. (1996). Family life. In M. C. Holbrook (Ed.), *Children with visual impairments: A parent's guide* (pp. 129–158). Bethesda, MD: Woodbine House.

Boykin, W., & Toms, F. (1985). Black child socialization. In H. P. McAdoo & J. L. McAdoo (Eds.), *Black children: Social, educational, and parental environments.* Beverly Hills, CA: Sage Publications.

Brazelton, T. B., & Cramer, B. G. (1990). *The earliest relationship: Parents, infants, and the drama of early attachment.* New York: Addison-Wesley Publishing.

Brigance, A. H. (1991). *BRIGANCE Diagnostic Inventory of Early Development—Revised (BDIED-R).* North Billerica, MA: Curriculum Associates.

Brown, C., & Bour, B. (1986) *Movement analysis curriculum.* Tallahassee, FL: Florida State Department of Education.

Brown, D., Simmons, V. Methvin, J., Anderson, S., Boigon, S., & Davis, K. (1991). *Oregon project for visually impaired and blind preschoolers.* Medford, OR: Jackson County Education Service District.

Brown, K. A., Wacker, D. P., Derby, K. M., Peck, S. M., Richman, D. M., Sasso, G. M., Knutson, C. L., & Harding, J. W. (2000). Evaluating the effects of functional communication training in the presence and absence of establishing operations. *Journal of Applied Behavior Analysis, 33,* 53–71.

Bruder, M. B. (2001). Natural environments: Expanding and enhancing learning opportunities for infants and toddlers. Presentation at Early Childhood Intervention Statewide Conference, April 30–May 2, 2001, Austin, TX.

Brugge, J. (1996). The inner ear: Vestibular apparatus (Chapter VII). Unpublished teaching manual for course entitled "Hearing and Balance"—University of Wisconsin. (www.neurophys.wisc.edu/h&b/index/htm/).

Bruner, J. S. (1974). From communication to language: A psychological perspective. *Cognition, 3,* 225–287.

Bruner, J. S. (1982). The organization of action and the nature of the adult–infant transaction. In E. Tronick (Ed.), *Social interchange in infancy: Affect, cognition and communication* (pp. 23–35). Baltimore: Paul H. Brookes.

Bruner, J. S. (1973). Competence in infants. In J. Anglin (Ed.), *Beyond the information given: Studies in the psychology of knowing.* New York: Norton.

Bruner, J. S. (1982). The organization of action and the nature of the adult-infant transaction. In E. Tronick (Ed.) *Social interchange in infancy* (pp. 23–35). Baltimore, MD: University Park Press.

Bunker, L. K. (1991). The role of play and motor skill development in building young children's self-confidence and self-esteem. *Elementary School Journal, 91,* 467–471.

California Deaf-Blind Services (2002). Neurological visual impairment. Fact sheet #022: (www.sfsu.edu/~cadbs/Eng022.html).

California Department of Education (1997).

Program guidelines for students who are visually impaired (rev. edition). Sacramento, CA: California Department of Education.

Callier-Azusa Scale (1978). Dallas: University of Texas at Dallas, Callier Center for Communication Disorders.

Cambourne, B. (1988). *The whole story: Natural learning and the acquisition of literacy in the classroom.* Auckland, NZ: Ashton Scholastic.

Campbell, P. H. (1982). *Introduction to neurodevelopmental treatment.* unpublished manuscript.

Campbell, P. H. (1983). Basic considerations in programming for students with movement difficulties. In M. Snell (Ed.), *Systematic instruction of the moderately and severely handicapped* (2nd ed.). New York: Charles E. Merrill Publishing.

Carnegie Corporation of New York (1994). *Starting points: Meeting the needs of our youngest children.* New York: Author.

Carr, E. G. (1994). Emerging themes in the functional analysis of problem behavior. *Journal of Applied Behavior Analysis, 27,* 393–399.

Carr, E. G. & Durand, V. M. (1985). Reducing behavior problems through functional communication training. *Journal of Applied Behavioral Analysis, 18,* 111–126.

Carriero, P., & Townsend, S. (1987). Routines: Understanding their power. In D. Frans (Ed.), *Teaching curriculum goals in routine environments* (pp. 1–13). Edmonton, Alberta, Canada: Cone Learning Systems.

Castellano, C., & Kosman, D. (1997). *The bridge to braille: Reading and school success for the young blind child.* Baltimore: National Organization of Parents of Blind Children.

Chan, S. (1992). Families with Asian roots. In M. Hanson & E. Lynch (Eds.), *Developing cross-cultural competence: A guide for working with young children and their families.* Baltimore: Paul Brookes.

Chen, D. (1997a). *Vision tests for infants.* (video). New York: AFB Press.

Chen, D. (1997b). *What can baby see? Vision tests and intervention strategies for infants with multiple disabilities* (video). New York: AFB Press.

Chen, D. (1999a). Center-based programs for infants with visual impairments and their families: "Natural" or "unnatural" learning environments? *Journal of Visual Impairment & Blindness, 93* (6), 390–392.

Chen, D. (Ed.), (1999b). *Essential elements in early intervention: Visual impairment and multiple disabilities.* New York: AFB Press.

Chen, D., & Dote-Kwan, J. (1995). *Starting points.* Los Angeles: Blind Childrens Center.

Chen, D., & Dote-Kwan, J. (1998). Early intervention services for young children who have visual impairments with other disabilities. In S. Z. Sacks & R. K. Silberman (Eds.), *Educating students who have visual impairments with other disabilities* (pp. 303–338). Baltimore: Paul H Brookes.

Chen, D., & Dote-Kwan, J. (1999). Conveying high expectations. In K. E. Wolffe (Ed.), *Skills for success: A career education handbook for children and adolescents with visual impairments* (pp. 47–76). New York: AFB Press.

Chen, D., & Schacter, P. H. (1997). *Making the most of early communication with infants, toddlers and preschoolers whose multiple disabilities include vision and hearing loss.* (video companion booklet). New York: AFB Press.

Cheng, L. L. (1993). Asian-American cultures. In D. E. Battle (Ed.), *Communication disorders in multicultural populations,* (pp. 38–77). Stoneham, MA: Butterworth-Heinemann.

Chimm, S.-H. (1989). *Introduction to Cambodian culture.* San Diego, CA: San Diego

State University Multifunctional Service Center.

Chomsky, N. (1965). *Aspects of the theory of syntax.* Cambridge, MA: MIT Press.

Clarke, K. (1988) Barriers or enablers? Mobility devices for visually impaired and multihandicapped infants and preschoolers. *Education of the Visually Handicapped, 20*(3), 115–130.

Cohen, R. A. (1992). Family issues—professional viewpoint. In R. L. Pogrund, D. L. Fazzi, & J. S. Lampert (Eds.). *Early focus: Working with young blind and visually impaired children and their families.* New York: AFB Press.

Corn, A. L. (1983). Visual function: A theoretical model for individuals with low vision. *Journal of Visual Impairment & Blindness, 77*(8), 373–377.

Corn, A. L., & Ferrell, K. A. (2000). External funding for training and research in university programs in visual impairments: 1997–1998. *Journal of Visual Impairment & Blindness, 94,* 374–384.

Corn, A. L., Hatlen, P., Huebner, K.M., Ryan, F., & Siller, M. (1995). *The national agenda for the education of children and youths with visual impairments, including those with multiple disabilities.* New York: AFB Press.

Corn, A. L., & Silberman, R. K. (1999). Personnel preparation programs in visual impairments: A status report. *Journal of Visual Impairment & Blindness, 93,* 755–769.

Council for Exceptional Children. (2000). *National plan for training personnel to serve children with blindness and low vision.* Reston, VA: Council for Exceptional Children.

Cowley, G. (2000). For the love of language. *Newsweek, Fall/Winter,* 12–15.

Cratty, B. (1971). *Movement and spatial awareness in blind children and youth.* Springfield, IL: Charles C. Thomas.

Crossman, H. L. (1992). *Cortical visual impairment presentation, assessment, and management.* (Monograph Series No. 3). North Rocks, New South Wales, Australia: The Royal New South Wales Institute for Deaf and Blind Children.

Cryotherapy for Retinopathy of Prematurity Cooperative Group (1990). Multicenter trial of cryotherapy for retinopathy of prematurity: One year outcome structure and function. *Arch Ophthalmol, 108,* 1408–1416.

Curran, E. (1988). *Just enough to know better: A braille primer.* Boston: National Braille Press.

Curry, S. A., & Hatlen, P. H. (1988). Meeting the unique educational needs of visually impaired pupils through appropriate placement. *Journal of Visual Impairment & Blindness, 82*(10), 417–424.

Cutsforth, T. D. (1951). *The blind in school and society.* New York: AFB Press.

D'Andrea, F. M., & Farrenkopf, C. (Eds.). (2000). *Looking to learn: Promoting literacy for students with low vision.* New York: AFB Press.

D'Arcangelo, M. (2000). How does the brain develop? A conversation with Steven Petersen. *Educational Leadership, 58*(3), 68–71.

Davidson, P., & Harrison, G. (1997). The effectiveness of early intervention for children with visual impairments. In M. Guralnick (Ed.), *The Effectiveness of Early Intervention* (pp. 483–495). Baltimore: Paul H. Brookes.

DePaepe, P., Reichle, J., & O'Neill, R. (1993). Applying general-case instructional strategies when teaching communicative alternatives to challenging behavior. In J. Reichle & D. P. Wacker (Eds.), *Communicative alternatives to challenging behavior: Integrating functional assessment and intervention strategies* (pp. 237–262). Baltimore: Paul H. Brookes.

Derman-Sparks, L. (1989). *Anti-biased curriculum: Tools for empowering young children.* Washington, D.C.: National Association for the Education of Young Children.

Dietz, S. & Ferrell, K. A. (1993). Early services for young children with visual impairment: From diagnosis to comprehensive services. *Infants and young children, 6*(1), 68–76.

Dodge, K. A. (1983). Behavioral antecedents of peer social status. *Child Development, 54*, 1386–1399.

Donnellan, A. M., Mirenda, P. L., Mesaros, R. A. & Fassbender, L. L. (1984). Analyzing the communicative functions of aberrant behaviors. *Journal of the Association for the Severely Handicapped, 9*, 201–212.

Dorf, M. (1985). *Instruction manual for braille transcribing* (3rd ed.). Washington: Library of Congress.

Dote-Kwan, J. (1995). Impact of mothers' interactions on the development of their young visually impaired children. *Journal of Visual Impairment & Blindness, 89*, 47–58.

Dote-Kwan, J., Chen, D., & Hughes, M. (2001). A national survey of service providers who work with young children with visual impairments. *Journal of Visual Impairment & Blindness, 95*, 325–337.

Duke-Elder, S., & Cook, S. (1963). *System of Ophthalmology* (Vol. III, part 1) (pp. 292–316). London: H. Kingston.

Dunnett, J. (1997). Neilson's Little Room: Its use with a young blind and physically disabled girl. *Journal of Visual Impairment & Blindness, 91*(2), 145–150.

Eisenberg, A. (1982). *Language development in cultural perspective: Talk in three Mexican homes*. Unpublished dissertation. Berkley, CA: University of California, Berkley.

Erin, J. (1990). *A unique learner: A manual for instruction of the child with visual and multiple disabilities*. Austin, TX: Education Service Center, Region XIII.

Erin, J. (1996). Functional vision assessment and instruction of children and youth with multiple disabilities. In A. Corn and A. Koenig (Eds.), *Foundations of low vision: Clinical and functional perspectives* (pp. 221–245). New York: AFB Press.

Erin, J. (2000). Students with visual impairments and additional disabilities. In A. J. Koenig & M. C. Holbrook (Eds.) *Foundations of education* (2nd ed.), Vol. 2: *Instructional strategies for teaching children and youths with visual impairments* (pp. 720–752). New York: AFB Press.

Espezel, H., & Jan, J. E. (1996). The use of melatonin to treat sleep-wake-rhythm disorders in children who are visually impaired. *Journal of Visual Impairment & Blindness, 90*(1), 43–51.

Falvey, M. A. (1986). *Community-based curriculum: Instructional strategies for students with severe handicaps*. Baltimore: Paul H. Brookes.

Farber, S. (1982). A multisensory approach to neurorehabilitation. In S. Farber (Ed.) *A multisensory approach* (pp. 115–176). Philadelphia: W.B. Saunders Company.

Fazzi, D. L. (1993). *Examining young blind children's perceptions of relationships within the social network*. Unpublished dissertation. Los Angeles: University of California, Los Angeles.

Fazzi, D. L. (1995) Orientation and mobility for young children with multiple disabilities. In D. Chen & J. Dote-Kwan (Eds.) *Starting points: Instructional practices for young children whose multiple disabilities include visual impairment* (pp. 89–98). Los Angeles: Blind Childrens Center.

Fazzi, D. L. (1998). Facilitating independent travel for students who have visual impairments with other disabilities. In S. Z. Sacks & R. K. Silberman (Eds.) *Educating students who have visual impairments with other disabilities* (pp. 441–468). Baltimore: Paul H. Brookes.

Fazzi, D. L., & Petersmeyer, B. A. (2001). *Imagining the possibilities: Creative approaches to orientation and mobility instruc-*

tion for persons who are visually impaired. New York: AFB Press.

Ferrell, K. A. (1985). *Reach out and teach: Meeting the training needs of parents of visually and multiply handicapped young children.* New York: AFB Press.

Ferrell, K. A. (1996). Your child's development. In M.C. Holbrook (Ed.), *Children with visual impairments: A parent's guide* (pp. 73–96). Bethesda, MD: Woodbine House.

Ferrell. K. A. (1998). *Project PRISM: A longitudinal study of developmental patterns of children who are visually impaired (final report).* Greeley's Division of Special Education, University of Northern Colorado.

Ferrell, K. A. (2000). Growth and development of young children. In M. C. Holbrook & A. J. Koenig (Eds.) *Foundations of education.* Vol. 1: *History and theory of teaching children and youths with visual impairments* (2nd ed.), (pp. 111–134). New York: AFB Press.

Ferrell, K. A., & Muir, D. W. (1996). A call to end vision stimulation training. *Journal of Visual Impairment & Blindness, 90,* 364–365.

Feuerstein, R., Rand, Y., Hoffman, M., & Miller, R. (1980). *Instrumental enrichment.* Baltimore: University Park Press.

Foster, A., & Gilbert, C. (1997). Epidemiology of visual impairment in children. In D. Taylor (Ed.), *Paediatric Ophthalmology* (2nd ed.). Oxford: Blackwell Science.

Fraiberg, S. (1968). Parallel and divergent patterns in blind and sighted infants. *Psychoanalytic Study of the Child, 23,* 264–300.

Fraiberg, S. (1977). *Insights from the blind.* New York: Basic Books.

Franklin, A., & Boyd-Franklin, N. (1985). A psychoeducational perspective on black parenting. In H. P. McAdoo & J. L. McAdoo (Eds.), *Black children: Social, educational, and parental environments.* Beverly Hills, CA: Sage Publications.

Freeman, D. (1972). *Corduroy.* New York: Penguin Putnam.

Furuno, S., O'Reilly, K. A., Hosaka, C. M., Inatsuka, T. T., Allman, T. L., & Zeisloft, B. (1979). *Hawaii early learning profile (HELP): activity guide. Enrichment Project for Handicapped Infants.* Palo Alto, CA: VORT Corp.

Gallimore, R., Weisner, T. S., Kaufman, S., & Bernheimer, L. P. (1989). The social construction of ecocultural niches: Family accommodation of developmentally delayed children. *American Journal on Mental Retardation, 94,* 216–230.

Gallivan-Fenton, A. (1994). Integrated transdisciplinary teams. *Teaching Exceptional Children, 26*(3), 16–20.

Galloway, A. (1981). *Orientation and mobility readiness for the preschool deaf-blind child* (pp. 51–59). San Gabriel Valley School for Multiply Handicapped.

Gesell, A. (1946). *The child from five to ten.* New York: Harper & Row.

Gessell, A. (1970). The ontogenesis of infant behavior. In P. H. Mussen (Ed.), *Carmichael's Manual of Child Psychology* (3rd ed.). New York: Whiley Press.

Gollnick, D. M., & Chinn, P. C. (1990). *Multicultural education in a pluralistic society.* Columbus, OH: Macmillan.

Gollnick, D. M., & Chinn, P. C. (1994). *Multicultural education in a pluralistic society* (4th ed.). Columbus, OH: Macmillan.

Gollnick, D. M. & Chinn, P.C. (2002). *Multicultural education in a pluralistic society* (6th Ed.). Upper Saddle River, NJ: Merrill.

Greey, M. (1994). *Honouring diversity: A cross-cultural approach to infant development for babies with special needs.* Toronto: Centennial Infant and Child Centre.

Greeley, J. (1997). Developmentally supportive care: Hospital to home for the infant with deaf-blindness. In *Workshop Proceedings, Vol. 1, The individual in a changing society* (pp. 292–301). Reno, NV: Hilton/Perkins Program.

Greeley, J., & Anthony, T. (1995). Play interaction with infants and toddlers who are deafblind: Setting the stage. *Seminars in Hearing, 16*(2), 1985–1991.

Greenspan, S. I., & Meisels, S. J. (1996). Toward a new vision for the developmental assessment of infants and young children. In S. J. Meisels & E. Fenichel (Eds.), *New visions for the developmental assessment of infants and young children* (pp. 11–26). Washington, DC: Zero to Three/National Center for Infants, Toddlers, and Families.

Greenspan, S., & Wieder, S. (1997). Learning to interact. *Scholastic Early Childhood Today, 12*(3), 23–24.

Guide to toys for children who are blind or visually impaired (2002). New York: AFB Press.

Hagood, L. (1997). *Communication: A guide for teaching students with visual and multiple impairments*. Austin, TX: Texas School for the Blind and Visually Impaired.

Hanson, M. J., & Lynch, E. W. (1995). *Early intervention: Implementing child and family services for infants and toddlers who are at risk or disabled* (2nd ed.). Austin, TX: Pro-Ed.

Harrell, L. (1992). Hospitalization issues. In R. L. Pogrund, D. L. Fazzi, & J. S. Lampert (Eds.) *Early Focus: Working with young blind and visually impaired children and their families*. New York: AFB Press.

Harry, B. (1992). Developing cultural self-awareness: The first step in values clarification for early interventionists. *Topics in Early Childhood Special Education, 12*(3), 333–350.

Harry, B., Kalyanpur, M., & Day, M. (1999). *Building cultural reciprocity with families: Case studies in special education*. Baltimore: Paul H. Brookes.

Hatlen, P. H. (February, 1990). Testimony presented to the Least Restrictive Environment Study Team of the Los Angeles Unified School District for the Joint Action Committee of Organizations Of and Serving the Visually Handicapped.

Hatlen, P. (1996). The core curriculum for blind and visually impaired students, including those with additional disabilities. *RE:View, 28*, 25–32.

Hatlen, P. H., & Curry, S. A. (1987). In support of specialized programs for visually impaired children: The impact of vision loss on learning. *Journal of Visual Impairment & Blindness, 81*(1), 7–13.

Hatton, D. D. (2001). Model registry of early childhood visual impairment: First-year results. *Journal of Visual Impairment & Blindness, 95*, 418–433.

Hatton, D. D., Bailey, D. B., Burchinel, M. R., & Ferrell, K. A. (1997). Developmental growth curves of preschool children with visual impairments. *Child Development, 68*, 788–806.

Hauser-Cram, P., & Krauss, M. W. (1991). Measuring change in children and families. *Journal of Early Intervention, 15*, 304–313.

Hazekamp, J., & Huebner, K. M. (1989). *Program planning and evaluation for blind and visually impaired students: National guidelines for educational excellence*. New York: AFB Press.

Heath, S. B. (1983). *Ways with words: Language, life and work in communities and classrooms*. Cambridge, UK: Cambridge University Press.

Herring, J. (1996). Adjusting to your child's visual impairment. In M. C. Holbrook (Ed.), *Children with visual impairments: A parent's guide* (pp. 129–158). Bethesda, MD: Woodbine House.

Hill, E. W. (1986). Orientation and mobility. In G. T. Scholl (Ed.), *Foundation of education for blind and visually handicapped children and youth* (pp. 315–340). New York: AFB Press.

Hill, E. W., Dodson-Burk, B., & Smith, B. (1989). Orientation and mobility for infants who are visually impaired. *RE:view, 21*(2), 47–59.

Hill, E. W., & Ponder, P. (1976). *Orientation and mobility techniques: A guide for the practitioner.* New York: AFB Press.

Hill, E. W., Rosen, S., Correa, V. I., & Langley, M. B. (1984). Preschool O&M: An expanded definition. *Education of the Visually Handicapped, 16*(2), 58–71.

Hill, E. W., Smith, B., Dodson-Burk, B., & Rosen, S. (1987). O&M for preschool visually impaired children. In *AER Yearbook* (pp. 8–12). Washington, DC: Association for Education and Rehabilitation of the Blind and Visually Impaired.

Holbrook, M. C. (1996). *Children with visual impairments: A parent's guide.* Bethesda, MD: Woodbine House.

Holmgren test for color blindness (1995–1996). Southbridge, PA: American Optical Company.

Holstrom, G., el Azizi, M., Jacobson, L., & Lennerstrand, G. (1993). A population based prospective study of the development of ROP in prematurely born children in the Stockholm area of Sweden. *British Journal of Ophthalmology, 77,* 417–423.

Holzhauser-Peters, L., & Husemann, D. A. (1988). Alternative service delivery models for more efficient and effective treatment programs. *Clinical Connection, 3*(2), 16–19.

Huebner, K. M., Prickett, G., Welch, T. R., & Joffee, E. (Eds.). (1995). *Hand in hand: Essentials of communication and orientation and mobility for your students who are deaf-blind.* New York: AFB Press.

Hutchinson, D. A. (1974). A model for transdisciplinary staff development. In *A nationally organized collaborative program for the provision of comprehensive services to atypical infants and their families* (Technical Report No, 8). New York: United Cerebral Palsy Association.

Hyvarinen, L. (1995–1996). *Vision testing manual.* Orlando, FL: Vision Associates.

Isenberg, S. J. (1989). *The eye in infancy.* Chicago: Year Book Medical Publishers.

Jan, J., Robinson, G. C., Scott, E., & Kinnis, C. (1975). Hypotonia in the blind child. *Developmental Medicine and Child Neurology, 17,* 35–40.

Joe, J. R., & Malach, R. S. (1998). Families with native American roots. In M. Hanson & E. Lynch (Eds.) *Developing cross-cultural competence: A guide to working with young children and their families* (2nd ed.), (pp. 127–164). Baltimore: Paul H. Brookes.

Joffee, E. (1988). A home-based orientation and mobility program for infants and toddlers. *Journal of Visual Impairment & Blindness, 82*(7), 282–285

Johnson, K., Griffin-Shirley, N., & Koenig, A. (2000). Active learning for children with visual impairments and additional disabilities. *Journal of Visual Impairment & Blindness, 94,* 584–594.

Johnson-Martin, N., Jens, K., & Attermeier, S. (1986). *The Carolina curriculum for handicapped infants and infants at risk.* Baltimore: Paul H. Brookes.

Kalyanpur, M. & Harry, B. (1999). *Culture in special education: Building reciprocal family–professional relationships.* Baltimore: Paul H. Brookes.

Kasai, T. (1991). An empirical note on tonic neck reflexes: Control of the upper limb's proprioceptive sensation. *Perceptual and Motor Skills, 72,* 955–961.

Kastein, S., Spaulding, I., & Scharf, B. (1980). *Raising the young blind child: A guide for parents and educators.* New York: Human Science Press.

Kekelis, L. S. (1992). Peer interactions in childhood: The impact of visual impairment. In S. Z. Sacks, L. S. Kekelis, & R. J. Gaylord Ross (Eds.), *The development of social skills by blind and visually impaired students: Exploratory studies and strategies* (pp. 13–35). New York: AFB Press.

Kekelis, L. S., & Sacks, S. Z. (1988). Mainstreaming visually impaired children into regular education: The effects of visual impairment on children's interactions with peers. In S. Z. Sacks, L. S. Keke-lis, & R. J. Gaylord-Ross (Eds.), *The development of social skills by visually impaired children*. San Francisco: San Francisco State University.

Kirk, S. A. (1992). Social focus: Developing socioemotional, play, and self-help skills in young blind and visually impaired children. In R. L. Pogrund, D. L. Fazzi, & J. S. Lampert (Eds.), *Early focus: Working with young blind and visually impaired children and their families* (pp. 61–65). New York: AFB Press.

Klein, M. D. (2001). Early communication development and role of caregiver-child interaction. On-line learning module. Northridge, CA: California State University, Northridge, Department of Special Education.

Klein, M. D., & Chen, D. (2001). *Working with children from culturally diverse backgrounds*. Albany, NY: Delmar.

Klein, M. D., Chen, D., & Haney, M. (2000). *Promoting learning through active interaction*. Baltimore: Paul H. Brookes.

Koenig, A. J. (1996). Growing into literacy. In M. C. Holbrook (Ed.), *Children with visual impairments: A parents' guide* (pp. 227–257). Baltimore: Woodbine House.

Koenig, A. J., & Holbrook, M. C. (2000a). Assuring quality literacy instruction in braille literacy programs. *Journal of Visual Impairment & Blindness, 94,* 677–694.

Koenig, A. J., & Holbrook, M. C. (2000b). Literacy skills. In A. J. Koenig & M. C. Holbrook (Eds.), *Foundations of education: Instructional strategies for teaching children and youths with visual impairments* (2nd ed.) (pp. 264–329). New York: AFB Press.

Kohn, M. L. (1977). *Class and conformity* (2nd ed.). Chicago: University of Chicago Press.

Kukla, D., & Thomas, T. (1978) *Assessment of auditory functioning of deaf-blind multi-handicapped children*. South Central Regional Center for Services to Deaf-Blind Children.

Lamb, G. (1996). Beginning braille: A whole language-based strategy. *Journal of Visual Impairment & Blindness, 90*(3), 184–189.

Lampert, J. S. (1992). Movement focus: Orientation and mobility in young blind and visually impaired children. In R. L. Pogrund, D. L. Fazzi, & J. S. Lampert (Eds.), *Early focus: Working with young blind and visually impaired children and their families* (pp. 61–65). New York: AFB Press.

Langley, M. B. (1980). *Peabody functional vision inventory for the multiple and severely handicapped*. Chicago: Stoelting.

Langley, M. B. (1998). *Individualized systematic assessment of visual efficiency*. Louisville, KY: American Printing House for the Blind.

LaPrelle, L. L. (1996). *Standing on my own two feet*. Los Angeles: Blind Childrens Center.

Leong, S. (1996). Preschool orientation and mobility: A review of the literature. *Journal of Visual Impairment & Blindness, 90*(2), 145–153.

Laskowski, E. R, Newcomer-Aney, K., & Smith, J. (1997). Refining rehabilitation with proprioception training: Expediting return to play. *The Physician and Sports Medicine, 24*(10), 89–98.

Lerner, P. S. (1995). Attention deficit disorder—attention deficit hyperactivity disorder: A developmental approach. (www.add_adhd.org/attention_deficits_ADHD.htm. Accessed 02–12–02).

Levack, N. (1994). *Low vision: A resource guide with adaptations for students with visual impairments* (2nd ed.). Austin. TX: Texas School for the Blind and Visually Impaired.

Lieberman, A. F. (1993). *The emotional life of the toddler*. New York: The Free Press.

Linder, T. (1993). *Transdisciplinary play-based assessment: A functional approach to working with young children*. Baltimore: Paul H. Brookes.

Luangpraseut, K. (1989). *Laos, culturally speaking*. San Diego: San Diego State University Multifunctional Service Center.

Lueck, A. H. (1998). Incorporating unique learning requirements into the design of instructional strategies for students with visual and multiple impairments: The basis for an expanded core curriculum. *RE:View, 30,* 101–116.

Lueck, A. H., Chen, D., & Kekelis, L. S. (1997). *Developmental guidelines for visually impaired infants: A manual for infants birth to two*. Louisville, KY: American Printing House for the Blind.

Lynch, E. W., & Hanson, M. J. (1992). *Developing cross-cultural competence*. Baltimore: Paul H. Brookes.

Lynch, E. W., & Hanson, M. J. (1998). *Developing cross-cultural competence: A guide for working with young children and their families* (2nd ed.), Baltimore: Paul H. Brookes.

Lyon, S., & Lyon, G. (1980). Team functioning and staff development: A role release approach to providing integrated educational services for severely handicapped students. *Journal of the Association for the Severely Handicapped, 5*(30), 250–263.

Mace, F. C., & Roberts, M. L. (1993). Factors affecting selection of behavioral interventions. In J. Reichle & D.P. Wacker (Eds.), *Communicative alternatives to challenging behavior: integrating functional assessment and intervention strategies* (pp. 113–133). Baltimore: Paul H. Brookes.

Mahoney, G., Boyce, G., Fewell, R. R., Spiker, D., & Wheeden, C. A. (1998). The relationship of parent–child interaction to the effectiveness of early intervention services for at-risk children and children with disabilities. *Topics in Early Childhood Special Education, 18,* 5–17.

Maida, S. O., & McCune, L. (1996). A dynamic systems approach to the development of crawling by blind and sighted infants. *RE:View, 28,* 119–135.

March of Dimes Perinatal Data Center (2000). *1999–2000 March of Dimes Birth Defects Foundation*.

Marks, S. B. (1998). Understanding and preventing learned helplessness in children who are congenitally deaf-blind. *Journal of Visual Impairment & Blindness, 92,* 200–211.

McCollum, J. A., & Hughes, M. (1988). Staffing patterns and team models in infancy programs. In J. B. Jordan, J. J. Gallagher, P. L. Hutinger, & M. B. Kanes (Eds.), *Early childhood special education: Birth to three* (pp. 129–146). Reston, VA: Council for Exceptional Children.

McCuspie, P. A. (1992). The social acceptance and interaction of visually impaired children in integrated settings. In S. Z. Sacks, L. S. Kekelis, & R. J. Gaylord Ross (Eds.), *The development of social skills by blind and visually impaired students: Exploratory studies and strategies*. New York: AFB Press.

McGee, J. J. & Menolascino, F. J. (1991). *Beyond gentle teaching: A nonaversive approach to helping those in need*. New York: Plenum Press.

McGonigel, M., Woodruff, G., & Roszmann-Millican, M. (1994). The transdisciplinary team: A model for family-centered early intervention. In L. J. Johnson, R. J. Gallagher, M. J. Montagne, J. B. Gordon, J. J. Gallagher, P. L. Huntinger, & M. B. Karnes, (Eds.), *Meeting early intervention challenges: Issues from birth to three* (2nd ed.). Baltimore: Paul H. Brookes.

McGraw, M. B. (1943). *Neuromuscular maturation of the human infant*. New York: Hafner.

McGregor, D., & Farrenkopf, C. (2000). Recreation and leisure skills. In A. J. Koenig & M. C. Holbrook (Eds.), *Foundations of education: Vol. II: Instructional strategies for teaching children and youths with visual impairments* (2nd ed.), (pp. 653–678). New York: AFB Press.

Mesaros, R. A. (1995). Comprehensive positive behavior support for young children with significant behavior problems. In D. Chen & J. Dote-Kwan (Eds.), *Starting points: Instructional practices for young children whose multiple disabilities include visual impairment* (pp. 79–88), Los Angeles: Blind Childrens Center.

Miles, B. (1998). Talking the language of the hands to the hands: The importance of hands for the person who is deafblind. Monmouth, OR: DB-LINK. The National Information Clearinghouse on Children Who Are Deaf-Blind. (http://www.tr. wou.edu/dblink/hands2.htm).

Milian, M. (2000). Multicultural issues. In M.C. Holbrook & A. J. Koenig (Eds.), *Foundations of education.* Vol. 1: *History and theory of teaching children and youths with visual impairments,* (2nd ed.). (pp. 197–217). New York: AFB Press.

Miller, D. D. (1985). Reading comes naturally: A mother and her blind child's experiences. *Journal of Visual Impairment and Blindness, 79,* 1–4.

Morgan, E. (1995) *The VIISA Curriculum.* Logan, UT: SKI*HI Institute, Hope, Inc.

Morse, M.T. (1999). Cortical visual impairment: Some words of caution. *RE:View, 31*(1), 21–26.

Munoz, M. L. (1998). *Language assessment and intervention with children who have visual impairments: A guide for speech-language pathologists.* Austin, TX: Texas School for the Blind and Visually Impaired.

Murphy, D.L., & Bernas-Pierce, J. (1995). Blind Babies Foundation registry of early childhood visual impairment in central and northern California. In J. Bernas-Pierce (Ed.), *The Hoyt-Akenson selected readings in pediatric ophthalmology: A resource for professionals working with children who are visually impaired.* San Francisco: Blind Babies Foundation.

Nash, J. M. (1997, February 3). Fertile minds. *Time, 149,* 48–56.

National Association for the Education of Young Children. (1996). *Guidelines for preparation of early childhood professionals.* Washington, DC: Author.

National Center for Health Statistics (1999). *Births: Find data for 1997.* Hyattsville, MD: NCHS.

National Center for Health Statistics (1994 - 1995). *National health interview survey on disability.* Hyattsville, MD: NCHS.

National Center for Health Statistics (1998). *Vital statistics of the United States Vol. I, Natality.* Hyattsville, MD: NCHS.

National Information Center for Children and Youth with Disabilities (December, 2001). *General information about visual impairments: Fact sheet number 13.* Washington, D.C.: Author. (Retrieved on February 19, 2002 from http://www.nichcy. org/pubs/factshe/fs13txt.htm.)

NEC*TAS (1991). *Guidelines and recommended practices for the individualized family service plan* (2nd ed.). Betshesda, MD: Association for the Care of Children's Health.

Newborg, J., Stock, J. R., Wnek, L., Guidubaldi, J., & Svinicki, J. (1984). *Battelle developmental inventory.* Allen, TX: DLM/Teaching Resources.

Nielsen, L. (1990). *Are you blind?* Copenhagen, Denmark: SIKON.

Nielsen, L. (1992). *Space and self.* Copenhagen, Denmark: SIKON.

Norton, D. G. (1990). Understanding the early experiences of black children in high risk environments: Culturally and ecologically relevant research as a guide to support for families. *Zero-to-Three, Vol X(4),* 1–7.

Ochs, E. (1982). Talking to children in Western Samoa. *Language in Society, 11,* 77–104.

Olson, M. R. (1981). *Guidelines and games for teaching efficient braille reading.* New York: AFB Press.

O'Neill, R. E., Horner, R. H., Albin, R. W., Storey, K., & Sprague, J. R. (1990). *Func-*

tional analysis of problem behavior: A practical assessment guide. Sycamore, IL: Sycamore Publishing Company.

O'Neill, R. E., & Reichle, J. (1993). Addressing socially motivated challenging behaviors by establishing communicative alternatives: Basics of general-case approach. In J. Reichle & D. P. Wacker (Eds.), *Communicative alternatives to challenging behavior: Integrating functional assessment and intervention strategies* (pp. 113–133). Baltimore: Paul H. Brookes.

Orel-Bixler, D. A., Haegerstrom-Portnoy, G., & Hall, A. (1989). Visual assessment of the multiply handicapped patient. *Optometry & Vision Services, 69*, 530–536.

Orel-Bixler, D. (1999). Clinical vision assessments for infants. In D. Chen (Ed.), *Essential elements in early intervention: visual impairment and multiple disabilities* (pp. 107–156). New York: AFB Press.

Paclawskyj, T. R., & Vollmer, T. R. (1995). Reinforcer assessment for children with developmental disabilities and visual impairments. *Journal of Applied Behavior Analysis, 28*, 219–224.

Palazisi, M.A. (1986). The need for motor development programs for visually impaired preschoolers. *Journal of Visual Impairment & Blindness, 80*, 573–576.

Palmer, E. A., Flynn, J. T., & Hardy, R. J. (1991). The Cryotherapy for ROP Cooperative Group: Incidence and early course. *Ophthalmology, 98*, 1628–1640.

Parette, H. P., & Petch-Hogan, B. (2000). Approaching families: Facilitating culturally/linguistically diverse family involvement. *Teaching Exceptional Children, 33(2)*, 4–10.

Parks, S., Furuno, S., O'Reilly, T., Inatsuka, C. M., Hosaka, & Zeisloft-Falbey, B. (1994). *Hawaii early learning profile (HELP): HELP (birth to three)*. Palo Alto, CA: VORT Corporation.

Parsons, S. (1986a). Function of play in low vision children (Part 1): A review of the research and literature. *Journal of Visual Impairment & Blindness, 80(3)*, 627–630.

Parsons, S. (1986b). Function of play in low vision children (Part 2): Emerging patterns of behavior. *Journal of Visual Impairment & Blindness, 80*, 777–784.

Parsons, S. (1979). *Parsons visual acuity test*. South Bend, IN: Bernell Corporation.

Paysse, E. A., Lindsey, J. L., Coats, D. K., Contant, C., & Steinbuller, P. G. (1999). Therapuetic outcomes of diode laser photocoagulation versus cryotherapy for threshold retinopathy of prematurity. *Journal of AAPOS, 4*, 234–240.

Pearce, R. S. (1992). Early childhood development. In R. L. Pogrund, D. L. Fazzi, & J. Lampert (Eds.), *Early focus: Working with young blind and visually impaired children and their families*. New York: AFB Press.

Peters, M. (1985). Racial socialization of young black children. In H. P. McAdoo & J. L. McAdoo (Eds.), *Black children: Social, educational, and parental environments*. Beverly Hills, CA: Sage Publications.

Piaget, J. (1952a). *The origins of intelligence*. New York: International Universities Press.

Piaget, J. (1952b). *The origins of intelligence in children*. Translated by M. Cook. New York: International Universities Press.

Piaget, J. (1954). *The construction of reality in the child*. New York: Basic Books.

Pogrund, R. L., Fazzi, D. L., Lampert, J. S. (Eds.) (1992). *Early focus: Working with young blind and visually impaired children and their families*. New York: AFB Press.

Pogrund, R., Healy, G., Jones, K., Levack, N., Martin-Curry, S., Martinez, C., Marz, J., Roberson-Smith, B., & Vrba, A. (1993). *Teaching age-appropriate purposeful skills (TAPS): An orientation and mobility curriculum for students with visual impairments*. Austin, TX: Texas School for the Blind and Visually Impaired.

Pogrund, R. L., & Rosen, S. J. (1989). The preschool blind child *can* be a cane user. *Journal of Visual Impairment & Blindness, 83*, 431–439.

Pogrund, R.L., & Strauss, F.A. (1992). Approaches to increasing assertive behavior and communication skills in blind and visually impaired persons. In S.Z. Sacks, L.S. Kekelis, & R.J. Gaylord-Ross (Eds.), *The Development of Social Skills by Blind and Visually Impaired Students* (pp. 181–194). New York: American Foundation for the Blind.

Quinn, M. M., Gable, R. A., Rutherford, R. B., Nelson, C. M., & Howell, K. W. (1998). *Addressing student problem behavior. Part I: An IEP team's introduction to functional behavioral assessment and behavior intervention plans.* Washington, DC: Center for Effective Collaboration and Practice.

Recchia, S. L. (1997). Play and concept development in infants and young children with severe visual impairments: A constructivist view. *Journal of Visual Impairment & Blindness, 91*(4), 401–416.

Rettig, M. (1994). The play of young children with visual impairments: Characteristics and interventions. *Journal of Visual Impairment & Blindness, 88*(5), 410–420.

Risjord, C., Wilkinson, J., & Stark, M. L. (2000). *Instruction manual for Braille transcribing* (4th ed.). Washington, D.C.: The Library of Congress, National Library Service for the Blind and Physically Handicapped.

Robinson, G. C., Jan, J. E., & Kinnis, C. (1987). Congenital ocular blindness in children: 1945 to 1984. *American Journal of Diseases of Children, 147*, 1321–1324.

Rogow, S. M. (2000). Communication and language: Issues and concerns. In B. Silverstone, M. A. Lang, B. P. Rosenthal, & E. E. Faye (Eds.), *The Lighthouse handbook on vision impairment and vision rehabilitation: Vol. 1. Vision Impairment* (pp. 395–408). New York: Oxford University Press.

Rosetti, L. (2001). *Enhancing early identification of infants and toddlers at risk.* Presentation at Early Childhood Intervention Statewide Conference, April 30–May 2, 2001, Austin, TX.

Russo, R. J., & Self, J. F. (2001). What is cortical visual impairment? Presented at California Transcribers and Educators of the Visually Handicapped Statewide Conference, San Francisco, CA.

Sack, R. L., Blood, M. L., Hughes, R. J., & Lewy, A. J. (1998). Circadian-rhythm sleep disorders in persons who are totally blind. *Journal of Visual Impairment & Blindness, 92*(3), 145–162.

Sacks, S. Z., & Silberman, R. K. (2000). Social skills. In A. J. Koenig & M. C. Holbrook (Eds.), *Foundations of education. Vol. 2. Instructional strategies for teaching children and youths with visual impairments* (2nd ed.) (pp. 616–652). New York: AFB Press.

Sacks, S. Z., & Silberman, R. K. (2000). Social skills in vision impairment. In B. Silverstone, M. A. Lang, B.P. Rosenthal, & E. E. Faye (Eds.), *The Lighthouse handbook on vision impairment and vision rehabilitation:* Vol. 1. *Vision Impairment* (pp. 377–394). New York: Oxford University Press.

Salcedo, P. (1986). Coping with the coping process. *Bridges, 3,*1–2.

Salend, S. J., & Taylor, L. (1993). Working with families: A cross-cultural perspective. *Remedial and Special Education, 14,* 25–32.

Sanford, L., & Burnett, R. (1996). The years ahead. In M.C. Holbrook (Ed.), *Children with visual impairments.* Bethesda, MD: Woodbine House.

Schneckloth, L. H. (1989). Play environments for visually impaired children. *Journal of Visual Impairment & Blindness, 83*, 196–201.

Segal, J. (1993). Speech and language development. In D. Chen & J. Dote-Kwan (Eds.) *First steps: A handbook for teaching young children who are visually impaired,* (pp. 69–81). Los Angeles: Blind Childrens Center.

Seligman, M. (1975). *Helplessness on depression, development, and death.* San Francisco: W. H. Freeman.

Sherman, C. (2000). Sensory integration dysfunction is controversial diagnosis. *Family Practice News 10*(3), 40.

Shon, K. H. (1999). Access to the world by visually impaired preschoolers. *RE:View, 30,* 160–173.

Shonkoff, J. P., & Hauser-Cram, P. (1987). Early intervention for disabled infants and their families: A quantitative analysis. *Pediatrics, 80,* 650–658.

Silberman, R. K. (1986). Severe multiple handicaps. In G. T. Scholl (Ed.), *Foundations of education for blind and visually handicapped children and youth: Theory and practice* (pp.145–164). New York: AFB Press.

Silberman, R. K., Corn, A. L., & Sowell, V. M. (1996). Teacher educators and the future of personnel preparation programs for serving students with visual impairments. *Journal of Visual Impairment & Blindness, 90,* 115–124.

Skellenger, A.C., Hill, M., & Hill, E. (1992). The social functioning of children with visual impairments. In S.L. Odom, S.R. McConnell, & M.A. McEvoy (Eds.), *Social competence of youth with disabilities: Issues and strategies for intervention* (pp. 165–188). Baltimore: Paul H Brookes.

Skellenger, A. C., & Hill, E. W. (1997). The preschool learner. In B. B. Blasch, W. R. Weiner, & R. L. Welsh (Eds.), *Foundations of orientation and mobility* (2nd ed.) (pp. 407–438). New York: AFB Press.

Smith, M. (1998). Joseph's coat: People teaming in transdisciplinary ways.

SEE/HEAR, Spring, 1998. Austin, TX: Texas School for the Blind and Visually Impaired.

Smith, M., & Levack, N. (1996). *Teaching students with visual and multiple impairments: A resource guide.* Austin. TX: Texas School for the Blind and Visually Impaired.

Sonksen, P., Levitt, S., & Kitsinger, M. (1984). Identification of constraints acting on motor development in young visually disabled children and principles of remediation. *Child Care Health and Development, 10,* 273–286.

Steendam. M. (1989). *Cortical visual impairment in children.* Enfields, New South Wales, Australia: Royal Blind Society of New South Wales

Swenson, A. M. (1999). *Beginning with braille: Firsthand experiences with a balanced approach to literacy.* New York: AFB Press.

Taylor, D. (ed.) (1997). *Paediatric ophthalmology* (2nd ed.). Oxford, UK: Blackwell Science.

Taylor-Peters, P. (1992). Behavioral focus: Developing positive strategies for behavior management of young blind and visually impaired children. In R.L. Pogrund, D.L. Fazzi, & J.S. Lampert (Eds.), *Early focus: Working with young blind and visually impaired children and their families* (pp. 70–79). New York: AFB Press.

Tharp, R., & Gallimore, R. (1988). A theory of teaching as assisted performance. In R. Tharp & R. Gallimore (Eds). *Rousing minds to life* (pp. 27–70). New York: Cambridge University Press.

Thomas, C. C., Correa, V. I., & Morsink, C. V. (2001). *Interactive teaming: Enhancing programs for students with special needs* (3rd ed.). Upper Saddle River, NJ: Merrill Prentice Hall.

Thomas, A., & Chess, S. (1977). *Temperament*

and development. New York: Brunner/Mazel.

Thorp, E., & Brown, C. (1987). *The family experience: A module of Project Year One—A comprehensive training package for infant service providers*. Washington, D.C.: George Washington University School of Education and Human Development, Department of Special Education, Infant Education Program.

Timmins, S. (1997). *Early development in children with severe visual impairment: Needs assessment for kindergarten and strategies for remediation*. Ontario, Canada: Author.

Topor, I. (1999). Functional vision assessments and early interventions. In D. Chen (Ed.), *Essential elements in early intervention: Visual impairment and multiple disabilities* (pp. 157–206). New York: AFB Press.

Topor, I., & Erin, J. (2000). Educational assessment of vision function in infants and children. In B. Silverstone, M. Lang, B. Rosenthal, & E. Faye (Eds.), *The Lighthouse handbook on vision impairment and vision rehabilitation* (pp. 821–831). New York: Oxford University Press.

Trawick-Smith, J. (1997). Cognitive development in infancy. In *Early childhood development* (pp. 165–191). Columbus, OH: Merrill/Prentice Hall.

Trelease, J. (1995). *The read-aloud handbook*. New York: Penguin.

Trief, E., Duckman, R., Morse, A. R., & Silberman, R. K. (1989). Retinopathy of prematurity. *Journal of Visual Impairment & Blindness, 83*(10), 500–504.

Troughton, M. (1992). *One is fun*. Brantford, Ontario, Canada: Author.

Turnbull, A. P., & Turnbull, H. R. (1997). *Families, professionals and exceptionality: special partnership* (3rd ed). Upper Saddle River, NJ: Prentice Hall.

U.S. Census Bureau, (1999). *Poverty in the United States: 1998*. Washington, D.C.: Author.

Utley, B. L., Roman, C., & Nelson, G. L. (1998). Functional vision. In S. Z. Sacks & R. K. Silberman (Eds.), *Educating students who have visual impairments with other disabilities* (pp. 371–412). Baltimore: Paul H. Brookes.

Vision screening project. (1980). Parsons, KS: University of Kansas Bureau of Child Research.

Vygotsky, L. S. (1962). *Thought and language*. Cambridge, MA: MIT Press.

Vygotsky, L. S. (1978). *Mind and society*. Cambridge, MA: Harvard University Press.

Walker, E., Tobin, M., & McKennell, A. (1991). *Blind and partially sighted children in Britain: The RNIB survey* (pp. 65–71). London: HMSO Publications.

Warren, D. H. (1994). *Blindness and children: An individual differences approach*. New York: Cambridge University Press.

Warren, D. (2000). Developmental perspectives. In B. Silverstone, M. Lang, B. Rosenthal & E. Faye (Eds.) *The Lighthouse handbook on vision impairment and vision rehabilitation* (pp. 325–337). New York: Oxford University Press.

Weiner, W. R., & Sifferman, E. (2000). A demographic study of certified orientation and mobility specialists. *RE:View, 32*, 39–45.

Wheeler, L. C., Floyd, K., & Griffin, H. (1997). Spatial organization in blind children. *ReView, 28*, 177–181.

Wilbarger, J., & Stackhouse, T. M. (1998). *Sensory modulation: A review of the literature*. Littleton, CO: The KID Foundation.

Witte, L. (1993). Precane devices in a residential school setting. *Journal of Visual Impairment & Blindness, 87*, 205–206.

Wolffe, K. E. (Ed.) (1999). *Skills for success: A career education handbook for children and adolescents with visual impairments.* New York: AFB Press.

Woodruff, G., & McGonigel, M. (1988). Early intervention team approaches: The transdisciplinary team. In J. B. Jordan, J. J. Gallehger, P. L. Hutinger, & M. B. Karnes (Eds.), *Early childhood special education: Birth to three* (pp. 163–181). Reston, VA: Council for Exceptional Children.

Wormsley, D. P., & D'Andrea, F. M. (Eds.) (1997). *Instructional strategies for braille literacy.* New York: AFB Press.

Early Focus touches on many topics in the areas of early intervention and the early education of children who are blind or visually impaired that each could fill a book of its own. This section points the way for professionals and family members of young visually impaired children to obtain additional information and to find the products mentioned in this book. The sources of information listed here are just a sampling of the many resources available for learning more about working with young children who are blind or visually impaired.

The first section lists books, periodicals, videos and other information sources, as well as a listing of assessment tools and curricula. The second section is a listing of organizations and agencies, including sources of information and referrals, professional membership organizations, and membership organizations for parents and other consumers. Finally, there are sources of products such as publications and adapted products and materials.

For additional information and sources of products, see the *Directory of Services for Blind and Visually Impaired Persons in the United States and Canada,* published by the American Foundation for the Blind and available on its website, www.afb.org.

PUBLICATIONS AND VIDEOS

Books

The following books may be helpful for readers who wish to obtain further information on a variety of topics related to young children who are blind or visually impaired and their families. These books cover a wide range of topics, including, among others, early intervention; children with visual impairments, hearing impairments, cerebral palsy, multiple impairments, and other disabilities; typical and atypical development; ophthalmology; and inclusion.

Accardo, P. J., & Whitman, B. Y. (1996). *Dictionary of developmental disabilities terminology.* Baltimore: Paul H. Brookes.
AFB directory of services for blind and visually impaired persons in the United States and Canada (26th ed.). (2001) New York: AFB Press.
Alexander, R., Boehme, R., & Cupps, B. (1993). *Normal development of*

functional motor skills: The first year of life. Tucson, AZ: Communication Skill Builders.

Anderson, W., Chitwood, S., & Hayden, D. (1997). *Negotiating the special education maze: A guide for parents and teachers* (3rd ed.). Betheseda, MD: Woodbine House.

Bailey, I. L., & Hall, A. (1990). *Visual impairment: An overview.* New York: AFB Press.

Batshaw, M. L. (Ed.) (1997). *Children with disabilities* (4th ed.). Baltimore: Paul H. Brookes.

Bernstein, J. (1988). *Loving Rachel: A parent's journey from grief.* Boston: Little, Brown.

Blakely, K., Lang, M. A., & Kushner-Sosna, B. (1995). *Toys and play: A guide to fun and development for children with impaired vision.* New York: Lighthouse International.

Brazelton, T. B. (1992). *Touchpoints: The essential reference. Your child's emotional and behavioral development.* Menlo Park, CA: Addison-Wesley Longman.

Bredekamp, S., & Copple, C. (Eds.). (1997). *Developmentally appropriate practice in early childhood programs* (rev. ed.). Washington, DC: National Association for the Education of Young Children.

Bricker, D. (1993). *Assessment, evaluation, and programming system (AEPS) for infants and children.* Baltimore: Paul H. Brookes.

Bricker, D., Pretti-Frontczak, K., & McComas, N. (1998). *An activity-based approach to early intervention* (2nd ed.). Baltimore: Paul H. Brookes.

Browne, B. C., Jarrett, M. H., Hovey-Lewis, C. J., & Freund, M. B. (1995). *Developmental playgroup guide.* Tucson, AZ: Communication Skill Builders.

Bureau of Education for Exceptional Students, State of Florida (1983). *Project IVEY: Increasing visual efficiency:* Vol. V-E. Tallahassee, FL: Florida Department of Education.

Capute, A. J., & Accardo, P. L. (Eds.) (1996). *Developmental disabilities in infancy and childhood. Vol. 2. The spectrum of developmental disabilities* (2nd ed.). Baltimore: Paul H. Brookes.

Casey-Harvey, D. G. (1995). *Early communication games. Routine-based play for the first two years.* Tucson, AZ: Communication Skill Builders.

Cassin, B., Solomon, S., & Rubin, M. (Eds.) (1990). *Dictionary of eye terminology.* Gainesville, FL: Triad Publishing.

Cavallaro, C. C., & Hanley, M. (1999). *Preschool inclusion.* Baltimore: Paul H. Brookes.

Chang, H. N. L., Muckelroy, A., & Pulido-Tobiassen, D. (1996). *Looking in, looking out: Redefining child care and early education in a diverse society.* San Francisco: California Tomorrow.

Charkins, H. (1996). *Children with facial difference: A parents' guide.* Bethesda, MD: Woodbine House.

Chen, D., & Dote-Kwan, J. (1995). *Starting points: Instructional practices for young children whose multiple disabilities include visual impairment.* Los Angeles: Blind Childrens Center.

Chen, D. (1999). *Essential elements in early intervention: Visual impairment and multiple disabilities.* New York: AFB Press.

Coling, M. C. (1991). *Developing integrated programs: A transdisciplinary approach for early intervention.* Tucson, AZ: Communication Skill Builders.

Cook, R. E., Tessier, A., & Klein, M. D. (1999). *Adapting early childhood curricula for children with special needs* (5th ed.). Upper Saddle River, NJ: Merrill/Prentice Hall.

Cratty, B. J. (1970). *Perceptual motor development in infants and children.* New York: Macmillan.

Cratty, B. J., & Sams, T. A. (1968). *The body image of blind children.* New York: AFB Press.

Dickerson, M. L. (2002). *Small victories: Conversations about prematurity, disability, vision loss, and success.* New York: AFB Press.

Dodson-Burk, B., & Hill, E. W. (1989). *An orientation and mobility primer for families and young children.* New York: AFB Press.

Fazzi, D. L., & Petersmeyer, B. A., (2001). *Imagining the possibilities: Creative approaches to orientation and mobility instruction for persons who are visually impaired.* New York: AFB Press.

Ferrell, K. A. (1985). *Reach out and teach: Meeting the training needs of parents of visually and multiply handicapped young children.* New York: AFB Press.

Finnie, N. R. (1975). *Handling the young cerebral palsied child at home* (2nd ed.). New York: E. P. Dutton.

Fraiberg, S. (1977). *Insights from the blind: Comparative studies of blind and sighted infants.* New York: Basic Books.

Geralis E. (Ed.) (1998). *Children with cerebral palsy: A parents' guide.* Bethesda, MD: Woodbine House.

Goldberg, S. (1982). *Ophthalmology made ridiculously simple.* Miami: Medical Master.

Grisham-Brown, J. (2000). *Reach for the stars, planning for the future: A transition process for families of young children.* Louisville, KY: American Printing House for the Blind.

Hagood, L., (1997). *Communication: A guide for teaching students with visual and multiple impairments.* Austin, TX: Texas School for the Blind and Visually Impaired.

Hanson, M. (1988). *Beyond tracking: Enhancing vision development from birth to one year of life.* Bridgeview, IL: Vision Unlimited.

Hanson, M. J. (1996). *Atypical infant development* (2nd ed.). Austin, TX: Pro-Ed.

Hanson, M. J., & Lynch, E. W. (1995). *Early intervention: Implementing child and family services for infants and toddlers who are at risk or disabled* (2nd ed.). Austin, TX: Pro-Ed.

Hayes, D., & Northern, J. L. (1996). *Infants and hearing.* San Diego, CA: Singular Publishing Group.

Hazekamp, J., & Huebner, K. M. (1989). *Program planning and evaluation for blind and visually impaired students: National guidelines for educational excellence.* New York: AFB Press.

Holbrook, M. C. (Ed.) (1996). *Children with visual impairments: A parent's guide.* Bethesda, MD: Woodbine House.

Holbrook, M. C., & Koenig, A. J. (Eds.) (2000). *Foundations of education* Vol. I, (2nd ed.). New York: AFB Press.

Huebner, K. M., Prickett, J. G., Welch, T. R., & Joffee, E. (Eds.) (1995). *Hand in hand: Essentials of communication and orientation and mobility for your students who are deaf-blind.* New York: AFB Press.

Hyvarinen, L. (1988). *Vision in children: Normal and abnormal.* Lake City, FL: Vision Associates.

Isenberg, S. J. (1989). *The eye in infancy.* Chicago: Year Book Medical Publishers.

Jose, R. T. (1993). *Understanding low vision.* New York: AFB Press.

Klein, M. D. (1988). *Pre-sign language motor skills.* Tucson, AZ: Communication Skill Builders.

Klein, M. D., Chen, D., & Haney, M. (2000). *Promoting learning through active interaction: An early communication curriculum.* Baltimore: Paul H. Brookes.

Koenig, A. J., & Holbrook, M. C. (Eds.). *Foundations of education* Vol. II, (2nd ed.). New York: AFB Press.

La Prelle, L. L. (1996). *Standing on my own two feet.* Los Angeles: Blind Childrens Center.

Levack, N. (1991). *Low vision: A resource guide.* Austin, TX: Texas School for the Blind and Visually Impaired.

Lowenfeld, B. (1971). *Our blind children* (3rd ed.). Springfield, IL: Charles C. Thomas.

Lueck, A. H., Chen, D., & Kekelis, L. (1997). *Developmental guidelines for infants with visual impairment: A manual for early intervention.* Louisville, KY: American Printing House for the Blind.

Lynch, E. W., & Hanson, M. J. (1998). *Developing cross-cultural competence* (2nd ed.). Baltimore: Paul H. Brookes.

Margetik, C., Calvello, G., Bernas-Pierce, J., & Murphy, D. (1999). *Off to a good start: Access to the world for infants and toddlers with visual impairments.* San Francisco: Blind Babies Foundation.

McClannahan, C. (1989). *Feeding and caring for infants and children with special needs*. Rockville, MD: American Occupational Therapy Association.

McNamara, A., de Juan, E., & Varley, M. (1991). *Understanding retinopathy of prematurity* Mountain View, CA: IRIS Medical Instruments.

Meisels, S. J., & Shonkoff, J. P. (1990). *Handbook of early childhood intervention*. New York: University of Cambridge Press.

Nielsen, L. (1992a). *Educational approaches for visually impaired children*. Lake City, FL: Vision Associates.

Nielsen, L. (1992b). *Space and self: Active learning by means of the Little Room*. Lake City, FL: Vision Associates.

Nielsen, L. (1993). *Early learning step by step: Children with vision impairment and multiple disabilities*. Lake City, FL: Vision Associates.

Parent Early Childhood Education Series. (1993). Louisville, KY: American Printing House for the Blind and Overbrook School for the Blind.

Project year one: A comprehensive training package for infant service providers: The famliy experience, the neonatal expeience, and the community experience [Resource Manuals]. (1988). Washington, DC: George Washington University, School of Education and Human Development, Department of Special Education, Infant Education Program.

Rogow, S. M. (1988). *Helping the visually impaired child with developmental problems*. New York: Teachers College Press.

Rossetti, L. M. (1990). *Infant-toddler assessment: An interdisciplinary approach*. Austin, TX: Pro-Ed.

Rossetti, L. M. (1996). *Communication intervention: Birth to three*. San Diego, CA: Singular Publishing Group.

Rothenberg, B. A. (1995). *Understanding and working with parents and children from rural Mexico*. Menlo Park, CA: CHC Center for Child and Family Development Press.

Sacks, S. Z., & Silberman, R. K. (Eds.) (1998). *Educating students who have visual impairments with other disabilities*. Baltimore: Paul H. Brookes.

Sacks, S. Z., Kekelis, L. S., & Gaylord Ross, R. J. (1992). *The development of social skills by blind and visually impaired students: Exploring studies and strategies*. New York: AFB Press.

Simmons, S. S., & Maida, S. O. (1992). *Reaching, crawling, walking . . . Let's get moving. Orientation and mobility for preschool children*. Los Angeles: Blind Childrens Center.

SKI*HI Institute. (1993). *A resource manual for understanding and interacting with infants, toddlers, and preschool age children with deaf-blindness*. Logan, UT: Hope.

Smith, M., & Levack, N. (1997). *Teaching students with visual and multiple impairments*. Austin, TX: Texas School for the Blind and Visually Impaired.

Sroufe, L. A. (1996). *Emotional development: The organization of emotional life in the early years.* New York: Cambridge University Press.

Stratton, J. M., & Wright, S. (1993). *On the way to literacy: Early experiences for visually impaired children.* Louisville, KY: American Printing House for the Blind. [handbook and 18 storybooks]

Swallow, R., & Huebner, K. M. (1987). *How to thrive, not just survive.* New York: AFB Press.

Tingey, C. (1989). *Implementing early intervention.* Baltimore: Paul H. Brookes.

Tuttle, D. W. (1984). *Self-esteem and adjusting with blindness.* Springfield, IL: Charles C. Thomas.

VandenBerg, K. A., & Hanson, M. J. (1993). *Homecoming for babies after the neonatal intensive care nursery: A guide for professionals in supporting families and their infants' early development.* Austin, TX: Pro-Ed.

Vaughan, D., Asbury, T., & Tabbara, K. F. (1999). *General ophthalmology* (15th ed.). East Norwalk, CT: Appleton and Lange.

Warren, D. H. (1984). *Blindness and early childhood development* (2nd ed., rev.). New York: AFB Press.

Warren, D. H. (1994). *Blindness and children: An individual differences approach.* New York: Cambridge University Press.

Watkins, S. (1989). *A model of home intervention for infant, toddler, and preschool aged multihandicapped sensory impaired children: The INSITE model.* Logan, UT: Hope.

Watkins, S., & Clark, T. C. (1992). *The SKI*HI model: A resource manual for family-centered, home-based programming for infants, toddlers, and preschool-aged children with hearing impairment.* Logan, UT: Hope.

Booklets, Pamphlets, Articles and Fact Sheets

The list below identifies booklets and pamphlets that may be of interest to readers. Many are directed at family members of young children who are visually impaired. The sources of many of these booklets and pamphlets will be found in the section on Organizations and Agencies. Some are available at no cost and some may be purchased for a minimal fee.

Baby care basics. (1988). Skillman, NJ: Johnson & Johnson Baby Care Products Company.

Ballard, J., Ramirez, B., & Zantal-Weiner, K. (1989). *Public Law 94-142, Section 504, and Public Law 99-457: Understanding what they are and are not.* Reston, VA: Council for Exceptional Children.

Brody, J., & Webber, L. (1994). *Let's eat:. Feeding a child with visual impairment.* Los Angeles: Blind Childrens Center.

Chen, D., & McCann, M. E. (1993). *Selecting a program: A guide for parents of infants and preschoolers with visual impairment.* Los Angeles: Blind Childrens Center.

Chernus-Mansfield, N., Hayashi, D., Horn, M., & Kekelis, L. (1986). *Heart to heart: Parents of children who are blind and visually impaired talk about their feelings.* Los Angeles: Blind Childrens Center.

Children with visual impairments: A parent's guide. Watertown, MA: National Association for Parents of Children with Visual Impairments.

Early years (a series of booklets). Toronto, Ontario, Canada: Canadian National Institute for the Blind.

Equals in partnership: Basic rights for families of children with blindness or visual impairment. Watertown, MA: National Association for Parents of Children with Visual Impairments.

Ferrell, K. A. (1984). *Parenting preschoolers: Suggestions for raising young blind and visually impaired children.* New York: AFB Press.

Getting to know your newborn. (1987). Skillman, NJ: Johnson & Johnson Baby Care Products Company.

Harrell, L. (1984). *Touch the baby.* New York: AFB Press.

Hedgecock, H., Hudson, E., Del Castillo, E., Stotland, J., & Sael, E. (n.d.). *Legislative handbook for parents.* Beloit, WI: National Association for Parents of Children with Visual Impairments.

Hefner, M. A., Thelin, J. W., Davenport, S. L. H., & Mitchell, J. A. (1988). *CHARGE syndrome: A booklet for families.* Columbia, MO: Quota Club.

Hug, D., Chernus-Mansfield, N., & Hayashi, P. (1987). *Move with me: A parent's guide to movement development for visually impaired babies.* Los Angeles: Blind Childrens Center.

Kekelis, L. (1984). *Talk to me: A language guide for parents of blind children.* Los Angeles: Blind Childrens Center.

Kekelis, L. (1985). *Talk to me II: Common concerns.* Los Angeles: Blind Childrens Center.

Kushner-Sosna, B., Moore, J. A., & Lang, M. A., (1992). *Technology for tots: Using computers with preschool children who have visual impairments.* New York: Lighthouse International.

Meyers, L., & Lansky, P. (1991). *Dancing cheek to cheek: Nurturing beginning social, play, and language interactions.* Los Angeles: Blind Childrens Center.

O'Mara, B. (1989). *Pathways to independence: Orientation and mobility skills for your infant and toddler.* New York: The Lighthouse International.

Pediatric visual diagnosis fact sheets. (1998). San Francisco: Blind Babies Foundation.

Preschool learning activities for the visually impaired child. Watertown, MA:

National Association for Parents of Children with Visual Impairments.

Recchia, S. (1987). *Learning to play: Common concerns for the visually impaired preschool child.* Los Angeles: Blind Childrens Center.

Schmitt, P., & Armenta-Schmitt, F. (1999). *Fathers: A common ground.* Los Angeles: Blind Childrens Center.

Strickling, C., (1998). *Impact of vision loss on motor development: Information for occupational and physical therapists working with students with visual impairments.* Austin, TX: Texas School for the Blind and Visually Impaired.

Uriegas, O. (1996). Almost 100 motor activities for infants and toddlers. *SEE/HEAR, 1*(4), Fall, pp. 6-7. Austin, TX: Texas School for the Blind and Visually Impaired and Texas Commission for the Blind.

Vores, J. K., & Pearson, N. A. *Early childhood development chart.* Austin, TX: Pro-Ed.

When you have a visually impaired student in your classroom: A guide for teachers (2002). New York: AFB Press.

Journals and Newsletters

The journals and newsletters listed in this section are available on a regular basis for professionals and families.

Awareness
National Association for Parents of Children
with Visual Impairments
P.O. Box 317
Watertown, MA 02471
(617) 972-7441 or (800) 562-6265

CHARGE Accounts
CHARGE Syndrome Foundation
2004 Parkdale Boulevard
Columbia, MO 65202-3121
(573) 499-4694 or (800) 442-6704
www.chargesyndrome.org

Exceptional Parent
Psy-Ed Corp.
65 East Route 4
River Edge, NJ 07661
(201) 489-4111
(201) 489-0074
www.eparent.com

Future Reflections
National Organization of Parents of Blind Children,
Division of National Federation of the Blind
1800 Johnson St.
Baltimore, MD 21230
(410) 659-9314

Journal of Visual Impairment & Blindness
AFB Press
11 Penn Plaza, Suite 300
New York, NY 10001
(717) 632-3535 or (888) 522-0220
www.afb.org/JVIB/main.asp

**National Newspatch: Quarterly Newsletter
for Educators of Visually Impaired Preschoolers**
Oregon School for the Blind
700 Church Street, S.E.
Salem, OR 97310
(503) 378-3820

RE:view
Heldref Publications
1319 18th Street, N. W.
Washington, DC 20036-1802
(202) 296-6267 or (800) 365-9753

Sibling Information Network Newsletter
991 Main Street
The University of Connecticut
East Hartford, CT 06108
(203) 282-7050

The Special Edge Newsletter
Resources in Special Education (RISE)
c/o Parents Helping Parents
3041 Olcott Street
Santa Clara, CA 95054
(408) 727-5775
fax: (408) 727-0182
www.php.com

VIP Newsletter
Blind Children's Fund
311 West Broadway, Ste. 1
Mt. Pleasant, MI 48858
(989) 779-9966
Fax: (989) 779-0015
www.blindchildrensfund.org

Young Exceptional Children
Division for Early Childhood, Council for Exceptional Children
Sopis West
1380 Lawrence St., Suite 650
Denver, CO 80204
www.dec-sped.org/yec

Videotapes

Some of the following videos provide valuable and encouraging overviews of early intervention topics for parents of young visually impaired children and other family members. Others are more technical and are directed mainly at professionals.

Building blocks: Foundations for learning for young blind and visually impaired children (1991). [Video in English and Spanish]. New York: AFB Press.

Can Do video series. Louisville, KY: Visually Impaired Preschool Services.

Chen, D., Klein, M. D., & Haney, M. (2000). *Promoting learning through active interaction. Supporting early communication with infants who have multiple disabilities* [video & booklet]. Baltimore: Paul H. Brookes.

Chen, D. (1997). *What can baby hear? Auditory tests and interventions for infants with multiple disabilities* [video & booklet]. Baltimore: Paul H. Brookes.

Chen, D., Brekken, L., & Chan, S. (1997). *Project CRAFT: Culturally responsive and family focused training.* Baltimore: Paul H. Brookes.

Chen, D. (1998). *What can baby see? Vision tests and interventions for infants with multiple disabilities* [video & booklet]. New York: AFB Press.

Chen, D., & Orel-Bixler, D. (1997). *Vision tests for infants.* [video & booklet]. New York: AFB Press.

Chen, D., & Schachter, P. H. (1997). *Making the most of early communication: Strategies for supporting communication with infants, toddlers, and preschoolers whose multiple disabilities include vision and hearing loss* [video & booklet]. New York: AFB Press.

Fish, M. E. (1990). *Getting there: A look at the early mobility skills of four young blind children.* San Francisco: Blind Babies Foundation.

Heart to heart: Conversations with parents of blind children and Dom Deluise. (1988). Los Angeles: Blind Childrens Center.

Helping your child learn video series. Verona, WI: BVD Promo Services.

Let's eat: Feeding a child with visual impairment. (1994). Los Angeles: Blind Childrens Center.

MacConnachie, J. (1988). *Raising a little cane: Trends in teaching cane travel to preschoolers.* 405 3rd Street, LaGrande, Oregon 97850.

Moore, S. (1985). *Beginnings: A practical guide for parents and teachers of visually impaired babies* [Video and booklet]. Louisville, KY: American Printing House for the Blind.

Moses, K. (1974). *The mourning theory and family dynamics: A presentation for the parents and families of impaired children.* Peoria, IL: Regional Resource Center VII.

Welch, T. P., (1995). *Hand in hand: It can be done!* New York: AFB Press.

Wolffe, K. E., & Sacks, S. Z. (2000). *FOCUSed on: Social skills.* [Video and study guide.] New York: AFB Press.

Assessments and Curricula

The following selected assessment tools and curricula may be useful for professionals working with young children with visual impairments. Publishers or sources for many of these are identified in more detail in the section on "Sources of Assessment and Curricula."

Anthony, T. (1992). *Inventory of purposeful movement behaviors.* Denver, CO: Colorado Department of Special Education, Special Education Services Unit.

Anthony, T. (1993). *Early intervention: Orientation and mobility checklist* (rev. ed.). Denver, CO: Colorado Department of Special Education, Special Education Services Unit.

Birth to 3 years & multihandcapped vision kit. Baby screen kit #C1358. Lake City, FL: Vision Associates.

Battelle developmental inventory. Allen, TX: DLM/Teaching Resources.

Barraga, N. (1980). *Program to develop efficiency in visual functioning.* Louisville, KY: American Printing House for the Blind.

Bayley, N. (2001). *Bayley scales of infant development* (2nd ed.). San Antonio, TX: The Psychological Corporation.

Bricker, D., Squires, J., & Mounts, L. (1999). *Ages and stages questionnaires (ASQ)—A parent-completed child-monitoring system* (2nd ed). Baltimore: Paul H. Brookes.

Brigance diagnostic inventory of early development—revised. (1991). North Billerica, MA: Curriculum Associates.

Brigance diagnostic inventory of early development—revised: APH tactile sup-

plement. (1991). Louisville, KY: American Printing House for the Blind.

Brown, C., & Bour, B. (1986). Volume V-K: Movement analsyis and curriculum for visually impaired preschoolers. In: *A resource manual for the development and evaluation of special programs for exceptional students*. Tallahassee, FL: Florida Department of Education.

Brown, D., Simmons, J., Methvin, J.,Anderson, S., Boignon, S., & Davis, K. (1991). *The Oregon project for visually impaired and blind preschoolers* (5th ed). Medford, OR: Jackson County Education Service District.

Callier-Azusa Scale. (1978). Dallas: Callier Center for Communication Disorders, University of Texas at Dallas,

Chen, D., Friedman, C. T., & Calvello, G. (1990). *Parents and visually impaired infants* (PAVII) [Guidelines & Materials]. Louisville, KY: American Printing House for the Blind.

Davis, J. A., & Langley, M. B. (1980). *Peabody model vision project* [Curriculum]. Chicago: Stoelting.

Dodson-Burk, B., & Hill, E. W. (1989). *Preschool orientation and mobility screening*. Alexandria, VA: Association for Education and Rehabilitation of the Blind and Visually Impaired, Division IX.

Early Education Unit, Special Education Division, California Department of Education (1997). *First look: Vision evaluation and assessment for infants, toddlers, and preschoolers, birth through five years of age*. Sacramento: Publications Division, California Department of Education.

Exsted, R., Lastine, D., & Paul, B. (1996). *Individualized, comprehensive, evaluation of functional use of vision in early childhood (I-CEE). An evaluation protocol*. Fairbault, MN: Minnesota Resource Center for Blind and Visually Impaired Students.

Fewell, R., & Langley, M. B. (1984). *DASI-II Developmental activities screening inventory*. Austin, TX: Pro-Ed.

Furuno, S., Inatsuka, T. T., O'Reilly, K. A., Hosaka, C. M., Zeisloft-Falbey, B., & Allman, T.L. (1985). *Hawaii early learning profile (HELP) activity guide*. Palo Alto, CA: VORT Corporation.

Furuno, S., O'Reilly, K. A., Inatsuka, T. T., Hosaka, C. M., & Falbey, B. Z. (1993). *Helping babies learn: Developmental profiles and activities for infants and toddlers*. Tucson, AZ: Communication Skill Builders.

Hill, E. W. (1981). *The Hill performance test of selected positional concepts*. Chicago: Stoelting.

Hill, E. W. (1987). *Preschool orientation and mobility project for visually impaired children: Final report, Grant No. G008401385* [Curriculum]. Washington, DC: HCEEP. (ERIC Document No. 292 259).

Johnson-Martin, N. M., Jens, K. G., Attermier, S. M., & Hacker, B. J.

(1991). *The Carolina curriculum for infants and toddlers with special needs* (2nd ed.). Baltimore: Paul H. Brookes.

Langley, M. B. (1980). *Functional vision inventory for the multiply and severely handicapped.* Chicago: Stoelting.

Langley, M. B. (1998). *Individualized systematic assessment of visual efficiency for the developmentally young individual (ISAVE).* Louisville, KY: American Printing House for the Blind.

Lighthouse House, Apple, Umbrella Series Flashcard Test (1980). Escondidio, CA: Lighthouse International.

Morgan, E., & Watkins, S. (1989). *Assessment of developmental skills for young multihandicapped sensory impaired children.* Logan, UT: Hope.

Morgan, E. C. (Ed.). (1995). *Resources for family-centered intervention for infants, toddlers and preschoolers who are visually impaired: VIISA Project* (2nd ed.). Logan, UT: SKI-HI Institute, Hope, Inc.

Newborg, J., Stock, J. R., Wnek, L., Guidubaldi, J., & Svinicki, J. (1984). *Batelle developmental inventory.* Allen, TX: DLM Teaching Resources.

Nielsen, L. (1992a). *Educational approaches for visually impaired children.* Lake City, FL: Vision Associates.

Nielsen, L. (1992b). *Space and self: Active learning by means of the Little Room.* Lake City, FL: Vision Associates.

Nielsen, L. (1993). *Early learning step by step: Children with vision impairment and multiple disabilities.* Lake City, FL: Vision Associates.

Parent's preschool visual development checklist (1995). Santa Ana, CA: Optometric Extension Program Foundation, Inc.

Parsons visual acuity test (1979). South Bend, IN: Bernell Corporation.

Pogrund, R., Healy, G., Jones, K., Levack, N., Martin-Curry. S., Martinez, C., Marz, J., Roberson-Smith, B., & Vrba, A. (1995). *TAPS: Teaching age-appropriate purposeful skills. An orientation and mobility curriculum.* Austin, TX: Texas School for the Blind and Visually Impaired.

Reynell-Zinkin scales: Developmental scales for young visually handicapped children. Chicago: Stoelting.

Vision Screening Project (1980). *The infant vision checklist.* Parsons, KS: University of Kansas Bureau of Child Research.

ORGANIZATIONS AND AGENCIES

The items in this section are a selection of national organizations that provide information, assistance, and referrals; operate toll-free hotlines; and publish materials that are valuable sources of information for parents of infants and preschool children who are blind or visually impaired and the professionals who work with them. A complete listing of agencies and organizations serving persons who are blind and visually impaired is included in the *AFB Directory of Ser-*

vices for Blind and Visually Impaired Persons in the United States, which is also avilable on their website, *www.afb.org.*

American Association of the Deaf-Blind
814 Thayer Avenue
Silver Spring, MD 20910
(301) 588-6545
www.tr.wou.edu/dblink/aadb.htm
The American Association of the Deaf-Blind is a consumer organization of deaf-blind persons. It is involved in advocacy activities, conducts service programs, acts as a referral service, maintains a library of materials on deaf-blindness, and holds a convention annually for deaf-blind persons and their families.

American Council of the Blind
1155 15th Street, N.W., Suite 720
Washington, DC 20005
(202) 467-5081 or (800) 424-8666
Fax: (202) 467-5085
www.acb.org
The American Council of the Blind is a consumer organization that provides referrals; scholarships; leadership and legislative training; consumer advocacy support; assistance in technological research; consultative and advisory services to individuals, organizations, and agencies; and program development assistance. Its special interest affiliate of the American Council of the Blind—Parents promotes the sharing of resources and information and produces an informative newsletter for parents of children who are blind or visually impaired.

American Foundation for the Blind
11 Penn Plaza, Suite 300
New York, NY 10001
(212) 502-7600 or (800) 232-5463
TDD: (212) 502-7662
Fax: (212) 502-7777
www.afb.org
The American Foundation for the Blind (AFB) acts as an information clearinghouse for people who are blind or visually impaired and their families, professionals, organizations, schools, and corporations. AFB stimulates research and mounts program initiatives to improve services to visually impaired persons, including the National Initiative on Literacy and the AFB Textbook and Instructional Materials Solutions Forum; advocates for services and legislation; maintains the M. C. Migel Library

and Information Center and the Helen Keller Archives; provides information and referral services; operates the National Technology Center and the Career and Technology Information Bank; produces videos; and publishes books, pamphlets, the *Directory of Services for Blind and Visually Impaired Persons in the United States and Canada,* the *Journal of Visual Impairment & Blindness,* and *AccessWorld: Technology and People with Visual Impairments.*

American Printing House for the Blind
1839 Frankfort Avenue, P.O. Box 6085
Louisville, KY 40206
(502) 895-2405 or (800) 223-1839
www.aph.org
The American Printing House for the Blind (APH) is a national organization that publishes books in braille, large-print, and audiotape formats; manufactures educational aids for persons who are blind or visually impaired; modifies and develops computer-access equipment and software; maintains an educational research and development program concerned with educational methods and aids; and provides a reference catalog service for volunteer-produced textbooks in all media for students who are visually impaired and for information about other sources of related materials.

Association for Education and Rehabilitation of the Blind and Visually Impaired
4600 Duke Street, Suite 430
Alexandria, VA 22304
(703) 823-9690
Fax: (703) 823-9695
www.aerbvi.org
The Association for Education and Rehabilitation of the Blind and Visually Impaired (AER) is a professional membership organization that promotes all phases of education and work for persons of all ages who are blind and visually impaired. AER organizes conferences and workshops, maintains job exchange services and a speakers bureau, holds continuing-education seminars, and is involved in legislative and advocacy projects. AER also publishes *RE:view,* a quarterly journal for professionals working in the field of blindness: a newsletter, *AER Reports;* brochures; and videotapes. It has a division that addresses the educational needs of infants and preschoolers, another that focuses on the needs of students with multiple disabilities, and an orientation and mobility division. There are state and regional chapters in the U.S. and Canada.

Association for Persons with Severe Handicaps
29 West Susquehanna Avenue, Suite 210
Baltimore, MD 21204
(410) 828-8274
www.tash.org
The Association for Persons with Severe Handicaps (TASH) is an advocacy organization for professionals who work with infants, children, and youths who have severe disabilities and their families. TASH holds an annual national conference, publishes the *Journal of the Association for Persons with Severe Handicaps* and the *TASH Newsletter,* and has a committee on early childhood that meets at the annual conference. There are state and regional TASH chapters.

Blind Children's Fund
311 West Broadway, Suite 1
Mt. Pleasant, MI 48858
(989) 779-9966
Fax: (989) 779-0015
www.blindchildrensfund.org
The Blind Children's Fund is an organization of parents and teachers that promotes activities and programs that benefit the growth, development, and education of children who are visually impaired. It also publishes pamphlets and books and holds symposia.

Canadian National Institute for the Blind
1931 Bayview Avenue
Toronto, Ontario M4G 3E8
Canada
(416) 486-2500
www.cnib.ca
The Canadian National Institute for the Blind (CNIB) fosters the integration of persons who are blind and visually impaired into the mainstream of Canadian life and promotes programs for the prevention of blindness.

Council for Exceptional Children
1920 Association Drive
Reston, VA 22091-1589
(703) 620-3660 or (888) 232-7733
www.cec.sped.org
Division of Early Childhood
www.dec-sped.org
The Council for Exceptional Children (CEC) is a professional organiza-

tion for practitioners serving infants, children, and youths who have disabilities. CEC holds an annual national conference and publishes two journals: *Exceptional Children,* which contains research and scholarly articles; and *Teaching Exceptional Children,* which contains articles on strategies and practices. The Division on Visual Impairments (DVI) publishes the *DVI Quarterly* and has a stand in the annual national CEC conference. The Division of Early Childhood (DEC) has a separate annual conference and state DEC chapters. It also publishes two journals: *Journal of Early Intervention,* which contains scholarly articles; and *Exceptional Young Children,* which contains articles on early childhood special education strategies and practices.

DB-LINK (The National Information Clearinghouse on Children Who Are Deaf-Blind)
345 North Monmouth Avenue
Monmouth, OR 97361
(800) 438-9376
www.tr.wou.edu/dblink
D-B LINK serves as a federally funded clearinghouse that provides information and copies of written materials related to infants, children, and youths who have both visual and hearing impairments. It publishes the newsletter *Deaf-Blind Perspectives.*

Federation for Children with Special Needs
1135 Tremont Street, Suite 420
Boston, MA 02120
(617) 236-7210
(800) 331-0688
Fax: (617) 517-2094
www.fcsn.org
The Federation for Children with Special Needs supports organized parent-to-parent efforts to enable parents to work more effectively with professionals in educating children with disabilities. It serves the Parent Training and Information Centers funded under the Individuals with Disabilities Education Act.

Foundation Fighting Blindness
(formerly the National Retinitis Pigmentosa Foundation)
11435 Cronhill Drive
Owings Mills, MD 21117-2220
(888) 394-3937
The Foundation Fighting Blindness conducts public education programs, supports research related to the prevention and treatment of re-

tinitis pigmentosa, maintains a network of affiliates across the country, and conducts workshops and referral and donor programs.

Hadley School for the Blind
700 Elm Street
Winnetka, Illinois 60093
(312) 446-8111; (800) 323-4238
www.hadley-school.org
The Hadley School for the Blind is an accredited home-study school. Its Parent/Child program offers parents of children who are visually impaired free correspondence courses on assessing a child's abilities, developing an infant's sensory skills, and using sensory aids in teaching a child, as well as courses in braille. It also provides a series of free booklets and periodicals.

Helen Keller National Center for Deaf-Blind Youths and Adults
111 Middle Neck Road
Sands Point, NY 11050
(516) 944-8900 (voice and TDD)
www.helenkeller.org/national/contact.htm
The Helen Keller National Center for Deaf-Blind Youths and Adults provides services and technical assistance to individuals who are deaf-blind and their families and maintains a network of regional and affiliate agencies.

**National Association for Parents of Children
with Visual Impairments**
P.O. Box 317
Watertown, MA 02471
(617) 972-7441 or (800) 562-6265
Fax (617) 972-7444
www.napvi.org
The National Association for Parents of Children with Visual Impairments (NAPVI) provides support to parents and families of children who are visually impaired; operates a national clearinghouse for information, education, and referral; promotes public understanding of the needs and rights of children who are visually impaired; supports state and local parents' groups and workshops that educate and train parents about available services, and their children's rights; and publishes the newsletter *Awareness,* for parents. NAPVI has chapters in many regions or states.

National Association for Visually Handicapped (*NAVH*)/New York
22 West 21st Street
New York, NY 10010
(212) 889-3141
Fax: (212) 727-2931
www.navh.org

National Association for Visually Handicapped
(*NAVH*)/San Francisco
3201 Balboa Street
San Francisco, CA 94121
(415) 221-3201
Fax: (415) 221-8754
www.navh.org
The National Association for Visually Handicapped (NAVH) produces and distributes large-print reading materials; offers counseling to persons with low vision, their families, and the professionals who work with them; acts as an information clearinghouse and referral center; sells low vision devices; and publishes *In Focus* for children and *Seeing Clearly* for adults.

National Center for Education in Maternal and Child Health
2000 15th Street North, Ste. 701
Arlington, VA 22201-2617
(703) 524-7802
Fax: (703) 524-9335
www.ncemch.org
The National Center for Education in Maternal and Child Health provides information services to parents and professionals on maternal and child health. It operates a resource center containing books, journals, articles, teaching manuals, brochures, fact sheets, and audiovisual materials and annually publishes *Reaching Out: A Directory of Organizations Related to Maternal Health*.

National Coalition for Deaf-Blindness
c/o Perkins School for the Blind
175 North Beacon Street
Watertown, MA 02172
(617) 972-7334
The National Coalition for Deaf-Blindness advocates on behalf of deaf-blind persons and provides information to consumers and professionals.

National Council of State Agencies for the Blind
206 N. Washington Street, Suite 320
Alexandria, VA 22314
(703) 548-1885
The National Council of State Agencies for the Blind promotes communication among agencies serving persons who are severely visually impaired.

National Early Childhood Technical Assistance System
CB #8040
500 NCNB Plaza
Chapel Hill, NC 27599
(919) 962-2001
The National Early Childhood Technical Assistance System provides technical assistance on the implementation of P.L. 99–457.

National Federation of the Blind
1800 Johnson Street
Baltimore, MD 21230
(410) 659-9314
Fax: (410) 685-5653
www.nfb.org
The National Federation of the Blind (NFB) is a national consumer organization with affiliates in all states. It monitors legislation affecting blind people, assists in promoting needed services, works to improve social and economic conditions of blind persons, provides evaluation of present programs and assistance in establishing new ones, grants scholarships to blind persons, and conducts a public education program. It maintains a Parents Division. NFB publishes the *Braille Monitor* and *Future Reflections*.

**National Information Center for Children
and Youth with Disabilities**
P.O. Box 1492
Washington, DC 20013-1492
Voice/TTY/TDD: (800) 695-0285
Fax: (202) 884-8441
www.nichcy.org
The National Information Center for Children and Youth with Disabilities serves as a national information clearinghouse on subjects related to children and youths with disabilities. It provides information and referral to national, state, and local resources and disseminates numerous free publications.

**National Library Service for the Blind
and Physically Handicapped**
Library of Congress
1291 Taylor Street, N.W.
Washington, DC 20542
(202) 707-5100 or (800) 424-8567
www.loc.gov/nls
The National Library Service (NLS) for the Blind and Physically Handicapped conducts a national program to distribute free reading materials in braille and on recorded disks and cassettes to persons who cannot utilize ordinary printed materials because of visual or physical disabilities.

**National Organization for Persons with Albinism
and Hypopigmentation**
1530 Locust Street, Suite 29
Philadelphia, PA 19302
(215) 454-2322 or (800) 473-2330
www.albinism.org
The National Organization for Persons with Albinism and Hypopigmentation (NOAH) publishes brochures and books to educate the public about albinism and hypopigmentation, encourages research on prevention and treatment of the diseases, holds conferences, maintains a speakers bureau, and provides support to persons with albinism or hypopigmentation and their families.

National Organization for Rare Disorders
100 Route 37, P.O. Box 8923
New Fairfield, CT 06812-8923
(203) 746-6518 or (800) 999-6673
TTY/TDD: (203) 746-6927
Fax: (203) 746-6481
www.rarediseases.org
The National Organization for Rare Disorders serves as an information clearinghouse on thousands of rare disorders. It brings together families with similar disorders for mutual support. It promotes research, accumulates and disseminates information about special drugs and devices, and maintains a database on rare diseases.

**National Technical Assistance Consortium for Children
and Young Adults Who Are Deaf-Blind**
Western Oregon University
Teaching Research
345 North Monmouth Avenue

Monmouth, OR 97361
(503) 838-8391; TTY/TDD: (503) 838-8821
Fax: (503) 838-8150
www.ntac@wou.edu or www.tr.wou.edu/ntac
National Technical Assistance Consortium (NTAC) provides technical assistance to families and agencies serving children and young adults who are deaf-blind. NTAC is a federally funded consortium project of Teaching Research and The Helen Keller National Center.

Office of Disease Prevention and Health Promotion
U.S. Department of Health and Human Services
Office of Public Health and Science, Office of the Secretary
200 Independence Avenue SW., Room 738G
Washington, DC 20201
(202) 401-6295
Fax: (202) 205-9478
odphp.osophs.dhhs.gov
The Office of Disease Prevention and Health Promotion refers medical professionals and the public to appropriate health organizations, provides health-related information, and maintains a library and an internal database.

Office of Special Education Programs
Preschool Grants Office
Office for Special Education and Rehabilitative Services
U.S. Department of Education
400 Maryland Avenue, S.W.
Washington, DC 20202
(202) 205-5507
www.ed.gov/offices/OSERS/OSEP/index/html
The Office of Special Education Programs provides general information on P.L. 99–457 and information about how to contact the individual state government bodies administering it.

SOURCES OF EDUCATIONAL MATERIALS, PUBLICATIONS, AND PRODUCTS

The following selected organizations are a small sample of those providing educational materials, publications, and products related to visual impairment. This section highlights sources of professional assessments and curricula for young children who are visually impaired, sources of braille and print-braille materials for young children, and sources of daily living products and other materials.

Sources of Assessments and Curricula

American Optical Company

P.O. Box 8020

Southbridge, MA 01550

(508) 764-5000 or (800) 358-8258

Fax: (508) 764-5010

The American Optical Company sells the Holmgren Test for Color Blindness which can be used as part of a functional vision assessment.

American Printing House for the Blind (APH)

1839 Frankfort Avenue, P.O. Box 6085

Louisville, KY 40206

(502) 895-2405 or (800) 223-1839

www.aph.org

American Printing House publishes assessments, curricula, videos, and other materials related to young children who are blind or visually impaired.

Optometric Extension Program

1921 East Carnegie Ave., Suite 3-L

Santa Ana, CA 92705

(949) 250-8070

Fax: (949) 250-8157

www.oep.org

Optometric Extension Program provides patient information pamphlets on vision related topics, including the *Parents' Guide and Checklist: A Reference Guide for Preschool Children's Vision Development.*

Paul H. Brookes

Box 10624

Baltimore, MD 21285-0624

Paul H. Brookes publishes assessments; curricula; and a variety of books, videos, and other materials related to children with disabilities, including those with visual impairments.

Stoelting Company

620 Wheat Lane

Wood Dale, IL 60191

(630) 860-9700

Fax: (630) 860-9775

www.stoelting.com/tests/index.htm

Stoelting Company publishes concept and vision assessment tools.

Texas School for the Blind and Visually Impaired
1100 West 45th Street
Austin, TX 78756-3494
(512) 454-8631
Fax: (512) 206-9452
www.tsbvi.edu
Texas School for the Blind and Visually Impaired publishes and sells professional books, assessments, curricula, and videotapes.

Vision Associates
4209 US Highway 90 West #312
Lake City, FL 32055
(407) 352-1200
www.visionkits.com
Vision Associates sells vision assessment kits and materials, books, and infant development materials, including the LEA Near and Distance Tests and the Hiding Heidi Low Contrast Test.

Sources of Braille and Print–Braille Books

American Action Fund for Blind Children and Adults
18440 Oxnard Street
Tarzana, CA 91356
The American Action Fund for Blind Children and Adults offers print–braille books on loan for preschoolers through 4th graders. An application is required; it can be obtained by writing to the American Action Fund.

American Printing House for the Blind
1839 Frankfort Avenue, P.O. Box 6085
Louisville, KY 40206-0085
(502) 895-2405 or (800) 223-1839
www.aph.org
American Printing House offers a series of print–braille books in its "On the Way to Literacy" series. These books are available for purchase only. The books are part of a larger series that includes a guidebook for parents and teachers.

National Braille Press
Children's Book-of-the-Month Club
88 St. Stephens Street
Boston, MA 02115

(617) 266-6160 or (888) 965-8965
Fax: (617) 437-0456
www.nbp.org
The Children's Braille Book-of-the-Month Club provides regular-print picture books with plastic braille over each page to members on a monthly basis. Individual books can also be ordered by nonmembers.

National Library Service for the Blind and Physically Handicapped
Library of Congress
1291 Taylor Street, N.W.
Washington, DC 20542
(202) 707-5100; (800) 424-8567
www.loc.gov/nls
The National Library Service (NLS) for the Blind and Physically Handicapped conducts a national program to distribute free reading materials in braille and on recorded disks and cassettes to persons who are visually impaired and physically disabled who cannot utilize ordinary printed materials. Materials are available on loan through regional libraries throughout the United States. Registration is required and can be initiated through a local public library.

Seedlings
P.O. Box 2395
Livonia, MI 48151-0395
(800) 777-8552
www.seedlings.org
Seedlings offers a variety of braille and print–braille books for purchase only. Also, other braille books are offered with print written above the braille words. Seedlings offers a small collection of books in uncontracted braille.

American Action Fund for Blind Children and Adults
Twin Vision Lending Library
1800 Johnson Street, Suite 100
Baltimore, MD 21230
(410) 659-9315
www.actionfund.org
Twin Vision Lending Library serves blind parents and blind children by lending Twin Vision Books and other braille publications written on the preschool to junior-high reading level. Twin Vision Books publishes children's books that combine print and braille on facing pages so that blind and sighted people can read together.

Sources of Products and Other Materials

American Thermoform Corporation
1758 Brackett Street
LaVerne, CA 91750
(909) 593-6711 or (800) 331-3676
Fax: (909) 593-8001
www.atcbrleqp.com
American Thermoform Corporation sells items such as braille printers and embossers, Thermoform machines, brailon paper, and labels.

Blind Babies Foundation
5016 Mission Street
San Francisco, CA 94112
(415) 586-6140
Fax: (415) 586-6279
www.blindbabies.org
Blind Babies Foundation provides educational materials, publications, and videos about young children with visual impairments.

Blind Childrens Center
4120 Marathon Street
Los Angeles, CA 90029-3584
(323) 664-2153 or (800) 222-3566 or (800) 222-3567 in California
Fax: (323) 665-3828
www.blindchildrenscenter.org
Blind Childrens Center provides educational publications in English and Spanish and videotapes about young children.

Exceptional Teaching Aids
20102 Woodbine Avenue
Castro Valley, CA 94546
(415) 582-4859 or (800) 549-6999
www.exceptionalteaching.com
Exceptional Teaching Aids manufactures and distributes educational materials and equipment for visually impaired students, including tutorial and other educational software programs; braille materials for reading readiness, math readiness, and math practice; and books on cassette.

Handiworks
10232 Glenoaks Blvd.
Pacoima, CA 91331
(818) 890-3685 or (800) 331-6123
Fax: (818) 890-1678
www.handiworks.com
Handiworks distributes cane holders for folding canes (of all sizes) to carry them on the belt at the waist when not in use. Other products to assist individuals who are blind or visually impaired with organization and smart travel are available.

Howe Press
Perkins School for the Blind
175 North Beacon Street
Watertown, MA 02172
(617) 924-3490
Fax: (617) 926-2027
Howe Press manufactures and sells the Perkins Brailler, as well as other tools, materials, and equipment for producing braille.

Independent Living Aids
27 East Mall
Plainview, NY 11803-4404
(800) 537-2118
www.independentliving.com
Independent Living Aids sells adapted games and other recreational items along with materials to make adaptations for skills of daily living, such as Puff Paint, Wikki Stix, and so on.

Lighthouse International
111 E. 59th Street
New York, NY 10022-1202
(212) 821-9200 or (800) 829-0500
www.lighthouse.org
Lighthouse International sells publications, brochures, videos, and adaptive materials for daily-living skills.

Lighthouse Professional Products
938-K. Andreasan Drive
Escondido, CA 92029
(800) 826-4200
Fax: (800) 368-4111

LS&S
P.O. Box 673
Northbrook, IL 60065
(847) 498-9777 or (800) 468-4789
Fax: (847) 498-1482
www.lssgroup.com
LS&S sells household products for adapted daily-living skills as well as adapted recreational materials.

MaxiAids
42 Executive Blvd.
Farmingdale, NY 11735
(800) 522-6294
Fax: (631) 752-0689
www.maxiaids.com
MaxiAids sells products for people with disabilities, including adaptive devices for daily living and low vision devices.

SpecialEd Solutions
PO Box 6218
San Antonio, TX 78209
(877) 324-2533 or (210) 828-3785
www.SpecialEd.com
SpecialEd Solutions sells sensory-stimulation equipment for children with visual or multiple impairments such as noisy boxes and noisy boards (resonance boards).

INDEX

Behavioral support (*continued*)
  positive focus of, 254–255
  reinforcement in, 274, 277, 279–282, 284
  scheduling, 271, 276, 278, 280–281, 283
  for sensory input needs, 274–277
  social strategies, 272, 274, 276–277, 279, 281, 284
  for tangible objects, need for, 282–283
  team approach, 284–286
Bilateral coordination, meaning of, 318
Binocular vision, meaning of, 76
Birth defects, 8–10
  leading causes, 8–9
Birthweight
  and birth defects, 8
  ethnic minority births, 10
Body awareness, 131–132
  assessment of, 131–132
  body mapping, 348–349, 367, 370–371
  and concept development, 131
  early signs of, 342
  motor development activities, 324–325
  orientation and mobility (O&M) activities, 367–370
  and spatial relations, 348–349, 367
Bonding. *See* Attachment
Bottle-feeding, 228–229
Braille instruction, 179–181
  contracted versus uncontracted approach, 168–169
  for parents, 168
  prebraille skills, 179–181, 182–183, 430
  reading aloud, 174
Braille materials
  alphabet, example of, 169
  braille blocks, 167
  braillewriter, 177–178
  environmental labels, 165–166, 170
  learning by family/teachers, 168–169
  making print-braille books, 166
  object books, 175
  print-braille books, 166
  resources for books, 482–483
  slate and stylus, 177
  storage of books, 167

Braillewriter, 177–178
Breast-feeding, 228–229
Brigance Diagnostic Inventory of Early Development-Revised, 149
Broken Wheel test, 78

Calendar boards, 147
Callier-Azusa Scale, 315–316
Cancer, retinoblastoma, 68
Canes, 385–386, 388–394
  adaptations for, 393
  early use, pros/cons of, 389–391
  long cane, teaching use of, 391–393
  pre-cane skills, 388–389
  tactile information from, 366
  types of, 385–386
Caregiver–child interaction, 189–191
  assessment of, 202, 204
  attachment, 191, 197–198
  and autonomy of child, 191, 198
  and children with visual impairment, 195, 197, 202–203
  and responsiveness to infant, 190–191
  supportive services for, 205–207
  and temperament of child, 190
Carolina Curriculum for Infants and Toddlers, 341
Caseload size, 14, 427–428
Cataracts
  features of, 65
  treatment of, 65
Center-based programs
  class size, 427–428
  features of, 422–425
  inclusion programs, 423
  for young children, 423–424
CHARGE association, features of, 65–66
Cheerio test, 78
Child find services, 4, 407–409
Child-rearing
  and cultural differences, 34–37
  and religion, 42
  and scarce resources, 40–41
Class size, 428–429
Clinical eye examination, components of, 73

Cultural diversity (*continued*)
  and religion, 42, 45–46, 48
  and teacher cultural competence, 13, 34
Cultural diversity and intervention
  center-based services, tips for, 47–48
  and culturally competent
    interventionist, 13, 34
  and family beliefs about learning, 44–45
  home-based services, tips for, 47
  interventionist skills and strategies, 41,
    49–51
Culture
  characteristics of, 33
  definition of, 32
Cytomegalovirus (CMV), and visual
    impairment, 62

Daily living skills
  age range for, in sighted children, 225
  daily activities, scope of, 223
  dressing, 233–235
  eating skills, 228–231
  food preparation activities, 239
  home tips, 226
  household chores, 237–239
  leisure activities. *See* Recreation and
    leisure activities
  organizational skills, 235–237
  personal hygiene skills, 226–228
  priority skills, identification of, 219–222
  toileting, 231–232
Daily living skills instruction
  backward chaining, 240–241
  for children with multiple disabilities,
    242–243
  demonstration, 241
  modeling, 241
  motoring, 241
  partial participation, 222
  reinforcement, 242
  routines, 241–242
  task analysis, 240
Deferred imitation, 125
Delayed visual maturation (DVM), 87
Democratic child rearing, 36
Demonstration

daily living skills instruction, 241
  and learning, 157–158
DeMorsier's syndrome, features of, 67
Diagnostics Assessment Procedure, 85
Direct service model, 14
Discipline of child, and cultural diversity,
    36–37, 42
Discrepancy analysis, behavioral
    assessment, 264–265
Disequilibrium, in Piaget's theory, 111
Divergence, meaning of, 76
Dramatic play, 194, 201
Dressing
  organizing clothing, 236–237
  skills development activities, 233–235
Drug-exposed infants, and visual
    impairment, 9, 64
Dyspraxia, 309, 311

Early intervention
  age range for, 1–2
  assessment, accommodations for,
    412–413
  best practices, 4
  effectiveness of, 2–5
  federal laws related to, 5–7, 405–406,
    414–415
  in natural environment, 13–14
  process of, 3
Early intervention services
  child find services, 4, 407–409
  and cultural diversity, 412
  ecological approach, 411
  family-centered approach, 411
  Individualized Family Service Plan
    (IFSP), 410
  Interagency Coordinating Councils
    (ICCs), 411
  specialized versus generalized services,
    12
Eating, skills development activities,
    228–231
Echo bucket, 273
Echolalia, 145–146
Echolocation, 359–362
  affecting factors, 360–361

sound signals, 359–360
teaching activities, 361–362
Ecological approach, early intervention services, 411
Education for All Handicapped Children Act (P.L. 94–142), 5, 405–406
Educational materials
literacy materials, 163, 165–170, 173–178
sources for, 481–486
toys/play materials, 193–194, 206, 208
writing materials, 177–178
See also Braille materials
Educational vision specialists
cultural competence of, 13, 34
role of, 69, 79, 428–431
shortage of, 13, 414
Electroculograms (EOG), 74
Electrodiagnostic tests, 74
Electronic communication devices, 147
Electro-optical devices, 77
Electroretinograms (ERG), 74
Environmental adaptations
as behavioral support activity, 272, 276, 278–279, 281, 283–284
for infants, 398–399
for movement/exploration, 401, 402–403
for preschoolers, 401–404
for recreation and leisure activities, 248–249
for safety, 398, 400, 401–402
for toddlers, 400–401
Environmental awareness
children with multiple disabilities, 374
in community, 373, 375–376
in home, 372–373
in school, 373
Environmental cues, 96–101
color, 100–101
contrast, enhancement of, 100
glare minimization, 98
lighting, 96, 98
space as organizer, 99
time for visual tasks, 99–100
types of, 59

Environmental mapping
children with visual impairment, 303
and spatial organization, 295–296
Esotropia, assessment of, 81
Ethnic minorities
low/very-low/preterm births, 10
See also Cultural diversity
Extended family, 38
Eye
normal development of, 52–54
See also Vision and visual development
Eye movement, assessment of, 84
Eye preference, 76
Eye pressure assessment, 73

Facial expression, teaching of, 214–215
Family-centered approach
as best practice, 4
orientation & mobility (O&M) instruction, 330, 403
See also Home-based program
Family of child with visual impairment, 16–51
advocacy role, 436–437
braille, learning of, 168–169
and center-based programs, 423
child in home environment. *See* Daily living skills
cultural differences. *See* Cultural diversity
grief, stages of, 18–20
home-to-school transition, 30
hospital-to-home transition, 28–30
and hospitalization of child, 26–28
professional partnership, requirements of, 26
reactions to child, 18–23
school-to-school transition, 30–31
supportive communication to, 24–27
Family structure, and cultural differences, 38
Farsightedness. *See* Hyperopia (farsightedness)
Fathers
birth of impaired child, reaction to, 21–22

Natural environment (*continued*)
  See also Environmental adaptations;
    Environmental awareness;
    Environmental cues
Near point vision, assessment of, 83
Nearsightedness. *See* Myopia
    (nearsightedness)
Negative reinforcement, 266–267
New Programmed Instruction in Braille
    (Ashcroft, Sanford, & Koenig), 168
Nystagmus, features of, 67

Object books, 175
Object permanence, 115–116, 341, 345–347
  aiding development of, 122–124, 346
  importance of, 115
  signs of, 341
  visual impairment, effects of, 115–116,
    345–346
Object recognition charts, 78
Observation, learning by, 44
Ocular reflexes, assessment of, 83
Optical devices
  hand-held magnifiers, 365
  introduction to, 365
Optic nerve, assessment of, 73
Optic-nerve hypoplasia, features of, 67
Optokinetic nystagmus drum, 73, 74, 76
Optometrist
  low-vision evaluation, 75–77
  role of, 69, 74–79
Oregon Project for Visually Impaired and
    Blind Preschool Children, 315
Oregon Skills Inventory, 355
Organizational skills, development
    activities, 235–237
Organizations for blind/visually impaired,
    listing of, 471–480
Orientation, meaning of, 327–328
Orientation and mobility (O&M)
    assessment, 394–404
  developmental function assessment,
    396–397
  team approach, 395
Orientation and mobility (O&M)
    instruction

for body awareness, 367–370
for concept development, 366–367
for environmental awareness, 372–376
environment and infants, 397–399
environment and preschoolers, 401–402
environment and toddlers, 400–401
family-centered approach, 330, 403
focus areas of, 330
in functional context, 381–382
hearing to facilitate movement, 357–362
human guide technique, 377–378
mobility devices, 382–394
for motor development, 321–322
for preschoolers, 355–356
program, development activities, 329
protective techniques, 379–380
self-help instruction, 353
self-initiation, encouragement of,
    354–355
and sensory development. *See* Sensory
    systems
social skills, 354
spatial relations, 370–371
for tactile information, 366
team approach, 330
trailing, 380–381
verbal communication in, 353
visual skills, 363–365
for young children, 376–377
Orientation and mobility (O&M)
    specialists, role of, 69, 431–432
Outdoor activities, 246

Parallel play, 193
Parents. *See* Caregiver–child interaction;
    Family of child with visual
    impairment
Parsons Visual Acuity Test, 82
Partial participation, in daily living skills,
    222
Peabody Functional Vision Inventory for
    Multiple and Severely Handicapped,
    81, 82–83
Pediatric ophthalmologist, role of, 69, 70–74
Peer interactions
  assessment of, 203–204